from Archer Taylor

Chicago - 1938

HARVARD STUDIES
IN COMPARATIVE LITERATURE

I. THREE PHILOSOPHICAL POETS
LUCRETIUS, DANTE, AND GOETHE
BY GEORGE SANTAYANA

II. CHIVALRY IN ENGLISH LITERATURE
CHAUCER, MALORY, SPENSER, AND SHAKESPEARE
BY WILLIAM HENRY SCHOFIELD

III. THE COMEDIES OF HOLBERG
BY OSCAR JAMES CAMPBELL, JR.

IV. MEDIAEVAL SPANISH ALLEGORY
BY CHANDLER RATHFON POST

V. MYTHICAL BARDS AND
THE LIFE OF WILLIAM WALLACE
BY WILLIAM HENRY SCHOFIELD

VI. ANGEVIN BRITAIN AND SCANDINAVIA
BY HENRY GODDARD LEACH

VII. CHAUCER AND THE ROMAN POETS
BY EDGAR FINLEY SHANNON

VIII. SPENSER AND THE TABLE ROUND
BY CHARLES BOWIE MILLICAN

IX. EGER AND GRIME
BY JAMES RALSTON CALDWELL

X. VIRGIL THE NECROMANCER
BY JOHN WEBSTER SPARGO

XI. CHAUCER'S USE OF PROVERBS
BY BARTLETT JERE WHITING

XII. ENGLISH LITERATURE AND CULTURE
IN RUSSIA (1553–1840)
BY ERNEST J. SIMMONS

XIII. D'EDMOND SPENSER A ALAN SEEGER
POÈMES ANGLAIS TRADUITS EN VERS FRANÇAIS
BY FERNAND BALDENSPERGER

XIV. PROVERBS IN THE EARLIER ENGLISH DRAMA
WITH ILLUSTRATIONS FROM CONTEMPORARY FRENCH PLAYS
BY BARTLETT JERE WHITING

HARVARD STUDIES

IN COMPARATIVE LITERATURE

FOUNDED BY

WILLIAM HENRY SCHOFIELD

XIV

PROVERBS IN THE EARLIER ENGLISH DRAMA

LONDON: HUMPHREY MILFORD
OXFORD UNIVERSITY PRESS

HARVARD STUDIES IN COMPARATIVE LITERATURE
VOLUME XIV

PROVERBS IN THE EARLIER ENGLISH DRAMA

WITH ILLUSTRATIONS FROM CONTEMPORARY FRENCH PLAYS

BY
BARTLETT JERE WHITING

CAMBRIDGE
HARVARD UNIVERSITY PRESS
1938

PRINTED AT THE HARVARD UNIVERSITY PRESS
CAMBRIDGE, MASS., U.S.A.

To

MY MOTHER AND FATHER

PREFACE

In this volume the proverbs and other proverbial material found in the earlier English drama are studied in relation to their context. The documents considered are the Biblical plays, moralities, interludes, early comedies and early tragedies. The overwhelming majority * of the extant plays written before the rise of the University Wits are treated, as, indeed, are a number of plays of later composition. Thus it has been possible to trace an unbroken line of usage within a definite literary type from earlier than 1400 to later than 1600. With few exceptions the plays have never before been discussed in terms of their proverbial lore, and they are but scantily represented in the principal dictionaries of English proverbs.

For purposes of comparison with the Biblical plays, moralities and interludes I have examined a large number of similar French plays and the result, while marked more by contrast than likeness, is not without value. Early French comedies and tragedies did not seem to afford enough points of contact to make their inclusion warrantable. The French plays, with the exception of a single group, had not, so far as I am aware, been searched for proverbs before, and the Appendix contains one of the most substantial contributions to our collections of proverbs from French medieval and renaissance texts to be made in recent years.

Because of its origin and its very nature the proverb

* Thomas Garter's *The Most Virtuous and Godly Susanna* (1578, Malone Society Reprints, 1936 [1937]) was not reprinted in time for me to introduce it at the end of chapter one. In this play the sententious remarks outnumber all the other sayings, a situation unusual in plays of the same type, but the Vice is true to his class in that he uses more than half the sayings.

as such must be considered an intrusive element in formal pieces of literature. Its presence can be justified on several grounds: it serves to impart moral advice in a simple and effective fashion, it is ornamental, or it is used to characterize an individual or a class. In early and relatively unsophisticated literature its didactic function is prominent, but the instructive and ornamental aspects of its use, as taught by ancient and medieval writers on rhetoric and poetic, and as practised by ancient and medieval authors, eventually found their way into the limbo of extinct literary devices. When more and more of an author's skill was devoted to artistic characterization, the proverb came to be recognized as an admirable means by which to separate an individual, or even a social class, from all others. Whether or not this device was justified in specific cases, it is here that the proverb found its most natural place in formal, written literature, where popular sayings were used to give a humorous reality to the speech of those who employed them.

Proverbs owe their birth not to the pen but to the tongue, their appeal is not to the eye but to the ear, and in literature they fit most convincingly into dialogue. We expect, then, to find proverbs freely used in the drama, and the extent to which they appear in Elizabethan plays has often been noted. Contemporary observation of the trait is clearly shown in Henry Porter's charming play *The Two Angry Women of Abington*, where the abuse of proverbs is subjected to a trenchant satire, the burlesque of which has been too often overlooked by commentators.

The present study points out that the use of proverbs had been conventionalized before the English drama developed into its most characteristic forms and that the popularity of homely sayings at the height of the Elizabethan period was no more than a continuation along familar paths. Since many of my general problems here are akin to those of my earlier volume, *Chaucer's Use of Proverbs*, I quote a paragraph from the preface to that book:

"A threefold division of proverbial material is followed in this volume: proverbs, proverbial phrases, and sententious remarks. I consider as proverbs sayings which are, or appear to be, popular in origin, or which have become thoroughly popular in use, while sententious remarks show clearly their learned origin. A proverbial phrase is not ordinarily a directly monitory piece of wisdom. I have segregated the comparisons from the other proverbial phrases. For a further discussion of the matter of definition I may refer to my article in *Harvard Studies and Notes in Philology and Literature*, XIV (1932), 273 ff. It is sometimes very hard to distinguish between a proverb and a sententious remark, and I can scarcely hope that all my readers will agree with all my decisions. Inevitably, too, some readers will feel, and perhaps rightly, that I have put in things which should have been left out and left out things which should have been put in. Many people, I have discovered, hold very definite views as to what does or does not constitute a proverb in a particular instance. It is especially difficult to feel secure about the identification of proverbs in another language than one's own. In general I have tried to be inclusive rather than exclusive."

Certain matters of procedure and mechanics must be explained here. Titles of plays and names of characters, outside of direct quotations, are given modern spellings and conventional forms. The quotations, however, are intended to reproduce their originals exactly save in the following particulars: every line of poetry begins with a capital, contractions are expanded silently, except for the symbol for "and" when it occurs other than at the beginning of a line, and occasional dots and bars have been dropped. Indeed, too much conservatism may have been shown in reproducing the idiosyncrasies of scribes and printers.

The plays, or groups of plays, are numbered consecutively throughout the volume, and for convenience of reference the assigned number is printed in the upper left-hand corner of the right-hand page. Dates for the composition of the plays are given in most instances after the titles. These dates can be established with certainty in very few cases, and again and again I have been forced to accept the guesses, of varying degrees of precision and plausibility, made by modern editors, by the authors of such useful handbooks as Eduard Eckhardt's *Das englische Drama im Zeitalter der Reformation und der Hochrenaissance* (Berlin, 1928), and even, though rarely, by myself. So elusive and unsatisfactory are the dates that I have not hesitated on more than one occasion to violate an apparent, or even actual, chronological arrangement.

The edition used is indicated after the title and here, as in the notes, London is to be understood as the place of publication when no other is given, and the customary abbreviations for the Early English Text Society are used after the first occurrence. The discussion of each play is preceded by a brief statistical summary which gives the length of the play and the amount of proverbial material which it contains. Wherever possible the editor's count is accepted, even in the case of the Malone Society Reprints, although the editorial policy of numbering every line of print sometimes exaggerates the length of a play by over two hundred lines. Otherwise the count is my own and has been checked and corrected by my friend Professor Harold Ogden White. The four numbers which indicate the amount of proverbial material are arranged in this order: proverbs, proverbial comparisons, other proverbial phrases, and sententious remarks. Thus the figures for the Towneley Plays are to be understood as follows:

12,276 lines: 24 (proverbs); 89 (proverbial comparisons); 66 (other proverbial phrases); 32 (sententious remarks).

The count includes every occurrence of a saying, even though a particular saying may have appeared more than once in the same play.

A necessary insistence on mechanical details ought not to obscure the fact that the material from which this book springs is rich in human interest. We have before us a mass of proverbs taken from a particular section of English literature. Our authors had two things in common, their literacy and their lack of genius. Some of them were certainly sophisticated, but they all knew, and this fact is part of the strength of the most minor Tudor writings, the language and thought of the English people of their age. In their use of proverbs they followed, wittingly or unwittingly, a convention which they themselves created and enforced, but the proverbs they used came from the folk from which they sprang and to which they were so close. Even when they were most learned — learned in a way that is half miraculous and half pitiful — when they gave stark renderings of Biblical lore or fumbling paraphrases of classical wisdom, even then they were expressing the verities which seemed natural to them and to their audiences. They understood the humor of proverbs, but the humor was of the grass roots and thus far more than feeble giggle or silly smile. The triteness of proverbs has been recognized by many wise and polished people, but their very triteness, coming in part from selection, has a depth which the wise and polished do not always plumb. The proverbs which fill the following pages, too much, perhaps, like rich plums in a flabby batter, bring us nearer to a comprehension of the philosophy of a truly vital people than do most pages written by and for a highly cultured class. If the reader comes from this book with a sense of the living surge and sweep of a sound folk the author will be happy, doubly happy, indeed, because of his slight share in the realization.

A portion of this book is the revision of a chapter in my doctoral dissertation written under Professor George Lyman Kittredge; and it is owing to his kindness and that of Professor Fernand Baldensperger that the volume appears in the Harvard Studies in Comparative Literature. Professor Harold Ogden White was kind enough to read the proof, and I am endebted to him, as well as to other friends, for numerous corrections and emendations. My wife assisted me in many ways.

Some of the sayings and words presented hereafter are frank and free beyond the normal usage of the drawing-room. Should anyone question my failure to expurgate, I could do no better than reply in the language of our sanest and most tolerant man of letters:

For this ye knowen al so wel as I,
Whoso shal telle a tale after a man,
He moot reherce as ny as evere he kan
Everich a word, if it be in his charge,
Al speke he never so rudeliche and large,
Or ellis he moot telle his tale untrewe,
Or feyne thyng, or fynde wordes newe.
He may nat spare, althogh he were his brother;
He moot as wel seye o word as another.

B. J. W.

Lowell House,
Cambridge, Massachusetts,
March 14, 1938.

CONTENTS

PROVERBS IN THE EARLIER ENGLISH DRAMA

CHAPTER I

THE BIBLICAL PLAYS

PART I

ENGLISH BIBLICAL PLAYS

THE FIRST problem in any study of the English Biblical drama is one of arrangement, since the various plays have so suffered through re-working and transmission that no satisfactory date for the first appearance of a given cycle is possible. It has seemed best to arrange the plays in the order used by J. E. Wells,[1] especially since that order has been justified by the evidence brought forward in the following pages. Such of the non-cyclic plays as contain no proverbial matter may be ruled out of court at once.[2] The plays considered in this chapter are dramatizations of various portions of the Bible, made for the education and edification of the common people. At first, no doubt, these plays remained close to their Biblical originals, but gradually, however started and however developed, there came to be interjected first bits of humor, then comic scenes, until finally we have whole plays, such as the Towneley *Second Shepherds' Play*, which contain far more original farce than derivative religious history. There are few things more edifying and instructive than proverbs, and it would not be unreasonable to expect that the writers of the religious plays might find proverbs of value in driving home to their uneducated audience the fundamental principles behind the Biblical stories. The following pages will show that this is so far from being the case that the serious religious plays contain almost no proverbs, and, what is even more strange, few more sententious remarks than their immediate sources rendered inevitable. Comic scenes alone contain popular proverbs and proverbial phrases to any marked extent, and even here, with the exception of a group of plays in the Towneley cycle and the second Coventry play, there are relatively few. A comparison will make this clear. The four principal cycles contain nearly seven thousand more lines than are found in Chaucer's works, including the *Romaunt*, and yet Chaucer uses over four times as many proverbs,[3] a third again as many comparisons, twice as many other proverbial phrases, and over four times as many sententious remarks.[4] Only in comparisons is any approach made to Chaucer, and it must not be forgotten that a few of the Towneley plays contain a disproportionate amount of all the proverbial material in the four cycles.

The authors of the religious plays, then, did not use proverbs for purposes of instruction, but rather to enliven the dialogue in the comic scenes in an effort, perhaps, to give it realism. We may say that the comic characters are singled out by their use of proverbs. The matter is vague, but we can be more specific in certain of the Towneley plays where an attempt is made to characterize shepherds and other rustics by their use of homely sayings. So far as individuals are concerned we shall see a tendency to make Joseph, husband of Mary, a sententious figure, especially in the Coventry play where he is depicted as a veritable proverb-monger.

At the end of this chapter (pp. 43 ff.) I deal with a number of miscellaneous plays based on the Bible, two of which, *Godly Queen Hester* (pp. 43 ff.) and Wager's *Mary Magdalene* (pp. 52 ff.), contain Vices borrowed from the moralities, judgment on whose behavior must be suspended until Chapter Two.

An interesting stage in the development of the religious drama is illustrated by 'The Ceremonial Verses for Palm-Sunday' (T. Wright and J. O. Halliwell, *Reliquiae Antiquae*, II [1845], 241 ff.), written about 1300, in which a man taking the part of 'bysschop Cayface' sings a Latin trope and speaks in both Latin and English. We find him introducing his remarks with a proverb:

> A wel sooth sawe sothlich ys seyd,
> Ech god game ys god y-pleyed,
> Lovelyche and lyȝt ys leve. (II, 241)

He had already made use of a sententious remark in justification of Jesus's death:

> Hit com to sothe that ich tho seyde,
> Betere hit were that o man deyde,
> Than al volk were y-lore. (II, 241, cf. 242)

1

THE CHESTER PLAYS

[Ed. H. Deimling and Dr. Matthews, Early English Text Society, Extra Series, LXII, CXV, 1893, 1916]

11,341 lines: 0; 25; 14; 15

The Chester plays, dating from the middle of the fourteenth century,[5] are usually held to represent a more primitive stage in the development and secularization of the religious drama than any of the other cycles. It is of interest and importance, therefore, to see to what extent proverbial material is found in this extensive cycle. The striking fact which confronts us is the complete absence of proverbs and the relative scarcity of other proverbial matter. In seven of the plays there is no such material whatever, and it is scanty enough in the remaining eighteen. God, in lamenting the fall of Lucifer and the lesser angels, calls out against Pride in a sententious passage beginning:

> Ah! wicked pryde aye work thee wo! (I, 19, i, 253)

Lucifer subsequently laments that

> Pride cast me downe, I wis,
> From heaven right to hell. (I, 27, ii, 167 f.)

Adam, the first man, gives us the first instance of a sententious outburst against women:

> Now all my kinde by me is kent,
> To flee womans intisement;
> Whoe trustes them in anye intent,
> Truly he is decayved. (I, 34, ii, 349 ff.)

God rebukes Cain for his ingratitude, and in so doing incites that thrifty agriculturalist to fratricide:

> Wottes thou not well that for thy deed,
> If thou doe well, thou may have meede;
> If thou doe fowle, fowle for to spede,
> And sicker thereof to be? (I, 43, ii, 581 ff.)

The restraint of Noah's remark when his wife has once been brought aboard is comical enough, and may well have been intended sententiously:

> It is good to be still. (I, 58, iii, 244)

Joseph in The Nativity uses some sententious material, all of a lugubrious nature. He is, not unnaturally, perturbed to find his wife with child, and he places the blame on disparity in years:

> Well I wist an old man and a may
> Might not accord by no way. (I, 110, vi, 125 f.)

Later he hails the approach of the tax collector with a familiar plaint:

> Poore mens waile is ever in weere. (I, 120, vi, 402)

In the same play the emperor Octavian comments on the certainty and unpredictability of Death:

> I must dye I wot not what daye. (I, 117, vi, 327)

At the conclusion of their unfortunate affray with Trowle, the first shepherd remarks, somewhat philosophically:

> But I must needes hold the harme that I have.
> (I, 144, vii, 302)

Jesus makes three statements which must be considered sententious, the first to Satan, and the others to Peter:

> Bread mon lyves not onely bie. (I, 220, xii, 62)

> Whosoeuer with Sword smiteth gladly,
> With Sword shall perish hastely. (II, 278, xv, 342 f.)

> Flesh is frayle and fallinge aye. (II, 351, xviii, 517)

The second thief is sententious on the cross:

> Make not thy frend thy foe! (II, 310, xvi, 712)

There is perhaps an echo of a common proverb ('boot cometh after bale') in the remarks addressed to God by the Rex Saluatus in The Last Judgment (xxiv) when he says,

> After Bale Boot thou bringes,
> And after Teene tyde Tydinges,
> (II, 431, xxiv, 113 f.; cf. I, p. 97, v, 286)

to which we may add the 'after Langour sendeth Lee' (II, 432, xxiv, 142) of the Regina Saluata.

These are all the sententious remarks and the proverbial phrases, mainly conventional comparisons, are few in number. The sparse humor of the Chester cycle is largely of the ranting sort typified by Herod, and it is in the mouths of the ranters that many, if not most, of the proverbial phrases are found. Obviously no attempt is made to inculcate virtue by means of proverbial material, since there are no proverbs and as few sententious remarks as any work based on Scripture could possibly contain. There appears, however, a weak kind of characterization in the use of proverbial phrases in the speeches of the semi-comic, ranting characters.

2

THE YORK PLAYS

[Ed. Lucy Toulmin Smith, Oxford, 1885]
13,069 lines: 3; 64; 26; 13

The longest of the cycles, that of York, which has been dated as early as 1340–1350, represents, as does the Chester cycle, a fairly early state in the development of the religious drama, and like that cycle contains little proverbial material. There are but three proverbs in the entire cycle. When we consider that the Isaac of the York play is more than thirty years old (p. 58, x, 80 ff.) we can feel that he has reason to know the truth of the matter when he tells his father that

Lyff is full swete. (p. 65, x, 279)

If we emend the last word but one from *aftir* to *askis*, the ingratiating remarks of the second shepherd to the infant Jesus gain both sense and proverbial force:

For I haue herde declared
Of connyng clerkis and clene
That bountith askis rewarde. (p. 122, xv, 116 ff.)

In the play dealing with the dream of Pilate's wife the knocking soldier tries to pacify the beadle, who is angered at his noise, by saying:

Wordis are as þe wynde. (p. 280, xxx, 236)

Sentențious remarks are more frequent. Adam, as in the Chester play, places much of the blame at Eve's door:

> Nowe god late never man aftir me
> Triste woman tale. (p. 34, vi, 149 f.)

The first lady makes a thoroughly feminine reply:

> Be stille, Adam, and nemen it na mare,
> It may not mende. (p. 34, vi, 155 f.)

Noah's wife, like the proverbial old dog, feels little confidence in her ability to conform to new ways:

> I lyffe ouere lange þis lare to lere. (p. 50, ix, 148)

After Abraham tells Isaac that they must go to make their offering together, he shuts off further discussion for the time with the words:

> Bott all þe soth is noȝt to sayne. (p. 59, x, 106)

Joseph replies to Mary's statement that her coming child is his and 'þe kyngis of blisse':

> Na, selcouthe tythandis than is þis,
> Excuse þam wele there women can. (p. 107, xiii, 161 f.)

In the end, however, when the angelic visitor has put things in their true light he becomes very solicitous for Mary:

> For litill thyng will women dere. (p. 111, xiii, 305)

Symeon, in the Temple, calls upon the Lord to send him a sight of the blessed babe:

> Great wo is wroght vnto mans harte,
> Whan he muste want that he wolde haue. (p. 438, xli, 157 f.)

In a later scene in the Temple the first Magister expresses his profound conviction that under certain circumstances children should be seen and not heard:

> For where maistiris are mette
> Childre wordis are noȝt to charge. (p. 161, xx, 119 f.)

Three of Jesus's more familiar statements occur in the cycle, the third one, in this instance, being reported by Malchus while making the timid Peter deny his Lord:

> A man lyvis noght in mayne and mode
> With brede allone. (p. 180, xxii, 75 f.)

> Whoso schall othir blame,
> Loke firste þam-selfe be clene. (p. 196, xxiv, 85 f.)

> For he þat strikis with a swerd with a swerde schall be streken.
> (p. 259, xxix, 148)

Peter was forced to undergo a severe verbal castigation from a woman who heaped racy, if not strictly proverbial, comparisons upon his head. Peter's reply is feeble, but no doubt the best he could produce at a trying moment:

> {For women are crabbed,
> {þat comes þem of kynde. (p. 259, xxix, 130)

Caiaphas, in the same play, stands for due process of law and prevents a soldier from striking Jesus, saying:

> Itt is no burde to bete bestis þat are bune.
> (p. 263, xxix, 245)

Pilate's wife bids her son carry to his father an account of her warning dream; the boy agrees to go, but declares that he must have a nap first:

> For he hase myster of a morne slepe þat mydnyght is myssand.
> (p. 278, xxx, 196)

The soldiers who were left to guard the tomb find themselves in an embarrassing predicament when they awake to discover Jesus risen and the tomb empty. They propose to lie and say that a hundred armed men, though not in buckram, to be sure, overpowered them. The first soldier, however, says, Tell the truth; if Pilate slay us

> We dye but onys. (p. 414, xxxviii, 338)

We find that the authors of the York plays made use of proverbial material mainly in the shape of comparisons, which are more than twice as numerous as in the Chester cycle, and which color the extravagant language of the ranters. In one place, however, the application is a little more subtle. Joseph's use of proverbial phrases and sententious remarks provides him with whatever individuality he possesses, but we are still far from the Joseph of the Coventry play.

3

THE TOWNELEY PLAYS

[Re-edited by G. England, with Introduction by A. W. Pollard, EETS., ES., LXXI, 1897]
12,276 lines: 24; 89; 66; 32

The Towneley cycle, or, at least, one member of that cycle, has long received most of the favorable literary criticism vouchsafed to the early religious drama. There is justice in this fact, since here is evident the work of a man who, following the comic muse, possessed whatever measure of genius was allotted to the English drama before the middle of the sixteenth century. Much controversy has raged about the exact amount of the cycle which should be attributed to the 'Wakefield Master,' and, although opinions based on a single stylistic point are never conclusive, it is possible that an examination of the proverbial material will throw light on the question. For the sake of completeness I shall call attention to the number and nature of the proverbial phrases in the various plays.

This cycle contains far more genuine proverbial material than any of the others, which would seem to indicate that parts of it, at least, were written by a man who had a fondness for proverbs. It consists of thirty-two plays, all but three (vii, xvii, and xxxii) of which contain something germane to the present investigation. At first glance, then, it would appear that the proverbial material is not likely to serve as a very accurate means of differentiation. We must remember, however, to take both quality and quantity into consideration, and we may plausibly believe that a play which contains no more than a proverbial comparison or two was not composed by a writer who ordinarily uses many proverbs.

When we examine the twenty-nine plays in question, we discover that some contain far less proverbial material than others. Thus three plays contain but a single proverbial phrase,[6] and eight others but little more,[7] and most of these are conventional comparisons which are Biblical or literary rather than popular. Other plays contain an occasional sententious remark. In the play of Abraham and Isaac, which has a single comparison,[8] Abraham feels bound to prepare to carry out God's harsh command:

And it is good that I be war,
To be avised full good it were. (p. 43, iv, 113 f.)

The plays in which Joseph appears are quite free from proverbs, although in The Annunciation,[9] Joseph philosophizes on ill-matched marriages like his own, and attacks women in a fashion which we have observed in the other cycles:

It is ill cowpled of youth and elde. (p. 91, x, 170)

Now who wold any woman trow?
Certys, no man that can any goode. (p. 91, x, 174 f.)

I blame the not, so god me saue,
Woman maners if that thou haue. (p. 92, x, 209 f.)

Ffor yong women wyll nedys play them
With yong men, if old forsake them,
Thus it is sene always. (p. 95, x, 302 ff.)

In The Flight Into Egypt, in addition to a single comparison,[10] Joseph quiets Mary's lamentations with the statement:

Now leyfe mary, be styll!
This helpys noght;
It is no boytt to grete,
Truly withoutten trayn. (p. 163, xv, 90 ff.)

This is similar to his reply to her in The Play of the Doctors when she complains of her heart 'as heuy as any lede': [11]

Mowrnyng, Mary, may not amend. (p. 192, xviii, 202)

Earlier in the same play one of the doctors had said,

Where masters ar mett,
Chylder wordys ar not to charge. (p. 189, xviii, 91 f.)

These plays show far less proverbial material than the corresponding ones in the Coventry[12] and Ludus Coventriae cycles,[13] and certainly they are not the work of a man who is anxious to use proverbs wherever possible. The one homely phrase[14] in The Crucifixion is overwhelmed by its more conventional brothers.[15] The only piece of sententious wisdom in the play lies in the commendation which the fourth executioner lavishes on his comrade:

Ye ar wise, withoutten drede,
That so can help youre self at nede,
Of thyng that shuld be done. (p. 260, xxiii, 74 ff.)

In The Resurrection, Mary Jacobi reflects that 'the sothe is not to hyde' (p. 317, xxvi, 376). A soldier comforts himself with the thought that 'we dy bot oones' (p. 320, xxvi, 481), and there are two proverbial phrases.[16] In Thomas of India [17] the Apostles disbelieve that Mary Magdalene has seen their Lord, and Paul is vigorous in the attack:

> And it is wretyn in oure law
> 'Ther is no trust in womans saw,
>   No trust faith to belefe;
> Ffor with thare quayntise and thare gyle
> Can thay laghe and wepe som while,
>   And yit nothyng theym grefe.
>
> In oure bookes thus fynde we wretyn,
> All manere of men well it wyttyn,
>   Of women on this wyse;
> Till an appyll she is lyke —
> Withoutten faill ther is none slyke —
>   In horde ther it lyse,
>
> Bot if a man assay it wittely,
> It is full roten inwardly
>   At the colke within;
> Wherfor in woman is no laghe,
> Ffor she is withoutten aghe,
>   As crist me lowse of syn.' (pp. 338 f., xxviii, 29 ff.)

Thomas, in his turn, accuses his fellows of having been duped by a spirit when they thought to see the Christ:

> Ye ar as women rad for blood / and lightly oft solaced.
> (p. 347, xxviii, 233)

Lazarus, in the play which bears his name,[18] is raised from the dead only to hold forth dismally on the horrors of death, and some of his remarks are thoroughly and typically sententious:

> Ther is none so styf on stede,
>   Ne none so prowde in prese,
> Ne none so dughty in his dede,
>   Ne none so dere on deese,
> No kyng, no knyght, no Wight in wede,
>   Ffrom dede haue maide hym seese,
> Ne flesh he was wonte to fede,
>   It shall be Wormes mese. (p. 390, xxxi, 111 ff.)

Amende the, man, whils thou art here,
  Agane thou go an othere gate;
When thou art dede and laide on bere,
  Wyt thou well thou bees to late. (p. 392, xxxi, 182 ff.)

The plays already dealt with contain almost no homely proverbial material to set them apart from the ordinary run of medieval religious verse, but those which remain draw on the popular store in differing degrees. Noah and the Ark has a fair number of earthy comparisons and racy miscellaneous proverbial phrases,[19] but even the memorable fight which took place, as the blissful undergraduate once put it, 'between Noah and a man named Uxor,' fails to evoke a single proverb. The play of Herod the Great contains a number of interesting proverbial phrases, most of which are used by the titular hero, who is characterized by rant and verbal violence.[20] There are three proverbial phrases, two of them homely enough, in The Talents,[21] and the second Torturer delivers himself of a sententious discussion of Fortune:

As fortune assyse / men wyll she make;
Hir maners ar nyse / she can downe and vptake;
  And rych
She turnes vp-so-downe,
And vnder abone,
Most chefe of renowne
  She castys in the dyche. (p. 291, xxiv, 379 ff.)

Pilate makes the same excuse for a nap which we have found his son using in an earlier cycle (see p. 10 above):

He has myster of nyghtys rest that nappys not in noynyng!
(p. 281, xxiv, 65)

After the lively dice game in which Pilate takes more advantage of his rank than of luck, the third Torturer assails dicing, which often leads to murder:

Thus sorow is at partyng / at metyng if ther be laghter.
(p. 292, xxiv, 397)

Here is little enough, but six remaining plays contain proverbs as well as other proverbial material.

Cain and his boy speak all the proverbs in The Killing of Abel. Garcio, who springs upon the reader of the religious plays almost unawares, says that he is more than ready to fight:

Yai, with the same mesure and weght
That I boro will I qwite. (p. 11, ii, 51 f.)

The mock aside was to be overdone in drama, but few can fail to be amused by Garcio's commentary on Cain's self-proclaimed pardon, especially when he anticipates one of the characters in The Second Shepherds' play with his acid

Ill spon weft ay comes foule out.
(p. 21, ii, 435; cf. p. 135, xiii, 587)

Cain makes use of a number of proverbial phrases [22] and one proverb, which he applies to Abel when his sanctimonious brother asks that he sacrifice with him:

Let furth youre geyse, the fox will preche. (p. 12, ii, 84)

His only sententious remark grows out of his thrifty reluctance to part with any of his property:

And it is better hold that I haue
Then go from doore to doore & craue. (p. 13, ii, 142 f.)

The excellent First Shepherds' Play,[23] unduly obscured by its more brilliant companion, is rich in proverbs. The sayings are divided evenly enough among the three shepherds, with something left over for Jack Garcio.[24] The first Shepherd [25] opens the play with a series of gloomy sententious statements which serve to indicate the sad situation in which he finds himself. There is no stability in earthly affairs:

Now in hart, now in heyll / now in weytt, now in blast,
 Now in care,
Now in comforth agane,
Now is fayre, now is rane,
Now in hart full fane,
 And after full sare.

Thus this Warld, as I say / farys on ylk syde,
Ffor after oure play / com sorows vnryde;
Ffor he that most may / When he syttys in pryde,
When it comys on assay / is kesten downe wyde,
 This is seyn;
When ryches is he,
Then comys pouerte,
Hors-man Iak cope
 Walkys then, I weyn. (pp. 100 f., xii, 4 ff.)

Later he declares that his poverty is due to his marriage:

It is sayde full ryfe,
'A man may not wyfe
And also thryfe,
 And all in a yere.' (p. 103, xii, 96 ff.)

When the Shepherds decide that the best singer shall begin the song, he remarks, sensibly enough:

Now prayse at the partyng. (p. 108, xii, 267)

He finds ready means to dismiss the queries which arise after the angelic message:

Nothyng is inpossybyll
Sothly, that god wyll. (p. 112, xii, 373 f.)

The second Shepherd is less sententious,[26] and his only proverb is to be echoed in The Second Shepherds' Play:

Ffyrst must vs crepe / and sythen go.
(p. 103, xii, 100; cf. p. 135, xiii, 591 f.)

The third Shepherd tells his quarreling companions that they 'fysh before the nett!' (p. 104, xii, 139).

When he gives the infant Jesus a bottle as his offering he says,

> It is an old by-worde,
> It is a good bowrde,
> For to drynk of a gowrde. (p. 115, xii, 481 ff.)

The comment which he makes about the quarrel of his companions seems proverbial:

> It is far to byd hyte
> To an eg or it go. (p. 105, xii, 150 f.)

He tells his companions ironically that they

> Wold by thare wytt / make a shyp be drownde, (p. 105, xii, 145)

and also that

> And ye look well abowte / nawther more nor myn,
> So gose youre wyttys owte / evyn as It com In.
> (p. 105, xii, 172 f.)

No Biblical play contains so much proverbial material as The Second Shepherds' Play. The proverbs are shared in equally by the speakers, so that any characterization must be of a class and not of individuals. The first Shepherd has three proverbs:[27]

> He lernyd tymely to steyll / that couth not say nay.
> (p. 133, xiii, 524)

> Kynde will crepe /
> Where it may not go, (p. 135, xiii, 591 f.; cf. 103, xii, 100)

> Lo god makys ayre. (p. 135, xiii, 604)

The second Shepherd quotes three proverbs, two of which occur in his discussion of marriage:

> Be well war of wedyng / and thynk in youre thoght,
> 'Had I wyst' is a thyng / it seruys of noght.
> (p. 119, xiii, 92 f.)

> Thou may cach in an owre
> That shall [savour] fulle sowre
> As long as thou lyffys. (p. 119, xiii, 97 ff.)

He is warrantably doubtful of Mak:

> Ill spon weft, Iwys / ay commys foull owte.
> (p. 135, xiii, 587; cf. p. 21, ii, 435)

Most of his proverbial phrases occur in the description which he gives of his formidable wife,[28] and there may be something proverbial, as well as anti-feministic, in his apologue of the hen and her unhappy rooster:

> Sely capyle, oure hen / both to and fro
> She kakyls;
> Bot begyn she to crok,
> To groyne or [to clo]k,
> Wo is hym is of oure kok,
> Ffor he is in the shekyls. (p. 118, xiii, 67 ff.)

The third Shepherd [29] uses two proverbs:

> Men say 'lyght chepe
> Letherly for-yeldys.' (p. 121, xiii, 170 f.)

> Seldom lyys the dewyll / dede by the gate.
> (p. 123, xiii, 229)

He has some of the sententiousness of the first Shepherd in The First Shepherds' Play. He, too, inveighs against the instability of the world, and says that men are

> Now in weyll, now in wo. (p. 120, xiii, 125)

As they leave Mak's house the first time, he remarks sagely:

> Ffare wordys may ther be / bot luf is ther none.
> (p. 134, xiii, 569)

Mak's proverbial phrases are many and varied,[30] and his one proverb is fitting enough to a man in his recurrent domestic predicament:

> Bot we must drynk as we brew,
> And that is bot reson. (p. 132, xiii, 501 f.)

Mak's wife [31] is not without her proverb, and it applies but too well to her graceless husband:

> Bot so long goys the pott / to the water, men says,
> At last
> Comys it home broken. (p. 126, xiii, 317 ff.)

She is well aware of the wisdom of her sex, saying complacently,

> Yit a woman avyse / helpys at the last, (p. 127, xiii, 342)

and again,

> It is rewthe to beholde,
> Now in hote, now in colde,
> Fful wofull is the householde
> That wantys a woman. (p. 129, xiii, 418 ff.)

Caiaphas, the chief performer in The Buffeting,[32] quotes a Latin proverb:

> Et omnis qui tacet
> Hic consentire videtur. (p. 232, xxi, 143 f.)

He uses the following saying, which may echo Chaucer:

> As euer syng I mes,
> Whoso kepis the lawe, I gess,
> He gettis more by purches
> Then bi his fre rent.
> (p. 233, xxi, 159 ff.; cf. Chaucer, *CT*, I, 256)

He is afraid that Jesus may escape from Pilate's hands, for

> Gyftys marres many man. (p. 242, xxi, 439)

He attacks Jesus viciously, using several proverbial phrases in doing so, and it becomes necessary for Anna, a more restrained character, to remind him that

> All soft may men go far. (p. 234, xxi, 211)

Anna shows a happy optimism when he declares that therc was never a

Man so wyk / bot he myght amende.
When it com to the pryk. (p. 236, xxi, 262 f.)

The first Torturer gives impertinent advice to Jesus:

It is better syt still / then rise vp and fall.
(p. 229, xxi, 28)

Although there is little proverbial material in The Scourging,[33] it does contain one excellent proverb, which is applied to Jesus by the second Torturer:

This man, as myght I spede / that has wroght vs this wo,
How 'Iudicare' comys in crede / shall we teche, or we go.
(p. 247, xxii, 127 f.)

John, to whom falls the sad task of telling Mary that her son is in captivity, tries to prepare her by means of an ominous axiom:

The trouth shuld no man layn. (p. 252, xxii, 282)

The Judgment [34] has its share of proverbs and sayings, all spoken by the two demons and their boisterous ally Tutivillus. The first Demon reminds the damned souls that, however prosperous they may have been, they must not forget the truth of

Prase at the partyng. (p. 385, xxx, 584)

He anticipates the Satan of Heywood's *Four PP* in his opinion of woman:

She that is most meke,
When she semys full seke,
She can rase vp a reke
If she be well nettyld. (p. 372, xxx, 166 ff.)

The second Demon explains the severity of God:

Sir, it is saide in old sawes —
The longere that day dawes —
'Wars pepill wars lawes.' (p. 373, xxx, 193 ff.)

Tutivillus uses no proverbs, but he bubbles over with proverbial phrases; indeed, to his share fall three-fourths of those in the play.

On the basis of the proverbial material quoted above, and taking into consideration the nature as well as the quantity of the sayings, we may conclude that a man fond of using proverbs and homely sayings, whom we may, if we choose, call the 'Wakefield Master,' wrote The Killing of Abel, The First Shepherds' Play, The Second Shepherds' Play, The Buffeting, and The Judgment; wrote, or had a large share in, The Play of Herod; had a slight share in The Scourging and The Talents, and an even slighter share in Noah and the Ark. He seems to have felt that proverbs were of especial value in characterizing his rustics, such as Cain, Garcio, and the Shepherds of both the Shepherds' plays. We must note, too, that the proverbs are not brought in haphazardly but are woven into the dialogue deftly and surely.

4

LUDUS COVENTRIAE

[Ed. K. S. Block, EETS., ES., CXX, 1922]

11,331 lines: 12; 51; 24; 25

The Ludus Coventriae,[35] sometimes called the Hegge plays, from the earliest known owner of the manuscript, seems to date from the last quarter of the fifteenth century. This collection is later than other cycles, but few borrowings from them have been pointed out in it,[36] though the plays have been traced to a number of non-dramatic sources.[37] The collection, on the whole, is fairly rich in proverbial material, the bulk of which is concentrated in a few of the plays, especially those dealing with the woes of Joseph and the birth of Jesus.

The cycle opens with a Proclamation in which Herod's fate is forecast sententiously:

> In his most pride xal come gret tene. (p. 8, i, 236)

God emphasizes the cause of Lucifer's fall:

> Thu lucyfere ffor þi mekyl pryde
> I bydde þe ffalle from hefne to helle. (p. 18, ii, 66 f.)

In the same play Adam expresses his belief that Eve's (and only incidentally his own) pleasure in the apple is hardly worth the aftermath:

> Schort lykyng xal be longe bought. (p. 28, ii, 398)

Eve anticipates in part John Ball's proverb, when she tells Adam that

> ȝe must delve and I xal spynne. (p. 29, ii, 415)

There is one proverb in the declamation spoken by Moses on the Ten Commandments:

> By-ware of custom ffor he wyl dere. (p. 54, vi, 98)

He is sententious on the evil wrought by wicked tongues:

> Wykkyd worde werkyht oftyn tyme grett ill
> Be war þer fore of wykkyd langage
> Wyckyd spech many on doth spyll
> Therfore of spech beth not owt-rage. (p. 55, vi, 135 ff.)

One of the characteristics of this cycle is the large number of plays that deal with Mary and the incidents before the birth of Jesus. In the play about the Conception of Mary we find several changes rung on the proverb which prophesies that joy will follow sorrow. Anna says

> And þo þat departe in sorwe god make þer metyng glad.
> (p. 65, viii, 56)

Joachim is very unhappy and, in his anguish, remarks that

Shame makyth many man his hed for to hyde. (p. 67, viii, 106)

One of his shepherds encourages him:

Aftere grett sorwe mayster evyr gret grace growyht.
(p. 67, viii, 117)

Not long after, the saying is echoed by an angel:

Aftere grett sorwe evyr grett gladnes is had.
(p. 70, viii, 200)

Though the plays concerned with Joseph are full of proverbial material, the proportion put in the good old gentleman's mouth is less than in the Coventry play, where he is distinctly characterized by his use of proverbs.[38] Joseph does not become Mary's husband inadvertently or through any fault of his own. He protests against it from the first:

It is a straunge thynge An old man to take a ȝonge wyff.
(p. 88, x, 182)

An old man may nevyr thryff
With a ȝonge wyff so god me saue. (p. 91, x, 278 f.)

The bishop urges him to come forward and join in the test, but he replies,

Sere he may Euyl go þat is ner lame. (p. 90, x, 238)

Here, of course, may be no more than a matter-of-fact account of his condition. The bishop is a Job's comforter at best, and he warns Joseph of the scandal which may be spoken about his household:

And as we redyn in old sage
Many man is sclepyr of tonge. (p. 93, x, 346 f.)

In The Parliament of Heaven Veritas informs God the Father that

Twey contraryes mow not to-gedyr dwelle. (p. 99, xi, 64)

In Joseph's Return, Mary's husband finds her pregnant and he not unnaturally jumps to the conclusion that his trip had been 'en Cornouaille.' He reflects how men despise him and pities himself not a little:

> Here may all men þis proverbe trow
> Þat many a man doth bete þe bow
> Another man hath þe brydde. (p. 111, xii, 81 ff.)

A rather feeble consolation occurs to him:

> And ȝett many bettyr than I
> Ȝa. hath ben made cokolde. (p. 112, xii, 116 f.)

Mary, because she feels somewhat ashamed to have her condition seen by the people, 'and namely of men,' wants to visit cousin Elizabeth in Montana without delay:

> Pylgrymagys and helpyngys wolde be go in hast
> Þe more þe body is peynyd þe more is þe mede.
> (p. 116, xiii, 17 f.)

The astonishing and rather revolting Trial of Joseph and Mary, almost without counterpart in medieval drama, contains much proverbial matter, but none is put in the mouth of Joseph, who, although he is outrageously abused, has here a more serious and noble rôle than elsewhere in the cycle. The humor, if considerations of taste will permit us to call it that, and the proverbial sayings are all given to Sym Summoner and to the Detractors. The Summoner holds true to the common medieval conception of his calling. His advice to those who are called to court, including 'Malkyn mylkedoke' (p. 123, xiv, 10) and 'davy drydust' (p. 123, xiv, 21), is

> And loke ȝe rynge wele in ȝour purs
> Ffor ellys ȝour cawse may spede þe wurs.
> (p. 123, xiv, 25 f.)

The Detractors, who, for love or duty, bring the condition of Mary to the attention of the bishop, are unduly scurrilous in their language, and several of their remarks are proverbial though unseemly. The first plays with a familiar theme:

A ȝonge man may do more chere in bedde
To A ȝonge wench þan may An olde
Þat is þe cawse such lawe is ledde
Þat many a man is a kokewolde.
(p. 126, xiv, 69 ff.)

And feetly with help sche can consent
To set A cokewolde on þe hye benche.
(p. 127, xiv, 95 f.)

Mary affirms that she is pregnant without sin, and they ask if perchance she slept uncovered in the snow and conceived from a snowflake; if she did her offspring will need to beware of the sun. The reference to the fabliau [39] is obvious, but the idea may have become proverbial.

The temporarily unfortunate Salome, that prototype of Sarah Gamp, if not of Mrs. Harris, uses a proverb when she is first called in:

Whan women travayl grace doth growe. (p. 140, xv, 151)

Before she goes off duty she discovers that occasionally things work out otherwise for the midwife who does not recognize a miracle promptly.

In The Death of Herod, Death dilates upon his power and his impartiality:

All men dwellyng upon þe grownde
Be-ware of me be myn councel
Ffor feynt felachep in me is fownde
I kan no curtesy as I ȝow tel.
(p. 177, xix, 259 ff.)

Jesus is willing to leave the doctors in the Temple and go home with his mother:

> Euery childe xulde with good dyligens
> His modyr to plese his owyn wyl forsake.
> (p. 187, xx, 279 f.)

John the Baptist uses a common figure to make clear that the good go to Heaven and the bad to Hell:

> Corne þat is good men kepe it ful clene
> Chaff þat is sympyl is sett wul nere at nought.
> (p. 193, xxi, 170 f.)

Jesus, in The Temptation, rebukes Satan:

> Nott only be bred mannys lyff ȝitt stood
> But in þe wurde of God as I þe say.
> (p. 196, xxii, 92 f.)

And again, at the beginning of The Woman Taken in Adultery:

> Who so Aske mercy he xal haue grace.
> (p. 201, xxiii, 38)

The Consolators give much good advice in The Raising of Lazarus. Mourning, one of them tells the lamenting sisters, is of no avail:

> Holde ȝour pes
> All ȝour wepynge may not amende itt.
> (p. 214, xxiv, 137 f.)

And another dilates on the inevitability of death:

> Eche creature hens must depart
> Þer is no man but hens must wende.
> Deth to no wyht can be a frende
> All þinge to erth he wyl down cast.
> (p. 218 f., xxiv, 275 ff.)

In this cycle the story of the passion of Christ is divided into two plays, each containing a number of separate scenes. One proverb is spoken by the Demon who serves as Prologue to The First Passion Play:

In trost is treson. (p. 227, xxv, 58)

And he includes in a satirical description of fashionable attire the admonition:

þow poverte be chef; lete pride þer be present.
(p. 227, xxv, 75)

Judas demands his thirty pieces of silver:

In old termys I haue herd seyde
þat mony makyth schapman.
(p. 252, xxv, 624 f.)

Jesus, as in the other cycles, reproves Peter for cutting off the ear of Malchus:

Ffor he þat smyth with swerd with swerd xal be smete.
(p. 266, xxv, 1000)

Anna, in The Second Passion Play, ends a sententious description of 'meed' with a proverb:

Ffor mede doth most in euery qwest
And mede is mayster bothe est and west
Now trewly serys I hold þis best
With mede men may bynde berys.
(p. 326, xxvi, 1604 ff.)

We find in the same play an echo of the 'friend in need who is a friend indeed' in Jesus's address to Mankind in the Resurrection:

Such a frende fyndyst þou nevyr none
To help þe at þi nede. (p. 321, xxvi, 1430 f.)

Christ, in The Appearance to Cleophas and Luke, remarks:

Trewth dyd nevyr his maystyr shame. (p. 340, xxix, 113)

In The Assumption of the Virgin the Jews are discussing Jesus and the harm which his policies seem likely to cause. The bishop applauds the course which they have taken:

> Therfore oure wysdam was to schortyn his endyng
> Whoso clyme ouer hie he hath a foule fall.
>
> (p. 356, xxxii, 31 f.)

We notice that while none of the proverbial matter in this cycle is used for characterization in as marked a fashion as will be seen in the second Coventry play, we do find that proverbs are common in the scenes connected with the Holy Family. Elsewhere proverbial material is found mainly in the speeches of characters who are treated humorously or slightingly.

5

THE COVENTRY PLAYS

[Ed. Hardin Craig, EETS., ES., LXXXVII, 1902]
2092 lines: 8; 5; 3; 7

Only two of the plays which comprised the cycle played in Coventry are extant. Their present form shows evidence of a revision by Robert Croo in 1534, and they are doubtless the result of a process of accretion which had been in operation for two centuries before that date.[40] The first of these, The Pageant of The Shearmen and Taylors, is a combination of two plays: first, The Annunciation, Nativity and Adoration of the Shepherds, and, second, The Adoration of the Three Kings, the Flight into Egypt and the Slaughter of the Innocents. The two parts are divided by a dialogue between three Prophets.[41] There are several striking and humorous scenes in the play, such as the pathetic self-pity of Joseph, the rough freshness of the shepherds, and the ranting pride and rage of Herod. Proverbs are nowhere used to heighten or characterize the humor, nor do they occur in the serious portions of the play. Gabriel soothes Mary's misgivings; her cousin Elizabeth, barren and old, is with child:

> To God onpossibull nothyng mabe. (p. 4, l. 87)

Joseph's outcries at his wife's condition are reminiscent of what we have found in other plays:

> Wele-awey! womon, now may I goo,
> Be-gyld as many a-nothur ys.
> (p. 5, ll. 121 f.)
>
> All olde men, insampull take be me, —
> How I am be-gylid here may you see! —
> To wed soo yong a chyld.
> (p. 5, ll. 133 ff.)

The second play, The Pageant of the Weavers, which consists of the Prophet Play (ll. 1–176), the Purification (ll. 177–721), and the Disputation in the Temple (ll. 722–1192), is of far greater interest. Joseph, who is responsible for the humor, is characterized by his use of proverbs. He is reluctant to get Mary the doves which she needs for the offering in the temple, but melancholy proverbs convince him that he has little chance of evading the task:

> The weykist gothe eyuer to the walle. (p. 47, l. 447)
>
> Nedis mvste thatt nedis schall. (p. 47, l. 456) [42]
>
> He thatt ma worst of all
> The candyll ys lyke to holde. (p. 47, ll. 457 f.)

Mary gently advises him to be on his way if he is going at all, and he asks for sympathy and substantiation from the married men in the audience:

> For he thatt weddyth a yonge thyng
> Mvst fullfyll all hir byddyng,
> Or els ma he his handis wryng,
> Or watur his iis when he wold syng;
> And thatt all you do knoo. (p. 48, ll. 466 ff.)

Mary urges him again, and he grudgingly admits that he'll have to go:

> Loo! feyre wordis full ofte doth leyde
> Men cleyne agen there mynd. (p. 48, ll. 485 f.)

He departs at last, feeling himself ill-matched against such a wife and likely

> Eyuer the worse yend of the staff to haue,
> Att the lattur yend. (p. 49, ll. 504 ff.)

The doves are not easy to find:

> I loke fast and neuer the nere. (p. 49, l. 514)

A friendly angel aids him, and he brings them home, full of self-commendation, and a little testy at Mary's haste to be off to the temple:

> Ey! bloo a whyle, dame, I the pray!
> For soft and essele men goo far.
> (p. 50, ll. 550 f.; cf. p. 51, l. 575)

Once more, however, he is overcome:

> Soo full of feyre wordis these wemen be,
> Thatt men thereto must nedis agre.
> (p. 50, ll. 555 f.)

When Jesus shows signs of precocity, Joseph remarks proudly:

> Loo! fryndis, here doth apere,
> Yt ys eyrly scharp thatt wol be thorne.
> (p. 56, ll. 747 f.)

On the way from the temple he becomes weary and says,

> That man thatt canot goo before
> Nedis mvst cum behynd. (p. 58, ll. 804 f.)

He is greatly distressed by the disappearance of Jesus, but tries to be philosophic:

In sorro wasse there neyuer man more,
But mornyng ma nott ytt amend;
Mare, wyff, lett vs therefore
Take the grace that God woll send.
(p. 65, ll. 1021 ff.)

That the use of proverbs is intended to be a characterizing feature of Joseph is shown by the fact that no other speaker in the play uses a single one. There are a number of weak proverbial comparisons, and Simeon is sententious in commending his clerk for seeking information:

Sith thatt ye for knoleyge dothe make sute,
Your wyttis the bettur do I reypute.
(p. 44, ll. 351 f.)

These, however, serve but to emphasize the fact that Joseph, old, feeble, complaining, and sententious, is the proverb-monger of the play.

6

THE DUBLIN AND BROME ABRAHAM AND ISAAC PLAYS

[Ed. O. Waterhouse, *The Non-Cycle Mystery Plays*, etc., EETS., ES., CIV, 1909, 26 ff.; cf. pp. xliii ff.]
Dublin, 369 lines: 1; 1; 0; 0
Brome, 465 lines: 1; 3; 1; 0

The Dublin Abraham and Isaac, probably written in the neighborhood of 1458,[43] contains what may be an oblique reference to the well-known and much appreciated proverb, 'A woman will have her will.' Isaac tells Abraham that if his mother had known what was in store she would never have let him come, whereupon his father says:

þi modre may not haue hir wille all way.
(p. 31, l. 197)

The Brome play contains a passage which seems to have been written with the proverb 'Out of sight, out of mind' as a model. Isaac begs Abraham not to grieve for him:

> For, be I onys ded and fro ȝow goo,
> I schall be sone out of ȝowre mynd.
> (p. 44, ll. 201 f.)

7

THE CROXTON PLAY OF THE SACRAMENT

[Ed. O. Waterhouse, *The Non-Cycle Mystery Plays*, etc., EETS., ES., CIV, 1909, 54 ff.; cf. pp. liv ff.]

1007 lines: 0; 5; 2; 0

With the exception of the Digby Mary Magdalene, which is a hybrid, the only surviving English play which can lay claim to being a miracle, and that not in the strictest sense of the word, is the Croxton Play of the Sacrament. It contains a very considerable amount of humor (though probably much that is humorous to us was not so for its auditors), but has neither proverbs nor sententious remarks.

8

THE DIGBY PLAYS

[Ed. F. J. Furnivall, EETS., ES., LXX, 1896]

The so-called Digby Plays, four in number, seem to date from the last quarter of the fifteenth century.

8a

566 lines: 0; 5; 2; 1

The first play, which combines the Slaughter of the Innocents and the Purification, contains no proverbial material worthy of the name and only a little laughless humor connected with the killing of the children. The only passage which can be called sententious occurs when one of the mothers threatens the thrasonical Watkin:

> Women be ferse when thei list to assaile. (p. 13, l. 311)

8b

663 lines: 1; 2; 4; 4

The second play, which deals with the Conversion of St. Paul, is somewhat more elaborate in structure but contains even less humor than the first. The single proverb is directed at Saul by Jesus:

> Yt ys hard to pryke a-gayns the spore. (p. 34, l. 184)

There are four sententious remarks in Saul's sermon, three of them Latin, with English translations:

> Who-so in pride beryth hym to hye,
> With mys[c]heff shalbe mekyd. (p. 47, ll. 524 f.)

> Quanto maior es, tanto humilia te in omnibus:
> The gretter thou art, the lower loke thu be;
> Bere the neuer the hyer for thi degre. (p. 48, ll. 549 f.)

> Ex habundancia cordis, os loquitur;
> Who movyth yt oft, chastyte louyth non;
> Of the hartes habundans the tunge makyth locucion.
> (p. 48, ll. 561 ff.)
> Oculus est nuncius peccati, —
> That the Iey ys euer the messenger of foly.
> (p. 48, ll. 571 f.)

8c

2144 lines: 0; 18; 2; 2

The third play, much longer than the average Biblical play, treats the life of Mary Magdalene, and contains no proverbs whatever, while the bulk of the proverbial material consists of comparisons, most of them from the mouths of the comic characters. There are two sententious remarks, neither of them notable. The World speaks of Fortune:

> For þe whele of fortune with me hath sett his sentur.
> (p. 66, l. 312)

The king of Marcylle is distressed when his wife begs to accompany him on the long sea voyage to the Holy Land:

> A-las! þe wyttes of wommen, how þey byn wylld!
> And þer-of fallytt many a chanse. (p. 119, ll. 1702 f.)

8d

1631 lines: 0; 9; 1; 1

The fourth play, or plays (since The Burial of Christ and The Resurrection are distinct), is not in the Digby manuscript (see p. vii). It duplicates a part of the play of Mary Magdalene, but is far inferior, its dullness being alleviated by neither inspiration nor humor. There are a few weak comparisons and one sententious remark. The Second Mary tries to quiet Mary Magdalene's grief:

> It is bot in vayn
> Thus remedilesse to mak compleyn.
> (p. 209, ll. 1123 f.)

9

THE NORWICH PLAYS

[Ed. O. Waterhouse, *The Non-Cycle Mystery Plays*, etc., EETS., ES., CIV, 1909, 8 ff.; cf. pp. xxvi ff.]

A, 90 lines: 1; 0; 0; 0
B, 153 lines: 0; 1; 0; 0

The Grocer's Pageant of the Creation and Fall is the only surviving member of the Norwich cycle, and it exists in two distinct versions. The A text, representing a part of the play in the form in which it was presented in 1533, is very short and contains but one proverb. Unusually enough this is put in the mouth of God, who tells Adam, as he describes the dire consequences of touching the forbidden fruit:

> A warned man may live: who can yt denye?
> (p. 9, l. 36)

The B fragment, representing the text in use in 1565, is about twice the length of A, and has nothing of interest except one very learned proverbial phrase, used by the Holy Ghost, who tells Man (Adam) that it is God's intention to try him,

> As gold is tryed in the fyer. (p. 17, l. 128)

10

THE STONYHURST PAGEANTS (1610–1625)

[Ed. C. Brown, Hesperia, VII, Göttingen, 1920]
8740 lines: 10; 25; 24; 33

Mystery and miracle plays were acted until the end of the sixteenth century, long after they had ceased to have any part in dramatic development, but there was little or no real change in Biblical drama after 1400. What was composed thereafter was almost entirely on the basis of types and actual plays already in existence. We are, then, all the more surprised at the phenomenon of a cycle written after 1600. The Stonyhurst Pageants, so called from the fact that they are found in the library of Stonyhurst College in Lancashire, were certainly written between 1610 and 1625.[44] The author was a Roman Catholic who hoped, probably, to use his plays to fix, if not to replant, his faith in the hearts of those hearing them. There is no doubt that the plays were intended for public presentation; there is little less doubt that they never came upon a stage. The manuscript is defective, but the extant plays, the first of which is numbered six, deal with Old Testament events from Jacob to Naaman. The plays, with one exception, are completely without humor or any real interest, even to the student of the drama. The play which differs from the others is the incomplete pageant of Naaman, the last in the manuscript. Curiously enough, it is modeled on Plautus, and the author has taken proper names as well as situations from the Roman dramatist.[45]

Proverbial material is unequally scattered through the plays,[46] the bulk being found in Naaman. Indeed six of the ten proverbs, four of the twenty-five comparisons, seven of the twenty-four other proverbial phrases (and we may note that eleven of the remaining seventeen refer to a period of 'seven years') and nineteen of the thirty-three sententious remarks are in this single play of 1136 lines. Simeon, in the sixth pageant of Jacob, uses a proverb:

All that we sayd was but in guyle, & yet yt made fooles fayne.
(p. 1, l. 22)

There are two sententious remarks. Ada laments for the Caananites the fate which has fallen upon them, and reminds the sons of Jacob that they themselves may find like misery for 'fortune's mutable' (p. 2, l. 42). Isachar, however, is stern and merciless in reply:

As you haue deseru'd, you shall receiue.
(p. 2, l. 46)

The seventh pageant, that of Joseph, contains two proverbs, both used by Turnsol, one of the famine-pressed Egyptians, as he makes up his mind to turn his land over to the king in return for a supply of grain:

Lyfe is sweete. (p. 35, l. 882)
Make a vertue of necessity. (p. 35, l. 888)

Joseph's brothers do not have much faith in dreams; after little Joseph tells how the sun, moon, and eleven stars did obeisance to him, Simeon says:

> Dreames be seldome to be trusted. (p. 7, l. 52)

Reuben tries, a shade hypocritically perhaps, to console his father at Joseph's supposed death:

> And your will vnto gods resigne
> Who takes them first, whom he loues best.
> (p. 11, ll. 151 f.)

In the eighth pageant of Moses we find Pharaoh sending out his army in haste after the Hebrews, for

> Daunger's in delay. (p. 71, l. 825)

He had earlier expressed an intention to keep his royal eye on the oppressive measures being taken against the Israelites:

> For better will the seruants doe, when that their maister's by.
> (p. 53, l. 294)

Moses, before his death, advised his people at length, among other things exhorting them as follows:

> But when that good & bade's before you set, the good choose rather.
> (p. 94, l. 1542)

In the ninth pageant of Joshua, Grizo, one of the spies, reports that Jericho should be easily captured, as the inhabitants are all terrified:

> For sooner will the souldiers flye then fight that are faynt hearted.
> (p. 97, l. 38)

Achan, caught with the goods which he had salvaged from Jericho against the Lord's strict injunction, realizes too late the impossibility of concealment:

> I see no synne's so secret, but yt's knowne to god Almighty.
> (p. 104, l. 255)

The fourteenth pageant of Saul contains two sententious remarks. Phalech encourages the Philistines to fight manfully against the Hebrews:

> Yt ys better lyke valyant men to dye
> Then lyue as slaues. (p. 155, ll. 161 f.)

Saul admits to David that he has dealt unfairly with him:

> For good turnes thou hast done to me, & yll I haue the rendred.
> (p. 189, l. 1180)

In his pageant, the fifteenth, David finds it easy to philosophize over the sudden death of Uriah:

> Diuerse ys th' euent of warres: now this & now that man
> The sworde cutts off. (p. 201, ll. 80 f.)

Bruna, a woman sent by Joab, tells David that the banishment of Absalom will not bring Ammon back to life:

> And as waters do not returne, So on th' earth wee all dye
> Neuer to come agayne to lyfe. (p. 206, ll. 229 f.)

Benedad sends a boastful and threatening message to King Achab (the seventeenth pageant of Elias), and the king responds fittingly:

> For many haue had the foyle before the victory that bragged.
> (p. 249, l. 427)

The incomplete eighteenth pageant of Naaman contains six proverbs. Artemona, wife of Naaman, uses two. When her servant, Phronesium, says that she has ever deemed her mistress free of sorrow and care, she replies:

> No body can tell where
> The shoe doth pinch, but she that yt vpon her foote doth weare.
> (p. 265, ll. 81 f.)

She urges Naaman to take steps for his own cure. Nothing can be achieved without effort:

> You know th' olde sayinge well
> That one must first the nutts shell cracke before he eate the kernell. (p. 279, ll. 472 f.)

Strato, who is unwilling to believe that Naaman can be cured by following the advice of Phronesium, is gloomily confident that the end will justify his suspicions:

> The ende will all disclose. (p. 287, l. 743)

> Tyme truth will tell, & bringe all thinges to light. (p. 288, l. 750)

Phronesium urges her mistress to make the best of a bad situation:

> Make a vertue of necessity. (p. 268, l. 158)

The king of Syria, with more sense than Naaman himself possesses, speeds him off to Samaria to try whether or no the prophet can cure his leprosy:

> There's daunger in delay. (p. 286. l. 684)

Artemona uses five sententious remarks. Her husband's malady causes her to relinquish any hope of happiness:

> I well perceiue that womens hopes do ofter proue most vayne. (p. 263, l. 25)

She finds some consolation in the good qualities of her maid:

> And in her's truly verifyed: Such maners, & conditions
> As euery one ys of, such for the most part are their fortunes. (p. 264, ll. 37 f.)

None the less, she cannot let Phronesium console her:

> Whyther steales not griefe? None can be found that ys on all parts blessed. (p. 265, l. 84)

> It's easy good aduise to geue to others in their misery. (p. 268, l. 148)

She finds Naaman hard to move for his own good:

For thou as oone an Æthiops skyne with washinge white may make
As that same willfull folow persuade this voyage to vndertake.
(p. 279, ll. 496 f.)

Phronesium modestly advances the value of her counsel:

For that shallow witted ys, may some tyme counsell geue
That wholesome ys, & a seely mouse a Liones may releeue.
(p. 266, ll. 101 f.)

If her mistress will only reveal her trouble it may well help matters:

And many tymes th' impartinge of ones griefe vnto an other
Eyther quite taketh yt away, or makes yt seeme farre lesser.
(p. 266, ll. 103 f.)

She urges her very reasonably not to waste time desiring the impossible and lamenting the inevitable:

Syth that can not be done
Which you desyre, desyre that which may effected bee.
(p. 267, ll. 146 f.)

To grieue at that which no wayes can be holpen
No wisdome ys: for the thinge that's once done can neuer bee
Vndone agayne. (p. 268, ll. 156 ff.)

Naaman himself is lavish of moralization. His misfortune calls forth a long outburst against Fortune:

Oh! how inconstant, frayle, & mutable is humane felicyty?
How's he deceiu'd that groweth proud for fortunes smyle that's momentary?
He trust's vnto a staffe of reede, on fortune that relyeth
As by me may be seene, whom she so miserably deiecteth,
And headlonge hurleth downe from the top of the hiegh'st felicity
In to the gulffe of endlesse woes, & neuer dyinge misery,
And trampleth me vnder her feete after a most strange fashion.
But yt's in vayne for to complayne, sith she's without compassion.
(pp. 272 f., ll. 297 ff.)

Like many another ungrateful husband he finds the solicitude and suggestions of his wife an added discomfort:

For he that doth intend to lyue & lead a quiet lyfe
Must euer more contentted be to be ruld by his wyfe.
(p. 283, ll. 604 f.)

For there's no trust in women when as the matter ys so weighty.
(p. 283, l. 607)

Even when once undertaken, he finds the journey to Samaria hard to make:

I fynd . . . by experience that nothinge ys so easy
But yt will seeme hard vnto hym, that doth the same vnwillingly.
(p. 291, ll. 840 f.)

The king of Israel is vastly annoyed with his brother monarch for sending him a leper, and his wrath is such that Naaman fears that it may lead to a war between the two lands. This depresses him still more, for

Doubtfull ys th' euent of warres. (p. 295, l. 956)

It seems to him that the only recourse is to take safety in flight:

Lest we to late repent. (p. 297, l. 1010)

Leonidas, his companion in the journey, has felt from the first that the Samarian prophet offers the only possibility of cure, and he has chided the doubting Strato for his scorn of Phronesium's plan:

But you perhaps th' aduise esteeme that's sould at highest rate.
Yet scorne not theyrs that's easy prizd, or freely ys bestowed.
(p. 286, ll. 701 f.)

He agrees, however, about the attendant dangers, and need for deliberation:

All perills yt's good to cast. (p. 288, l. 754)

He hears with horror of the king of Israel's reception of Naaman. This attitude is most unlooked for, and yet

It's a true sayinge: that trouble sooner happeneth
And griefe of mynde vnto a man, then that which he desyreth!
(p. 297, ll. 990 f.)

Like Leonidas, the wise Syrian king feels that it would be foolish to ignore the story of the servant girl:

> And many tymes the symple & vnlearned
> A salue for some sores do fynd out, where of the wysest men
> And such as were esteem'd the best phisitions, did neuer dreame.
> (p. 285, ll. 669 ff.)

Comic relief is afforded by the squabbling servants, Bromia and Dorio, and the latter finds himself outmatched:

> I well perceiue a womans weapon her tongue is & her nayls.
> (p. 289, l. 786)

11

GODLY QUEEN HESTER (1525–1529)

[Ed. W. W. Greg, Materialen zur Kunde des älteren Englischen Dramas, V, Louvain, 1904]

1180 lines: 7; 1; 7; 9

If we date *Godly Queen Hester*, which was first printed in 1561, as early as 1525–1529, we do so because we accept the identification of Haman with Wolsey (cf. Greg, pp. viii ff.). So far as our investigation is concerned, the most striking thing about the play is the scarcity of proverbial phrases. Otherwise it offers little that is unusual. The Vice,[47] Hardy Dardy, uses more proverbs than anyone else, and, indeed, his first words are:

> A prouerbe as men say a dogge hath a day,
> When so euer that it chaunce. (p. 26, ll. 636 ff.)

He repeats the saying a few lines later:

> But as I say, a dogge hath a day. (p. 26, l. 646)

When Haman doubts Hardy Dardy's fitness for his service, the Vice at once concludes that his lack of wit is responsible and insinuates a very virtue therein:

Yet afole when it doth happe may somtyme chaunce to stoppe a gappe
When wyse men wyll not mell. (p. 27, ll. 660 f.)

He shows little sorrow when his master is dragged away to execution, and takes the opportunity to tell the story of Phalaris's brazen bull and its unfortunate maker:

I wene by god he made a rodde,
For his owne ars. (p. 41, ll. 1035 f.)

The three remaining proverbs deal with pride and ambition. Pride suggests the possibility of ill to himself — 'If pryde haue a fall' (p. 22, l. 524), and Ambition is afraid for Haman:

Sumtyme or tyde, he may for his pryde,
Suffer some shame. (p. 23, ll. 564 f.)

At the end of the play the complacent queen sums up Haman's career in general terms:

The hygher they clyme the deper they fall.
(p. 46, l. 1175)

The sententious remarks outnumber the proverbs, and are, for the most part, heavy and uninteresting. The play opens with the king's gentlemen discoursing, at the royal request, on the qualities most worthy of honor. The first gentleman's remarks are typical:

Me seames as vertue none can be so good,
Not ryches nor power, wisdome nor gentill bludde.
For wher vertue fayleth, the other be not suer,
But full vnstable, and longe cannot indure.
(p. 4, ll. 25 ff.)

The king expresses a belief in justice and a ruler's need to cherish it:

Quoque, si princeps malus populus coruet.
(p. 6, l. 93; cf. *Prov.* xi, 14)

Esther during the address which wins her the royal hand, once excuses her plain-speaking, or, perhaps, her wordiness, with 'veritie hath no pere' (p. 14, l. 304). When Pride enters it is with a song on his lips, and the song consists of a number of such sententious paradoxes as the following:

> Oft chance such rekning, that with their mouth thei sing,
> Though thei wepe in their hart. (p. 15, ll. 340 f.)

This thought leads him to a discussion of people who say one thing and do either another or nothing:

> They saye they can doe all, but when neede doeth befall,
> They begynne to starte. (p. 16, ll. 356 f.)

Haman's objection to Hardy Dardy is that he is a fool, and so unlikely to keep his master's secrets:

> Fooles largely will bourde and tell al theyr thought.
> (p. 27, l. 662)

Hardy Dardy's reaction to Haman's plan to kill all the Jews is insouciant enough for any Vice:

> It woulde greue any man yonge or olde of age
> Without his head to goe on pylgrimage.
> (p. 32, ll. 789 f.)

Ahasuerus feels no pity for Haman:

> He that deserues payne is worthy certaine,
> Euen for to haue it. (p. 41, ll. 1053 f.)

Later the king expounds the moral of the play at some length:

> My Lordes by this fygure ye may well se,
> The multitude hurte by the heades necligence,
> If to his pleasure so geuen is he,
> That he will no paine take nor dilligence,
> Who careth not for his cure ofte loseth credence,
> A prouerbe of olde sume time in vsage,
> Few men that serue but for theyre owne aduauntage.
> (p. 45, ll. 1162 ff.)

12

THE RESURRECTION OF OUR LORD (1530–1560)

[Ed. J. Dover Wilson and Bertram Dobell,
Malone Society Reprints, 1912 (1913)]
1321 lines: 0; 3; 1; 3

The Resurrection of Our Lord, first printed in 1912 from a defective manuscript, itself considerably later than the date of composition, is a pedestrian piece, devoid of grace, interest, and proverbs. Caiaphas tells Pilate that the disciples are probably stirring up trouble of some kind:

> A naughtie nature, never fcales want
> To studdye out myscheife, he ys in hit soe pregnant.
> (p. 4, ll. 112 f.)

When Mary Magdalene's wrath against the persecutors of her Lord reaches extravagant lengths, Mary Jacobi seeks to quiet her:

> For you doe but consume your hart with heavines
> About a thinge, that ys remedilesse. (p. 13, ll. 386 f.)

The pertinacity of Thomas's doubt finally brings a reproof from James:

> That heade, which thinkes, his owne reason the best
> Are most part with fancies, ys all possest.
> (p. 41, ll. 1276 f.)

13

John Bale

John Bale's best-known plays, *The Three Laws* and *King Johan*, will be considered among the moralities (see pp. 97 ff. below). His Biblical plays have little to recommend them to the reader.

13a

THE CHIEF PROMISES OF GOD UNTO MAN (1538)

[Tudor Facsimile Texts, 1908]
983 lines: 0; 5; 2; 2

The Chief Promises of God unto Man is indeed a tedious performance and is as lacking in proverbs as in humor. God, in chiding the children of Israel for their lack of obedience to him, points out that even

> An oxe knoweth hys lorde, an asse hys masters dewtye.
> (sig. D iii)

The Prophet Isaiah has a little more hope: the Israelites have a good king, and that promises something:

> Whan the prynce is good, the people are the better.
> And as he is nought, their vyces are the greatter.
> (sig. D iv)

13b

JOHN BAPTIST'S PREACHING IN THE WILDERNESS (1538)

[Ed. J. S. Farmer, *The Dramatic Writings of John Bale*, 1907, pp. 127 ff.]
493 lines: 0; 1; 2; 2

Of the two sententious remarks in *John Baptist's Preaching*, the soldier, who has been impressed by John's words, uses one:

> Experience doth show whereas are good monitions,
> May be avoided all jeopardy and danger. (p. 136)

The other expresses Jesus's desire to save all mankind:

> He is no good captain that from his army fall. (p. 145)

13c

THE TEMPTATION OF OUR LORD (1538)

[Tudor Facsimile Texts, 1909]
433 lines: 0; 0; 4; 0

The Temptation contains only four miscellaneous proverbial phrases, three of which are spoken by Satan.

14

JACOB AND ESAU (*c.* 1545)

[Tudor Facsimile Texts, 1908]
1750 lines: 6; 12; 17; 10

Jacob and Esau, like many of the plays of this period, is hard to date. Licensed for printing in 1557, the extant edition is of 1568, but the play itself was probably written in the 1540's, and there has been some desire to attribute it to Udall, or, at least, to his school. There is considerable proverbial material, but it is not used to characterize any one person, though, in general, the proverbs and proverbial phrases are spoken by the comic characters.

Jacob is the white-haired boy of most of the characters, and no one but Isaac has any good to say of Esau; even Ragau, loyal enough in deed, is anything but a worshipful admirer of his master in thought and speech. Zethar and Hanan, the two neighbors who have been awakened before their wonted hour of rising by Esau's lusty horn, deplore his wildness. Hanan says that it has been ever so from his childhood:

> Yong it pricketh (folkes do say) that wyll be a thorne.
> (sig. A iv, i, 2)

This very proverb provides the theme and refrain of the song which Abra, Rebecca's handmaiden and model of serving girls, sings in the third act. 'Then let her sweepe with a brome, and while she doth it, sing this song':

> It hath bene a prouerbe before I was borne,
> Yong doth it pricke that wyll be a thorne.
> Who will be euill, or who will be good,
> Who geuen to truth or who to falshood,
> Eche bodies youth sheweth a great likelihood.
> For yong doth it pricke that will be a thorne.
> Who so in youth will no goodnesse embrace,
> But folow pleasure, and not vertues trace,
> Great meruaile it is if such come to grace.
> For yong doth it pricke that will be a thorne.
> Suche as in youth will refuse to be tought,
> Or will be slacke to worke as he ought,
> When they come to age, their proofe will be nought.
> For yong doth it pricke that will be a thorne.
> If a childe haue bene giuen to any vice,
> Except he be guided by such as be wyse,
> He will therof all his lyfe haue a spice.
> For yong doth it pricke that will be thorne.
> It hath bene a prouerbe. &c. (sig. E ii[v], iv, 4)

Esau's shabby treatment of Ragau in the matter of the 'grosse and homely pottage' is enough to arouse the servant's anger and sorrow, so that we are not surprised at the characterization which he gives of his master:

> This prouerbe in Esau may be vnderstande:
> Clawe a churle by the tayle, and he will file your hand.
> (sig. C iv, ii, 3)

Old Deborra, the nurse, is appreciative of Abra's willingness and charm — 'There is not a pretier gyrle within this mile' — but for all that it seems likely to her that Abra's husband may catch a shrew:

> Cat after kinde (saith the prouerbe) swete milke wil lap,
> If the mother be a shrew, the daughter can not scape.

> Once our marke she hath, I maruell if she slippe:
> For hir nose is growing aboue hir ouer lippe.
> (sig. E iii, iv, 4)

This is a somewhat gloomy view for a woman to take of her own sex, but Deborra is a simple soul at best. When she sees Jacob decked out in Esau's fine clothing she is mightily impressed by the change it has made in him:

> Now I see apparell setteth out a man.
> (sig. E iv[v], iv, 8)

Mido, the little boy who leads the blind patriarch about, is one of Jacob's partisans, but none the less he uses a proverb which indicates his understanding, albeit an approving one, of the deception practised on Isaac:

> Now I see it true the blinde eate many a flye.
> (sig. F i [v], iv, 9)

When Rebecca laments the fact that Esau is the older son, Jacob strives to quiet her with a sententious remark:

> Mother, it is to late to wishe for that is past.
> (sig. B i, i, 3)

This is very like what poor old Isaac says to Esau when, much later in the play, he is forced to admit to his favorite son that his blessing is irretrievably gone:

> That is done and past, can not be called againe.
> (sig. F iv, iv, 4)
> Things done can not be vndone. (sig. F iv, iv, 4)

When Rebecca tries openly and volubly to persuade Isaac to put Jacob before Esau, little Mido speaks admiringly of his mistress's power of repartee, and there is probably as much genuine melancholy as satire in Isaac's reply:

> Yea, womens answeres are but fewe times to seeke.
> (sig. B iv[v], i, 4)

Mido seems to remember this when Rebecca swears Abra and himself to secrecy concerning her plot. Abra becomes indignant that she should come in the charge before Mido, and he replies in the best masculine vein:

> They say, women will euer be clattering.
> (sig. D iii, ii, 4)

Once Esau's belly is full of pottage he waxes sententious:

> Ah, sir, when one is hungry, good meat is much worth.
> And well fare a good brother yet in time of neede.
> (sig. C iv[v], ii, 3)

We have already noted Ragau's disgust at Esau's failure to share the pottage with him, but our sympathy recedes somewhat when he tells us that he had earlier provided surreptitiously for himself. Like Chaucer's Wife of Bath and Manciple, among many others, he has profited by good maternal advice:

> I tolde you at the fyrst, I woulde prouide for one:
> My mother taught me that lesson a good whyle agone.
> (sig. C iv[v], ii, 3)

Isaac regrets Esau's neglect of him, but he does not find it at all strange:

> But it is oft sene whome fathers do best fauour,
> Of them they haue lest loue againe for their labour.
> (sig. D iii[v], iii, 1)

Rebecca urges speed on Jacob in the execution of her nefarious scheme:

> Therfore whyle the tyme serueth, I thee warne,
> To slacke when all thinges are ready may do harme.
> (sig. F i, iv, 8)

15

Lewis Wager's *MARY MAGDALENE* (*c.* 1560)

[Tudor Facsimile Texts, 1908]
2136 lines: 8; 12; 11; 9

Lewis Wager's long play, *The Life and Repentance of Mary Magdalene,* is a curious mixture of mystery, miracle, and morality in which Infidelity and Malicious Judgment rub shoulders with Simon the Pharisee, Christ, and Mary Magdalene.

The first remarks of the Prologue are in Latin:

> Nulla tam modesta felicitas est
> Quæ malignantis dentes vitare possit. (sig. A ii)

He goes on to translate this and Wager thus initiates a favorite device of his, namely, the quoting and translating of sententious Latin phrases. There are nine more of these (sigs. A ii, B i, B ii, C ii, C ii[v], C iii, D i[v] [2], D ii[v], E i[v]), but they are not worth giving, nor have I included them in my count. Apart from this unusual number of Latin quotations there are an exceptionally high proportion of proverbs in relation to the rest of the proverbial material. There are two proverbs in the Prologue:

> For euill will neuer said well, they do say. (sig. A ii)

> A horse will kick if you touche where he is galled. (sig. A ii[v])

The rest are all spoken by the bad characters, and Infidelity, the Vice, leads with three. When Pride urges Mary to boast of her family she readily admits that she came of an honorable stock, but it is unlikely that she hears Infidelity's comment:

It is a stock (they say) right honorable and good,
That hath neither thefe nor whore in their blood.
(sig. D i)

Mary fears that her ill conduct will lead to public shame, but Pride suggests the possibility of keeping secrets, and Infidelity says:

Ye shal not kepe my counsel, if ye can not kepe your own.
(sig. D ii)

He hears that Jesus is to dine with Simon the Pharisee and he begins to plot mischief:

By God he shall haue soure sause it may hap.
(sig. G iv)

Carnal Concupiscence tells Infidelity to cure himself of his habit of winking:

He that loketh with one eie, & winketh with an other,
I would not trust (say they) if he were my brother.
(sig. C ii)

Mary's instruction in the fine art of self-adornment includes tight lacing in the waist. It may pain somewhat, but as Pride says:

Use will make the thyng easy. (sig. D i)

Malicious Judgment, one of the chief fomenters of the plots against Jesus, fears lest the Savior be granted too much time before he is checked:

There is euer peryll in muche delay. (sig. E i[v])

Each of the sententious remarks is spoken by an evil character, and Infidelity is handsomely in the lead with six out of the nine. Mary ought to waste no time in seeking her pleasures:

One thyng is this, you shal neuer be yonger in dede.
(sig. B ii)

He greets Pride as 'the spryng of iniquitie' (sig. B iii), a description which the latter is only too proud to use of himself:

> The beginning of syn, which doth man from God deuide
> Scripture calleth it nothyng els but pride. (sig. B iv[v])

Incidentally, Cupidity is not loath to contest the field with Pride, for he says:

> You know that my name is called Cupiditie,
> Whom Scripture calleth the roote of all iniquitie.
> (sig. B iv[v])

Infidelity has a poor opinion of women:

> This is a true prouerbe, and no fained fable,
> Few womens words, be honest, constant, and stable.
> (sig. D i[v])

> Such as wer harlots in their youth
> May vse to be baudes euermore for a truth. (sig. D ii[v])

> Women haue no soules, this saying is not newe.
> (sig. E iv[v])

Malicious Judgment is of the same mind:

> Womens heartes turne oft as doth the wynde.
> (sig. G iii[v])

Jesus himself is not exempt from the Vice's taunts, and Infidelity closes his part of the discussion at Simon's dinner party thus:

> But with fooles it is follie to vary. (sig. I i[v])

Part II

French Biblical Plays

At this point we can add to our appreciation of the use of proverbs in the English Biblical plays by means of a brief survey of some of the principal French plays belonging to this type. The French plays under consideration are *Le Mistère du Viel Testament*, Arnoul Greban's *Mystère de la Passion*, Simon and Arnoul Greban's *Mystère des Actes des Apostres*, and the *Miracles de Nostre Dame*. While these do not constitute all the early French Biblical plays they do run the gamut of the subject matter and they are certainly long enough to be representative. The only systematic study of the proverbs in the early French drama is in a doctoral dissertation [48] whose author set a chronological limit for himself antedating all of our texts save the *Miracles de Nostre Dame*. Our purpose will be best served by a succinct account of the plays in this chapter and the segregation of the French proverbial material in the Appendix. Rigid adherence to chronology would require us to start our discussion with the *Miracles de Nostre Dame*, but I prefer to begin with the later *Mistère du Viel Testament*,[49] since that is more comparable to the English plays.

The *Mistère* covers the Old Testament selectively with liberal additions in bulk and detail from non-Biblical sources. The principal surface differences from the English cycles are its intensive treatment of Old Testament themes, and its length, since its forty-nine thousand three hundred eighty-six lines (plus two thousand seven hundred twenty-four lines in interpolations) are more than all the English miracle and mystery plays put together, if we exclude the *Stonyhurst Pageants*. Direct influence of the French plays on the English plays is slight and mainly limited to the Chester cycle,[50] but the similarity in material and approach makes comparison feasible and valuable. The *Mistère*, like most of the English cycles, shows marked evidence of accretion.

Before making an examination of the proverbial material in the *Mistère* we must consider contrasts between the French and English cycles. In the English cycles we have observed that the proverbial material was often concentrated in a few plays. In the French cycle we find a strikingly different state of affairs, since all but two of the forty-five plays have proverbial material and the distribution is extraordinarily even. In the English plays we observed further that the bulk of the proverbs was spoken by comic or semi-comic characters. Here again the French cycle differs sharply. There is humor enough in the French plays, but it is almost exclusively occupational and given to non-Biblical characters. The principal comic figures illustrate this fact: the curiously named masons who construct the Tower of Babel;[51] the shepherds who, at various points, give homely details of their life;[52] Maudollé, the executioner, in the play of Joseph;[53] Gournay and his more hilarious colleagues in the play of Esther;[54] the soldiers who slaughter the Hebrew children in Egypt;[55] the gravediggers, strangely like Shakespeare's, in the episode in which Solomon solves the problem of a disputed inheritance;[56] the servants in Susanna's kitchen;[57] Monsieur Turelututu and his comrades in the army of Holofernes;[58] Saoul and Maudollé, the carpenters who build Haman's gallows;[59] and the impecunious artist who makes the statue of Octavian.[60]

The grimness of much of the humor is noticeable, as well as the absence of pagan potentates in comic rôles.

The humorous scenes contain very little proverbial material.[61] The French authors did not use proverbs for characterization, though inevitably some characters speak more than others. Hagar, in her small part, uses two proverbs,[62] and Rebecca is liberal with proverbial phrases.[63] Esau speaks two proverbs and one phrase,[64] and the interpolated speech of Envy, in the play of Joseph and his Brethren, is full of simple proverbial comparisons.[65] David makes use of a surprisingly large number of proverbial phrases and sententious remarks.[66] As one would expect, Solomon's connection with proverbs is emphasized. There is an uncommonly amusing scene in which Solomon entertains the queen of Sheba and others by reciting some of his proverbs, with an accompaniment of exclamations of admiration and delight from his auditors — 'Vella ung notable proverbe,'[67] 'Quel proverbe, Dieu souverain!'[68] 'C'est une noble parabolle,'[69] and 'Quelle parabolle notable!'[70] When the recitation is finished one of the minor characters says,

> Ce disner cy a esté plein
> De proverbes, joyeusetés,
> Chançons, jouxtes, beaulx ditz, dictez;
> C'estoit toute joye et liesse. (IV, 407, ll. 36493 ff.)

As the queen departs she makes a promise, 'Vos beaulx proverbes retiendray.'[71] As a matter of fact, Solomon had not distinguished himself with his proverbs, although his knowledge of the arts and crafts of Normandy is to be commended:

> La femme folle de costume
> A la langue plus fort tranchent
> Q'un fin rasouer de Guigant.
> (IV, 403, ll. 36372 f.)

There are eighty-two proverbs in the *Mistère*, few of which are repetitions. The most popular is 'Necessité n'a loy aucune,' [72] which appears four times. 'Nourriture passe aage' is used twice, once introduced by 'On dit bien vray que' [73] and once by 'Car on dit en commun langaige.' [74] The idea of 'Ung temps ne peult tousjours durer' [75] is echoed in 'Tousjours ne court pas une chance.' [76] The instability of the courtier's life, a favorite medieval theme, is expressed in two proverbs:

On dit ung mot qui partout court . . .
Que service de court
N'est pas heritage. (IV, 119, ll. 29819 ff.)

Vous ne sçavez combien
Grace de court a homme dure.
(VI, 54, ll. 45614 f.)

The *Mistère* is fairly rich in proverbial phrases, but they are neither interesting nor especially novel. The majority, one hundred thirty-two in number, are simple comparisons, most of which are drawn from the animal kingdom. The lion leads the list, as is eminently fitting, followed no less fittingly, perhaps, by the pig, and then by the wolf, dog, sheep, calf, and so on. The miscellaneous proverbial phrases, of which there are ninety-three, twenty-six of them representing references to 'seven years,' are of singularly little moment.

One hundred and fifty-nine sententious remarks are scattered through the *Mistère*, many of which are translations or paraphrases of Biblical lore. Certain ideas are extremely popular and the sententious remarks fall into rather definite groups. A favorite admonition is to the effect that there is no advantage in worrying about a thing which has taken place — 'Quant c'est faict c'est faict.' The inevitability of Death, its way of hitting suddenly and unexpectedly at rich and poor alike, is often noted, especially in the earlier plays. The transitoriness of 'bien mondain' is another melancholy favorite.

The nature and distribution of the proverbial material bears out the statement made earlier that in the *Mistère du Viel Testament* proverbs are introduced primarily for their simple and immediate didactic value and without any idea of their affording characterization or humor. The only author who is clearly fond of proverbs, and especially proverbial phrases, is the man who wrote the long interpolated passages in the separately printed *Moralite de la vendition de Ioseph* (*c.* 1538; see Rothschild, I, xxxi ff.). He scattered proverbial material with abandon but with neither taste nor skill.

The next play to consider, following the order of the Bible, is Arnoul Greban's *Mystère de la Passion* [77] in which the life and death of Our Lord, copiously interspersed with interminable scenes in Heaven and Hell, drags its slow course through thirty-four thousand five hundred and seventy-five lines. This grievous work contains twenty-eight proverbs, one hundred three comparisons, forty-seven other proverbial phrases, and fifty-five sententious remarks. If we compare these figures with those derived from the *Mistère du Viel Testament*, taking the greater length of the latter into consideration, we see that there are somewhat fewer proverbs, rather more proverbial phrases, and far fewer sententious remarks in Greban's play. The distribution, too, is different, and here the *Passion* permits comparison with the English plays. The humorous scenes in the French play may be divided into two groups, first, those in which devils are presented and which are usually set in Hell, and, second, those in which the lower classes, such as servants, messengers, guards, jailers, soldiers, seamen, and the like, appear. The humor, or at least the realism, of the second type is often interesting and refreshing, but there is little in the infernal scenes save dreary ranting monotony. The Hell scenes contain three proverbs, thirty-five comparisons, ten other proverbial phrases, and two sententious remarks. In the lower-class scenes we find ten proverbs, thirty-three comparisons, twenty-four other proverbial phrases, and three sententious remarks. Sententious remarks, obviously, are reserved for the serious scenes, but one hundred fifteen of the one hundred seventy-eight other sayings are in the humorous passages, which represent a decided minority of the lines of the play. The speech of the fiends is definitely characterized by the use of proverbial comparisons, some of them rather violent, while the lower-class characters use many proverbs and proverbial phrases, and a homely realism is thus obtained, especially by the use of miscellaneous proverbial phrases. Here, though by no means as pronounced, we find the same tendency to localize proverbial material in the comic scenes, and to fill ranting speeches with proverbial comparisons which we have observed in the English plays.

We need not pass judgment on the authorship or the relations between manuscripts and editions of the *Mystère des Actes des Apostres*,[78] usually held to be written by Simon Greban with the aid of his brother Arnoul.[79] Whoever the author, he was a man whose verses flowed rapidly and indefatigably, if not over smoothly, and the length of the *Actes* may be estimated as something above sixty-six thousand lines. In all this expanse we find fifteen proverbs, one hundred eighty-two comparisons, sixty-eight other proverbial phrases, and sixty-two sententious remarks. If Simon Greban be the main author his interest in proverbial material was far less than his brother's, and that lack of interest is especially evident in the proverbs. So far as the humorous scenes are concerned we find here too a considerable number set in Hell, though by no means as many in the second half of the play as in the first, and these passages contain forty-three comparisons, eight other proverbial phrases, and one sententious remark. In the lower class scenes we find one proverb, thirty-six comparisons, eight other proverbial phrases, and four sententious remarks. In addition to these well-defined groups, the Hebrew persecutors of the Apostles use a considerable amount of proverbial material, largely derogatory comparisons.

There can be no question concerning the distressing lack of proverbial material in this long play, but it does contain two passages, both toward the end, which are of extreme value in illustrating the development of the dramatic use of proverbs. We find in the *Actes des Apostres* two of those proverb-capping scenes which were to be the delight of many a later dramatist.

Two priests discuss the death of St. James with Agripart and Trotemenu, who are both well pleased by the sad event. When the rascals leave, the two priests confer as follows:

Le premier prebstre.
Tant gratte chieure que mal gist.

Le second prebstre.
Tant va le pot a leau quil casse.

Le premier prebstre.
Tant tardon que vient la becasse.

Le second prebstre.
Tant plus croist mal / tant plus contrainct.

Le premier prebstre.
Tant plus gelle / tant plus estrainct.

Le second prestre.
Plus crye on / plus bruyct le meffaict.

Le premier prestre
Or sus / ce qui est faict est faict /
Et ce qui aduiendra aduiendra. (II, fo. clxxxvii)

The second passage contains some of the conversation which followed the spectacular, literal, and well-deserved fall of Simon Magus:

Le premier cheualier Neron.
On dit que nul ne peult voller sans aesles /
Mais ie scay bien quelles luy ont failly.

Le second cheualier Neron.
Je scay trop bien quil est cheu faulte delles
De son tumber le corps mest tresailly.

Gerion.
De quelque vent a este accueilly
Dont a este a terre renuerse.

Daru.
Cest mal volle encores pis failly
Dung mauuais aer a este trauerse.

Martinien a part.
De tempter dieu nest pas licite
A son egal se doit on comparer.

Proces.
Sage est louurier quen raison sexcercite
Selon le faict fault loeuure preparer.

Martinien.
Selon lestat doit on lhostel parer
Cil qui bien vit a bien mourir apprent.

Proces.
Offense a dieu est forte a reparer
A sage tiens qui vers luy ne mesprent.
(II, fo. ccxx[v])

The first of these dialogues, unmixed as it is with non-proverbial material and containing proverbs rather than sententious remarks, is more interesting than the second, and, indeed, is one of the best examples of proverbial stichomythia before the middle of the sixteenth century. For the first English example of this kind see p. 139 below.

Finally we come to a group of religious plays, older, as already noted, than any of the French plays which we have hitherto considered, and which belong to a type scantily represented in English, the strict miracle play. Here I have examined the great collection of plays dealing with the miracles and beneficence of the Virgin Mary.[80] It consists of forty plays, composed mainly in the fourteenth century, which aggregate seventy thousand one hundred sixty-six lines. Although there is only one play (x) which contains no proverbial material, the total amount is very slight. There are in all the plays but thirty-one proverbs, fifty comparisons, one hundred and six other proverbial phrases, and seventy-nine sententious remarks. Many of these plays are lively and pleasing enough to read, but they are almost completely devoid of humor, and what little appears is often of the most elementary nature, such as scenes in which porters demand bribes before admitting visitors, or those in which two or more men discuss longingly their chance of getting a drink of something stronger than water. Such passages do not lend themselves especially to the use of proverbs, nor, in general, do we find proverbs in them.

We can sum up in a few words what the French plays have to tell us. The earliest plays which have been examined contain fewer proverbs than it is easy to imagine a fourteenth-century French writer introducing into any more or less independent work of the length of the *Miracles de Nostre Dame*. The *Mistère du Viel Testament*, which, in part at least, is probably older than the New Testament plays, uses proverbial material for purely didactic purposes and does not ordinarily employ it in humorous scenes. Arnoul Greban, in his *Mystère de Passion*, and the author, probably Simon Greban, of the *Mystère des Actes des Apostres* do not introduce an undue amount of proverbial material but do show a marked tendency to concentrate it in humorous scenes where it, and especially the proverbial phrases, emphasizes the ranting speech of the demons and hostile Hebrews, and the fresh realism of the speech of the lower-class characters. There is little or no attempt to characterize individuals by the use of proverbs as was done on several occasions in the English plays, and, despite the appearance of two proverb-capping scenes in the *Actes des Apostres*, the French dramatists are far behind their English colleagues in the exploitation of proverbial material.

CHAPTER II

THE MORALITIES

Part I

English Moralities

The thirty-eight plays treated in this chapter differ considerably from one another in length, interest, and literary merit, but they all belong to one rather loose dramatic type — the morality. We are not concerned here with the question of strict definition;[1] for our purpose the chief characteristic of most moralities is that in them a neutral, usually a universal, character is subjected to good and bad influences of one kind or another. We have in general, then, three groups of characters, Neutrals, Virtues, and Vices. The Vices, obviously dear to author and audience alike, are responsible for the humor and, though we may blush to confess it, the greater part of any interest which may lurk in the moralities. In addition they are all important so far as proverbial material is concerned, for, just as the sayings in the Biblical plays were largely limited to the humorous scenes, so in the moralities they are found most commonly in the speeches of the evil and comic characters. The Virtues often get a fair share of the sententious remarks, but seldom many of the proverbs and proverbial sayings. There are, inevitably, a number of exceptions to this rule. In *The Castle of Perseverance* and *Mankind* and, to a lesser degree, Lyndsay's *Satire of the Three Estates*, for example, the good characters employ about half of the proverbs, but ordinarily the preponderance is on the side of evil. Among the Vices one usually stands out from his companions and is often denominated the Vice *par excellence.* He is apt to be a merry, care-free rascal with most of the good jokes, and a schemer who is willing to deceive and abuse his own confederates. He it is who ordinarily uses far more proverbs and proverbial phrases than anyone else, and, indeed, their use may well be said to form a characterizing feature of the chief Vice. Outstanding examples are Freewill in *Hickscorner*, Fancy (if he be the Vice) in *Magnificence*, Infidelity in Bale's *Three Laws* (in interesting contrast to Sedition in *King Johan*, who uses far fewer), Avarice in *Respublica*, Courage in Wapull's *The Tide Tarrieth No Man*, and Idleness in *The Marriage of Wit and Wisdom.* Professor Morris P. Tilley in a discussion of this last play makes the following comment, which, so far as I know, is the first studied recognition of this marked tendency:

> Following what was probably an established dramatic convention, continued by Shakspere in the speech of his jesters, the author heightens the wit of Idleness, the Vice in his play, by giving him more than a liberal share of proverbs. Over against his *twenty-six*, the other characters share the remaining *twenty-eight*, with five the highest number given any one of them.
>
> The intention of the author in favoring Idleness with so large a share of proverbial wit and wisdom is obvious. He aims to have his main character win and hold, by his cleverness, the centre of interest in the play. In a similar way, in *Euphues*, Lyly lards with proverbs the speeches of his characters to emphasize their cleverness.[2]

Proverbs were obviously not introduced in the moralities for educational purposes but rather because they were considered humorous [3] and because a wealth of proverbial phrases was felt to increase the effect of low life realism which the Vices were expected to suggest. This is as definite a use of proverbs for characterization as one could ask for and there are few other instances in the moralities. Wit and Will, the neutral characters, employ the bulk of the proverbs in *The Marriage of Wit and Science* but even here the frolic Will uses most of the proverbial phrases. The only clear-cut case is in *Respublica* where People, representing the distressed lower classes, emphasizes his humble origin and rusticity by means of a liberal sprinkling of homely sayings.

The number of moralities whose titles are proverbs is worthy of note. We find W. Wager's two extant plays *The Longer thou Livest the more Fool thou art* and *Enough is as Good as a Feast* and we hear of his lost *'Tis Good Sleeping in a Whole Skin*; George Wapull's *The Tide Tarrieth No Man*; Ulpian Fulwell's *Like Will to Like, Quoth the Devil to the Collier* and Thomas Lupton's *All for Money*.

16

PRIDE OF LIFE (c. 1410?)

[Ed. O. Waterhouse, *The Non-Cycle Mystery Plays*, etc., EETS., ES., CIV, 1909, 88 ff.; cf. pp. lxiv ff.]
502 lines: 2; 3; 2; 4

The oldest preserved morality seems to be the fragmentary *Pride of Life*, the remnant of which has been mutilated by careless scribes. In his long speech the bishop says that it fares with men in the world as with

> Fiscis in a pol
> þe gret eteit þe smal. (p. 100, ll. 361 f.)

The king rejects the suggestion that he should go to church, uttering a proverb which has not been understood by all editors:

> Nay Churc nis no wyl cot,
> Hit wol abid þer.[4] (p. 102, ll. 425 f.)

There are several sententious remarks. The Prologue queries:

> Wat helpit to yilp mucil of his mit
> Or bost to mucil of his blys? (p. 89, ll. 37 f.)

The king (?) announces his intention of clinging to the root of his rest:

> I nil chong fer no new. (p. 92, l. 130)

His wife tries to quiet his foolish talk of living forever:

> Yet þogh þou be kinge
> Nede schalt haue ende;
> Deth ouercomith al thinge
> Hou-so-euer we wende. (p. 94, ll. 203 ff.)

The king's answer to this sensible statement is a typical piece of slander:

> Ʒe, dam, þou hast wordis fale,
> Hit comith þe of kinde;
> Þis nis bot women tale. (p. 94, ll. 207 ff.)

17

THE CASTLE OF PERSEVERANCE (c. 1425)

[Ed. F. J. Furnivall and A. W. Pollard, *The Macro Plays*, EETS., ES., XCI, 1904, 75 ff.]

3650 lines: 7; 45; 19; 45

The Castle of Perseverance is the earliest complete, or nearly complete, morality and it is also one of the longest, running as it does to three thousand six hundred fifty lines. So far as proverbial material is concerned this play differs widely from later plays of the same type. This is not to say that there is any lack of sayings, but their nature and distribution is peculiar. In a morality one naturally expects sententious remarks, but, even considering the length of this play, forty-five occurrences represent an unusually high level. The number of proverbial phrases is not excessive, but that the comparisons should outnumber all others nearly three to one is decidedly contrary to the later and general usage. Finally, with so much proverbial material the number of proverbs is low out of all proportion.

Then, too, we shall see in the later plays that the proverbs are usually spoken by the Vice and his associates, while here there is a fairly even division between Vices and Virtues.

The Bad Angel employs the two best proverbs. After having heard the Good Angel cry out against covetousness he tells Mankind:

> Ȝa! whanne þe fox prechyth, kepe wel ȝore gees!
> (p. 101, l. 804)

This is a beautiful example of the ancient and honored legal aphorism: When your case is bad, attack the other attorney. Later in dismissing the sound and pious counsel of such good ladies as Chastity, Industry, and Generosity, he remarks coarsely enough:

> Lete þe qwenys cakle!
> Þer wymmen arn, are many wordys:
> Let hem gone hoppyn with here hakle!
> Þer ges syttyn, are many tordys.
> (p. 156, ll. 2649 ff.)

The remaining proverbs are on a higher plane. Chastity declares that the man is foolish indeed who will not be warned by others:

> I lete a man no bettyr þanne a best,
> For no man can be war be oþer
> Tyl he hathe al ful spunne. (p. 155, ll. 2616 ff.)

Mankind, perhaps, showed a slightly mercenary and worldly spirit when he lamented the transitoriness of wealth:

> Tresor, tresor, it hathe no tak. (p. 166, l. 2987)

The remaining proverb, which is used three times, once by Justice and twice by Truth, clearly reflects the uncharitable, if amply justified, attitude which those good sisters take toward Mankind when the poor misled wretch is brought before the Supreme Bench:

> As he hath browyn, lete hym drynke.
> (p. 171, l. 3163)
>
> Lete hym drynke as he brewyth! (p. 174, l. 3275)
>
> As he hathe browne & bake,
> Trewthe wyl þat he drynke. (p. 175, ll. 3300 f.)

Because the sententious remarks in this play are so numerous and are used with so little reference to character or situation, there is no practical use in a detailed discussion of their relation to their context.[5] We may separate a series of sayings which grew out of the familiar proverb 'Bote after bale.' We find here three types:

1. þat in bowre þi bale schal bete. (Bad Angel, p. 88, l. 368)
   þou schalt be my bote of bale. (Mankind, p. 90, l. 445)
   Of bytter balys þou mayste me bete.
   (Good Angel, p. 116, l. 1314)
   Al þi bale schal torne þee to bote.
   (Penance, p. 119, l. 1404)

2. Boþe here bak & here blod, I brewe al to bale.
   (Gluttony, p. 106, l. 966)
   I brew to þee þyne bale. (Sloth, p. 147, l. 2339)
   Bytter balys þou hyr brewe! (World, p. 149, l. 2420)
   He brewyth hym-selfe a byttyr galle.
   (Patience, p. 154, l. 2577)
   Bitter balys I gynne to brewe. (Mankind, p. 166, l. 2984)
   Body! þou dedyst brew a byttyr bale.
   (Soul, p. 166, l. 3013)

3. May any bote þi balë brewe. (Shrift, p. 116, l. 1305)
   Sum bote of balë þou me brewe. (Mankind, p. 162, l. 2864)

Then there is a large group of sayings against covetousness and greed:

Haue he neuere so mykyl, ȝyt he wold haue more.
(First Flagbearer, p. 79, l. 88)

Hard a man is in age, & Covetouse be kynde.
(First Flagbearer, p. 80, l. 92)

Non est in mundo diues, qui dicit 'habundo.'
(Pleasure, p. 92, l. 506)

Tyl man be dyth in dethys dow,
He seyth neuere he hath I-now.
(Bad Angel, p. 101, ll. 813 f.)

Þer is no dysese nor debate
Þorwe þis wyde werld so rounde,
Tyde nor tyme, erly nor late,
But þat Coueytyse is þe grounde.
(Generosity, p. 150, ll. 2454 ff.)

Mankynde seyth he hath neuere I-nowe,
Tyl his mowthe be ful of clay.
(Generosity, p. 155, l. 2638 f.)

'More & more,' in many a place,
Certys þat song is oftyn songe.
(Mankind, p. 158, ll. 2716 f.; p. 159, ll. 2770, 2774)

'More & more' sey ȝyt, haue do.
(Covetousness, p. 159, ll. 2759, 2762)

For þou seydyst neuere 'I-now I-now.'
(Bad Angel, p. 169, l. 3116)

In opposition are a number of sayings used either satirically or by the bad characters:

And þou schalt fyndë, soth to sey,
Þi purs schal be þi best[ë] frende.
(Covetousness, p. 152, ll. 2521 f.)

A-forn mele, men mete schul tyle;
It is good, for al chaunce,
Sum good owhere to hyde.
(Mankind, p. 153, ll. 2538 ff.)

Peny-man is mekyl in mynde. (Mankind, p. 156, l. 2666)

Where-so I walke in londe or lede,
Peny-man best may spede:
He is a duke to don a dede
Now in euery place. (Mankind, p. 156, ll. 2671 ff.)

In Penyman is al his trust. (Good Angel, p. 157, l. 2678)

There are three sayings which deal with the covetous man's estate:

And his eyr aftyrward comyth euere be-hynde.
(First Flagbearer, p. 80, l. 103)

Man knowe not who schal be his eyr, & gouerne his good.
(Second Flagbearer, p. 80, l. 105)

Oftyn tyme I haue ȝou told,
Þo men, þat ȝe arn to lest be-hold,
Comynly schal ȝoure wonnynge wold,
And ben ȝoure next eyrys. (World, p. 163, ll. 2905 ff.)

The remaining sayings, which, it will be observed, are relatively few, are listed in the order of their occurrence:

To speke fayre be-forn, & fowle be-hynde.
(Backbiter, p. 97, l. 668)

Þus seyth Caton, þe grete clerke:
'Labitur exiguo quod partum tempore longo.'
(Covetousness, p. 103, ll. 868 f.)

Of Mankynde, getyth no man no good,
But if he synge 'si dedero.' (Mankind, p. 103, ll. 881 f.)

Þus Euery synne tyllyth in oþer,
And makyth Mankynde to ben a foole.
(Covetousness, p. 108, ll. 1035 f.)

For, whanne Lucyfer to helle fyl,
Pride, þer-of þou were chesun.
(Meekness, p. 140, l. 2096 f.)

In meselynge glotonye,
With goode metis & drynkys trye,
I norche my syster Lecherye.
(Gluttony, p. 144, ll. 2258 ff.)

Worldis wele is lyke a iij-foted stole;
It faylyt a man at hys most nede.
(Abstinence, p. 154, ll. 2599 f.)

Drery is my deth-drawth;
A-geyns me may no man stonde.
(Death, p. 160, ll. 2792 f.)

Þe grete fyschys ete þe smale. (Death, p. 161, l. 2821)

Do for ȝoure self whyl ȝe han spase!
(Mankind, p. 166, l. 2997)

Mercy pasë allë þynge. (Soul, p. 168, l. 3064)

Evyr at þe begynnynge
Thynke on ȝoure last endynge! (God, p. 186, ll. 3648 f.)

18

MANKIND (*c.* 1475)

[Ed. F. J. Furnivall and A. W. Pollard, *The Macro Plays*, EETS., ES., XCI, 1904, 1 ff.]

907 lines: 11; 7; 17; 7

Mankind contains a considerable number of proverbs, but here we find the miscellaneous proverbial phrases definitely in the ascendancy, a situation which we are to observe in most other moralities. It is worthy of note that in this play, as in *The Castle of Perseverance,* the good or neutral characters use nearly half of the proverbs.

Mercy tells New-guise that an economy of well-chosen words is superior to anything else:

Few wordis; few & well sett! (p. 5, l. 102)

She also advises Mankind, that

Mesure ys tresure. (p. 9, l. 230)

Later, Mercy laments that Mankind is so shifting, and above all so ready to listen to bad advice:

In trust ys treson. (p. 27, l. 743)

Early in the play Mankind, in a mood that is not to last, regrets that his flesh has sway over his soul:

Wher þe goode wyff ys master, þe goode-man may be sory.
(p. 8, l. 195)

His pious frame of mind passes ere long, and we find him hinting at the proverb which says, 'When the belly is full the bones will be at rest':

I xall slepe (?MS skepe), full my bely.
(p. 22, l. 581)

Among the bad characters New-guise uses two splendid Wellerisms:

'Ecce quam bonum & quam Jocundum,' quod þe deull to þe frerys.
(p. 12, l. 318)

'Beware,' quod þe goode wyff, when sche smot of here husbondis hede: 'be-ware!' (p. 23, l. 611)

The remaining proverbs are, in contradistinction to what we usually find, rather shreds and scraps than completed sayings. When Mischief says,

Pesse, fayer babys! ȝe xall haue a nappyll to-morow,
(p. 16, l. 420)

he certainly has in mind the proverb which declares that 'A child's love, if lost with a pear, may be gained with an apple.' And we have no trouble in recognizing 'Each man for himself and the Devil take the hindmost' in his

I be-schrew þe last xall com to hys hom.
(p. 26, l. 717)

The proverbs implicit in Naught's two remarks are easy to identify:

I xulde haue don bettur, hade I wyst.
(p. 25, l. 678)
My bolte ys schott. (p. 29, l. 775)

Mercy employs all but one of the seven sententious remarks. She begins the play with a monologue in which she repeats one saying three times:

The corn xall be sauyde, þe chaffe xall be brente.
(p. 2, ll. 43, cf. p. 3, ll. 46, 55)

She dislikes the bad characters, but she is able to take a mournful satisfaction in their future lot:

But such as þei haue sowyn, such xall þei repe.
(p. 7, l. 175)

Solomon she quotes with approbation:

'Vanitas vanitatum,' all ys but a vanyte.
(p. 28, l. 760)

Part of her natural philosophy is that a worthy petition ought to be granted:

> Aske mercy, & hawe. (p. 32, l. 856)

Mankind ought to be more careful about whom and what he believes:

> Þe prowerbe seyth / 'Jacula prefata minus ledunt.'
> (p. 33, l. 875)

The remaining sententious remark is addressed penitently and hopelessly by Mankind to Mercy:

> The prowerbe seyth 'þe trewth tryith þe sylfe.'
> (p. 31, l. 831)

19

WISDOM (*c.* 1460)

[Ed. F. J. Furnivall and A. W. Pollard, *The Macro Plays*, EETS., ES., XCI, 1904, 35 ff.]

1168 lines: 9; 5; 7; 5

Wisdom, which in plot is among the simpler moralities, contains relatively little proverbial material, but there are more proverbs than proverbial phrases or sententious remarks. Though there are as many Vices as mind could desire, this play has no Vice; the rôle of suborner to wickedness is taken by Lucifer, who uses three proverbs. In his suave way he acknowledges that man may occasionally pray and fast:

> All thynge hat dew tymes. (p. 49, l. 401)

A man, however, should not try to distinguish himself by means of ascetic habits:

> Who clymyt hye, hys fall gret ys. (p. 50, l. 444)

He rejoices when Mind, Will, and Understanding decide to follow his advice, and he assures them that it is not he alone who will be pleased:

> Gode lowyt a clene sowll & a mery. (p. 51, l. 494)

The remaining proverbs are spoken by Will and Understanding. Will remarks complacently of himself:

> Wyll, for dede oft ys take. (p. 43, l. 221)

In his enthusiasm over his group of lechers he produces two Wellerisms, which, if not strictly proverbs, are of distinction:

> They may sey with tenker, 'I trow lat a-mende.'
> (p. 60, l. 755)
>
> Thre fortherers of loue; hem schrew I! quod Bete.
> (p. 60, l. 762)

Understanding also likes Wellerisms. Falseness, he says, is now

> Clepyde wysdom: 'ware þat!' quod Wyly.
> (p. 55, l. 607)

Understanding boasts of the perjury and deceit of his retainers, the false Jurors:

> Wyche wey to þe woode wyll þe hare,
> They knewe, & þey at rest sett als tyghte.
> (p. 60, ll. 744 f.)

He alludes to the trusting proverb of the spendthrift, 'Spend and God will send,' when he says:

> I hoope of a goode yer,
> For euer I trost Gode wyll send.
> (p. 62, ll. 827 f.)

Lucifer utters a sententious remark akin to many in *The Castle of Perseverance*:

> So to couetyse he xall wende,
> For þat enduryth to þe last ende.
> (p. 53, ll. 532 f.)

Understanding has saved his money and is well pleased with the fact:

> Ryches makyt a man equall
> To hem sumtyme his souereyngis were.
> (p. 54, ll. 590 f.)

> Wo wyll haue law, must haue monye.
> (p. 57, l. 669)

Mind calls for the exile of Will's lecherous band:

> Wer vycis be gederyde, euer ys sum myschance.
> (p. 61, l. 769)

Wisdom tries to turn Mind from his evil courses by warning him of his inevitable fate:

> Dethe, to euery creature certen ys.
> (p. 64, l. 880)

20

Henry Medwall's *NATURE* (*c.* 1486–1500)

[Tudor Facsimile Texts, 1908]
2922 lines: 5; 10; 26; 21

Henry Medwall, the first English dramatic author whose name has come down to us,[6] was reasonably fond of proverbial material, especially miscellaneous proverbial phrases and sententious remarks. In *Nature* none of the few proverbs are spoken by the virtuous characters, though the neutral character, Man, uses two. The World bids Man pay no heed to Reason or Innocence:

> Theyr wordys be but wynde. (sig. B iii[v])

Pride wrests an old proverb awry in both form and sense when he says of his son:

> I begate the horson in bast
> It was done all in hast
> Ye may se there was no waste. (sig. C ii[v])

Man is pleased with his foresight in not being off with the old love before he is assured of the new:

It ys good to be sure euer more. (sig. F ii[v])

His final repentance is accompanied by the belief that, as was inevitable, he has paid for his wisdom:

Wyt ys nothyng worth / tyll yt be dere bought.
(sig. I ii[v])

When Man commands Bodily Lust to marshal his defensive forces against Reason, Bodily Lust has his doubts about the response of such kittle cattle to discipline:

I had leuer kepe as many flese
Or wyld hares in an opyn lese
As undertake that. (sig. G ii[v])

Ten characters share the twenty-one sententious remarks. Of these Reason uses five. He sends Man into the world with good counsel concerning speech and action:

And let thy world [*word*] be cousyn to thy dede.
(sig. B iii)

After Man's repentance he tells him to seek God's mercy without fear:

God ys mercyable yf ye lust to craue
Call for grace and sone he wyll yt send.
(sig. E ii[v])

Also he must fight off his Vices by following the corresponding Virtues:

Quia contraria contrariis curantur, *etc.*
(sig. E iii[v])

Unfortunately this regimen is of no avail and Man returns to his gay friends, but when age creeps on him he seeks Reason again and begins to lament his wasted years. Reason has small comfort at first:

A thyng don / can not be called agayn.
(sig. H iii[v])

Soon, however, he sends Man back to the Virtues once more, telling him that he ought to be able to recognize them, as he knows their opposites very well:

> Of .ii. contrarys there ys but one lernyng
> That ys to say whan thou knowyst well that on
> The other contrary ys knowen anon. (sig. H iv)

The World makes three efforts to impress his importance on Man:

> Also he must nedys / do as the worlde doth.
> (sig. B ii[v])
> For euery man / clepyth hym wyse
> That doth after the comen gyse. (sig. B iv[v])
> Thynke that ye be here / a worldly man
> And must do as men / that in the world dwell.
> (sig. B iv[v])

Man's first reformation is accompanied by a sound if transitory resolution:

> Man wythout reson ys but blynde. (sig. E i[v])

Before long we find him using his philosophy less worthily as a consolation for having failed to acquire a new mistress 'at the tother syde of the water':

> That we can not haue we must forgo
> There ys none other remedy. (sig. F ii[v])

The self-satisfaction, not untouched by fear, with which he views his sorry defensive preparations against Reason is rather pathetic:

> I dout and drede
> The wurst as wyse men do. (sig. H i)

Sensuality's welcome of Pride is not unreminiscent of Chanticleer's famous translation of 'Mulier est hominis confusio':

> Ye[*Pride*] be radix viciorum . Rote of all vertew.
> (sig. C iii[v])

The same saying is used more seriously by Meekness:

> The rote of all syn / ys Pryde ye know well.
> (sig. H iv[v])

To it we may well add Occupation's similar characterization of Idleness:

> For yt ys the very moder and maysters of syn.
> (sig. I ii)

Sensuality sees no good reason why a person should not look out for himself:

> A well drawen man ys he / and a well taught,
> That wyll not gyue hys hed for nought. (sig. C ii)

He also says that there is no need to fear Covetousness's influence with Man as yet:

> Mary whan hys hed waxeth hore
> Than shalbe good season
> To folow couetyse and hys way. (sig. D iv[v])

Gluttony serves to illustrate the proverb that 'When the belly is full the bones would be at rest':

> And whan I am well fed
> Than get I me to a soft bed
> My body to repose. (sig. G i[v])

He confesses, too, that he often leads to Lust:

> For hote drynkys and delycate refeccyon
> Causeth flesshely insurreccyon. (sig. G ii)

Later Abstinence boasts that she is followed by Chastity (sig. I iii). Pride believes that forewarning leads to forearming:

> I am glad ye warn me thus in seson
> I shalbe the better ware. (sig. F iii[v])

Liberality, speaking of Prodigality and Avarice, urges the middle way:

> Take the myd way / bytwyxt theym two
> And fle thextremytees. (sig. I ii[v])

21

THE WORLD AND THE CHILD (1522)

[Tudor Facsimile Texts, 1909]
976 lines: 1; 6; 8; 3

Few moralities contain so little proverbial material as *The World and the Child,* and in none is the distribution less characteristic. The single proverb, which is none too popular, is spoken by Conscience:

> But syr measure is in all thynge. (sig. B iii)

Conscience also warns Manhood sententiously against Pride:

> Nay syr beware of pryde and you do well
> For pryde lucyfer fell in to hell. (sig. B i)

In addition he gives Manhood advice already familiar to us:

> Alwaye or ye begyn thynke on the endynge
> For blame. (sig B iii[v])

Folly, a singularly pale figure to serve as Vice, suggests the inevitable consequence of Pride:

> Folye before and shame behynde. (sig. C iii[v])

22

John Rastell's *THE NATURE OF THE FOUR ELEMENTS* (after 1517)

[Tudor Facsimile Texts, 1908]
1439 lines: 2; 6; 8; 3

John Rastell's doleful play, which he called 'a new interlude and a mery,' the incomplete *Nature of the Four Elements,* contains very little proverbial material. The Vice, Sensual Appetite, is true to form in that he employs the two proverbs. The first of these is a fine Wellerism with which he announces his too long delayed entrance:

> Well hyet quod hykman when that he smot
> Hys wyffe on the buttockes with a bere pott.
> (sig. B ii)

The other serves as an insult to Studious Desire and Experience, whom he greets thus:

> The mo knauys the worse company. (sig. C v[v])

The Messenger, whose long dull opening speech is an ominous portent of what is to follow, makes use of a sententious remark:

> For wysedome and foly is as it is takyn
> For that one callyth wysedome another callyth foly.
> (sigs. A ii[v]–A iii)

Studious Desire promises Humanity that he will try to find Experience and bring him for a good long talk,

> For cunnyng is the thynge that wolde be sought.
> (sig. B ii)

Humanity excuses himself feebly to Sensual Appetite and Ignorance for consorting with Studious Desire and Experience:

> O syr ye know ryght well this
> That when any man is
> In other mens company
> He must nedes folow the appyte
> Of such thynges as they delyte
> Som tyme amonge perdy. (sig. E ii[v])

23

HICKSCORNER (1497–1512)

[Tudor Facsimile Texts, 1908]
1027 lines: 4; 7; 12; 4

Just why Hickscorner should have given his name to the play which bears it is rather a mystery, since he is of far less importance than his companions in mischief, Freewill and Imagination. There are not many proverbs in the play, indeed only four, and Freewill uses two of these. We come upon numerous references to theft, arrest, and prison, above all Newgate, and so we are not surprised to find Freewill's first proverb just such a one as a criminal would love:

> But a frende in courte is worthe a peny in purs.
> (sig. B iv[v])

If, as we often hear, sudden conversion is a sign of melodrama, then there are few more melodramatic plays than *Hickscorner*, but Freewill's change of heart leaves the reader somewhat cold as docs his pious urging of Imagination to join him at the mourner's bench:

> Hyt is better be tyme than to late. (sig. C v[v])

Imagination expects to get on in the world:

> For ye knowe well there is crafte in daubynge.
> (sig. A vi)

The fourth proverb, suggested rather than given, is used by Hickscorner of Wanton Sybyl:

> For she is trusty at nede. (sig. A viii)

The outstanding position of the Vice, in this case Freewill, in the employment of proverbial material, especially of proverbial phrases, is seldom better illustrated than here, where he speaks eleven out of nineteen.

The sententious remarks are all used by the Virtues. Pity has three, as when she laments the way of the world:

Fewe frendes pouerte dooth fynde. (sig. A iii[v])

Later she remarks:

Lo, lordes, they may curs the tyme they were borne
For the wedes that ouer groweth the corne, (sig. B ii[v])

and again:

All trouth is not best sayd. (sig. B iii[v])

It is Contemplation who delivers the customary attack on Fortune:

For fortune wyll tourne her whele to swyfte
That clene fro thy welthe she wyll the lyfte.
(sig. C ii)

24

WEALTH AND HEALTH (before 1557)

[Ed. W. W. Greg, Malone Society Reprints, 1907]
964 lines: 2; 1; 9; 5

Wealth and Health is not rich in proverbial material. Liberty is surprised that Wealth and Health start to leave at his approach. Don't they recognize their old friend? If not, he has the answer:

Loe, out of syght out of remembryng
Absence is cause of straungnes.
(sig. B i, ll. 199 f.)

Will, who conceals as long as possible the fact that his full name includes Ill-, speaks candidly enough of himself:

Ylwyl cannot say wel. (sig. D iii, l. 840)

Wealth also offers self-characterization:

Welth hath no pere. (sig. A ii, l. 19)

Health, on the contrary, has a different opinion:

> Welth is nothing sure. (sig. A ii, l. 31)

Health chides Wealth for his arrogance in taking credit to himself for mortal happiness. Man's prosperity lies rather in

> The grace of god that passeth all thyng.
> (sig. A iii[v], l. 101)

Later Remedy makes a similar reference to

> The grace of God, which is our chief forderance.
> (sig. C iii, l. 584)

Wealth, having been chided by Health, is glad to get a little of his own back at the expense of Liberty, who has declared himself 'the better' of Health and Wealth:

> Such presumptuouse wordes wyll haue a fall.
> (sig. B i[v], l. 241)

25

John Skelton's *MAGNIFICENCE* (1515–1520)

[Ed. R. L. Ramsay, EETS., ES., XCVIII, 1908]
2567 lines: 15; 21; 60; 25

John Skelton's *Magnificence* is a dull and disappointingly un-Skeltonic play, but it does contain much proverbial material, with an unusually large proportion of miscellaneous proverbial phrases. The proverbs are spoken in the main by the neutral and bad characters.

The play opens with much commendation of Measure, some of it from that worthy's own mouth:

> Measure is treasure. (p. 5, l. 125)

Magnificence, too, thinks more highly of Measure than his subsequent behavior indicates:

> Measure is a meane nother to hy nor to lawe. (p. 7, l. 188)
> Yet Mesure is a mery mene. (p. 13, l. 380)

Measure uses two other proverbs. Liberty wishes the continuance of free will, and Measure asks chidingly:

> But haue ye not herde say that Wyll is no Skyll?
> (p. 6, l. 148)

Again Measure warns the ebullient Liberty:

> Yet beware of 'Had I wyste!' (p. 7, l. 211)

Poor Liberty hears this same proverb from Felicity at a later time:

> Yet it is good to beware of 'had I wyst.'
> (p. 44, l. 1395)

Magnificence, with truly regal whim, is not always pleased with his tricky advisers, and becomes angry at Fancy, even when the rogue is representing himself to be Largess:

> Wel, wyse men may ete the fysshe, when ye shal draw the pole.
> (p. 10, l. 300)

With two exceptions the remaining proverbs are spoken by Fancy and Counterfeit Countenance. Fancy says that he is nobody's fool:

> In faythe, els had I gone to longe to scole,
> But yf I coulde knowe a gose from a swanne.
> (p. 10, ll. 298 f.)

He can distinguish between things and occasions:

> Ye, Syr, a blaunched almonde is no bene.
> (p. 13, l. 381)

Left with the stage to himself he does not hesitate to confess the lightness of his character:

> With a pere my loue you may wynne,
> And ye may lese it for a pynne.
> (p. 32, ll. 1016 f.)

Counterfeit Countenance decks out a monologue on his own popularity with three proverbs:

> It is euyll patchynge of that is torne. (p. 15, l. 447)
>
> When the noppe is rughe, it wolde be shorne. (p. 15, l. 448)
>
> It is moche worthe that is ferre fet. (p. 15, l. 455)

Cloaked Collusion finds little to merit respect in the remarks of his fellow in rascality, Counterfeit Countenance:

> Thy wordes be but wynde. (p. 19, l. 578)

When Magnificence doubts his ability to win the favor of Carnal Delectation, Courtly Abusion tells him that gold will accomplish his end:

> Money maketh marchauntes, I tell you, over all. (p. 49, l. 1574)

At the beginning and at the end of the play we find the Virtues using most of the sententious remarks. Felicity comments on the instability of worldly affairs:

> Howe after a drought there fallyth a showre of rayne,
> And after a hete oft cometh a stormy colde. (p. 2, ll. 12 f.)

Poverty places the responsibility for this state of affairs at Fortune's door:

> Syr, remembre the tourne of Fortunes whele,
> That wantonly can wynke, and wynche with her hele.
> Nowe she wyll laughe; forthwith she wyll frowne;
> Sodenly set vp and sodenly pluckyd downe;
> She dawnsyth varyaunce with mutabylyte,
> Nowe all in Welth, forthwith in Pouerte;
> In her promyse there is no sykernesse;
> All her Delyte is set in Doublenesse. (p. 63, ll. 2022 ff.)

She warns that past happiness cannot be recalled:

> Yesterday wyll not be callyd agayne. (p. 63, l. 2031)

The Epilogue to the play consists of a tiresome repetition of this theme, which is valiantly labored by Redress, Circumspection, and Perseverance. The remarks of the first give a sufficient idea of the remainder:

> Nowe well, nowe wo, nowe hy, nowe lawe degre;
> Nowe ryche, nowe pore, nowe hole, nowe in dysease;
> Nowe Pleasure at large, nowe in captyuyte;
> Nowe leue, nowe lothe, now please, nowe dysplease;
> Now ebbe, now flowe, nowe increase, now dyscrease:
> So in this worlde there is no Sykernesse,
> But fallyble Flatery enmyxyd with Bytternesse.
> (p. 79, ll. 2512 ff.)

Apparently not satisfied with the praise given him in proverbs, Measure applies three sententious remarks to himself:

> Oracius to recorde in his volumys olde,
> With euery condycyon Measure must be sought.
> (p. 5, ll. 114 f.)

> There is no surfet where Measure rulyth the feste.
> (p. 5, l. 139)

> For defaute of Measure all thynge dothe excede.
> (p. 8, l. 217)

Felicity fears that excess liberty which becomes license:

> Lyberty makyth many a man blynde. (p. 3, l. 52)

Adversity tells how he creeps up on the unsuspecting:

> And in theyr moste truste I make them ouerthrowe.
> (p. 59, l. 1885)

Faulty upbringing leads to most mischief:

> For there is nothynge that more dyspleaseth God
> Than from theyr chyldren to spare the rod
> Of correccyon. (p. 60, ll. 1928 ff.)

Adversity turns Magnificence over to the tender mercies of Poverty, who takes a certain grim pleasure in the falls of the mighty:

He dynyd with Delyte, with Pouerte he must sup.
(p. 61, l. 1965)

He woteth not what Welth is that neuer was sore.
(p. 61, l. 1971)

I fynde it wryt,
In Welth to beware; and that is Wyt. (p. 61, ll. 1974 f.)

Of the naughty characters, indeed of all the characters, Fancy is richest in sententious remarks. In fact, if we were to follow the general rule, namely, that the Vice speaks more proverbial material than any other character, then we should find that *Magnificence*, contrary to some opinions, has a Vice, and that Fancy fills the part. He is not sure if Magnificence is a fool:

But ofte tymes haue I sene wyse men do mad dedys.
(p. 10, l. 302)

He is as ready, though not as repetitious, as Measure in commending himself, here in his feigned rôle of Largess:

For Largesse stynteth all maner of stryfe. (p. 13, l. 367)

Magnificence is a niggard indeed if he economizes in any way:

What! sholde you pynche at a pecke of grotes,
Ye wolde sone pynche at a pecke of otes.
(p. 13, ll. 384 f.)

In his amusing scene with his hawk he says the best he can of the bird:

Eche thynge is fayre when it is yonge.
(p. 31, l. 971)

He bridles somewhat at Folly's declaration that Fancy leads most wretches to folly. It seems to him an unfair and unrestrained accusation:

A peryllous thynge, to cast a cat
Vpon a naked man and yf she scrat.
(p. 41, ll. 1298 f.)

Cloaked Collusion refuses to show deference to Crafty Conveyance. Let the knave come if he wants to see him:

> Tushe! he that hath nede, man, let hym rynne.
> (p. 26, l. 786)

Counterfeit Countenance fits a sententious remark into his monologue:

> All thynge is worse whan it is worne.
> (p. 15, l. 451)

Liberty does not think that Felicity ought to be too particular and complaining:

> And so as ye se it wyll be no better,
> Take it in worthe suche as ye fynde.
> (p. 45, ll. 1438 f.)

He also uses the common alliterative phrase 'bote of all my bale' (p. 64, l. 2070), a variant of which had occurred to Cloaked Collusion earlier:

> I brewe moche bale. (p. 24, l. 744)

Courtly Abusion has no very high respect for female virtue, though he admits the existence of female discretion:

> Ye, for *omnis mulier meretrix si celari potest.*
> (p. 50, l. 1586)

26

YOUTH (after 1528)

[Tudor Facsimile Texts, 1908]
787 lines: 1; 7; 8; 4

We know little enough concerning the author of *Youth*, but we can be certain of the title of at least one book in his library, and that is *Hickscorner*, which he pillaged freely and unintelligently. He lets his Riot call himself 'as mery as a kinge,' a proverbial phrase which Freewill had claimed in the earlier play. Another curious phrase which may possibly be proverbial occurs in both plays. Hickscorner remarks, 'ye whan my soule hangeth on the hedge cast stones' (sig. B ii), and Youth says much the same thing:

When my soule hangeth on the hedge once
Then take thou and caste stones. (sig. C ii)

The only proverb in *Youth* is part of Riot's attack on Charity's effort to keep Youth pious:

A yonge sainte an olde deuyll. (sig. C ii)

Charity tells Youth that beauty, strength, and wealth are of no lasting value:

What shal it be whan thou shalt flyt
For the wealth into the pyt
Therfore of it be not to boolde
Least thou for think it whan thou art old
Ye maye be lykened to a tre
In youth floryshyng with royallte
And in age it is cut downe
And to the fyre is throwne
So shalt thou but thou amende
Be burned in hel without ende. (sig. A ii)

He assures him that God is but waiting for his petition:

O yet remember cal to thi minde
The mercy of God passeth al thyng
For it is wryten by noble clerkes
The mercye of God passeth all werkes
That witnesseth holy scrypture sainge thus
Miseratio domini super omnia opera eius.
(sig. A ii[v])

Charity also welcomes the ill usage which Pride and Riot lavish on him:

The more sorowe the more mede. (sig. B iv[v])

The two evil counselors do not always agree. Pride tells Youth to take a wife. 'God forbid!' cries Riot. Flesh is cheap and

> Ouer muche of one thinge is nought. (sig. B ii[v])

27

EVERYMAN (*c.* 1500)

[Tudor Facsimile Texts, 1912]
921 lines: 8; 3; 2; 8

When we consider the lack of humor in *Everyman* (or, perhaps better, *The Summoning of Everyman*), we are not surprised to find a lack of proverbial phrases, which, as we have seen, are likely to be found in the remarks of comic characters. It is strange, however, to come upon eight proverbs, mostly occurring in the passages in which Everyman is seeking aid from his faithless friends and attributes. Even grim Death uses a proverb:

> For wete you well the tyde abydeth no man.
> (sig. A iv)

Everyman calls upon his old crony Fellowship to

> Be . . . a good frende at nede, (sig. A v[v])

but he finds him wanting, and it is only at the end of the play that he discovers Good Deeds willing to promise:

> Thou shalte fynde me a god frende at nede.
> (sig. D iii)

Fellowship is ready enough to stand by Everyman until he discovers the nature of his old friend's journey, and then, while he is willing to admit that 'promyse is duyte' (sig. A v[v]), he finds it a duty easy to avoid.

Everyman uses a variant of the same proverb later when Strength deserts him:

> Wyll you breke promyse / that is dette.
> (sig. D ii[v])

Everyman counts on the support of his relatives:

> For kynde wyll crepe where it may not go.
> (sig. A vi[v])

He soon sees that there is no trust in them, nor in any of those who have been deceiving him with pretty speeches:

> Loo / fayre wordes maketh fooles fayne.
> (sig. B i[v])

His pathetic hope carries him to Goods, who ought to be able to help him:

> For it is sayd euer amonge
> That money maketh all ryght / that is wronge.
> (sig. B ii[r–v])

The Messenger, who opens the play, sums up its purport in a sententious remark:

> This story sayeth man in the begynnynge
> Loke well & take good hede to the endynge.
> (sig. A ii)

Death uses familiar words in introducing himself to Everyman:

> I am dethe that no man dredeth
> For euery man I rest and none spareth.
> (sig. A iii[v])

Fellowship's early remarks are almost indignantly opposite to his later course:

> For he that wyll saye and nothynge do
> Is not worthy with good company to go.
> (sig. A v[v])

Everyman regrets to see his old friend depart:

> Partynge is mournynge. (sig. A vi[v])

But he can give an explanation:

> It is sayd in prosperyte men frendes may fynde
> Whiche in aduersytye be full vnkynde.
> (sig. A vi[v])

Kindred, like Fellowship, is ready to aid until he finds out the nature of the need:

> For ouer his kynne a man may be bolde.
> (sig. B i)

Confession encourages Everyman with the thought of God's compassion:

> Aske god mercy and he wyll graunte truely.
> (sig. B iv[v])

At the end Everyman is dismayed to see his capacities fall away as the grave yawns. He has put his trust too much in what is transitory and fickle:

> He that trusteth in his strength
> She hym deceyueth at the length.
> (sig. D ii[v])

28

Sir David Lyndsay's *THE THREE ESTATES* (*c.* 1535)

[In F. Hall's *Sir David Lyndesay's Works*, Part iv, pp. 377 ff., EETS., ES., XXXVII, 1869]
4630 lines: 9; 23; 36; 20

The longest of the moralities is Sir David Lyndsay's *Pleasant Satire of the Three Estates.* This forerunner of *Back to Methuselah* and *Strange Interlude* is four thousand six hundred thirty lines long, and modern playgoers are put to shame by the information that king and court sat through a performance lasting nine hours.[7] Despite its excessive length it has less proverbial material than many a shorter play.[8] Lyndsay's language is racy and natural enough in all conscience, but its raciness is achieved not so much by a wealth of proverbial phrases as by a vulgarity and obscenity of vocabulary that outdoes even the other moralities. Not only is the proverbial material scanty, but it is spread out in a way foreign to most of the plays. There is more in the speeches of the bad characters than in those of the good, but little or no concentration. This fact is strikingly illustrated when we note that of the nine proverbs two are used by the virtuous characters, or rather one saying is used twice, and the rest by the bad, but there is a separate speaker for each proverb. Fourteen characters use the twenty sententious remarks, Deceit having three, Falset two, Diligence two, Good Counsel two, and John-the-Commonweal two. I can see no reason to do more than list the various sayings in the order of their occurrence.

Proverbs

For als lang leifis the mirrie man
As the sorie, for ocht he can. (Wantonness, p. 380, ll. 106 f.)

Sa that ȝe be nocht ane ȝoung sanct,
And, sync, ane auld deuill. (Placebo, p. 384, ll. 233 f.)

We will tak it, perchance,
Howbeit that wee say nay. (Danger, p. 386, ll. 305 f.)

Ouhen freinds meits, harts warmis,
Quod Iok, that frelie fude. (Falset, p. 398, ll. 643 f.)

Be suir that mair belangis to the pleuch.
(Correction, p. 439, l. 1695)

I cair nocht that: als gude luife cums as gais.
(Sensuality, p. 440, l. 1726)

Ouha ever beis hangit with this cord
Neids never to be dround. (Pardoner, p. 454, ll. 2096 f.)

Ȝit sumthing mair belangis to the pleuch.
(Good Counsel, p. 474, l. 2556)

Quhen fuillis ar fow, then ar thay faine.
(Folly, p. 534, l. 4274)

Sententious Remarks

Thocht ȝoung oppressouris at the elder leiris.
(Diligence, p. 378, l. 28)

Let euerie man keip weill ane toung,
And euerie woman tway. (Diligence, p. 379, ll. 76 f.)

The buik says Omnia probate,
And nocht for to spair. (Placebo, p. 385, ll. 269 f.)

Till tak our tyme, quhill wee may get it.
(Falset, p. 401, l. 711)

Kings sould of gude exempils be the well;
Bot, gif that ȝour strands be intoxicate,
In steid of wyne, thay drink the poyson fell:
Thus pepill follows, ay, thair principate.
(Verity, p. 415, ll. 1056 ff.)

And wee twa meit againe this nicht,
Thy feit salbe with fourtie hands. (Deceit, p. 435, ll. 1570 f.)

And for to mix his iustice with mercie.
(Good Counsel, p. 446, l. 1884)

Ane consuetude against the common weill
Sould be na law. (Pauper, p. 452, ll. 2015 f.)

This parting dois me paine. (Sensuality, p. 472, l. 2511)

Now, into peace, ȝe sould provyde for weirs.
(Good Counsel, p. 474, l. 2557)

Qui non laborat non manducet,
This is, in Inglische toung or leit:
Quha labouris nocht he sall not eit. (John, p. 475, ll. 2600 ff.)

To plaint on Preistis, it is na bourd.
(John, p. 479, l. 2720; cf. p. 452, ll. 2029 f.)

To speik of Preists, be sure it is na bourds.
(Parson, p. 481, l. 2773)

I let ȝow wit, my Lords, it is na bourds
Of Prelats for till speik sic wantoun words.
(Spirituality, p. 482, ll. 2781 f.)

Ȝe are bot ane estait, and we ar twa;
Et vbi maior pars ibi tota. (Temporality, p. 484, ll. 2835 f.)

Howbeit that Nunnis sing nichts and dayis,
Thair hart waitis nocht quhat thair mouth sayis.
(Prioress, p. 514, ll. 3663 f.)

I wait weill, ȝe will never thryfe
Farther nor the fourth air. (Deceit, p. 529, ll. 4086 f.)

Fairweil! For I am to the widdie wend;
For quhy falset maid never ane better end.
(Falset, p. 533, ll. 4240 f.)

Sum seiks to warldlie dignities,
And sum, to sensuall vanities.
Quhat vails all thir vaine honours,
Nocht being sure to leife twa houris?
Sum greidie fuill dois fill ane box;
Ane vther fuill cummis, and breaks the lox,
And spends that vther fuillis hes spaird,
Quhilk never thocht on them to wairde.
Sum dois as thay sould never die.
Is nocht this folie? Quhat say ȝe?

(Folly, p. 543, ll. 4482 ff.)

29

John Bale's *THE THREE LAWS* (1538)

[Tudor Facsimile Texts, 1908]

2040 lines: 5; 13; 20; 7

Few champions of the Reformation were such masters of obloquy and scurrility as was John Bale, Bishop of Ossory, who lived from 1495 until 1563, and of his equals in this respect no one wrote for the stage. Only two of his moralities have survived, and while he is best known for *King Johan*, the shorter *Three Laws* is on the whole more lively. In this play the Vice, Infidelity, assisted by other equally vicious characters, is able to distort and corrupt the laws of Nature, Moses, and Christ, but is overthrown in the end by Vindicta Dei. Nothing indicates the general nature of the play better than the stage direction at the end: 'Lete Idolatry be decked lyke an olde wytche, Sodomy lyke a monke of all sectes, Ambycyon lyke a byshop, Couetousnesse lyke a pharyse or spyrituall lawer, false doctryne, lyke a popysh doctour, and hypocresy lyke a graye fryre. The rest of the partes are easye ynough to coniecture' (sig. G i[v].)

Infidelity, the Vice, runs true to form in the proportion of the proverbial material which is given to him.

He not only employs four of the five proverbs, but also seventeen of the proverbial phrases and three of the sententious remarks. He hints at a likely but unsavory love affair between Sodomy and Idolatry:

> Where hungry dogges lacke meate,
> They wyll durty puddynges eate,
> For wante of befe and conye. (sig. B iv[v])

His mind runs on lust, and he is certain that Evangel is a cuckold, and willing to agree to the latter's scandalous attack on the relations of 'the popes oyled swarme' with their female parishioners:

> Yea, poore marryed men, haue very moch a do,
> I counte hym wysest, that can take a snatche and to go.
> (sig. E i)

He greets the two children, False Doctrine and Hypocrisy, on whom he counts to overthrow Christ's Law, with:

> As good is a becke, as is a dewe vow garde.
> (sig. E ii)

It is False Doctrine who uses the last proverb in calling the faithful up to participate in Infidelity's pardon:

> Who first speake first spede. (sig. E viii)

Infidelity acknowledges himself to have at least one feminine fault:

> The worst fault I haue, I am hastye now and than,
> But it is sone gone, I toke it of a woman. (sig. C vi)

His belief is firmly fixed in the hope that

> Into the dytche, the blynde the blynde maye lede.
> (sig. D iv)

Evangel assures him that he believes only too strongly in his mocking words:

> As thu art, thu speakest, after they hartes abundaunce.
> (sig. D vii[v])

This warning has no effect on Infidelity, who shortly after makes a wretched pun on the common title of a priest 'Dane Johan, Dane Robert' and so on, and thus drags in a reference to the old, more or less sententious, prophecy:

> Their nomber is soch, as hath ronne ouer all
> The same Danes are they, men prophecy of playne,
> Whych shuld ouer ronne, thys realme yet ones agayne.
> (sig. D viii)

Vindicta Dei, who puts all right in the end, has no fear of Infidelity:

> Whan the stronger come, the weaker must nedes bowe.
> (sig. F iv)

Christian Faith exhorts all to be faithful to their native land and not follow the ways of 'Reygnolde Pole,' for even

> A dogge to hys frynde, wyll neuer be vnlouynge.
> (sig. F viii[v])

The Law of Nature rounds all off with a pregnant warning:

> Who lyueth without lawe, shal perysh without lawe.
> (sig. F viii[v])

30

John Bale's *KING JOHAN* (1536)

[Ed. J. H. P. Pafford, Malone Society Reprints, 1931]
2645 lines: 8; 28; 31; 10

The Malone Society edition of *King Johan*, with its careful and well-arranged reproduction of the manuscript, casts much new light on the composition and revision of the play. The editor is able to suggest (pp. xxii ff.) plausibly enough that Bale had written the play by the autumn of 1536, that he recast it in 1538, and that long years later he revised it again in the hope of producing it before Queen Elizabeth in 1561. For our purposes the most interesting fact is that in revising the passage dealing with John's submission, humiliation, and murder (pp. 78–107), Bale introduced five of the play's eight proverbs (p. 96, ll. 1874, 1883, p. 98, l. 1917), three proverbial phrases (p. 87, l. 1716; p. 94, l. 1840; p. 106, l. 2096), and one sententious remark (p. 94, l. 1834). Had it not been for this revision the play would have been singularly weak in proverbs. As usual we find most of the proverbs and proverbial phrases spoken by the bad characters, but unlike Infidelity in *The Three Laws*, Sedition, the Vice of the present play, does not use an overwhelming majority. Sedition has nothing but contempt for England and observes her sorrow with derision:

> Yt is as great pyte, to se a woman wepe
> As yt is to se, a sely dodman crepe
> Or as ye wold say, a sely goose go barefote.
> (p. 10, ll. 175 ff.)

Clergy complains bitterly to the easily swayed Nobility that the king's levies on the church are such

> That an abbeye turneth to a graunge.
> (p. 28, l. 572)

England can see little good to come from the churchmen, either high or low, cardinal or archbishop, and she expresses her opinion by means of two proverbs:

> Lyke lorde lyke chaplayne, neyther barrell better herynge.
> (p. 96, l. 1874)

Sedition mocks her and counsels the Cardinal to force John to make still larger grants:

> As the saynge is, he fyndeth that surely bynde.
> (p. 96, l. 1883)

When he sees that this scheme is not going to work he cynically expresses a popular belief in two closely allied proverbs:

> No grote no Pater noster, no penye no placebo.
> (p. 98, l. 1917)

It is unusual for the godly and serious characters to use proverbs, but Imperial Majesty is an exception to the general rule, and he rebukes Clergy, who insists on putting personalities before principles:

> The crowe wyll not chaunge her hewe.
> (p. 118, l. 2347)

The unholy characters speak all but three of the sententious remarks. England finds a Biblical description of the clergy:

> As christ dothe saye, blynd leaders of the blynd.
> (p. 3, l. 34)

King John rebukes Nobility for his large and unwise donations to the church, and when he is told that they had been made with the best intentions, replies that

> The intente ys nowght, which hath no sewer grovnde.
> (p. 24, l. 480)

Verity realizes that she can be a troublemaker, albeit a necessary one:

> Treuthe ingendereth hate. (p. 112, l. 2208)

Sedition is more than rude to the king:

> Gesse at a ventur, ye may chance þe marke to hytt.
> (p. 14, l. 263)

His opinion of women finds a ready niche in the rich literature of anti-feminism:

> It is a worlde to heare, a folysh woman reason.
> (p. 94, l. 1834)

Once in the toils he longs to be free and far away:

> I woulde I were now, at Rome, at the sygne of the cuppe
> For heauynesse is drye. (p. 124, ll. 2446 ff.)

The absence of a divine origin for the woes of husbands with erring wives is implicit in his answer to a question about his abode. He lives, he says,

> Amonge such people, God ded neuer make
> Not only cuckoldes, as but suche as folowe the popes lawes.
> (p. 128, ll. 2523 f.)

Dissimulation is proud of his duplicity:

> Thowgh I seme a shepe, I can play the suttle foxe.
> (p. 34, l. 708)

When he feels the pangs of his own poison in his vitals he calls out, no doubt with memory of the value of friends in need:

> Helpe now at a pynche. (p. 105, l. 2074)

Sedition's wickedness is too much for his own fellow-workers in the vineyard of evil, and Private Wealth explains his continued existence thus:

> Wher herbes are pluckte vpp, þe wedes many tymes remayne.
> (p. 39, l. 817)

31

John Redford's *WIT AND SCIENCE* (*c.* 1545)

[Ed. J. O. Halliwell[-Phillipps], Shakespeare Society, XXXVII, 1848]

1079 lines: 5; 2; 2; 5

John Redford's *Wit and Science* is an early and excellent example of the educational morality, the aim of which was to direct the child to proper studies and to keep him from wanton and destructive self-indulgence. The hero, Wit, is safely united to Science after sundry rather pleasant vicissitudes along the primrose path. Redford's play inspired two later and greatly altered versions, *The Marriage of Wit and Science* (*c.* 1569–1570) and *The Marriage of Wit and Wisdom* (*c.* 1570). The relationship between the two later plays and their joint or several relationships to their prototype are confused, and my remarks are naturally limited to the proverbial material which they contain. One thing is certain: Redford did not suggest the rather extensive use of proverbs in which the later authors indulged.

Reason feels assured that young Wit is a fitting match for his daughter Science. The boy must be tested, however, and

> Thende of hys jornay wyll aprove all. (p. 2)

Idleness speaks of herself with a pretty impersonality:

> Ye shall se her tryde,
> Nother idle nor well ocupyde. (p. 20)

Once she has beguiled Wit, she tells her son, Ignorance, that Wit, in Ignorance's coat, is as much a fool as himself:

> Won foole keepe another. (p. 31)

Experience, the mother of Science, reminds her that there is no trusting in sudden love such as Wit's had been:

> But that it is true thys proverbe old,
> Hastye love is soone hot and soone cold! (p. 36)

After Wit is redeemed he avows himself ready to follow Experience's counsel:

> Once warne half armd, folk say. (p. 53)

The sententious remarks, in the main, are spoken by the good characters. Instruction is distressed by Wit's headstrong desertion:

> When wytes stand so in ther owne conceite,
> Best let them go tyll pryde at hys heyghte
> Turne and cast them downe hedlong agayne. (p. 7)

Later, none the less, he is willing and glad to speak words of cheer to the hero:

> After stormy clowdes cumth wether clere. (p. 45)

Honest Recreation has no love for her rival, Idleness, and gives her the traditional characterization:

> For that common strumpet, Idellnes,
> The verye roote of all vyciousnes. (p. 16)

Idleness, contrary to the more usual complacence of the vicious under such accusations, is inclined to take this charge amiss and asks querulously:

> Am I the roote, sayst thow, of vyciousnes? (p. 17)

Reason is glad that Wit accepted his merited chastisement from Shame, for if he had resisted

> I wold have thowght than that Wyt had bene,
> As the sayeng is and daylye seene,
> Past shame once, and past all amendment. (p. 45)

We have here a meagre amount of proverbial material, and, if we look ahead we find that those who adapted Redford's play took over little enough of it. In *The Marriage of Wit and Science* we find eighteen proverbs, two of which are taken from Redford. The saying about 'hot love soon cold' which Experience utters in *Wit and Science* is spoken by Wit in *The Marriage of Wit and Science*, and he adds to it the proverb, 'Out of sight, out of mind' (see below, p. 140). As in the earlier play

Idleness declares herself 'neither idle nor well occupied,' but in the later instance she calls her remark a proverb (see below, p. 141). No one of the fourteen proverbs in *The Marriage of Wit and Wisdom* had appeared in either of the two earlier plays. The four proverbial phrases in *Wit and Science* do not turn up in the later plays, and the only duplication between the thirty-two proverbial phrases in *The Marriage of Wit and Science* and the forty-nine in *The Marriage of Wit and Wisdom* is far from significant, consisting as it does in the remark of Will in the first play (sig. E iii[v]) that servants 'runne with leaden heeles,' and a reference by Idleness in the second (p. 58) to 'some leaden heeled lubber.' The five sententious remarks in *Wit and Science* do not figure among the thirteen in *The Marriage of Wit and Science*, and in *The Marriage of Wit and Wisdom*, which contains ten, we find the familiar statement (p. 58) that Idleness is the 'mother of wise (*vice*),' a statement made this time by Idleness.

We observe that while the author of *The Marriage of Wit and Science* borrowed somewhat from Redford, the author of *The Marriage of Wit and Wisdom* borrowed from no one, for neither of the two correspondences between his play and the others need be considered anything but a coincidence. Not only does the proverbial material fail to duplicate, but the persons who use most of the proverbial material are not the same in the various plays. In *Wit and Science* there is no evidence whatever that Redford used proverbs other than as they came to mind. In *The Marriage of Wit and Science*, however, Wit and his *alter ego* Will, who had not been in Redford's play, are the only characters to use more than a single proverb. Wit uses eight and Will five. It is unusual to have the neutral character thus signaled out by his, or their, penchant for proverbs. When we come to consider the proverbial phrases we find that Will, despite his fewer proverbs, runs away with the show as he speaks twenty-one out of thirty-two, while Wit speaks but five. The sententious remarks in this play are divided fairly, Nature using four, Will three, Wit and Experience two each, and Science and Recreation one each. In *The Marriage of Wit and Wisdom* we find an entirely different situation. Idleness, instead of being an evil female character, is the Vice and as such produces most of the proverbial material. He is responsible for seven of the fourteen proverbs, thirty-one of the forty-nine proverbial phrases, but only one of the ten sententious remarks. Wit uses three proverbs, no proverbial phrases, and two sententious remarks. None of the other characters deserve consideration, unless it be Good Virtue with two proverbs and one sententious remark, or Indulgence with five proverbial phrases.

The only deductions which can be drawn from these observations are clear enough and, though Mr. Tannenbaum ("Comments on the Marriage of Wit and Wisdom," *Philological Quarterly*, IX [1930], 338 ff.) holds that F. Merbury, who may have written *The Marriage of Wit and Wisdom*, also wrote *The Marriage of Wit and Science*, the evidence from the proverbs is against it. However an author striving to make two plays out of one might vary the plot, no writer of moralities was likely to shift the bulk of his proverbial material from the neutral characters to the Vice. *The Marriage of Wit and Science* and *The Marriage of Wit and Wisdom* will be taken up at length in their chronological positions.

32

Richard Wever's *LUSTY JUVENTUS* (*c.* 1550)

[Tudor Facsimile Texts, 1907]
1168 lines: 0; 2; 6; 9

The bitterly Protestant morality, *Lusty Juventus*, perhaps best known for its appearance in a garbled and misnamed form in the play *Sir Thomas More* (iv, 1), is decidedly weak in proverbial material. There are few proverbial phrases and nothing that can be called a proverb, although one or two of the sententious remarks are found elsewhere in truly popular form. The Messenger who acts as prologue speaks of the need for early education:

> An order to bring vp youth, Ecclesiasticus doth write,
> An vntamed horse wyl be hard saith he
> And a wanton chylde wilfull wyll be. (sig. A i[v])

The Devil, also using a common sententious saying for his own purposes, remarks on the unnatural way in which the young are accepting the new religion:

> For if they wil not folow my waies when they are yong
> It is hard turning them when they come to age.
> (sig. B iii[v])

The Messenger refers to the frailty of youth who may be easily led to evil by Nature:

> That Nature hath ingrafted, is hard to kyll.
> (sig. A i[v])

Juventus, who comes in singing a pleasing song, complains thereafter that his companions have failed to keep a rendezvous with him. He hopes, however, to profit by their treachery:

> Against another tyme they haue taught me wyt.
> (sig. A ii[v])

He is more than pleased to be a friend to anyone who greets him:

> Old acquaintaunce wyll soone be remembred.
> (sig. C ii[v])

Hypocrisy, the Vice, introduces himself to Juventus as Friendship, and reproaches him for his lack of recognition. At first he accuses him of wilfully ignoring an old friend:

> But now I perceue that promocion
> Causeth both man, maners and fashion,
> Greatly for to chaunge. (sig. C iii)

He then alters his tune somewhat, and says that he himself had almost forgotten his old friend:

> By longe absense brought out of memory.
> (sig. C iii[v])

When Juventus fears the reproaches of Good Counsel and Knowledge, the Vice tells him that the best defense is offense:

> Byd them plucke the beame out of there owne eye.
> (sig. D i)

Juventus bears the phrase in mind and directs it at Good Counsel when an opportunity occurs:

> But you wil not see the beames in your owne eyes.
> (sig. E ii[v])

33

ROBIN CONSCIENCE (*c.* 1550)

[In W. C. Hazlitt, *Remains of the Early Popular Poetry of England*, III, 1866, 225 ff.]

339 lines: 0; 4; 1; 7

It is perhaps dignifying *The Booke in Meeter of Robin Conscience* beyond its deserts to call it a morality, but the little dialogue is not without interest. In it the pious and Protestant Robin rebukes at length, and with no apparent success, his father Covetousness, his mother New Guise, and his sister Proud Beauty. There are no proverbs, and four of the sententious remarks are introduced in the margin by the author. Robin tries to lure his father into the paths of charity:

> Father, yov haue enovgh, if yov haue not too mvch.
> (III, 229, l. 39)

He fears that his mother's love of fashionable garb will lead her into even more evil ways:

> Svch a tree, svch frvte from it dooth proceed.
> (III, 240, l. 205)

As for his sister, Solomon had expressed it centuries before:

> Salomon declareth this by the beavtifvl rovt,
> A faire woman withovt discrete manners (saith he)
> Is like a ring of golde on a Swines snovt.
> (III, 242, ll. 247 ff.)

It is evident that the author has no hope for the mother's conversion, for his comment at the end of Robin's plea is gloomy:

> She deuils are hard to tvrne. (III, 240)

He is even more pessimistic about the sister:

> To talke well with some women dooth as mvch good,
> As a sicke man to eate vp a loade of greene wood.
> (III, 247)

Two of the frequent marginal notes are sententious. Of the father's love for treasure the author asserts:

> Where a mans hart is, there is his God.
> (III, 231)

Proud Beauty refuses to believe Robin's pleasant prognostications that her self adornment will lead to 'halters and stinkings and . . . baldnes of head,' but the author adds hopefully:

> Feare and shame much sin doth tame.
> (III, 246)

34

RESPUBLICA (1553)

[Ed. L. A. Magnus, EETS., ES., XCIV, 1905]
1938 lines: 20; 11; 44; 17

Of the plays which were written to bolster the tottering Catholic faith in England, *Respublica* is perhaps the most interesting, especially for our present purpose. Not only is the Vice, Avarice, full of old saws, as is fitting to his rôle, but People, 'representing the poore Commontie,' is given a very considerable number of homely sayings, most of which bring out his character as the standard-bearer of the masses.

Avarice intends, as he tells us in his opening speech, to deceive Respublica and get as much from her as possible. His pickings may seem of little importance to her, but

> Manye a smale makith a greate. (p. 4, i, 1, 109)

He must lay aside for the future:

> Store (thei saie) is no sore. (p. 4, i, 1, 116)

He is fearful lest thieves break in and steal, and his running comments do not encourage Insolence, Oppression and Adulation, who wish to gain his attention. Adulation finally takes heart of grace from a remark which, though not addressed to him, might well embolden an unfortunate suitor:

> Therefore catche that catche maye, hardely, & spare not.
> (p. 6, i, 3, 172)

Avarice agrees to help them once he is established as Policy at Respublica's court, and Oppression, who is in a great hurry to get his fingers in the pie, receives a well-merited rebuke:

> You will over the hedge ere ye comme att the stile.
> (p. 9, i, 3, 262)

Gold enough is soon in Avarice's possession, and he addresses his sweet bags as tenderly as an indulgent mother her children. He knows their yearning after repose in his chest:

> When the bealie is full, the bones woulde bee att reast.
> (p. 26, iii, 4, 757)

As he is cooing to his darlings he observes Adulation watching, and at once leaps to the worst conclusion:

> Ye can see no grene cheese / but your teethe wyll watier.
> (p. 26, iii, 4, 763)

He is no more happy to see Oppression, whom he greets uncharitably:

> The mo knaves the merier.
> (p. 26, iii, 5, 777)

None of them may come too near for the parley lest they mistake his money bags for fat black sausage:

> For suche hongrye doggs will slabbe vp sluttishe puddinges.
> (p. 28, iii, 6, 853)

If they want booty, let them serve themselves, and that without delay, for the sun won't always shine:

> While time is laie on lode,
> Consider ye have but a tyme of hey Making,
> And harvest is not mued withowte peines taking.
> (p. 30, iii, 6, 901 ff.)

What is more, the world moves on:

> Tyme willnot tarye. (p. 30, iii, 6, 904)

Although Avarice uses more proverbs than any other Vice of our acquaintance, he is being but true to type, and it is People who is the most unusual character in the play. This is not the first time that we have found rural characters speaking in dialect, but not before nor after are we to find a rustic figure as thoroughly characterized by the use of proverbs as is People. He is suspicious of Respublica's councilors from the outset. Adulation affirms that reforms are well under way, but this does not content People:

> Yea, iche heare his vaire wordes: but what beeth we the neare?
> (p. 24, iii, 3, 711)

He will wait before he applauds:

> Whan Is fynde ytt, chil beleve yt.
> (p. 24, iii, 3, 718)

He continues in the same ungracious vein:

> Than chil beleve een still / that vaine woordes beeth but tales.
> (p. 25, iii, 3, 727)

Even the smooth-tongued Avarice cannot content and beguile him. Change in itself is of no merit:

> As goode ner a whitt as ner the better.
> (p. 33, iv, 3, 1014)

It's all very well for Oppression to say that it takes time to bring about amelioration, but what about his plight in the meantime?

> While the grasse shall growe, the horse shall sterve.
> (p. 37, iv, 4, 1120)

He is none too tractable in the face of their threats. He asks if he may have 'leave to thinke' (p. 38, iv, 4, 1163), and when this is denied, retorts:

> þought is free,
> And a catt, þey zaith, maie looke on a king, pardee.
> (p. 38, iv, 4, 1165 f.)

Apart from those of Avarice and People there are but two proverbs. The Prologue is confident that right will prevail:

Tyme trieth all. (p. 2, l. 27)

Adulation tries to persuade Avarice to cease worrying about his money. Such preoccupation is unhealthy:

It prolongethe the life of Manne to bee merye.
(p. 30, iii, 6, 895)

The sententious remark about time and truth occurs five times in the play. The Prologue declares:

Tyme bringeth truth to lyght, (p. 2, l. 27)

and shortly after refers to

Veritee, the daughter of sage old Father Tyme.
(p. 2, l. 33)

Adulation, with anything but admiration, refers to the lady in much the same language:

Of the generall Veritee, Olde tymes daughter.
(p. 42, v, 2, 1201)

When she announces herself as 'dame Veritee' Avarice asks in horror 'What? the daughter of Tyme?' (p. 55, v, 9, 1699). An earlier remark of Avarice's had been of similar purport:

And tyme hathe this one vngracious propertee
To blab at length & open all that he dothe see.
(p. 30, iii, 6, 908 f.)

Avarice is given three sententious remarks. His abuse of Adulation is typical of the Vice's attitude toward his partners in ill-doing:

Youe the-Crowe-is-white youe, youe the-swanne-is-blacke youe.
(p. 6, i, 3, 184)

He quotes the Distichs of Cato as a spur to the others to make hay while the sun shines:

Remembre this verse, UT SINT OMNIA SALVA,
FRONTE CAPILLATA, POST HEC OCCASIO CALVA.
(p. 30, iii, 6, 918 f.)

When Oppression asks to have this 'fyne rag of rhetorike' expounded, he is chided for his lack of Latin, but is instructed all the same:

Forsouthe, sir, yt was of the goddesse occasyon.
She weareth a greate long tuffet of heare beefore,
And behinde hathe not one heare / neither lesse nor more.
Whereby is taught youe that, when Occasyon ys,
Ye muste take yt be tyme / or of your purpose mysse.
(pp. 30 f., iii, 6, 927 ff.)

His Latin is not exhausted and he finds some with which to reproach Respublica when, at long last, she sends him into exile:

I now see, HONORES MUTANT MORES,
But as semeth here, RARO IN MELIORES.
(p. 49, v, 6, 1509 f.)

Oppression is the only other evil character to use sententious remarks, one of which is revealing enough:

Eche man snatche for hymselfe.
(p. 11, i, 3, 315)

He is both surprised and angry at People's complaint:

Thow canst not see, thow wretch / canst thow whan thow art well?
(p. 38, iv, 4, 1149)

Despite his many proverbs, People speaks but two sententious remarks. He is philosophical, even if he complains, and is willing to

Take what God shall send. (p. 25, iii, 3, 737)

When Avarice and Insolence call him rude and foolish, he replies with dignity and reserve:

Thoughe zome bee starke bedlems, yet wise volkes beeth no dawes.
(p. 36, iv, 4, 1112)

The Prologue is well aware of the wickedness of the world and the sensitive prejudices of many:

In dede, no man speaketh wordes so well fore pondred,
But the same by some meanes maye be misconstrued.
(p. 1, ll. 9 f.)

Respublica laments that things in the world change, and evidently not for the better:

What yearethlye thinge is permanent or stable?
(p. 15, ii, 1, 439)

Mercy and Truth pity the sad state of Respublica, languishing so long in misfortune, but Truth is able to see the silver lining:

But as meate & drinke & other bodylye foode
Is never founde to bee, so pleasaunte nor so goode
As whan fretting hongre / & thrifte hathe pincht afore;
And as health after sickenes is sweeter evermore,
So after decaye & aduersytee overcome [ms. evercome]
Welth and prospiritee shalbe double welcome.
(p. 44, v, 3, 1341 ff.)

When the day of reckoning comes Mercy, true to her name and nature, pleads for the culprits:

[It is muche] more glorie & standith with more skyll,
Loste shepe to recover, then the scabye to spill.
(p. 60, v, 10, 1859 f.)

Justice is inexorable, however, and Nemesis summons Avarice by his true name and title:

Now, the plague of Comonweales, as all men doo note,
Come foorth, Avarice. (p. 61, v, 10, 1894 f.)

35

JOHN THE EVANGELIST (before 1557)

[Ed. W. W. Greg, Malone Society Reprints, 1907]
653 lines: 0; 3; 6; 4

The feeble little play *John the Evangelist*, which may even be as early as 1520 (see Greg, p. vi), is chiefly characterized by its smattering of Latin phrases. One of its four sententious remarks is in that language and is spoken by Eugenio to Irisdision:

> Than is Caton false / and that he endytes
> For he sayth (Nec te collaudas / nec te culpaberis ipse)
> Great laudacyons loueth these hypocrytes
> (Qui se colaudat) &c. (sig. A ii[v], ll. 41 ff.)

Eugenio also makes a statement, which, coupled with Erasmus's famous observation, seems to indicate that English osculation was by way of becoming proverbial:

> The curtesye of Englande is ofte to kys
> And of it selfe it is lechery where pleasure is.
> (sig. B i, ll. 222 f.)

In one of his infrequent appearances Saint John comments on the unsteadfastness of worldly goods:

> Rychesse . . . is mutable.
> (sig. B i[v], l. 252)

Evil Counsel gives what out of its immediate context would be excellent advice:

> Whan a man hath inowe
> Let hym parte with his neyghboures.
> (sig. C i[v], ll. 504 f.)

36

W. Wager's *THE LONGER THOU LIVEST THE MORE FOOL THOU ART* (1559–1560)

[Tudor Facsimile Texts, 1910]
1990 lines: 11; 9; 16; 23

W. Wager shows a marked partiality for the use of proverbs as the titles of his plays. Of his four plays concerning which we have information, the two which have survived completely have proverbial titles and a third which suffered in the kitchen of Warburton's feckless cook was prophetically named *'Tis Good Sleeping in a Whole Skin.*

The Longer thou Livest the more Fool thou art is apparently the earliest of Wager's plays, and it certainly exhibits a less developed taste for proverbial material than does *Enough is as Good as a Feast.* The title proverb occurs six times (sigs. A ii[v], A iv[v], D ii[v], D iii, F iii, G i). There are only five other proverbs, two of which are spoken by Wrath. He remarks on the folly of an attempt to educate Moros, the silly hero of the play. Of what use are books to such a one?

> A foole will delight more in a bable. (sig. C iv)

He is not surprised when Moros rises to great heights of prosperity:

> They say that fooles are fortunable. (sig. E ii)

Here he is echoing a remark previously made by Fortune herself:

> Fortune can exalte fooles. (sig. D iv[v])

Piety is aghast at the crew which Wrath proposes to gather about the wealthy Moros, which include Impiety, Cruelty, and Ignorance:

> Such a Master, such seruaunts in deede. (sig. E ii)

Incontinence also uses a proverb apropos of Moros's wild use of his newly acquired sword:

> It is a prouerbe wise and auncient,
> Beware how you geue any edge toole,
> Vnto mad men that be insipient,
> Vnto a yonge childe, and vnto a foole. (sig. D i)

There are an unconscionable number of sententious remarks in the play. The Prologue sets the pace:

> To be a good man it is also expedient,
> Of good Parents to be begotten and borne,
> In deede to all men it is most euident,
> That a pleasaunt Rose springeth of a sharpe Thorne,
> But commonly of good Seed procedeth good Corne,
> Good Parents in good manners do instruct their childe,
> Correcting him when he beginneth to grow wilde.
> (sig. A ii)

However, he goes on, one must not count too much on environment and nurture:

> Bringing vp is a great thing, so is dilligence,
> But nothing, God except, is so strong of Nature,
> For neither councell, learninge nor sapience,
> Can an euill nature to honest manners allure.
> (sig. A ii[v])

Discipline is the prize user of sententious remarks, most of which are directed at fools in general and Moros in particular. There would be little point in doing more than group his dreary drivel:

> *Quales quisque sibi natos eduxit habebit.*
> As one bringeth vp, his Children saith he,
> So shall he haue them, wise or without wit. (sig. A iv)

> The wise man willeth, an Asse to haue a scourge.
> (sig. B ii[v])

> Vexation they say giueth intelligence. (sig. B ii[v])

> For conuersation with persons of vertue
> Altereth nature sometime for a suertie. (sig. C i)

Custome may all kinde of manners bring forth.
(sig. C i)

Beate a foole in a morter saith the wise man,
And thou shalt not make him leaue his folly.
(sig. D ii[v])

A foole vttereth his angre in hast. (sig. F iii[v])

Where much angre is, strength is past. (sig. F iii[v])

As fayer legges to a cripple are vnseemelie,
So to a foole honor is vndecent. (sig. F iii[v])

As snow in haruest is vntimelie,
So is it a plague where a foole is regent. (sig. F iii[v])

Idleness does not believe that Discipline and Piety will make notable progress in the education of Moros:

Doting fooles thinke to make Corne to grow
Vpon grauell, where earth there is none.
(sigs. C i[v]–C ii)

When Incontinence calls him 'the parent of all vice' (sig. C ii) he repeats the charge with quiet pride:

The parent of all vice thou diddest me call.
(sig. C ii)

He has few good words for his own colleagues, paying his respects to Wrath as follows:

Wrath and Madnesse they say be all one,
Sauing that Madnesse doth still remaine:
But wrath in fooles will soone be gone,
Yea and as soone it wil come againe. (sig. C ii[v])

Like Discipline, Piety directs his remarks against fools:

Better it is to meete a she Beare,
When she is robbed of her whelpes,
Then with a foole that rule doth beare. (sig. E ii)

For a madde man hauing in his hand edge toole,
Seketh both him selfe and other to kill,
So a cunning man without wisdom is but a foole.
(sig. G iii[v])

Moros, to whom we owe, for his tags of old songs and ballads (sigs. A iii[r-v], D ii), a greater debt by far than to Discipline and Piety, expresses two parallel and singularly wise opinions:

> Much on the Spitte is past abstinence. (sig. B ii)
>
> In all thinges there is a meane. (sig. F ii[v])

Exercitation has little hope of improving Moros:

> While a plant of a Tree is yonge and tender,
> You may cause it to grow croked or right:
> So a childe, while knowledge is but slender,
> You may instructe whereto you will by might:
> But after the Plante is growne to a tree,
> To any bowinge it will not geue place:
> So yonge folkes when to age growne they be,
> Waxe stubborne and be of an indurate face.
> (sig. C i)

Fortune characterizes herself:

> I aduaunce and I plucke downe againe.
> (sig. D iii[v])

37

W. Wager's *ENOUGH IS AS GOOD AS A FEAST* (*c.* 1565)

[Ed. Seymour De Ricci, Henry E. Huntington Facsimile Reprints II, New York, 1920]
1545 lines: 23; 12; 11; 14

Enough is as Good as a Feast is a border-line play, one which is as much an interlude as a morality. Few early plays, and certainly no other of Wager's, are so rich in proverbs. The proverb which furnishes the title occurs eight times (sigs. A iii, A iii[v], B i[v], C ii, C iv, D ii[v], G ii, G ii[v]) in addition to its appearance on the title-page. The remaining fifteen proverbs are divided among eight speaking parts. Covetous, the Vice, is given but one which appears when he chides Temerity and Inconsideration for their slight respect:

> Soon ripe soon rotten. (sig. C iii)

He does, however, make use of a number of proverbial phrases.

The Prologue apologizes for belaboring the point of the play:

> Few woords to wise men are sufficient.
> (sig. A ii[v])

Another proverb outside the action is found in a song:

> The longest liuer pay all. (sig. B ii)

Worldly Man, who comes to a worse end than most neutral characters, uses four proverbs, two of them together in his entering speech:

> A common saying better is enuy then rueth,
> I had rather they should spite then pitty me:
> For the olde saying now a dayes proueth trueth,
> Naught haue naught set by as dayly we see.
> (sig. A iii)

He defends his mercenary point of view against Heavenly Man:

> For money as men say winneth bothe Citties and townes.
> (sig. B i)

He gains a short period of grace, but is soon led to his old ways, and glories in his bad reputation:

> A common saying the Fox fareth the better and not the worse:
> When that the good wife dooth him ban and cursse.
> (sig. E iv[v])

Enough appears from his own proverb and uses three others. He warns Worldly Man against his seeming friends:

It is an olde prouerbe and of an ancient time:
Which saith, it is not all Golde, that like Golde dooth shine.
(sig. D ii[v])

The promises and boasts of Covetous and the others are not necessarily reliable:

The greatest bosters are not the best giuers:
Nor the ernest preachers are the best liuers.
(sig. D iii[v])

He sees little real hope for Worldly Man's salvation:

But it is an olde saying and a true certainly:
It wil not out of the flesh that is bred in the bone verily.
(sig. D iii[v])

When Covetous is most alarmed at Worldly Man's defection, Temerity in two proverbs deplores precipitate action:

Haste maketh waste Brother Couetouse ye wot:
No looue so soon colde, as that is moste hot.
(sig. B iii[v])

The Physician who tries to revive Worldly Man, and is sent off without his pay, hurls two sayings at his patient and his patient's servants:

A common saying in deed, that is like vnto like:
A wicked M[aster] for wicked seruants, God must needs strike.
(sig. F iv)

Inconsideration thinks that Covetous talks rather too freely:

They say it is perelouse with edge tooles to iest.
(sig. C ii)

The sententious remarks, like the proverbs, are divided without consideration for the categories of the speakers. Covetous uses three, two of which are descriptive of his own character:

Couetouse (saith the wise man) is the root of all euil.
(sig. B iv)

I am the root of all wickednes and sin. (sig. G i)

Covetous pretends to agree with Enough and rebukes Worldly Man for his greed, but he spoils the effect by suggesting that what is true for many need not be true for all:

For euery man is not called after one sorte.
(sig. D iii)

One of Contentation's four sayings is a sententious variant of the title proverb and a second is another attack on the covetous man:

Inough serueth them not til that they haue more.
(sig. B i)

For the more he hath, the more stil he dooth require.
(sig. G ii)

True wealth, he tells Worldly Man, is a thing of the spirit and not the purse:

A minde wel content,
Is great riches as wise king Salomon dooth say.
(sig. B i[v])

He is sorry to see Worldly Man borne away on the devil's back, but no one who courts evil company can escape infection:

He that toucheth pitch, shalbe defiled with the same.
(sig. G i[v])

Heavenly Man refuses to humor Worldly Man's pettishness:

Tobe angry without a cause, without mends must be eased.
(sig. A iv)

He warns him, as Contentation had done, that no one dare trust to worldly wealth for more than a brief space:

> As for the treasure that you possesse heer,
> Through ficklenes of Fortune soon fadeth away:
> The greatest of renown and moste worthy Peer,
> Somtime in the end falleth to misery and decay.
> (sig. B i)

He emphasizes the dangers of such trust by an appropriate borrowing from Scripture:

> It is as easy for a Cammel through an Nedles eye to thrust,
> As for him that on riches hath fixed his minde:
> The way to eternall saluation to finde. (sig. E i)

The Prologue declares that rash and ready speakers lay up trouble for themselves and others:

> When, where, and to whome they speak they must note:
> Before that any thing passe out of their throte.
> (sig. A ii[v])

Precipitation boasts that he leads Worldly Man into the snare of Inconsideration, and the latter then teaches him

> Neither to consider his beginning:
> Neither at the end what shall be the winning.
> (sig. C iii[v])

During Worldly Man's brief period of conversion and grace he is full of edifying resolutions and words:

> I finde it true as the wise king Saloman dooth say,
> It is better to haue a little with the fear of the Lord
> Then to haue much treasure and yet go astray.
> (sig. C iv)

Shortly thereafter he falls into the hands of Covetous and Precipitation and hails them as friends without regard to Enough's admonition:

> Be not rash in taking a freend Aristotle dooth say.
> (sig. D ii[v]

37a

W. Wager's *THE CRUEL DEBTOR* (*c.* 1566)

[Malone Society Collections, I, 4 (1911), 315 ff.;
II, 2 (1923), 142 ff.]

265 lines: 0; 0; 3; 5

The four surviving leaves of Wager's play, *The Cruel Debtor*, contain several sententious remarks, but do not represent enough of the play to warrant any generalization. Four of the sententious remarks are found in a single leaf. I give them in the order of their occurrence.

He that putteth hym selfe in forewarde
Can not be sure, but putteth hym selfe id hazard.
(Simulation, II, 2, 143, ll. 1 f.)

It is ma< > to medle betwene men in theyr fury,<
They know not theyr owne father when they be angry<.
(Rigor, II, 2, 143 f., ll. 33 f.)

To deceiue such one as is knowen deceiuable
Is no deceyte. (Rigor, II, 2, 144, ll. 54 f.)

Lo here see, he that to deceiue al, hys mind doth cast
By some meane is deceyued hym selfe at the last.
(Rigor, II, 2, 144, ll. 60 f.)

The hygher that any man presumeth to clyme
The sorer is hys hurte whan he chaunceth to fall.
(Ophiletis, I, 4, 320, ll. 97 f.)

38

IMPATIENT POVERTY (before 1560)

[The Tudor Reprinted and Parallel Texts, 1909]

1095 lines: 4; 2; 13; 8

The amount of proverbial material in *Impatient Poverty* is not unusual, but its disposition is somewhat out of the ordinary. Here, although we find Envy and

Misrule using nine out of fifteen proverbial phrases, they have no proverbs or sententious remarks. Peace quotes a popular proverb to Impatient Poverty, at the same time trying to make it appear learned:

> Take hede my frende thus sayth the texte
> In lyttle medlynge standeth great rest. (p. 6)

He also warns Prosperity to have a care of dangers ahead:

> Yet I saye beware of had I wyst. (p. 24)

Abundance claims that he makes most of his harsh bargains because of the importunity of his victims. They beg for aid and

> Me thincke it is a good dede
> To helpe a man at hys nede. (p. 11)

He can see no valid reason to lower himself from his substantial rank and he expresses his opinion with a proverb apparently drawn from football:

> Euer with th[e] strongest part renneth the ball. (p. 14)

Peace employs five of the eight sententious remarks. He urges Prosperity to give freely to good causes:

> For euerye peny that so is spente
> God wyll sende the double. (p. 10)

He also tells him to shun Envy and Misrule, the sooner the better:

> It is [b]etter to forsake them betyme then to late. (p. 24)

When he declares roundly that

> Open synne muste do open punishemente, (p. 34)

he is but echoing the Summoner's earlier, but hypocritical, remark:

> Open synne must haue open penaunce. (p. 32)

Again when he says that

> Many a man doth decay for lacke of good forewitte,
> (p. 35)

he may well have taken a hint from the lesson which bitter experience had taught Poverty:

> Make a sure foundacyon, or ye set vp the rofe
> Of a good & vertuous beginning cometh a good ending.
> (p. 31)

Peace's last remark will not sound unfamiliar to us:

> Soueraynes here may ye se proued before you al
> Of thys wanton worlde the great fragilyte
> Euer mutable of the turnyng as a bal
> Nowe flode of ryches nowe ebbe of pouerte
> What shulde men set by this worldes vanyte
> Thynke on this lesson and do it not forget
> The gayest of vs al is but wormes meate. (p. 35)

Nor, indeed, will we be surprised at Conscience's earlier warning to Abundance to repent before it is too late:

> Yesterdaye thou canst not agayne call. (p. 14)

39

Ulpian Fulwell's *LIKE WILL TO LIKE, QUOTH THE DEVIL TO THE COLLIER* (*c.* 1568)

[Tudor Facsimile Texts, 1909]
1237 lines: 44; 14; 17; 5

When Ulpian Fulwell wrote his morality he chose a proverb, *Like Will to Like, quoth the Devil to the Collier*, for the title, and explained his choice in the Prologue:

> Sith pithie prouerbs in our English tung doo abound,
> Our author thought good such a one for to chuse:
> As may shew good example and mirth may eke be found,
> But no lasciuious toyes he purposeth to vse. (sig. A ii)

We have found few plays with as large a percentage of proverbs as this, and that remains true even after we have observed that thirty out of the forty-four proverbs are accounted for by occurrences of the title proverb in one form or another. Fulwell introduced the saying on nearly every page of his play, ranging in form from the full version (sigs. A ii, A iv, B ii, C ii, D i, D i[v], E i[v], E iv[v]) to such sententious remarks as

> Cicero in his book de amicitia these woords dooth expresse,
> Saying nothing is more desirous then like is vnto like,
> (sig. A ii)

and

> Similis similem ubi quærit, (sig. B i[v])

through such other forms as: 'And the Deuil with the Colier, the theef that seeks the theef' (sig. A ii[v]), 'The Colier and the Deuill wil be, / Much like to like alway' (sig. B i), 'Like wil euer to like goe' (sig. D i), 'Like wil euer to like' (sig. B ii[v]), 'Like wil to like alway' (sigs. A iv[v], D i[v]), 'Like to like alway' (sig. A iv), 'Like wil neuer from like' (sig. E iii[v]), 'Like with like wil euer agree' (sig. B i), 'Like with like reward obtain' (sig. F ii), 'As like to like wel coupled then' (sig. F ii), 'Like wil to like' (sigs. A iv[v], B ii, C ii, C ii[v]), 'Like to like' (sig. F ii), 'Like wil vnto like' (sig. A ii), 'Like vnto like' (sig. A ii[v]).

The Prologue uses another proverb:

> Diuers men of duiers mindes be. (sig. A ii)

Nichol Newfangle, the Vice, enters complaining of the lack of recognition on the part of the audience:

> I am no sooner out of sight but quite out of minde.
> (sig. A ii[v])

In his conversation with Lucifer he acknowledges the latter's power:

When the deuil wil haue it so: it must needs so be.
(sig. B i)

His remaining proverbs are found in a single passage, which serves to forecast the way in which sayings are piled on sayings in such later plays as Henry Porter's *Two Angry Women of Abington*:

Such Carpenter such chips,
And as the wise man saith, such letice such lips.
For like maister like men, like tutor like Scholer.
(sig. C ii)

Although Nichol leads in use of proverbial material, Tom Tosspot is a close second to him. Tom is very much pleased to meet Nichol, especially since he was not expecting to do so:

It is an olde saying, that mountains and hills neuer meet,
But I see that men shall meet though they doo not seek.
(sig. B ii)

Like many talkative people, he is an advocate of taciturnity:

Few woords are best among freends this is true.
(sig. B ii[v])

After he and Rafe Roister have selected Nichol to decide which of the two is the greater knave, the judge's behavior makes him begin to repent the choice:

So for our own tailes we haue made a rod.
(sig. B iii[v])

Another time, you may be sure, he will be wiser:

And ere I leap once I wil look twice.
(sig. B iii[v])

After the two fine fellows have lost their goods in pursuit of pleasure and the 'land of the two-legged mare' which Nichol has promised them, they come in and the stage direction says that Rafe 'must cursse and ban.' Tom's comment is proverbial:

Wel be as be may is no banning. (sig. D iv[v])

Rafe uses but two proverbs and those in repentance for the course of life which has reduced him to beggary:

Now the horsse is stolen I shut the stable doore. (sig. E i[v])

Time tarieth no man but passeth stil away. (sig. E i[v])

He is equally sententious:

But the time past cannot be called again this is no nay. (sig. E i[v])

Take time while time is for time dooth flee. (sig. E i[v])

Virtuous Life employs a sententious remark:

Sith the thing praise woorthy need no praise at all. (sig. D ii[v])

Nichol, in his silly song, affords us a dietary saying:

Butter is no bone meat. (sig. C iii)

Tom is able to account for the predicament in which he and Rafe find themselves:

Vicious persons beholde not the net. (sig. E ii)

40

NEW CUSTOM (1559–1573)

[Tudor Facsimile Texts, 1908]

1075 lines: 10; 5; 6; 2

The only known edition of *New Custom* was not printed until 1573, but the strong anti-Catholic sentiment indicates that it was probably written some time before that date, while references to the reign of Queen Mary place its composition after 1558. When compared with the number of other sayings, proverbs bulk large; we find six out of the ten spoken by Perverse Doctrine, who is described as 'an olde Popishe priest,' and who combines the rôles of Vice and neutral character since, after causing great trouble, he ends by being converted to the true and new belief. He is much annoyed by the way that mere boys preach the new learning and interpret the Bible:

> Youthe is rashe they say, but olde men hath the knowledge.
> (sig. A iii[v])

When New Custom introduces himself as Primitive Constitution, Perverse Doctrine remarks that he thought it must be some such thing of nought:

> Like Lettuse like lippes, a scabd horse for a scald squire.
> (sig. B iii[v])

He recognizes that the reformers have the upper hand but he hopes for better things to come. The pendulum swings, and it may

> Chaunce that a dogge hath a daye. (sig. D i[v])

He leaves Ignorance at the tavern lining his cap against the rain. He himself might well have stayed,

> But as the prouerbe saith it is good to keepe still.
> One head for the reckning bothe sober and wise.
> (sig. D ii)

With Ignorance such a dolt he has to do all the work:

> For neede they say maketh the olde wife, and man both to trudge.
> (sig. D ii)

Perverse Doctrine also utters five out of the six miscellaneous proverbial phrases.

The Prologue begins his speech with a proverb:

> All thinges be not soe as in sight they doe seeme.
> (sig. A ii)

Shortly after he uses another:

> For many heades, many wittes wee doe plainely see.
> (sig. A ii[v])

New Custom alone of the good characters is at all proverbial in speech. When Perverse Doctrine urges that the study of Duns and the Questionists is better than being idle, he retorts:

> They say better to be idle then to do harme.
> (B ii[v])

Cruelty with his ordinary elegance of speech swears 'by goddes guttes' that he will destroy the heretic varlet, Light of the Gospel. Ignorance tells him that he had better use counsel as well as impetuosity:

> For moe wittes as you knowe, may do better then one.
> (sig. C iv[v])

Light of the Gospel strengthens New Custom with a sententious remark of scriptural origin:

> Faith moueth mountaines. (sig. B iv[v])

Cruelty hopes to overthrow the upholders of heresy. In some cases, however, he would forgive rather than punish:

> I wote that sometime the wisest may fall.
> (sig. C iii)

41

ALBION KNIGHT (*c.* 1566)

[Ed. J. P. Collier in the Shakespeare Society's Papers, I (1844), 55 ff.]

396 lines: 1; 4; 3; 2

The three hundred ninety-six lines which are all that survive of the political morality, *Albion Knight*, are not crowded with sayings. It is significant, however, that every bit of proverbial material in the play is spoken by Injury, the Vice, or his companion in misdeeds, Division. Justice censures Injury for his 'lyght apparaile' and the Vice asks, much hurt:

> Apparell, good syr, what faulte is that
> Though grey be her cote why blame ye the wild cat?
> (p. 57)

Injury also uses both the sententious remarks. He tells Albion that he will be universally railed at as 'halfe a man and halfe a wyld goose.' Albion, not unnaturally, demands an explanation and gets it:

> And for because ye study but for the begynnynge
> And never provide for a sure endyng
> Begynnyng lyke a man ye take great assay
> At last lyke a wyld goose even but to flye awaye.
> (p. 59)

Injury fears lest Justice's brother, Peace, may arrange a match between his daughter Plenty and Albion (p. 66). We may find here, no doubt, an echo of the proverb, 'Peace breedeth plenty.'

42

THE STORY OF KING DARIUS (1565)

[Tudor Facsimile Texts, 1909]
1614 lines: 1; 6; 17; 2

Although *King Darius* contains elements of both mystery play and morality, the later element may be fairly said to predominate. There is little proverbial material for a play of more than sixteen hundred lines. Of the seventeen miscellaneous proverbial phrases seven are expressions of worthlessness and four indicate distance. The only thing at all characteristic is that Iniquity, the Vice, uses ten of the seventeen, but he utters no other proverbial material. The only proverb in the play occurs in a song at the end in which the auditors are urged to cleave to Constancy and to

> Spurne not agaynst the prycke. (sig. H iv[v])

Partiality is fierce against Equality, especially in urging Iniquity to attack him:

> Let hym haue as good as he doth brynge. (sig. C i)

The first claimant for King Darius's prize to the proponent of the wisest sentiment chooses to attack wine and sums up his argument in one line:

> Thus wine maketh men to haue a small wyt.
> (sig. G iii[v])

43

THE TRIAL OF TREASURE (1567)

[Tudor Facsimile Texts, 1908. Sig. E iii is wanting, but the missing portion is found in Hazlitt's Dodsley, III, 1874, 296 ff.]

1042 lines: 4; 7; 8; 12

The Trial of Treasure is not rich in proverbial material. In his opening speech Lust expounds his philosophy of existence:

> Therfore a litle mirth is worth much sorow some say.
> (sig. A iii)

He accuses Just of wearing drab clothes in contrast with his own, and, indeed, of being lousy. Just is not slow to reply:

> It is not golde alwayes that doth shine,
> But corrupting Copper of small valuation.
> (sig. A iii[v])

Lust plans to follow the advice of Æsop:

> It is good to be wittie and wyse. (sig. B iii)

When Treasure is taken from him he yields with as good grace as possible:

> He must needs go, that is driven by the devil's drift.
> (Hazlitt's Dodsley, III, 297)

Just uses two sententious remarks, the first an attack on idleness:

> Where idelnes is Lust parteth the stake.
> (sig. A iv[v])

The other is a learned version of the proverb which tells us that 'Pride goes before and Shame comes after':

> Elation and Pride, no commoditie doth bring,
> But is often knowen the forerunner of shame.
> (sig. C i)

Sapience has no belief in the permanence of worldly goods:

> For treasures here gotten are vncertaine and vaine,
> But treasures of the mynde do continually remaine.
> (sig. B iv[v])

He also reminds Just of the various fates of the unwise, some of whom are over-ambitious and

> Clime till they fall downe againe. (sig. C i)

Lust complains that

> Fortune is variable, (sig. B ii[v])

and quotes Thales on the virtue of Treasure:

> I perceiue that she is a true frende at neede.
> For I haue proued her according as Thales doth saye
> And I perceiue that her bewtie can not decaye.
> (sig. D iv)

Lust does not monopolize Thales. We find sour Visitation rebuking the Vices:

> Thou neuer remembrest Thales his sentence,
> Who willeth men in all thinges to kepe a measure,
> Especially in loue to incertaintie of treasure.
> (sig. E i[v])

Time speaks impersonally about himself:

> You know that all such things are subject to time.
> (Hazlitt's Dodsley, III, 296)

> Time cannot tarry.
> (Hazlitt's Dodsley, III, 297)

> Remember that Time turneth all things about:
> Time is the touchstone the just for to try.
> (Hazlitt's Dodsley, III, 300)

Although Inclination, the Vice, speaks eight of the fifteen proverbial phrases, he has in addition only a single sententious remark:

> He that can flatter shalbe well beloued. (sig. D ii)

The song at the end of the play opens with the following:

> Take hede in tyme, and note this well,
> Be ruled alwaies by councell. (sig. E iv)

44

LIBERALITY AND PRODIGALITY (?1567–1568)

[Ed. W. W. Greg, Malone Society Reprints, 1913]
1352 lines: 4; 9; 9; 11

While *Liberality and Prodigality* was not printed, so far as we know, until 1602, the nature of the play makes an earlier date, perhaps 1567–1568 (cf. Greg, p. v), not unlikely. There is a proverb in the Prologue:

> The Prouerbe is, *How many men, so many mindes.*
> Which maketh proofe, how hard a thing it is,
> Of sundry mindes to please the sundry kindes.
> (sig. A iii, ll. 1 ff.)

Vanity comments approvingly on Money's praise of himself:

> Money makes masteries, old prouerbs declare.
> (sig. B iii[v], l. 234)

The gallant Captain Welldone, temporarily out of fortune's favor, would not willingly ask for aid, but he finds two proverbs which indicate his need:

But need doth make, the Prouerbe saith, th'old wife to trot for woe.
Yet whom starke need doth pinch, at length the diuel driues to go.
(sig. D ii, ll. 647 f.)

The Prologue contains a sententious remark warning against ambition:

Lest perking ouer-hie, with shame wee fall.
(sig. A iii, l. 25)

Still another is used impersonally in a song:

But fading pleasures in the end,
Are bought with fasting pain.
(sig. F i[v], ll. 1132 f.)

There are three passages about Fortune. The first is directed at the goddess by Virtue:

Whilome hath bin taught that fortunes hold is tickle,
She beares a double face, disguised, false, and fickle,
Full fraughted with all sleights, she playeth on the pack,
On whom she smileth most, she turneth most to wracke.
(sig. B i[v], ll. 116 ff.)

The second is used by Liberality:

But this is sure, and that most sure, that Fortune is vnsure,
Her selfe most fraile, her giftes as fraile, subiect to euery shewre:
And in the end, who buildeth most vpon her suerty,
Shall finde himselfe cast headlong downe, to depth of miserie.
(sig. D i[v], ll. 630 ff.)

In the third case Fortune is speaking of herself:

For as she list to fauour, els to frowne,
She hoyseth vp, or headlong hurleth downe.
(sig. E ii[v], ll. 965 f.)

Fortune makes use of another saying as she prepares for her contest with Virtue:

Time posts away, and words they be but vaine.
(sig. B iv, l. 287)

Tenacity, with his rustic accent and miserly ways, comes up to Fortune's court to seek Money, but fears lest missing it he will be

> A foole returnd, like as a foole I came.
> (sig. B ii, l. 146)

He has no bribe to offer to Vanity:

> Poore men, deare zonne, must craue of courtesie.
> (sig. B ii[v], l. 176)

Liberality cannot endure Tenacity, for, he says,

> Contraries cannot agree.
> (sig. B iv[v], l. 321)

Vanity, frivolous though he may be, is a learned fellow and has Latin at his beck and call:

> Quod differtur, non aufertur.
> (sig. E ii[v], l. 936)

We find the more or less customary praise of Reason, this time delivered by Equity:

> Where reason rules, there is the golden meane.
> (sig. E iv[v], l. 1090)

45

THE MARRIAGE OF WIT AND SCIENCE (1569–1570)

[Tudor Facsimile Texts, 1909]
1287 lines: 18; 9; 23; 13

The relation of *The Marriage of Wit and Science* to John Redford's *Wit and Science* and to *The Marriage of Wit and Wisdom* has already been discussed (see pp. 104–106 above). The proverbs in this play are numerous, thirteen out of eighteen being used by either Wit or Will. In this play we find one of those proverb-capping dialogues which we have already noted in the French religious drama (see pp. 61 ff. above) and which were to be popular in later plays:

Witte. Both blame and shame, rashe boldnes doth breede.
Will. You must aduenture both, spare to speake, spare to speede,
What tell you me of shame, it is shame to steale a horse.
Witte. More hast then good speede, makes many fare the worse.
Will. But he that takes not such time while he maye,
Shal leape at a whyting when time is a waye.
Witte. But he that leapes before he loke, good sonne,
Maye leape in the myre, and mysse when he hath done.
(sig. C iii[v]–C iv)

As the play opens, Wit confesses to his mother, Nature, that he is most inconstant, and finds himself too readily moved by prevailing causes:

Much like the nayle that last came in, & dryues the former out.
(sig. A ii)

Wit tells Experience almost flippantly that he will be happy to entertain Instruction, Study, and Diligence:

The more company the merier. (sig. C i[v])

Incidentally, Will caps this proverb of Wit's with another:

It is a good faulte to haue more then enowe.
(sig. C i[v])

Tediousness brags mightily as he prepares to do battle with Wit, but this does not perturb our hero:

Great bost small rost. (sig. D ii)

After dancing with Recreation, Wit shows more temperance in mirth than we might have expected:

Enoughe is enoughe. (sig. D iv)

When Science fails to recognize him after his disguise by Idleness, he reproaches her with the same proverb relative to hasty love which had been applied to him in

Redford's play (see p. 103 above), and adds to it yet another:

> An old sayd sawe it is, and to true I finde,
> Soone hot, sone cold, out of sight, out of mind.
> (sig. E i[v])

In addition to those already quoted, Will uses two proverbs. He warns Wit not to let his wife get control:

> Or elles the graye Mare, wil be the better horse.
> (sig. B ii[v])

He makes a rather scandalous suggestion to Wit, and when the latter asks, I fear rhetorically, what he means, he replies:

> One masse for a penye, you know what is what.
> (sig. C iii[v])

Five other characters use one proverb each. Nature warns Wit that man achieves the higher qualities only by toil and intellect, and

> This by toyle and practise of the mind,
> Is fet full farre god wot and bought full deare.
> (sig. A iii)

We have here a somewhat curious application of the proverb 'Far fet and dear bought is good for ladies.' Science doubts if Wit's readiness to marry her within an hour will lead to good:

> Such haste myght hapelye turne to wast to sum.
> (sig. B iii[v])

Reason, too, opposes undue haste:

> Pause a while,
> Or els this hast of yours will you beguile. (sig. C i)

Experience re-echoes the sentiment:

> This hedlong hast, may soner misse then hit. (sig. C i)

Idleness uses a proverb which she had spoken in Redford's play (see p. 103 above):

> There laye and there bee, the prouerbe is verified,
> I am neither idle, nor yet wel occupied. (sig. E i)

The sententious remarks are divided evenly enough. Nature, who has had but one proverb and one proverbial phrase, uses four — all addressed to Wit. She urges him to make known his plans that she may aid him:

> He salues the sore that knowes the pacient best.
> (sig. A ii)

She can't do everything, however, and refuses to attempt the impossible:

> Why should I challenge that I cannot doe?
> (sig. A iii)

There is a power above her which rules her and through which she will give Wit a love of knowledge and of self-improvement:

> Good groundes are tilde, as well as are the worste
> The rankest flower will aske a springyng tyme,
> So is mans wit vnperfit at the first. (sig. A iii[v])

Wit should never forget that he must apply himself ardently if he is to succeed:

> The worthiest things ar wonne with pain in tract of time alwaies.
> (sig. A iii[v])

Wit hopes to accomplish much and, counting on the assistance of Time, plans to get along without labor:

> Time worketh all with ease, and gyues the greatest dynt
> In tyme softe water dropes can hollowe hardest flynt.
> (sig. A iv)

He prepares to attack Tediousness with assurance despite the unlikelihood, to be verified all too soon, of success:

Unlikely thinges are brought to passe, by courage now and then.
(sig. D ii)

Will boasts himself to be a man of few words who refuses to

Make a brode tree, of euery litell shrubbe, (sig. B i)

but amusingly enough he uses fifteen lines and eight proverbial phrases to say it. He has a low opinion of the sense and virtue of women:

Fayre wordes are wont oft times, fayre women to allure.
(sig. B iv[v])

Women are best pleased, tyll they be vsed homely.
(sig. C iv)

Experience, true to the lessons which she gives herself, is slow to believe in Wit's protestations of love for Science:

There are that promise fayre, and meane as well,
As any heart can thinke, or tongue can tell,
Which at the first are hot, and kindle in desyre,
But in one month or twayne, quit quenched is the fyre.
Such is the trade of youth whome famies force doth lede,
Whose loue is only at the plonge & cannot longe procede.
(sig. C iv[v])

It will be observed that Experience expresses here sententiously what she had conveyed by means of a proverb in *Wit and Science* (see p. 103 above). She goes on in much the same vein:

Who breaketh promise, wil not sticke likewyse to breake his othe.
(sig. C iv[v])

When Wit is restored from the death-like swoon into which Tediousness cast him he is in despair, but Recreation comforts him with the thought that there is always another day and things are bound to improve. No one can hope to win always:

Not euery foyle doth make a fal, nor euery foyle doth slaye.
(sig. D iii)

46

THE MARRIAGE OF WIT AND WISDOM (*c.* 1570)

[Ed. J. O. Halliwell[-Phillipps], Shakespeare Society, XXXI, 1846]
1265 lines: 14; 10; 39; 10

The proverbial material in *The Marriage of Wit and Wisdom* [9] has been collected and studied in Morris P. Tilley's "Notes on The Marriage of Wit and Wisdom," *The Shakespeare Association Bulletin*, X (1935), 45–57, 89–94. I am indebted to Professor Tilley's discussion for several particulars, and I give specific references hereafter to certain of his important identifications and comments. This is the third of the three 'marriage' moralities (see pp. 102 ff. and 138 ff. above) and, while it contains but slightly more proverbial material and that only in the greater number of miscellaneous proverbial phrases, the distribution is altogether different. *The Marriage of Wit and Wisdom* is here far more typical than are the earlier plays. Idleness, now not a vicious female but the Vice himself, uses seven of the fourteen proverbs, nine of the ten comparisons, twenty-three of the other proverbial phrases, but only one of the ten sententious remarks. In his introductory monologue he avows his intention of preventing Wit's marriage to Wisdom, and he is ready to work slowly to attain his result:

> Soft fier makes swet malt. (p. 13)

He brings Wit into the arms of Wantonness and finds profit for himself in the act:

> Ah! sirra! it is an old prouerb and a true,
> I sware by the roode!
> It is an il wind that bloues no man to good. (p. 23)

There is proverbial precedent for him to pick the sleeping Wit's pocket:

> The cook is not so sone gone
> As the doges hed is in the porigpot. (pp. 23 f.)

He favors the audience with two Wellerisms, the first of which expresses his resignation to the unwelcome attentions of Snatch and Catch:

> This is that must neades be,
> Quoth the good man, whenn he made his wyfe
> Pine the baskit. (p. 27)

It seems to me likely, though regrettable, that 'pine' represents a scribal telescoping of two words which give the saying as unsavory a sense as his second *sagwort* certainly has:

> Here is nuse, [quoth] the fox, when he lett a farte in the morninge. (p. 30)

Nothing seems likely to save him from the thieves, and so:

> Patiencs [Patience], perforce. (p. 27)

Having lost his money he is more philosophical than most rogues thus paid in their own wares:

> Euell gotten worse spent. (p. 28)

As Tilley points out (p. 90), Wit runs two proverbs together in speaking to Idleness:

> Thou art a mery fellowe and wise,
> And if thou kepe thy selfe warme. (p. 16)

When in prison he repents, too late, his folly:

> But I, alas! when steede is stolin,
> Doo shut the stable dore. (p. 55)

Good Nurture stresses the cares of those who have charge of the young:

> One greefe fales on anothers neck,
> And youth will haue his rueth. (p. 54)

Catch, once he has his eye on the purse of Idleness, declares of him:

> This is a craftee fox, but, by a herring toke. (p. 27)

The exact meaning is not clear (see Tilley, p. 51), but perhaps we may see here a garbled reference to the familiar incident in the *Roman de Renart* where Reynard gets his fill of fish by feigning himself to be dead by the roadside. When Isengrim, like the dupe he always is, blatantly repeats the trick he is severely mauled and all but killed. In the saying, perhaps, the rôles of fox and wolf have been reversed. This explanation is certainly far-fetched, but not, to complete the proverb, dear bought. Fancy says, with reference to herself:

> The rowling stone we se
> Doth neuer gather mosse. (p. 46)

The only character to use more than a single sententious remark is Wit, who escapes from one entanglement only to expose himself to fresh dangers:

> Like as the silly mariner,
> Amidst the wauing sea,
> Doth clime the top of mightie mast,
> Full oft both night and day;
> But yet at last, when happily
> He come from ship to shore,
> He seakes to saile againe as fresh
> As erst he did before;
> So likwise I, which haue escapte
> The brunts which I haue done,
> Am euen as fresh to venter now,
> As when I first begane.
> (pp. 46 f. [see Tilley, p. 91])

Once more he falls into the toils and bewails his failure to be guided by experience:

> The silly bird once caught in net,
> If she ascape aliue,

Will come no more so ny the snare,
Her fredome to depriue;
But rather she will leaue her haunt,
The which she vsed before. (p. 55)

The Prologue had foretold Wit's defeat by Fancy:

Then Fancy frames effects,
To bring his braine aborde,
And shelue his ship in hauens mouth,
Yere it the seas haue scoured.
(p. 6 [see Tilley, pp. 92 f.])

Snatch and Catch enter singing a song which begins:

I [It] hath bin told, ben told in, prouerbs old,
That souldiares suffer both hunger and cold,
That souldiares suffer both hunger and cold. (p. 25)

Catch, watching the furtive, harried glances of Idleness, discovers where the purse is hidden:

Vbi animus ibi oculus, where he loues there he lookes.
(p. 27)

Fancy is aware of her own defects, and declares, applying it to herself, that

Gold, with other metels mixt,
Must neades be full of drose. (p. 46)

Good Nurture laments Wit's second fall from grace:

Whereby I learne with paine
There is no greefe so fare gone past,
But may returne againe. (p. 55)

Idleness describes herself accurately enough:

Idlenis, the say, is the mother of Wise (Vice). (p. 58)

Severity welcomes Wit, at last retrieved, we hope, once and for all, with a heavy piece of meteorological and maritime moralizing:

The cloudes were nere so black,
But the brightnis of the sone
At last might put them back.

> The wind did neuer blowe so much,
> Where with the barke was tore,
> But that the wether was so calme
> To bring the ship to shore. (p. 59)

Wisdom emphasizes her love for Wit with a passing and incomplete comment on the undying affection of the turtle-dove:

> For why, allthough the turtle long
> Ware parted from her mate. (p. 61)

47

George Wapull's, *THE TIDE TARRIETH NO MAN* (1576)

[Tudor Facsimile Texts, 1910]
1854 lines: 38; 5; 7; 16

The large number of occurrences of proverbs in George Wapull's *The Tide Tarrieth No Man* is partly explained by the fact that Wapull, like Fulwell rather than Wager, worked his title-proverb well-nigh to death. It occurs twenty times (sigs. A ii, A ii[v], A iii, A iii[v], B iii, B iiii, C i, C ii[v], C iiii, D i, D i[v], D ii[v], E i[v], E ii[v], E iiii, G i, G ii[v]), in addition to a variant:

> For Tyde hath no byding,
> But ebbing and flowing,
> Comming and going,
> It neuer doth rest. (sig. A iii[v])

The allied proverb, 'Take time while time is,' with slight changes in one or two cases, is also frequent, turning up ten times (sigs. A iii[v], B ii[v], B iii, C i[v], C iiii, E iii, E iiii[v], F i, G ii[v]).

It is characteristic that Courage, the Vice, is responsible for the title proverb on eleven occasions, and for the other on six.

The Prologue explains the use and interpretation of the title-proverb:

> Which prouerbe right well might be applyed,
> To a better sence then it is vsed:
> There is time to aske grace, this may not be denyed,
> Of thy sinfull life so greatly abused.
> Let not that time then be refused,
> For that tyde most certayne will tarry no man,
> Thus taking the prouerbe, we rightly do scan.
> (sig. A ii[v])

Of the eight remaining proverbs, Courage uses three. He declares that there is no need of haste:

> A little while breaketh no square. (sig. B i)

A little later, however, he is urging the Courtier to waste no time in trying to borrow money:

> Now is the time of hap good or ill:
> Venture it therefore while it is hote. (sig. C ii[v])

Soon he becomes an even more urgent advocate of speed as he pushes Wanton toward her long-desired marriage:

> In delaying comes harmes. (sig. D ii[v])

This same sentiment is expressed in a song in which Courage takes part with Wanton, Wasteful, and Hurtful Help:

> But hurte comes in delayings. (sig. F i)

Both Good Neighborhood and Greediness state in part the proverb about 'a friend in need':

> That you will stand my friend if I neede. (sig. B iv)

> Why I lende my money like a friend for good will,
> And thereby doe helpe men at their neede.
> (sig. F iv[v])

The Courtier, who is by way of being a Latinist, combines a proverb with a sententious remark as he complains that his pretended friends have robbed him little by little:

> *Ninubula pluuia imbrem parit,*
> A miȝeling shower ingendreth great wet,
> Which saying *officium prouerbia non tarit,*
> Many a little maketh a great. (sig. E i)

After Wanton is safely married to Wasteful she sees no reason for saving money:

> Spend, and God will send, else the prouerbe lyes.
> (sig. E iiii)

Courage favors his friends with four sententious remarks. In his opening Skeltonics he points out that incongruities are often found together in nature:

> For as in the Bee,
> For certayne we see,
> Sweete honey and sting. (sig. A iii)

He falls in readily with Wanton's desire for a husband, and adds a reason to her own:

> But youthfull bewty will not alwayes last.
> (sig. D ii[v])

Like most Vices, he takes no pains to be polite to his assistants, and thus he tells Painted Profit and Feigned Furtherance:

> Needes knaues you must go, for so you came hether.
> (sig. D iv[v])

When Correction leads him off to execution he tries to be philosophical:

> Sithens there is no remedy, best is a short payne.
> (sig. G iv)

The Prologue, following Saint Augustine, compares avaricious people to hell:

> Neyther of them know when they are well.
> (sig. A ii)

Greediness expresses a characteristic fear of poverty:

> For once rich, and after in decay,
> Is a miserable thing, as Hyemes hath declared.
> (sig. B iii)

He is also aware of the folly of lamenting over an accomplished fact:

> Least of that misery I know the smart,
> Then is it to late any mone to make. (sig. B iii)

Without too much consistency, though no doubt the situation seems very different to him, he quotes with scorn what the Preacher says:

> Looke about in time quoth hee, or it be to late.
> (sig. F iii[v])

Painted Profit fears that accusations, especially when directed against himself, may get Feigned Furtherance into trouble:

> For appeaching oft, the appeacher disturbes.
> (sig. A iv)

He also exhibits evidence of early education:

> *Ne quisque sapit, qui sibi non sapit,*
> This saying I redde, when as I went to schoole,
> One not wise for himselfe, is but a very foole.
> (sig. B i)

Feigned Furtherance agrees:

> For who helpes not himselfe, before any other,
> I coumpt him a foole, if he were my brother.
> (sig. B i)

Hurtful Help agrees to accept the authority of Courage, but his reason is not notably deferential:

> Sometimes it is good a fooles minde to content.
> (sig. B i)

The Courtier has found to his sorrow and loss that the most warmly effusive friends are not always to be trusted:

> As with the poyson, which is moste delectable,
> The heart of man, is soonest infected:
> So the foe moste hurteth, who seemeth most amiable,
> And of all wise men, is to be detected.
> At this time this saying I haue elected,
> For that they which friendship, to me professed,
> In steade thereof, my hurte haue addressed. (sig. E i)

Wasteful, when his money runs out, shows himself unexpectedly ready to work for more, and he finds that he has to remind his wife Wanton that:

> As for pleasure there is a time,
> So for profite there is the like. (sig. E iii[v])

He is finally rescued from Despair, who is urging him to suicide, and his savior Faithful Few draws the inevitable moral from Wasteful's misspent youth:

> And although the beginning haue a pleasaunt sente,
> Yet of the ending, the taste is as ill. (sig. G ii[v])

48

Thomas Lupton's *ALL FOR MONEY* (1578)

[Tudor Facsimile Texts, 1910]
1574 lines: 4; 7; 8; 8

In Thomas Lupton's dull play, *All for Money*, the Vice, Sin, uses three of the four proverbs and three of the eight sententious remarks. A feature of the play is the very considerable number of Latin tags and quotations, some sententious, but most merely inept.

Nichol Never-out-of-the-Law hopes to cheat a neighbor out of a piece of land with the admirable intent of leaving it to his children. Sin sums the situation up by means of two proverbs, the first somewhat altered:

> It is a good winde that blowes no man to euill,
> But happie are those children whose father goes to the deuill.
> (sig. D iii)

Mother Croot, who has more than one colt's tooth in her old head, thinks that a young husband will rejuvenate her. Sin is willing to admit the need of heroic measures:

> When I was a boye it was an olde saying,
> That an olde sacke would lacke much clouting and patching.
> (sig. E i)

The other proverb serves to introduce Neither Money nor Learning who is disposed to be humble:

> By the olde prouerbe euerie man may not weare a fourde hood.
> (sig. C ii[v])

The very title of the play is a sententious remark, as the Prologue suggests when he says:

> Our Authour a pleasant Tragedie with paynes hath now made,
> Whereby you may peceyue, All thing is for money:
> For *Omnia pecunia effici possunt*, as in *Tullies* sentence is said.
> (sig. A ii[v])

Science, Theology, and Art wag their heads dolorously over the state of the world and the greed for gold. Science says:

> *Diues vix bonus*, a preatie saying and true,
> The riche man is scante good, this is the meaning.
> (sig. A iii[v])

No one can accuse Lupton of a lack of ingenuity. When Money enters 'there must be a chayre for him to sit in, and vnder it or neere the same there must be some hollowe place for one to come vp in' (sig. A iv).

Shortly thereafter Money feels ill at ease and is told that Pleasure is the occasion. 'Here money shal make as though he would vomit, and with some fine conueyance pleasure shal appeare from beneath' (sig. B i). This is too good a bit of stage business to drop, and Pleasure gives similar birth to Sin, the Vice, and Sin to Damnation. Damnation 'shal haue a terrible vysard' and Sin is somewhat moved by his offspring. He remarks:

They say Sinne is heauie, but he is heauier I sweare,
(sig. B ii)

and he adds two more sayings descriptive of his mixed emotions:

It must needes be good ground that brings forth such good corne.
(sig. B ii)

Yet the crowe thinkes her blacke birdes of all other the fairest.
(sig. B ii)

Money without Learning is the typical covetous man:

The more money I haue
The more I desire. (sig. C ii[v])

All for Money promises to aid Nichol Never-out-of-the-Law and sends him away speedily:

Go about thy busines, drie wood soone catcheth fire.
(sig. D iii[v])

Mother Croot, with some of the Wife of Bath's instincts but none of her charm, is more humble than Dame Alice would have been:

You may see Sir, olde women haue much clitter clatter.
(sig. D iv[v])

49

Nathaniel Woodes's *THE CONFLICT OF CONSCIENCE* (before 1581)

[Tudor Facsimile Texts, 1911]
2115 lines: 7; 4; 19; 18

For the sake of the citizens of Norwich one may hope that Nathaniel Woodes's sermons were not as tedious as his long and wearisome *Conflict of Conscience*,[10] which was printed in 1581 but probably written somewhat earlier. The proverbs are limited to the naughty characters, and the good characters use but four of the eighteen sententious remarks.

Hypocrisy, the Vice, has three proverbs. He is very angry, or pretends to be so, with Tyranny and Avarice for not having observed him when they first came on the scene:

> You could not see the wood for the trees.
> (sig. C ii[v])

He has occasion to mention Tyranny, and when he sees him coming at that very moment, he remarks:

> Sooner named, sooner cumme, as common Prouerbes say.
> (sig. D ii)

He tries to persuade Philologus, when the latter is before the Cardinal on a charge of heresy, to recant. The Cardinal, he intimates, is not likely to remain long as gracious as he now appears:

> It is euill waking of a Dog that doth sleepe.
> (sig. F iv[v])

Sensual Suggestion, whose sole part in the play is to make Philologus renounce his faith in favor of worldly riches and safety, employs three proverbs. In his insinuating address to Philologus he plays on the well strung harp of his vanity:

> A wise man sometime, of a fool may take counsell.
> (sig. F iii)

Things, he admits, seem bad either way:

> Howbeit of two euils, the least must be chused.
> (sig. F iii[v])

When Philologus argues that afflictions of this world are transitory and heavenly glory everlasting, Suggestion admits that he is right:

> But yet as they say,
> One Birde in the hande, is worth two in the bush.
> (sig. F iv)

The remaining proverb is Avarice's. We are scarcely startled to learn that he believes that

> Indeede you say trueth, the ende is worth all.
> (sig. C iv)

Hypocrisy lards his discourse with six sententious remarks. In his opening soliloquy he declares that tyrants demand praise and fair words:

> Tirannie with flatterie is easely pacifyed,
> Wheras Tom tell troth shall feele of his Sword.
> (sig. B iii[v])

With the same breath he quotes

> That olde said saw, and common by word:
> *Obsequium amicos*, by flateries friends are prepared:
> But *veritas ôdium parit*, as commonly is seene,
> For speaking the trueth, many hated haue beene.
> (sig. B iii[v])

Avarice meets with his castigation though not, perhaps, with his disapproval:

> Well may the Couctous be lykened to a drone,
> Which of the Bees labours, will spoile and wast make,
> And yet to get hony, no labour will take. (sig. C ii)

Tyranny and Hypocrisy come near to blows. The latter feels that he has been altogether too friendly and familiar:

> *Nimia familiaritas parit contemptum,*
> The olde prouerbe by mee is verefied,
> By too much famyliaritie contemned be some.
> (sig. C iii)

Once Philologus has determined to take the easy path to orthodoxy, Hypocrisy commends his wisdom in shaping his course by his own safety:

> He that will seeke eche man to content.
> Shall prooue him selfe at last most vnwise.
> (sig. G i)

Next to Hypocrisy in number of sententious remarks comes Avarice. He fears that it will be hard to recapture men who have tried his fruits and found them sour:

> The Fish once taken, and scaped from baight,
> Will euer heareafter, beware of the hooke,
> Such as vse hunting will spie the Hare straight,
> Though other discerne her not, yet on her shall looke.
> (sig. B iv[v])

He warns both Tyranny and Philologus against repentance that comes too late:

> Then wilt thou repent it, when it is to late.
> (sig. C ii)
> Then will you repent, it when it is to late.
> (sig. F i[v])

Early in the play Satan had begun to fear lest the powers of reformation completely destroy his earthly kingdom and he resolves to act without delay, else

> I shall repent it, when it is to late. (sig. A iii)

Avarice thinks that if Hypocrisy and Tyranny quarrel he himself may gain:

Two Dogges oftentimes one bone would faine catch,
But yet the thirde doo both them deceiue.
(sig. C iii[r-v])

Philologus, as wordy as his name implies, is heavily moralistic in his opening words with Mathetes:

Moreouer, we do vse to loath that thing we alway haue,
And doo delight the more in that which mostly we doe want.
(sig. B i[v])

For trouble bring forth pacience, from pacience dooth insue
Experience, from experience Hope, of health the ankor true.
(sig. B ii)

At the end of the play he is horror-struck at the infidelity which he had shown in recanting, believes that God can have no pardon for him, and dismisses his comforters as unqualified:

The healthfull neede not Phisicks art, and ye which are all haile,
Can giue good counsell to the sick, their sicknesse to eschew.
(sig. I i)

The Prologue has no use for idleness:

Idelnes more euills doth bring, into the minde of man,
Then labour great in longer tyme, againe expell out can.
(sig. A ii)

Tyranny's command of Latin sayings is not far behind Hypocrisy's:

Inter amicos omnia sunt communia they say,
Among friendes there is reconed no propertie.
(sig. C iv)

Conscience accuses Philologus of changing his faith in order to retain mundane prosperity, the very point

Which caused Christ himselfe to say, that with much lesser payne,
Should Camel passe through needles ey, then rich men Heauen obtayn.
(sig. G iii[v])

Suggestion, striving desperately to hold Philologus in error, declares that since Conscience is unable to enjoy worldly delights he opposes them for others,

As did the Foxe, which caught in snare, and scapt with losse of tayle,
To cut off theirs, as burthenous, did all the rest counsayll.
(sig. G iii[v])

50

THE THREE LADIES OF LONDON (1584) by R.W.

[Tudor Facsimile Texts, 1911]
1655 lines: 6; 10; 19; 9

Although there is no real evidence that *The Three Ladies of London* is by Robert Wilson, the R.W. on the play's title-page has long been taken to represent his name. As a morality this play has nothing to recommend it, and it contains little proverbial material.

Simplicity, not quite the fool he appears, tells Dissimulation that he believes Usury is full of 'beceite' even though

There is no beceite in a bagge pudding, is there? nor in a plaine pudding thy. (sig. D i)

'Beceite' for 'deceite' is an example of Simplicity's consistent verbal distortions and malapropisms which are occasionally mildly amusing. Conscience reminds the arrogant Lucre, who is bragging over her victory, that

Pride will haue a fall. (sig. D ii[v])

Dissimulation, true to his nature, tries to conceal his intrigues and proposes even to improve on the proverb which enjoins silence:

It is an olde prouerbe, tis good hauing a hach before the dore, but ile haue a doore before the hatch. (sig. E ii[v])

Lucre is unrepentant to the end and speaks saucily to the Judge:

In deniall stands triall. (sig. F ii[v])

Conscience employs two proverbs. When Lucre has her in the toils and sends Usury to collect an exorbitant rent, Conscience is resigned:

> We must haue pacience perforce seeing there is no remedy.
> (sig. C iii)

She is reduced to the scant life of a broom-seller, but since it is God's will she strives to take her lot well:

> Thus am I driuen to make a vertue of necessitie.
> (sig. D iv[v])

Conscience uses two of the nine sententious remarks. She tells Simplicity that together they must do their best, but she is not over confident:

> We will do what we can: But *vltra posse non est esse*, you know.
> (sig. B iv[v])

She refuses to bandy words with Lucre:

> Well well Lucar, *Audeo, et taceo,* I see and say nothing.
> (sig. D ii)

Simplicity, as we have observed before, exhibits on occasion a reasonable amount of penetration. Thus he is not deceived by Dissimulation and Fraud who are

> A couple of false knaues togither, a Theefe and a Broker.
> (sig. A iii[v])

When he falls into the hands of Constable Diligence he argues that his association with Fraud, Tom Beggar, and Wily Will was fortuitous and innocent:

> Why maister Constable if a sheepe goe among Wolues all day:
> Shall the sheepe be blamde if they steale any thing away.
> (sig. F ii)

Lucre is not impressed with the bookishness of Conscience. Display of knowledge doesn't mean everything:

> I haue seene so cunning a Clarke in time to proue a foole.
> (sig. D ii[v])

She also reminds Conscience that much of her misfortune is due to her own sharp tongue:

> If thou hadst kept thy tongue, thou hadst kept thy friend.
> (sig. E i)

The wretched Italian merchant Mercadore will do anything for prosperity's sake:

> For he dat will liue in the world, must be of the world sure.
> (sig. B ii[v])

Dissimulation preaches from much the same text:

> He that cannot lie, cog, dissemble, and flatter now a daies,
> Is not worthie to liue in the world, not in the Court to haue praise.
> (sig. B iii)

Love finds that she has yielded unwisely to the bland beguilings of Dissimulation and says sorrowfully:

> But now I mone too late. (sig. F i[v])

51

THE THREE LORDS AND THREE LADIES OF LONDON by R. W. (1590)

[Tudor Facsimile Texts, 1912]

2244 lines (poetry and prose): 12; 5; 7; 12

If Robert Wilson wrote *The Three Ladies of London* he almost certainly wrote *The Three Lords and Three Ladies of London* as well. This is a longer and, in part at least, a more tiresome play, despite the fact that it contains many more proverbs, though fewer proverbial phrases, than its predecessor.

Simplicity uses four proverbs. When he lays a wager of six ballads to 'six ierkes at your buttockes' that he can sing better than Wit, he answers his opponent's question about the keeper of the stakes, by saying:

Neither of your companions, for that's aske my fellow if I be a theefe.
(sig. C i)

Simony is playful when he meets with Dissimulation and Usury, remarking, and this is his only proverb, that they meet because they are not mountains:

And men may meete though mountaines cannot.
(sig. C iv[v])

Simplicity has no trouble in capping this proverb:

I see many of these old prouerbes prooue true, tis merrie when knaues meet. (sig. C iv[v])

He classes Fraud with a fox:

I see, a fox and a false knaue haue all one luck, the better for banning.
(sig. D i)

Dissimulation and his companion flee the approach of Nemo, the only person in the play who is capable of consistent good action, and are followed by Simplicity's comment:

Birdes of a fether wil flie together, but when they be taken
Then are they baken. (sig. E i)

The only other character to use more than one proverb is Policy. He, with more than one meaning, suggests that marriage between the Lords and Ladies will be advisable:

Mariage doth make amends for many a misse.
(sig. C iv)

The leader of the Castilian lords is Pride, followed by his page Shame, and the proverbial significance of these two is explained by Policy:

Shame followes *pride*, as we a prouerbe haue,
Pride goes before, and *shame* comes after.
(sig. G iv[v])

Dissimulation tries to worm his way back into Love's good graces. When she dismisses him with a proverb he finds a ready answer to it:

> *Loue.* Who once are burn'd, the fire will euer shun.
> *Dis.* And yet once burn'd to warme againe may prooue.
> (sig. D iv)

Pomp, one of the three lords, has no regard for Fortune, and, indeed, is so bold as to declare roundly:

> Fortune's a foole. (sig. E ii)

Simony, Dissimulation, and Fraud fear the coming of the Spaniards and plan flight, but not Usury, who knows where his home and friends are:

> Therfore here will I stay sure, to keepe what I haue, rather than be a traitor vpon hap and had I wist. (sig. F iv)

Shealty, the herald of the Spaniards, whose name Policy defines as 'an Irish word, signifieng liberty, rather remisnes, / Loosnes if ye wil' (sig. G iv), taunts the English in words which remind us of a common proverb:

> You crauen English on your donghills crowe.
> (sig. G iv[v])

Conscience speeds the Lords against the Spanish invaders:

> Daunger's in delay. (sig. F ii)

As in the proverbs, Simplicity leads in the use of sententious remarks. He is not ashamed to try to learn from the pages Wit, Will, and Wealth:

> Children can teach old folks. (sig. B iv[v])

He would be willing to have Wealth serve him, and finds potent arguments in favor of such an arrangement:

> Hadst not thou better serue a free man of the Citie, and learne a trade to liue another day, than to be a seruing boy in thy youth and to haue no occupation in thine age. (sig. C ii)

Simplicity, still with a touch of malapropism, is a great admirer of Time:

Ye may see Time dooth much, Time weares out yron horshooes: Time teares out milstones: Time seasons a pudding well, and Time hath made me a free man, as free to beare water and sell Ballades, as the best of our copulation. (sig. C iii)

He is well pleased with himself after he has bought the counterfeit gold from Fraud:

Wel, a man may see, he that's ordained to be rich, shal be rich. (sig. E iv)

In his anxiety to marry off the three Ladies, Nemo keeps them from the public eye:

As cunning chapmen do by curious wares,
Which seldome showen do most inflame the mind. (sig. E i[v])

He doesn't have too high an opinion of the sex:

Women weake are tempted soone with giftes. (sig. E ii[v])

Love and Lucre exchange doleful remarks on a world that once seemed better to them than it does now:

Love. Life but a breath, and follie but a flower . . .
Love. Sorrow remaines when ioy is but a blast
Lucre. A blast of wind is worldes felicitie. (sig. D ii)

Will explains to Wit the significance of *Pour temps* on Pleasure's shield:

The best pleasure of al lasts but a time. (sig. B iii)

The page boys make fun of Simplicity, telling him not to gape so at the shields, lest he swallow a fly. He asks if a fly can do hurt, and Wit answers:

Yea, haue ye not heard that the fly hath her spleene
And the Ant her gall? (sig. B iii[v])

Policy marvels at the ostentation of the Spaniards and wonders if their arrival will be followed by some great events, or

> Doo all these mountaines moue to breede a mouse?
> (sig. G i[v])

Desire makes a remark which might well have been taken as a motto for all the moralities:

> It is good to follow examples of good. (sig. I i[v])

52

LINGUA (1607)

[Tudor Facsimile Texts, 1913]
3133 lines (poetry and prose): 9; 8; 12; 15

The long Cambridge play, *Lingua*, ascribed to Thomas Tomkis, differs somewhat from the norm but is none the less an example of the late and degenerate morality. As is perhaps fitting to a university play, the proverbs and sententious remarks outnumber the proverbial phrases. There is but small favoritism shown in the distribution of the proverbial material. The heroine, Lingua, whose efforts to be elevated to the rank of a sense give its theme to the play, employs one proverb:

> He that will catch Eeles must disturbe the floud.
> (sig. A iv[v])

To stir up strife between the five senses, she leaves a crown and robe with an inscription dedicating it to the best of the five. Tactus finds it first and, after concealing it from Olfactus, sees one exit closed to him by the approach of Visus; turning in the other direction, he remarks:

> Theres more wayes to the wood then one.
> (sig. B iv[v])

There, however, he perceives Gustus, and decides to brazen it out:

> Well 'tis best to venture. (sig. C i)

A method springs to his mind:

> A sodaine lye hath best luck. (sig. C i)

Phantastes, who can produce a sonnet or a love-song at a moment's notice, also works three proverbs into his remarks. His page Heuresis asks him for the love letter ordered by Master Inamerato, and receives a beginning, with the sage comment that the end is easy enough:

> He that once begun well, hath halfe done, let him begin againe and there's all. (sig. D ii[v])

He turns a statement by Communis Sensus, the arbiter between the senses, into a proverb:

> *Communis Sensus.* *Memory* the season of your comming is very ripe.
> *Phantastes.* Had you staid a little longer 'twould have bin starke rotten. (sig. D iii[v])

His remaining proverb is more true than delicate:

> For none can weare Ciuet, but they are suspected of a proper badde sent, where the prouerbe springs, hee smelleth best, that doth of nothing smell. (sig. H iv)

Communis Sensus has little respect for Phantastes and greets one of the latter's ornate outbursts rudely:

> As the foole thinketh, so the bell clinketh. (sig. G iii[v])

Appetitus's single proverb fits his character neatly:

> I must finde you meate and the Diuell finde you cookes. (sig. K iv[v])

If there is a Vice in the play it is Mendacio. In his conventional boasting self-appraisal he uses a proverb:

> As for old-men they challenge my Company by authority. (sig. D i)

His sententious remarks are four in number, one of which occurs in the same passage:

Your Trauellers so dote vpon me as passes; O they haue good reason, for I haue carried them to many a good meale, vnder the Countenance of my familiarity. (sigs. C iv[v]–D)

He declares with unexpected truth that Remembrance is his only friend and finds a Latin saying to prove it:

Thou hast heard *Oportet mendacem esse memorem.* (sig. E iv)

A little later he seems, but only seems, to deny this:

This axiome, *A quick Inuention and a good Memory can neuer agree.* (sig. F i)

He urges Appetitus to

Catch occasion by the foretop. (sig. K ii)

Tactus is given as many sententious remarks as the Vice. He stumbles over the crown and robe at first and hits upon a most appropriate saying:

High thoughts haue slippry feete. (sig. B ii[v])

Once he thinks that he has the dignity for himself he feels it working through his veins:

They lie that say Complections cannot change. (sig. B iii)

He is in favor of moderation and control:

How rash is man on bidden (? hidden) armes to rush. (sig. C i[v])

In a brawl with the other senses he hopes to win in the end:

Ile make you late repent it. (sig. C iii)

Communis Sensus has a real appreciation of the value of time:

We cannot pluck the least fether from the soft wing of time. (sig. F ii)

He also is spared doubt as to the primary rôle of the eternal woman:

The last and feminine sense, the sense of speaking.
(sig. I iv)

At this point we may well note that Phantastes has an unkind comment for the sex:

Tis strange, that women being so mutable,
Will neuer change in changing their apparell.
(sig. I ii[v])

And even the gentle Somnus is not without his gall:

I haue more trouble to make one woman sleepe, then all the world besides they be so full of tattle. (sig. L iii[v])

To return tc Communis Sensus, we find him reprimanding Lingua for her inflated claims:

Those that seeke what is not theirs, oftentimes loose what's their owne. (sig. M iv[v])

Somnus's remaining sententious remark springs easily from his inner nature:

Better to sleepe then wake, and toile for nothing.
(sig. M i[v])

Finally we hear Visus speaking with more righteousness than assurance:

Right's more aduantage, then an host of soldiars.
(sig. C iii[v])

Part II

French Moralities

An examination of twenty-one French moralities, chosen arbitrarily because of their inclusion in the two principal collections of early French non-Biblical plays,[11] was productive of little save disappointment. French moralities are decidedly inferior to the English in readability because of the fact that while there are vicious characters in the French plays, the Vice himself can not be recognized [12] and the comic scenes which center about that hero are usually missing. Such humor as the French moralities contain is unusually flat, and we find a much sharper contrast between French morality and farce than we do between English morality and the interlude. With the absence of the Vice and the scarcity of humor goes a notable absence of proverbial material. Many of the French moralities are short, and these contain none or at most three or four proverbial passages. Among the longer ones [13] we may note *Charité* (Viollet Le Duc, III, 337 ff.), which runs to two thousand four hundred ninety lines, and contains five proverbs, of which Le Monde employs two, and four sententious remarks, of which Charité uses two. There are eleven comparisons, of which Charité uses four and Le Monde and L'Avaricieulx two each, and thirteen other proverbial phrases, of which Tricherie, L'Avaricieulx and La Mort use three each. There is nothing here which resembles the concentration of proverbial material which we have found in many of the English moralities.

Another play, *Enfans de Maintenant* (Viollet Le Duc, III, 1 ff.), of much the same length (two thousand eighty-six lines) contains three proverbs, used respectively by Instruction, Discipline, and Honte, and nine sententious remarks, four of which are enunciated by Instruction and three by Bon Advis. Six of these are in Latin and four ascribed to Cato of the Distichs, for whom the author had a great affection:

> Estudie ung petit livret
> Que fist autrefois Cathonnet,
> Qui est tout plain de bonnes meurs,
> Et n'est pas long et si est seurs. (III, 51, 74)

Of the ten comparisons, Le Fol and Discipline use two each; Finet and Luxure use three each and Maintenant two of the eleven other proverbial phrases. Here we may note a slight tendency to let the less respectable characters employ the proverbial phrases, but nothing at all striking.

If the plays which we have examined are at all typical, and nothing in Petit de Julleville's account of the others suggests the contrary, we must conclude that no comparison between English and French moralities about their use of proverbs is valid and that the English playwrights could not have gained even a hint for their consistent and even rather prominent use of proverbial material from across the Channel.

CHAPTER III

THE INTERLUDES

Part I

English Interludes

The small group of short comic plays, usually called interludes, are not especially distinguished by their use of proverbs. Even John Heywood, the preeminent practitioner of the art, and one whose interest in proverbs is well known, has but little to offer. Except for No Lover Nor Loved, the Vice of *A Play of Love*, and the impatient, suffering hero of *Johan Johan*, none of his characters are marked by their love of proverbs. Among the other plays we find the Plowman in *Of Gentleness and Nobility* and Celestina in *The Beauty and Good Properties of Women* using more sayings than any of the other characters. In *Jack Juggler* we have a titular hero who is a Vice, but despite that fact it is his dupe Jenkin Careaway who employs the bulk of the proverbs. *Tom Tyler and his Wife* alone of all the interludes is rich in proverbs, and it, indeed, contains more than many a longer morality, but no one of the characters uses a disproportionate number. The very plot of the play is based on an anti-feministic proverb and the number of sayings woven into the lively songs with which the play is filled are of especial interest.

One thing is certain: whatever the leading features of an interlude may be, a lavish use of proverbs is not among them.

The earliest trace of an interlude in English is, beyond doubt, the *Interludium de clerico et puella* [1] which has a very close connection with the *fabliau*, *Dame Siriȝ*, but this fragment of eighty-five lines contains nothing more proverbial than the comparison 'Yu hates me mar yan yayt dos chnief (l. 21).'

53

THE MANNER OF THE CRYING OF A PLAY (*c.* 1503)

[In W. M. Mackenzie, *The Poems of William Dunbar*, Edinburgh, 1932, pp. 170–174]
173 lines: 0; 2; 1; 0

Next to consider is the curious little monologue, variously entitled *The Manere of the Crying of ane Play* (Asloan MS) and *Ane littill Interlud of the Droichis Pairt of th*[*e Play*] (Bannatyne MS), which has been ascribed to William Dunbar, and the closest literary affinities of which seem to be with the French *monologues* and *sermons joyeux.*[2] Its proverbial content is of no interest.

54

John Heywood's *WITTY AND WITLESS*

[Ed. F. W. Fairholt, Percy Society, XX, 1846]
703 lines: 2; 0; 2; 1

The name of John Heywood is almost synonymous with 'interlude' so far as English literature is concerned. It is not my purpose at this time to enter into problems of authorship or dating, but to consider, in what is probably a reasonably chronological order, the six plays which he wrote or which are commonly attributed to him.[3] John Heywood, we may observe, was vastly interested in proverbs — he wove a considerable collection of them into a discussion of marriage; he worked them into several hundred epigrams; and he used them liberally in his long allegorical poem, *The Spider and the Fly*. It is not surprising, then, that the proverb hunter turns to Heywood's plays with pleasant anticipation of a rich quarry.

What may well be the earliest and what is certainly the least dramatic of Heywood's plays has come down to us only in manuscript and titleless. The title *Witty and Witless* is employed here out of deference to recent usage, though one may conjecture that the author called it *The Play of Wit*. This debate, for it is no more, contains little proverbial material, although it is by means of a proverb that Jerome draws John back from his surrender to folly. John had said that he felt it better to go to heaven a fool than to run the risk of going to hell a wise man:

> An old proverb makythe with thys, whyche I tak good,
> Better one byrd in hand then ten in the wood! (p. 24)

Jerome seized the saying and fitted it to his purpose, finally asking with triumph:

> Ten byrds in the wood, or one in hand alone,
> Whych chose ye now? (p. 26)

James, the apostle of folly, had earlier directed a sententious remark at John:

> But that wytt whych bostythe the full of his wynnyng,
> As thowghff he knewe th'end of thing at begynnyng,
> That wytt schall schow wyttless ympedyment. (pp. 7 f.)

55

John Heywood's *A PLAY OF LOVE*

[Tudor Facsimile Texts, 1909]
1577 lines: 6; 7; 15; 10

A Play of Love contains a Vice, No Lover Nor Loved, who talks in the Vice's traditionally proverbial vein, this despite the fact that he employs but two of the six proverbs and three of the seven comparisons. When we come to the fifteen other proverbial phrases we find him using eleven in his own right and quoting one. The sententious remarks, and this is by no means usual, are even more concentrated, as he speaks them all, four in his own right and six in reported conversation, mainly that of his erstwhile mistress.

Lover Loved returns successful from his search for someone to judge between himself and No Lover Nor Loved:

> The olde seyng seyth he that seketh shall fynde.
> (sig. C ii)

He counsels his opponent against too much confidence:

> Who shall wynne the ende, the ende at ende shall try.
> (sig. D ii[v])

When accused of going without food or sleep because of love he is at no loss for a reply:

> I dysdayne
> Fode and slepe, this prouerbe answereth you playne
> Loke not on the meat, but loke on the man. (sig. D iv)

No Lover Nor Loved is not over chivalrous. He finds it hard to agree with Lover Not Loved, who bemoans his fate as a rejected suitor:

Your payne is most if she say nay and take it
But if that she say nay and forsake it
Then is her payne a great way the greater.
(sig. C iii[v])

He rebukes Loved Not Loving when she presses her opponent for an answer:

Tary ye be to gredy
Men be not lyke women alway redy. (sig. D ii)

Lover Not Loved evidently had a proverb in mind when he included the following in a list of Love's servants:

Hast, wast, lust without lykyng or lyberte.
(sig. D i[v])

Five of the sententious remarks are repetitions of the same saying, couched, by the way, in dog Latin of high quality. No Lover Not Loved describes an early affair in which, thinking all the time to deceive the lady with false protestations, he finds himself served with the same sauce. He quotes the lady generously and, indeed, all but the second of the five occurrences of the saying are originally from her remarks:

For who so that mocketh shall surely stur
This olde prouerbe mockum moccabitur. (sig. B iv[v])

Wherby I thought her owne tale lyke a bur
Stack to her owne back mockum moccabitur. (sig. C i)

Wherwith I brought in moccum moccabitur. (sig. C i[v])

All my meanyng was
To gyue mock for mock. (sig. C i[v])

Defende the from mockes in tyme to come
By clappyng fast to thy snowt euery day
Moccum moccabitur for a nosegay. (sig. C i[v])

He is forced to quote her again at his own expense:

Lyke as a foole myght haue iettyd in a net
Beleuyng hymselfe saue of hym selfe onely
To be perceyued of no lyuyng body. (sig. C i[v])

Quotation is a favorite device with him. He tells his mistress that Dread had warned him against believing in the stability of her love:

> That if I wan your loue all in one howre
> I sholde lose it all agayne in thre or fowre.
> (sig. B iv[v])

He professes to be more than willing for reconciliation:

> Swete harte quoth I after stormy colde smertes
> Warm wordes in warm louers bryng louers warm hartes.
> (sig. B iv[v])

He applies a variant of Chaucer's favorite 'Pitee renneth soone in gentil herte' to Loved Not Loving:

> For I haue a mynde that euery good face
> Hath euer some pyte of a pore mans case.
> (sig. C ii)

He finds love and untruth not widely sundered:

> Louyng and lyeng haue we brought nowe hyther
> Louers and lyers to ley both to gyther. (sig. E i[v])

56

John Heywood's *THE PLAY OF THE WEATHER*

[Tudor Facsimile Texts, 1909]

1254 lines: 1; 5; 9; 8

The Play of the Weather, itself based on the proverbial inability of people to agree on meteorological conditions, contains less proverbial material than *A Play of Love*, and Merry Report, the Vice, fares poorly in the distribution. He is given four of the nine miscellaneous proverbial phrases, three of which hint at a connection between the knight's hunting horn and his wife's honor, and two of the eight sententious remarks.

The single proverb, spoken by the Wind Miller, is the earliest noted appearance of one of our most striking weather sayings:

> And now to mynde there is one olde prouerbe come
> One bushell of march dust is worth a kynges raunsome.
> (sig. C ii)

The Gentlewoman informs Merry Report that she has been brought up to love music, and receives this answer:

> Oft tyme yt is sene both in court and towne
> Longe be women a bryngyng vp & sone brought down.
> (sig. D i)

He listens to the Laundress, but is not impressed:

> Many wordes lyttell mater and to no purpose.
> (sig. D ii)

Merry Report calls the Water Miller a knave and is given the retort courteous:

> You shulde neuer call
> Your felow knaue nor your brother horeson
> For nought can ye get by it when ye haue done.
> (sig. B iv)

The Water Miller belittles the arguments of his rival, the Wind Miller:

> Thou spekest of all and consyderest not halfe.
> (sig. C ii[v])

The Merchant takes umbrage when Merry Report in a single breath calls him a parson and asks for his wife:

> I se ye speke more of dotage then knowledge.
> (sig. B ii)

The Wind Miller argues stoutly for wind rather than rain:

> And it is sayd syns afore we were borne
> That drought doth neuer make derth of corne.
> (sig. C ii)

In her youth the Laundress was as beautiful as the Gentlewoman and might have led just such a life as the latter does:

> But I feared parels that after myght fall.
> (sig. D i[v])

Jupiter's investigation shows him that men, like the gods, are divided on the question of acceptable weather:

> As longe as heddes from temperaunce be deferd
> So longe the bodyes in dystemperaunce be.
> (sig. D iv[v])

57

John Heywood's *THE PARDONER AND THE FRIAR*

[Tudor Facsimile Texts, 1909]
641 lines: 1; 2; 10; 1

The scanty proverbial material in *The Pardoner and the Friar* is divided evenly enough, with the Pardoner slightly in the lead. He employs the proverb, four of the miscellaneous proverbial phrases, and the sententious remark, while the friar has the two comparisons and two of the remaining six miscellaneous proverbial phrases, the other four going to the Parson.

The Friar threatens to knock the Pardoner on the costard, and the latter replies with a challenging Wellerism:

> Mary that wolde I se quod blynde hew. (sig. B iii)

The Pardoner also directs his sententious remark at his rival:

> I holde it best
> To kepe your tonge while ye be in rest. (sig. B iii)

58

John Heywood's *THE FOUR PP*

[Tudor Facsimile Texts, 1908]

1234 lines: 4; 3; 7; 10

In *The Four PP* the Pardoner uses all three of the comparisons, the Pothecary five of the seven other proverbial phrases, and the Pedlar five of the ten sententious remarks. The four proverbs are divided impartially between the four characters. The Pardoner tells the Palmer that he

> May lye by aucthoryte
> And all that hath wandred so farre
> That no man can be theyr controller.
> (sig. A iii[r-v])

The Pedlar explains why it takes women so long to dress: they have so much to put on that

> The lette is suche
> That spede is small whan haste is muche.
> (sig. B i[v])

Singing, suggests the Palmer, does not depend on good will alone:

> What helpeth wyll where is no skyll? (sig. B ii[v])

In his gibe at the Palmer, the Pothecary seems to be using a saying modeled on the proverb, 'Many kiss the child for the nurse's sake:'

> Suche is the payne that ye palmers take
> To kysse the pardon bowle for the drynke sake.
> (sig. C ii[v])

Even if the Pedlar cannot make any sales to his new comrades, he determines to stay with them for pastime's sake:

> Who may nat play one day in a weke
> May thynke hys thryfte is farre to seke. (sig. B ii)

He likes to drink and finds that it arouses a desire for sleep:

For wynkynge to drynkynge is alway lynkynge.
(sig. B ii)

He flatters the other three and urges them to give up wasteful liberty and form a totalitarian group:

All thynge decayed where is no hedde. (sig. B iv)

After the Palmer has won the contest, the others refuse to abide by the agreement and so he, always obliging, relieves them of the necessity. The Pedlar then delivers a homily on the equal value of different virtues:

One kynde of vertue to dyspyse another
Is lyke as the syster myght hange the brother.
(sig. E iii[v])

The Pothecary, who is as close to a Vice as anyone in the play,[4] counters this with the boast that he uses no virtue at all. The Pedlar replies:

That is of all the very worste waye
For more harde it is as I haue harde saye
To begynne vertue where none is pretendyd
Then where it is begonne the abuse to be mended.
(sig. E iii[v]–E iv)

The Palmer employs three sententious remarks, the first of which is a shrewd blow at the Pardoner:

Ryght selde is it sene or neuer
That treuth and pardoners dwell together.
(sig. A iii)

Despite the Pothecary's argument in favor of speedy death, the Palmer is not completely persuaded:

Yet better tary a thynge then haue it
Then go to sone and vaynly craue it. (sig. A iv)

He has no wish to win mastery over the others:

And sure I thynke that quietnesse
In any man is great rychesse. (sig. C i)

The Pardoner believes that, as is often said of fools, travel is not likely to have improved the Palmer's wit:

> Yet welcome home as wyse as ye wente. (sig. A ii)

He charges him with that weakness of argument which leads to personal abuse of one's opponent:

> For reason on your syde so farre doth fayle
> That ye leue sonyng and begyn to rayle. (sig. A iii)

59

John Heywood's *JOHAN JOHAN THE HUSBAND*

[Tudor Facsimile Texts, 1909]

678 lines: 2; 4; 13; 1

The unhappy husband has well nigh a monopoly of the proverbial material in *Johan Johan the Husband.* Of the twenty items, he uses sixteen, including both the proverbs and the sententious remark. He is loath to go for the priest, but what can a poor married man do?

> There is a prouerbe whiche trewe nowe preueth
> He must nedes go that the dyuell dryueth.
> (sig. A iv[v])

He misapplies his second proverb somewhat. He reminds Sir John that he had once served as his clerk, and never had priest a better, yet Sir John has not hesitated to eat up all the pie. This is all very well, but it has no real relation to the saying by means of which he had sought to introduce it:

> But nowe I se well the olde prouerbe is treu
> The parysshe preest forgetteth that euer he was clarke.
> (sig. B iii[v])

He asks the audience if a man does not have a right to

chastise his wife, and in so doing he makes a remark which seems perhaps more sententious than chivalrous:

> That is a poynt of an honest man
> For to bete his wyfe well nowe and than.
> (sig. A i[v])

We have in this play a very clear case of an individual deliberately characterized by the use of proverbial material, and the scarcity of such material elsewhere in the play makes the situation all the more evident.

The results of our examination of Heywood's plays are far from what we had anticipated. No sixteenth century writer is more closely identified with proverbs than is Heywood and yet in six plays, running to something over six thousand lines, we find only sixteen proverbs, twenty-one comparisons, fifty-six other proverbial phrases and thirty-one sententious remarks. If we glance back at some of the moralities, such as *The Castle of Perseverance* (p. 68 above), *Magnificence* (p. 85 above), *The Three Estates* (p. 94 above), or *Respublica* (p. 110 above), or look ahead at almost any of the comedies, we shall see that Heywood was positively chary of proverbs. Of his two Vice-characters, No Lover Nor Loved and Merry Report, only the former employs the many sayings characteristic of his class. It is true that John the husband is, in his small way, a proverb-monger, and this is original with Heywood, as there are no signs of it in John's French prototype, Pernet.[5] Even this, however, cannot alter our conclusion that either Heywood's interest in proverbs sprang up after his plays were composed or that he did not regard them as fitting decorations for the drama.[5a]

60

OF GENTLENESS AND NOBILITY (*c.* 1530)

[Tudor Facsimile Texts, 1908]
1176 lines: 4; 2; 9; 7

Of Gentleness and Nobility was long thought to be the work of John Heywood, but evidence has lately been produced in favor of its assignment to John Rastell, Heywood's father-in-law.[6]

The Plowman uses the bulk of the proverbial material in the play; three of the four proverbs are his, as are the two comparisons, five of the other proverbial phrases, and two sententious remarks. Next comes the Knight with one proverbial phrase and four sententious remarks, and finally the Merchant, who uses three proverbial phrases and one sententious remark. The Plowman has no intention of wasting his time talking when there is money to be saved:

> And I tell the playnly with out any bost
> A halpeny is as well sauid as lost. (sig. A v[v])

His idea of gentlemen is an old one, going back at least to that early English radical, John Ball:

> For when adam dolf and eue span
> Who was then a gentylman
> But then cam the churl and gederyd good
> And ther began furst the gentyll blood.
> (sig. A vi[v])

He vastly prefers black Maud, his wife, to the painted popinjays of the upper classes:

> Tote man for all sych venereall werk
> As good is the foule as the fayre in the derk.
> (sig. C i[v])

The Knight's reply to this last is, perhaps, a fair hit:

> Thow sayst trew, drafe is good Inough for swyne.
> (sig. C i[v])

The Knight expresses his philosophy of government clearly:

> For reason wyll euer it shuld so be
> Wyse men to haue folys in captyuyte. (sig. A ii)

This was aimed at the Merchant, who fought back, but later said much the same thing himself, directed this time at the Plowman:

> For it is almyghty goddys purueaunce
> Wyse men of folys to haue the gouernaunce.
> (sig. C iii[v])

The Knight accuses the Plowman of shifting the debate from sober arguments to threats of personal violence:

> Thow spekyst lyk a clerk that hath lyttyll wyt
> When a case is put yf he can not soyle it . . .
> Then wyll he answere hym thys wyse & sey
> Beware what ye sey syr now I aduyse you
> For it is treason or herysy that ye spek now.
> (sig. B iii[v])

The Knight argues that rich men ought to dress well, since their luxuries keep the poor occupied and out of

> Idylnes
> Whych is the moder of vyce and wretchydnes.
> (sig. C ii)

He agrees with the Merchant that the Plowman's obstinacy is invincible and that they might as well leave:

> Caton sayth this
> Contra verbosas noli contendere verbis
> Contend nor argu neuer in no matter
> With hym that is full of words and clatter.
> (sig. C ii)

The Plowman, in his restricted sphere, is as fond of a good table as is Chaucer's Franklin:

> There is no ioy nor pleasure in this world here
> But hyll bely fyll and make good chere. (sig. A vi)

All men, he claims, are brothers under God:

> The vylyst beggar that goth by the dore
> Had ye not both one god & creature
> Ye cam of one furst stok & progenye
> Both of adam & eue ye wyll not denye.
> (sig. B i)

61

THE BEAUTY AND GOOD PROPERTIES OF WOMEN or *CALISTO AND MELIBÆA* (*c.* 1530)

[Tudor Facsimile Texts, 1909]
1087 lines: 4; 5; 5; 16

The principal features of *The Beauty and Good Properties of Women* are that the sententious remarks alone outnumber all the rest of the proverbial material, and that Celestina, the old bawd, employs three quarters of the sayings in the play. She is unwilling to expend her energies for promises alone:

> Wordes are but wynd. (sig. A vi)

Money is what she wants:

> For money makyth marchaunt that must Iet.
> (sig. A vi)

In her plea to Melibæa she reminds her that death comes as readily to the young as to the old:

> For as sone goth to market the lambys fell
> As the shyppys / none so old but may lyff a yere
> And ther is none so yong but ye wot well
> May dye in a day. (sig. B iii)

Melibæa decides to follow Celestina's moderate suggestions but not until the morrow, for, as she says,

> To morow is a new day. (sig. C i[v])

Celestina's sententious remarks, for the most part, reveal her as a lady of fundamental propriety and kindness. She is anxious to aid Calisto at once:

> For long hope to the hart mych troble wyll do.
> (sig. A v[v])

Even the kindest old lady may feel the need of pay in addition to protestations:

> I have herd his wordes but where be his dedes.
> (sig. A vi)

Parmeno knows her past rather too well and so, always desirous for concord, she attempts to engage the tale-telling lad in song:

> Where armony is ther is amyte. (sig. A vi[v])

She gives the boy good counsel:

> Vse no slowth nature abhorryth idelnes.
> (sig. B i[v])

When she talks to Melibæa her moralizing is in full spate. She considers it folly to think of regaining youth:

> Folys are they that are past theyre passage
> To begyn agayn which be at the endyng
> For better is possession than the desyryng.
> (sig. B ii[v])

While young, however, one should take advantage of the gifts of fortune:

> Bewte shall passe at the last thys is truth.
> (sig. B iii)

She is strongly in favor of good deeds:

> We shuld not only lyf by bred here
> But by our good workys. (sig. B iii)

Her devious nature, added to her fear of Melibæa's wrath, keeps her from too blunt a statement of purpose:

> But what I must mone where I dare not say.
> (sig. B iii[v])

Melibæa's anger, and, we note with regret, her none too lady-like language, when she hears that it is for Calisto that her complacence is sought, brings only satisfaction to the subtle old bawd:

> Ther is no tempest that euer doth endure.
> (sig. B iv[v])

Her hopes are justified and the fact that Melibæa consents to compromise makes her certain of the future:

> Now know ye by the half tale what the hole doth meane.
> (sig. C i[v])

Once more she reflects on the transitoriness of human emotion:

> These women at the furst be angry & furyous
> Fayre wether comyth after stormys tempestyous.
> (sig. C i[v])

Sempronio, Calisto's servant, has no great respect for women, of whom he says, they are

> Semyng to be shepe and serpently shrewd.
> (sig. A iii)

> Therfore lo yt is an old sayeng
> That women be the dyuelles nettes and hed of syn
> And mannys mysery in paradyse dyd begyn.
> (sig. A iii[v])

He wonders why he should be more active than his master:

> It paseyth a meruell
> The master slow the seruant to be dylygent.
> (sig. A iv)

So long as Celestina's story of a sick person who requires her aid does not include the hated name of Calisto, Melibæa is sympathetic:

> For they that may hele sekefolk & do refuse theym
> Suerly of theyre deth they can not excuse theym.
> (sig. B iii[v])

Knowledge of the 'sick' man's name changes all that and, along with the pretty names, such as 'berdyd dame,' 'rybaud,' 'brut baud,' and the like which she hurls at Celestina, she has time to philosophize:

> It is not sayd I se well in vayn
> The tong of man & woman worst members be.
> (sig. B iv)

62

THERSITES (*c.* 1537)

[Tudor Facsimile Texts, 1912]
915 lines: 6; 12; 23; 2

Thersites, which has recently been ascribed to Nicholas Udall,[7] contains an unusually large number of miscellaneous proverbial phrases, seventeen of which are spoken by the titular hero. There is a proverb on the title-page:

> Thys Enterlude Folowynge
> Dothe Declare howe that the
> greatest boesters are not
> the greatest
> doers. (sig. A i)

Three of the six proverbs in the text are spoken by the mother of Thersites. She urges him not to force her to cure Telemachus of 'the wormes that do hym harme':

> Sonne ye be wise kepe ye warme. (sig. C iv)

She alters her opinion of Telemachus, however, and

finally expresses a wish that more parents brought their children up to be as mannerly:

> A chylde is better vnborne then vntaughte.
> (sig. D iii)

Though she loves Ulysses but little, she is not unwilling to visit him:

> It is good to set a candell before the deuyll.
> (sig. D iii[v])

The other proverbs, all in the vein of the saying on the title-page, express the soldier's opinion of Thersites:

> Cowardes make (may) speake apase
> St[r]ypes prouethe manne. (sig. E i)

> Maysters ye maye see by this playe in sighte
> That great barking dogges, do not most byte
> And oft it is sene that the best men in the hoost
> Be not suche, that vse to bragge moste. (sig. E i)

The mother of Thersites believes him when he says that he is fleeing from the persecution of a thousand horsemen:

> One against so manye, is no indyfferente matche.
> (sig. C ii)

The hero himself explains his sudden desire for reconciliation with his old foe Ulysses:

> Wroth maye not alwaye laste. (sig. C iv)

63

TOM TYLER AND HIS WIFE (before 1661)

[Ed. G. C. Moore Smith and W. W. Greg,
Malone Society Reprints, 1910]
927 lines: 18; 8; 17; 4

The date of the lively play of *Tom Tyler and His Wife*, which has received far less than its due from critics and literary historians, is unknown and the first extant edition is of 1661. This print says that the play is 'as it was printed and acted about a hundred years ago,' and there is no reason to doubt the general truth of the statement, though the date of composition is probably nearer 1550 than 1560. The play is unusually rich in true proverbs: indeed we may say that its plot is based on a proverb. The proverbial material is fairly evenly distributed among the principal characters and, in addition, is frequent in the songs which are characteristic of the play. The proverb which contains the play's ruling theme is uttered by the first character as he introduces himself:

> I Represent the part that men report,
> To be a plague to man in many a sort
> Destinie. I am, which as your Proverbs go,
> In wedding or hanging am taken for a fo.
>
> (p. 1, ll. 21 ff.)

The same proverb runs as a refrain through the song which Tom Tyler sings as he comes on the stage:

> *The Proverb reporteth, no man can deny,*
> *That wedding and hanging is destiny.*
> I am a poor Tyler in simple aray,
> And get a poor living, but eight pence a day,
> My wife as I get it, doth spend it away;
> And I cannot help it, she saith; wot ye why,
> For wedding and hanging is destiny.
> I thought when I wed her, she had been a sheep,
> At boord to be friendly, to sleep when I sleep.
> She loves so unkindly, she makes me to weep;
> But I dare say nothing god wot, wot ye why?
> For wedding and hanging is destiny.
> Besides this unkindnesse whereof my grief grows,
> I think few Tylers are matcht with such shrows;
> Before she leaves brawling, she falls to deal blows
> Which early and late doth cause me cry,
> That wedding and hanging is destiny.
> The more that I please her, the worse she doth like me,
> The more I forbear her, the more she doth strike me,
> The more that I get her the more she doth glike me;

Wo worth this ill Fortune that maketh me crie
That wedding and hanging is destinie.
If I had been hanged when I had been married,
My torments had ended, though I had miscarried;
If I had been warned, then would I have tarried;
But now all too lately I feel and crie,
That wedding and hanging is destinie.
(pp. 2 f., ll. 66 ff.)

Toward the end of the play Destiny appears again and uses a cognate of the saying:

If your fortune bee to hang on a tree,
Five foot from the ground, ye shall never be drownd.
(p. 22, ll. 782 f.)

It also appears incidentally in a later song, in which all the characters join, which consists of variations on the proverb that 'Patience conquers all':

Patience entreateth good fellows all,
Where Folly beateth to break their brawll,
Where wills be wilfull, and Fortune thrall,
A patient party perswadeth all.

Though Strife be sturdy to move debate,
As some unworthy have done of late.
And he that worst may the candel carry,
If Patience pray thee, do never varry.

If froward Fortune hap so awrie,
To make thee marry by Destenie,
If fits unkindly do move thy mood,
Take all things patiently, both ill and good.

Patience perforce if thou endure,
It will be better thou mayst be sure,
In wealth or wo, howsoever it ends,
Wheresoever ye go, be patient Friends.
(p. 25, ll. 888 ff.)

The additional proverb in the seventh line of this song is to be noted.

When Tom's wife Strife, an allegorical character in

name only, is invited by Tipple to drink and share a bit of bacon, she accepts gladly for

As long lives a merry heart as a sorrie. (p. 5, l. 159)

Poor Tom is driven from his hard-earned glass by his termagant spouse and complains of his lot to his friend Tom Tayler. This enterprising and sympathetic wife-tamer puts on Tom Tyler's clothes, and when Strife takes him for her husband he gives her a good thrashing, ending with the admonition to behave herself and to

Praise at thy parting. (p. 12, l. 410)

She remembers the proverb later after her silly Tom has confessed the deceit and received the drubbing he richly deserved for his blabbing, and she uses it complacently as she boasts to her friends of her victory:

It is an old saying, praise at the parting.
(p. 19, l. 667)

That was later, however, and she did no crowing after Tom Tayler had beaten her blue and caused her gall to burst. On the contrary, she lamented this apparent change in her doltish mate. Her sweet meat days are over:

Soure sauce is now my chear. (p. 12, l. 415)

Tayler tells Tyler the way to rule a wife:

And she will not be ruled, let her be cooled.
(p. 13, l. 458)

Strife's friends Sturdy and Tipple are as amazed at Tyler's transmogrification as is the lady herself, but Sturdy is none too sympathetic with her gossip's reversal and finds a proverb to explain the alteration:

The still Sow eateth up all the draffe.
(p. 15, l. 521)

Tom comes home, hopeful to get to bed without waking Strife, and tries to bluff it out when she takes a conciliatory tone:

> And now you may see, as the old sayings bee,
> God sendeth now, short hornes to a curst Cow.
> (p. 16, ll. 575 f.)

She says that she can't love a man who beats her and the simpleton surrenders at once. 'You can loue me, then, for it was Tom Tayler who beat you.' Strife's valetudinarian pose vanishes and she beats him until Sturdy, who with Tipple, comes in upon this edifying scene, tries to stop her:

> Enough is enough, as good as a feast.
> (p. 18, l. 658)

Tom escapes and Sturdy suggests that she and Tipple compose jointly a song telling the sad story of Tom. Strife starts them off, as no one knows the affair better than herself. This beautiful example of communal composition, which seems to have been overlooked by students of ballad origins, contains the line 'Though some be sheep, yet some be shrowes' (p. 20, l. 710) which doubtless refers to the proverb 'Better to marry a shrew than a sheep,' and a similar allusion is probably to be seen in the eighth line of Tom Tyler's song already quoted (p. 189 above), and certainly in the final song. Destiny appears again and gives Tyler cold counsel, and the latter decides that he can do little about his fate:

> Hap good hap, will, hap good, hap evil;
> Even hap as hap may. (p. 22, ll. 804 f.)

The play ends with a song which contains two proverbs, one of which we have seen already, and some sententious advice:

When sorrowes be great, and hap awry,
Let Reason intreat thee patiently.

Though pinching be a privie pain,
To want desire that is but vain.
Though some be curst, and some be kind
Subdue the worst with patient mind.

Who sits so hie, who sits so low?
Who feels such joy, that feels no wo?
When bale is bad, good boot is ny
Take all adventures patiently.

To marrie a sheep, to marrie a shrow,
To meet with a friend, to meet with a foe,
These checks of chance can no man flie,
But God himself that rules the skie.
(p. 26, ll. 909 ff.)

Sententious matter has appeared in some of the songs which we have quoted, and another, rendered in parts by Strife, Tipple, and Sturdy, contains little else:

Tom Tiler, Tom Tiler,
More morter for Tom Tiler.

As many as match themselves with shrowes,
May hap to carrie away the blowes,
Tom Tiler, Tom Tiler.

As many a Tyde both ebs and flowes,
So many a misfortune comes and goes,
Tom Tiler, Tom Tiler.

Though Tilers clime the house to tile,
They must come down another while,
Tom Tiler, Tom Tiler.

Though many a one do seem to smile,
When Geese do wink, they mean some gile,
Tom Tiler, Tom Tiler. (pp. 6 f., ll. 218 ff.)

Tipple admires Strife's easy way of handling her husband; she must have an excellent technique:

Good handling doth much. (p. 20, l. 724)

Sturdy also is envious, and Tipple reminds her that all things change:

> Alwaies the Seas
> Be not like mild, but wanton and wild
> Sometime more higher, then need shall require.
> (p. 20, ll. 729 ff.)

64

Thomas Ingelend's *THE DISOBEDIENT CHILD* (1560–1570)

[Tudor Facsimile Texts, 1908]
1538 lines: 4; 20; 9; 10

Thomas Ingelend's *Disobedient Child* contains few proverbs, an average number of sententious remarks, but an unusually large proportion of comparisons. The Priest, who furnishes a mild diversion by complaining about his negligent clerk, realizes that he is helpless:

> At this present there is no remedy
> But to take tyme, as it doth fall. (sig. D iii)

The Father uses two related proverbs to indicate that he will not forgive his son:

> But as he had brewed, that so he shulde bake.
> (sig. D iii[v])

> But my Sonne doubtles, for any thynge that I knowe
> Shall reape in such wyse as he dyd sowe. (sig. D iv)

The Son's servant, in the course of a complacent monologue, first expresses fear lest his master chide him for delay, but then decides not to worry:

> His wordes they be but onely wynde. (sig. E iii)

The Father does his utmost to persuade his son to study:

> For a man without knowledge (as I haue read)
> Maye well be compared to one that is dead.
> (sig. A iii[v])

He tells him, in addition, that he cannot hope to get along without work:

The Scriptures declare,
That he shoulde not eate, which wyll not laboure.
(sig. B ii)

He argues against marriage and fortifies his argument with an old and pertinent quotation:

True he shall fynde, that Hipponactes dyd wryte
Who sayde with a wyfe are two dayes of pleasure
The first is the ioye of the Maryage daye and nyght
The seconde to be at the wyfes Sepulture. (sig. D iv)

The Son, once become Husband, finds out that Father really did know best:

O mercyfull God, in what lamentable state
Is he, of whom the wyfe is the mayster?
(sig. F i[v])

It is somewhat hard for us to sympathize with him, however, because his wife's violence and abuse were called forth solely in an effort to make him do a little work.

The Maid cook, after a vain attempt to help her fellow worker understand *Domine labia aperies*, decides

That none is so deafe, as who wyll not heare.
(sig. C ii[v])

The speaker of the peroration drives home the moral of the play. Education must begin early:

For as longe as the twygge is gentell and plyent
(Euery man knoweth this by experience:)
With small force and strength it maye be bent
Puttynge therto but lytell dylygence.
But after that it waxeth somewhat bigger
And to cast his braunches largely begynneth,
It is scant the myght of all thy power,
That one bowghe thereof, easely bendeth,
This twygge to a chylde maye welle be applyed.
(sig. G iv)

He goes on to make the inevitable quotation from Solomon:

> Remember what writeth Salomon the wyse,
> Qui parcit Virgae, odith filium. (sig. G iv[v])

The song which brings the play to a rather dreary end is of morality all compact. We have an *ubi sunt* passage of twelve lines (sig. H ii), which mentions Solomon, Samson, Absalom, Jonathan, Caesar, Dives, Tully, and Aristotle. This cheerful vein is then further emphasized:

> O meate of wormes, O heape of duste,
> O lyke to dewe clyme not to hye:
> To lyue to morowe, thou canot not truste,
> Therfore now betyme helpe the nedye.
> (sig. H ii[v])

Nothing on earth is permanent or sure:

> The worlde doth gyue and take agayne.
> (sig. H ii[v])

65

THE NICE WANTON (1560)

[Tudor Facsimile Texts, 1909]
557 lines: 4; 2; 9; 9

The typographical disorder of the first edition of *The Nice Wanton* is illustrated by the proverb which Ishmael uses in suggesting that any spinning his sister does is likely to be with her 'heles vp wynd':

> For a good mouse hunt, is cat after kyng.
> (sig. A ii)

There can be no doubt but that 'kyng' is an error for 'kynd,' and the profusion of printer's errors must, however we regret it, keep us from feeling too confident that the type-setter had 'A cat may look at a king' in mind. It is quite possible that it is the printer rather than the author to whom we owe the proverbs on the title page:

> Early sharpe, that wyll be thorne,
> Soone yll, that will be naught.
> To be naught, better vnborne,
> Better vnfed, then naughtely taught.

There is but one other proverb, and that is spoken by the pious prig Barnabas, spiritual ancestor to Sir Charles Grandison, and the saying is characteristic of our hero, since by means of it he explains his success:

> But it is an olde prouerbe, you haue herd it I think
> That god wyl haue se, shall not wynke. (sig. C i[v])

The sententious remarks are handed about impartially enough. The Messenger uses one with which we are familiar:

> The prudent Prince Salomon, doth say,
> He that spareth the rod, the chyld doth hate.
> (sig. A i[v])

The same idea occurs to Eulalia, the kind neighbor who cannot resist her duty to tell Xantippe of the follies of her favorite son and daughter:

> He that spareth the rod, hateth the chyld truely.
> (sig. A iii)

When Eulalia finds Xantippe's sympathies so wholeheartedly against that 'mome' her studious son, she leaves without pursuing the matter:

> Better in time, then to late. (sig. A iii[v])

Barnabas is less sententious than his nature would suggest. He is shocked to see his sister singing in the street:

> Sobrenes becommeth maydes alway. (sig. A ii)

He ends the play with a figure which we have often found in the Youth-moralities:

> A yonge plant you may platte & bowe as ye wyll,
> Where it groweth strong, there wyll it abyde styll.
> (sig. C ii)

The fair Dalila takes part in a sufficiently curious dialogue:

> *Dalila.* Though ye do Ceteri nolunt,
> *Iniquity.* Peace Dalila, speak ye laten poore foole,
> *Dalila.* No, no, but a prouerbe I learned at scoole.
> (sig. A iv)

In her part-song with Iniquity she gives him sound advice:

> When ye haue your wyl,
> Ye were best lye styll. (sig. A iiii[v])

Ere long she speaks to him in a different vein:

> A knaue I found the, a knaue I leaue the here.
> (sig. B i[v])

The Magistrate, a very Daniel come to judgment, rebukes his bailie, none other than Iniquity, for attempting to bribe him to free Ishmael:

> Brybes (saith Salomon) blind the wise mans sight.
> (sig. B iii)

66

JACK JUGGLER (1562)

[Ed. W. H. Williams, Cambridge, 1914]
1062 lines: 6; 9; 17; 6

Jack Juggler is an amusing little play which affords a neat example of cross-breeding, in that the familiar and farcical scene from *Amphitruo* is put in operation by Jack Juggler, a Vice. Jack is sufficiently typical of the later Vice, but we observe, with some surprise, that most of the proverbs are spoken by the hapless Jenkin Careaway. Poor Jenkin, who has let bucklers, apples, and dice interfere with his duty, has devised an elaborate falsehood by means of which he hopes to escape just punishment. His artless prattle is doubly amusing to the audience which is aware of Jack's plot against him and so his first two proverbs mean more than he realizes:

> But I promise you I do curstlie feare
> For I feel a vengeable burning in my left ere
> And it hath byn a saying, of tyme long
> That swete mete woll haue soure sauce among.
> (p. 13, ll. 320 ff.)

He then knocks on his own door, and when Jack within bids him be gone, he threatens fight and then, fearing to be taken up on it, he wishes he hadn't. A cursed fatality pursues him:

> When a man hath most hast he spedith worst.
> (p. 14, l. 355)

Jack offers him a serving of fist meat which Jenkin declines, professing to have supped amply before, but Jack has an answer which constitutes his only proverb, and that a dietary one:

> This shalbe your Chise, to make your met digest.
> (p. 16, l. 382)

Jack's sophistry and assurance finally pursuade Jenkin that he is indeed not himself, and he then reviles his own carelessness:

> Thou woldest lyse thyne arse if it were loose.
> (p. 27, l. 619)

He uses another proverb in the speech at the end which serves as an epilogue to the play:

> Sumwhat it was sayeth the prouerbe olde
> That the Catte winked when here iye was out
> That is to saye no tale can be tolde

But that sum Englyshe maye be piked therof out
Yfso to serche the laten and ground of it men wil go aboute
As this trifling enterlud that before you hath bine rehersed
May signifie sum further meaning if it be well serched.
(pp. 43 f., ll. 993 ff.)

Two of the six sententious remarks are in the Prologue, and both consist of Latin quotations, one from the Distichs of Cato and the other from Ovid:

Interpone tuis interdum gaudia curis
Ut possis animo quemues sufferre laborem
Doo any of you knowe what latine is this . . . .
The two verses, which I rehersid before
I finde written in the boke of Cato the wyse
Emongs good precepts, of lyuing a thousand more
Which to folowe there, he doth all men auise
And they may be Englyshed, breflie in this wyse
Emongs thy carful busines, vse sume time mirth and ioye
That no bodilye worke, thy wyttes breke or noye.
(p. 2, ll. 1–14)

For, Quod caret alterna requie durabile non est
Nothing may endure (saith Ouyd) with out some rest.
(p. 3, ll. 27 f.)

Three of the remaining are Jenkin's. He is in great fear of his mistress, Dame Coy, 'an angrye piece of fleshe,' who may well owe her name to Chaucer's rime:

For she is as all other weomen bee
A verie cursed shrew. (p. 9, ll. 208 f.)

He later threatens Jack:

By my faith yf thou be angrie without a cause
You shall haue a mendes made with a cople of straus.
(p. 16, ll. 394 f.)

One way of the world does not please him in his rôle of epilogue:

And an olde saying it is, that most tymes myght
Force, strength, power, and colorable subtlete
Dothe oppresse, debare, ouercum and defeate ryght.
(p. 44, ll. 1007 ff.)

Dame Coy uses a single sententious remark and that, as it happens, is not true in her case. She is very angry at not being taken to supper:

> I saye nothing, but I thinke sum what I wis.
>
> (p. 28, l. 642)

It is with surprise, and almost with fascinated horror, that the reader of this thoroughly derivative farce comes gradually to realize that he is engaged with a clever, though not very subtle, attack on transubstantiation. This has a bearing on the date of composition. Though the date of printing is 1562, Mr. Williams, in his introduction, argues that it must have been written before 1552, because he is certain that it was by Udall and earlier than *Ralph Roister Doister*, which he assigns to that year. The implication of the 'allegory' is that people are being forced to express a belief in transubstantiation, and that points either to the reign of Henry or that of Mary and not to the more or less liberal years of Edward (1547–1553). The temptation is to say that it was written in Mary's reign by an imitator of Udall, rather than in Henry's days by the master himself. One hesitates to follow Mr. Williams (pp. xi ff.) when he finds allusions here to the sad story of Udall, the school boy, and the silver plate.

Part II

French Interludes

We are doubtless justified in treating as counterparts of our English interludes such French dramatic types as *farces*, *sotties*, *monologues*, and *sermons joyeux*. Taken together the French plays are shorter, more varied, more immoral, and more amusing than are the English. So far as proverbs are concerned, we find the same situation which we have already observed in the French drama: although almost every play contains some proverbial material it is, with the exception of one group of plays, seldom used systematically. An examination of more than one hundred and forty comic plays [8] shows only seven worthy of special mention, and four of these are *sotties*. Few of the other plays contain more than ten items of a proverbial nature and an unusually large number of these are comparisons. The seven exceptions can be discussed in brief space.

The central figure in *La Farce de la bouteille* [9] is characterized by the use of proverbs and sententious remarks. It is evident that the author felt no great respect for proverbs since the character who uses them is the *badin* and he, even among *badins*, bears away the bell for folly. The matter of the play consists of a mother's laments for the stupidity of her son and her consultation with a neighbor concerning his future. The *badin* enlivens the scene with speculations about his bottle and a series of irrelevant statements and unresponsive answers. The mother's feelings are easily understood:

> Sa poure teste ne repose
> Non plus que faict l'eau de la mer. (p. 14)

He employs eight sayings, most of them shrewd enough, but almost never applicable to the situation:

> Tel cuyde aucune foys monter
> Deux pas & qui en descent quatre. (p. 7)
>
> Bien souvent un bon taire
> Vaulx mieulx dix foys que tant parler. (p. 7)
>
> Beaucoup de gens pensent voler
> Deuant qu'il ayent aulcunes plumes;
> Que voules vous, c'est la coustume
> Des ieunes gens de maintenant. (p. 9)
>
> Signifiant que nul de sa vertu
> Ne doibt voler deuant qu'il ayt des elles. (p. 9)
>
> Tousiours n'est pas temps de se taire
> Aulcune foys fault paroller. (p. 11)
>
> Pleust a Dieu que l'on eust crible
> Le bon grain d'aueques la paille. (p. 12)
>
> Ases va qui fortune passe,
> Se dict on en commun langaige. (p. 14)
>
> Depuys qu'on chante trop matin,
> On dict que ce n'est pas bon signe. (p. 22)

He is well versed in Scripture, and this it is perhaps which leads the neighbor, in obvious desperation, to suggest:

> Faisons en un homme d'eglise,
> Ie n'y trouue aultre moyen. (p. 13)

The *Farce Nouvelle a cinq personnaiges, c'est assavoir Marchandise, et Mestier, Pou d'Acquest, Le Temps qui court et Grosse Despense* [10] (*c.* 1450) is a political satire which has several of the characteristics of a morality.[11] Whatever its exact *genre*, it contains two proverb-capping scenes which deserve notice.

> Mestier
> Tel cuide par trop embrasser
> Qui laisse eschaper son fardeau.

Marchandise
Tel cuide souvent menasser
Qui est frappé de son cousteau. (III, 59, 253)

The second passage is far more extensive and decidedly reminiscent of similar scenes in the *Mystère des Actes des Apostres* (see pp. 61 ff. above):

Mestier
Tel cuydoit bien avoir credit
En aulcun lieu, a toute gasté.

Pou d'Acquest
Pour ce qui s'est par trop hasté
De monter, il est cheu à val.

Marchandise
Pour peu de chose il vient beaucoup de mal.

Mestier
De moins que neant on faict maintes reproches.

Marchandise
Par icelluy qui les pechez rabat,
Une demarche nous mect en gros debat.

Pou d'Acquest
Voyre sans plus pour avoir une crosse.

Mestier
Fort à ferrer a tousjours fer qui loche.

Marchandise
Cheval hargneux une estable a par soy.

Pou d'Acquest
Passe partout souventes foys s'acroche
Et deschire ce qui est autour soy. (III, 59, 256)

The remaining plays are *sotties*, of which their editor, Picot, could write:

L'extrême diversité des vers qui se suivent, le brusque passage d'une idée à une autre, l'amoncellement des proverbes et des allusions satiriques sont les principaux mérites du genre.[12]

It is very true that the *sotties* contain more proverbs than the other plays of this general type, but even here we do not find them used as frequently or as skilfully as in many of the English plays. Let us consider, for example, *Les Menus Propos* [13] (before 1500), a play of five hundred and seventy-one lines. The characters in the play are three *sots* who recite couplets in turn with complete regularity and almost no thread of continuous sense. Of their remarks Picot says

> Les propos des trois sots méritent surtout d'être étudiés à cause du grand nombre de proverbes et de dictons populaires qu'ils renferment.[14]

The proverbs are many and interesting enough in themselves, but *Les Menus Propos* is only a little more dramatic in form than Heywood's *Dialogue Conteynyng the Number of the Effectuall Prouerbes in the Englishe Tounge*, and it is certainly less dramatic in sense.

The *Sottie du Monde* (1524) opens with a string of proverbs and sentențious remarks spoken, one each, by seven characters:

> Le Prestre *commence.*
> L'homme propose et Dieu dispose.
>
> Le Medecin.
> Fol cuide d'un, et l'autre advient.
>
> L'Orphevre.
> Du jour au lendemain survient
> Tout autrement qu'on ne propose.
>
> Le Bonnetier.
> En folle teste folle chose.
> Point n'est vray tout ce que fol pense.
>
> Le Cousturier.
> Au temps qui court n'y a fiance:
> Maintenant joye et demain pleur.
>
> Le Savetier.
> Aujourd'huy vos verrez monsieur,
> Et demain simple maistre Jehan.
>
> Le Cuisinier.
> Tel cuide vivre plus d'un an
> Qui meurt dans trois jours. (II, 328, ll. 1 ff.)

There are other proverbs in this play, but they are scattered and without significance.

Les Sobre Sotz entremellez avec les Syeurs d'Ais (1536) rejoices in a proverbial subtitle [15] and a proverb-capping scene in which the five *sots* all join:

> Le .IIIIe. Sot.
> Voyla que c'est que d'entreprendre
> Menger la lune a belles dens.
>
> Le .Ve. Sot.
> Tel se treuve en gros acidens
> Qui en pence bien eschaper.
>
> Le Premyer Sot.
> Tel ne sairoyt un coup frapper
> Qui toutefois se faict bien craindre.
>
> Le .IIe. Sot.
> Tel prent grand plaisir a veoir paindre
> Qui ne sairoyt bien faire un traict.
>
> Le .IIIe. Sot.
> Tel va bien souvent au retraict
> Qui de chier n'a poinct d'envye.
>
> (III, 57 f., ll. 57 ff.)

Here, too, although there is other proverbial material, it is thrown in without discrimination.

We may also quote a passage full of sayings from the *Farce Nouvelle . . . des Cris de Paris* (*c.* 1540), a play which, as a whole, has but slightly more coherence than *Les Menus Propos*:

> Le Second [Gallant]
> Belle maniere a au besoing
> Qui de sa voye a quelque apuy.
>
> Le Sot
> Belle doctrine prent en luy
> Qui de son poing faict un maillet.
> Vous avez laissé ce feuillet;
> Mais si l'ai ge bien retenu.

Le Second
Je voys vers vous tout frais venu:
Il ne doibt pas estre reprins.
De grant follie ung homme est prins
Qui se fuyt pour femme espouser.

Le Premier
Grande follie veult user
Qui tant se veult faire appeller.

Le Second
De follie se veult mesler
Qui a soy marier omet.

Le Sot
De grant folye s'entremet
Qui se chastie par aultruy.

Le Premier
Ma foy, nous n'en chevirons huy.
Escoute la, sotte memoire:
Qui plus ne veult bon conseil croire
En la fin voit son bien finé.

Le Second
Qui plus ne veult estre enseigné,
Il voit ou doit voir qu'il est nisse.

Le Premier
Qui plus ne veult qu'on le punisse,
Il veoit ce qu'il ne demandoit.

Le Sot
Qui plus hault monte qu'il ne doit,
Il voit ung clocher de plus loing.

Le Second
Escoute, ja n'est il besoing
De nous y rompre plus la teste.

Le Premier
Et non, car il n'est que une beste. . . .
Aussi ceste raison est vive,
Que a laver la teste d'ung asne
On n'y pert rien que la lescive.

(III, 146 f., ll. 397 ff.)

Finally Picot suggests that *Les Deulx Gallans et une Femme qui se Nomme Sancté* (*c.* 1485) is no more than a dramatization of the proverb:

> Qui n'a santé il n'a rien;
> Qui a santé il a tout. (I, 177)

The scenes which we have quoted are not without interest, but the fact that they are substantially all that more than one hundred and forty plays have to offer serves to make it emphatic that French writers of farce were not especially interested in proverbs. They used them, to be sure, but not in large numbers and almost never for characterization, except for a slight tendency to put them, usually without regard to context or action, into the speeches of persons of inferior mentality. We have already noticed that Heywood made less use of proverbs than might have been expected. It is possible, though not demonstrable, that French farce, which certainly influenced him, played a part here.

CHAPTER IV

EARLY ENGLISH COMEDIES

OUR INVESTIGATION so far has indicated clearly that proverbs and homely proverbial phrases are normally found only in comic scenes, although, as the interludes show, it is possible to have comic scenes which do not contain any appreciable number of sayings. The fifteen comedies treated in this chapter serve to bear out the general rule and, indeed, to strengthen it, as several of them, notably *The Bugbears*, *Misogonus*, *Damon and Pithias*, *Promos and Cassandra*, and *Fedele and Fortunio* are richer in proverbs and proverbial phrases than any plays which we have examined, and only Skelton's *Magnificence* and *Respublica* can be said to approach them at their lower limit.

Several writers of comedy borrowed the popular and ubiquitous Vice from the morality, so we find Politic Persuasion in John Phillips's *Patient Grissell*, and Common Conditions in the play of that name, spouting proverbs as indefatigably as any of their predecessors. On the other hand, Subtle Shift, in *Sir Clyomon and Sir Clamydes*, is not especially given to saws and sayings. In addition to the regular and denominated Vices there are a number of characters who are obviously modeled, in part at least, on the Vice and, like their prototype, revel in proverbs. Among these are Mathew Merygreeke, who uses about half of the proverbial material in Udall's *Ralph Roister Doister*, Cacurgus, in *Misogonus*, and Echo, in Gascoigne's *Glass of Government*. There is an exception in this group in the person of Diccon, the madcap troublemaker of *Gammer Gurton's Needle*, who uses few proverbs. Side by side with persons on whom the touch of the Vice is strong, we find others clearly characterized by their use of proverbs. The servant called B in Medwall's *Fulgens and Lucres* is an excellent example of this, and other proverb-mongers of the servant class are the maid Tibet Talk Apace in *Ralph Roister Doister*, Squartacantino in *The Bugbears*, and Rosko in Whetstone's *Promos and Cassandra*. Persons of relatively higher station markedly fond of proverbs are Aristippus in R. Edwards's *Damon and Pithias*, Captain Crackstone, who has perhaps a dash of the Vice in his composition, and Pedante, both in *Fedele and Fortunio*, and Phallax in *Promos and Cassandra*. Cassandra, in the last-named play may possibly be characterized by her use of proverbs. If so we face the rare spectacle of a serious, even tragic, figure falling back on proverbial wisdom as a support in moments of overwhelming disaster.

It is perhaps worth while to note the large number of proverbs and proverbial phrases, most of them original with the English authors, in the plays adapted from the Italian, of which Gascoigne's *Supposes* contains materially fewer than either *The Bugbears* or *Misogonus*.

67

Henry Medwall's *FULGENS AND LUCRES* (*c.* 1497)

[Ed. Seymour De Ricci, Henry E. Huntington Facsimile Reprints I, New York, 1920]

2385 lines: 4; 5; 17; 5

Henry Medwall's *Fulgens and Lucres* probably deserves the distinction of being called a comedy rather than an interlude, even though the main plot of the play leaves much to be desired. We are not especially interested in the prudent Lucres's choice of the honorable, though lowly born, Gayus Flaminius, but rather in the often genuinely amusing dialogue of the servants A and B who appear as a kind of prologue to get the play started and then calmly walk into the action themselves. Our examination of Medwall's morality *Nature* (see pp. 77 ff. above) divulged a measured fondness for proverbial material on the author's part, and the present play is in accord. There is about the same amount in both plays, except that, as is natural enough, there are four times as many sententious remarks in the morality. We find one important difference however: in *Fulgens and Lucres* Medwall definitely utilizes proverbial material as a means of characterization. The servant B employs two of the four proverbs, four of the five comparisons, eleven of the seventeen other proverbial phrases, and one of the five sententious remarks. He tells A not to be afraid lest the play will be full of flattery, but to see it and then

> Prayse at the parting euyn as ye fynde.
> (sig. A iv[v])

He wishes to marry Jone, the maid, but is under no illusions about the economy of matrimony:

> Ye god sende vs mery wether
> I may not wed and thryue all to gether. (sig. C v)

His wooing becomes so impetuous that Jone has to utter a warning to her ardent suitor:

> Fyrst ye shall
> Chepe or euer you by. (sig. C iv[v])

Cornelius, finally rejected by Lucres, is not sure that he can commend her method of breaking the news to the claimants:

I wot nere yet I wyll prayse as I fynde.
(sig. F vi[v])

B's somewhat pessimistic view of marriage appears in a sententious remark addressed to Jone:

I mene yf ye wolde be content
Or ony wyse agree
For to be my sacrament of penaunce
Ey god gyue it a very very vengeaunce
Of wedlocke I wolde haue sayde. (sig. C iv[r-v])

Gayus believes in the power of assiduity in love affairs:

For who so euer oweth obedyence
Vnto loue he hath greate nede
To attendaunce if he wyll spede. (sig. B iv)

He reminds Cornelius that they share a common ancestry:

Both he and I cam of adam and eue. (sig. F v[v])

He also refers to

Idelnes the causer of syn. (sig. F v[v])

A wonders if the whole truth will be disclosed in the play:

Trouth may not be sayde alway. (sig. A iv[v])

68

Nicholas Udall's *RALPH ROISTER DOISTER* (1534–1541)

[Ed. E. Flügel in C. M. Gayley, *Representative English Comedies, From the Beginnings to Shakespeare*, New York, 1912, pp. 87 ff.]
2044 lines: 17; 13; 28; 8

The proverbs in *Ralph Roister Doister* have been used as evidence to fix its date. When Professor J. W. Hales[1] found sayings in the play which were also in Heywood's

Dialogue he at once assumed that it must have been written after the *Dialogue* had appeared. To prove borrowing by means of proverbs is, as Flügel (p. 96) points out, to base one's proof on very unsteady ground. The number and allocation of proverbs in *Ralph Roister Doister* is just about what we should expect if the play were a morality, and despite the classical influence Mathew Merygreeke is a true Vice in his use of proverbs. He employs eight of the play's seventeen proverbs, five of its eight sententious remarks, and, we may note in addition, eighteen of the forty-one proverbial phrases. He is the first character to appear on the stage after the prologue is finished and his first lines contain two proverbs:

> As long lyveth the mery man (they say)
> As doth the sory man, and longer by a day.
> Yet the Grassehopper for all his Sommer pipyng,
> Sterveth in Winter wyth hungrie gripyng,
> Therefore an other sayd sawe doth men advise,
> That they be together both mery and wise.
> (p. 108, i, 1, 1 ff.)

A little later we find him teasing Roister Doister by threatening to leave him:

> The tyme away dothe waste,
> And the tide they say, tarieth for no man.
> (p. 111, i, 2, 10 f.; cf. 19)

He gives Roister Doister traditional advice on the method to pursue in wooing the widow, and he repeats the counsel later in the play:

> Wowers never speede well, that have a false harte.
> (p. 116, i, 2, 172)

> Ye may not speake with a faint heart to Custance.
> (p. 147, iii, 3, 109)

During the elaborate joking which follows the mock requiem Mathew runs two proverbs into a single line:

> Good happe is not hastie: yet in space cometh grace.
> (p. 146, iii, 3, 104)

A little later he urges Roister Doister to be cold and firm toward Custance:

> For one madde propretie these women have in fey,
> When ye will, they will not: Will not ye, then will they.
> (p. 152, iii, 4, 93 f.)

Roister Doister wants everything ready for his assault on Dame Custance, and Mathew shifts his remark into a proverb:

> *R. R.* For such chaunce may chaunce in an houre, do ye heare?
> *M. M.* As perchance shall not chaunce againe in seven yeare.
> (p. 160, iv, 3, 26 f.)

The titular hero of the play refers to another proverb in a dialogue with Mathew:

> *M. M.* But why speake ye so faintly, or why are ye so sad?
> *R. R.* Thou knowest the proverbe, bycause I can not be had.
> (p. 143, iii, 3, 11 f.)

He also employs a Wellerism to emphasize his intention to supplant Goodluck in Custance's affections:

> Backare quod Mortimer to his sowe.
> (p. 114, i, 2, 97)

Next to Merygreeke in the use of proverbs is Dame Custance's maid Tibet Talk Apace. She is, we observe at once, a lazy wench, and not at a loss to find proverbs to justify the slowness of her movements:

> No haste but good, . . . for whip and whurre
> The olde proverbe doth say, never made good furre.
> (p. 118, i, 3, 11 f.)

> Soft fire maketh sweete malt. (p. 118, i, 3, 14)

When Roister Doister offers to kiss her, as he kisses all whom he loves, she asks a saucy question:

> When dyd ye last kisse your cowe.
> (p. 122, i, 3, 110)

This has been thought to be an allusion to the common Wellerism, 'Every man to his taste,' and so on. The identification is perhaps borne out by Tibet's terse comment when old Madge Mumblecrust says that she'd never refuse a kiss from such a fine gentleman:

> They that lust: I will againe to my sewyng now.
> (p. 122, i, 3, 116)

The fact that Tibet prefers work to Roister Doister indicates strongly how little she fancies him. Christian Custance finds it hard to discover love in Roister Doister's attack. Yet Mathew had said he loved her and Mathew now reaffirms his master's affection: 'He loved a while even like a turtle dove.' Her answer is her single proverb:

> Gay love God save it, so soone hotte, so soone colde.
> (p. 176, iv, 8, 38)

Christian's intended, Gawyn Goodluck, is a little too willing to believe evil of his intended to augur well for her happiness with him. He uses two proverbs, one of her and the other at her:

> Ah surra, nowe I see truthe in the proverbe olde,
> All things that shineth is not by and by pure golde.
> (p. 177, v, 1, 13 f.)

> Yea Custance, better (they say) a badde scuse than none.
> (p. 179, v, 2, 28)

Mathew can be sententious at a moment's notice, as when he explains the need for haste to Roister Doister:

> Negligence in greate affaires ye knowe may marre all.
> (p. 111, i, 2, 17)

He is inclined to throw cold water on Roister Doister's ideas about the widow's wealth. The fortune which one marries has a way of shrinking during the very ceremony:

> Learne this one lesson of me afore,
> An hundred pounde of Marriage money doubtlesse,
> Is ever thirtie pounde sterlyng, or somewhat lesse.
> (p. 113, i, 2, 84 ff.)

But then:

> Wowers and Widowes are never poore.
> (p. 113, i, 2, 89)

The popular and more or less proverbial notion about female curiosity is expressed in his reply to Christian's statement that she has not read Roister Doister's fatal letter:

> Ye a woman? and your letter so long unredde.
> (p. 141, iii, 2, 69)

When she exhibits displeasure at seeing Roister Doister's crew at her door Mathew takes a high, if a trifle whining, moral stand:

> May not folks be honest, pray you, though they be pore?
> (p. 149, iii, 4, 2)

Dobinet Doughtie, Roister Doister's servant, comments sententiously on his master's evident ill success as a lover:

> So fervent hotte wowyng, and so farre from wiving.
> (p. 131, ii, 1, 17)

And again he prepares for any contingency:

> It is good to cast the wurst. (p. 134, ii, 3, 10)

When Gawyn's ill-founded and unkind doubts have been dissipated at last, their only begetter, Sym Suresby, apologizes, though not very abjectly, to Christian Custance. She forgives him, but with a moral generalization:

> Though hastie reportes through surmises growyng,
> May of poore innocentes be utter overthrowyng.
> (p. 180, v, 4, 21 f.)

69

GAMMER GURTON'S NEEDLE (before 1579)

[By Mr. S. Mr. of Art. Ed. H. F. B. Brett-Smith,
The Percy Reprints, II, Oxford, 1920]
1283 lines: 5; 13; 21; 3

Without entering into the controversy as to the authorship of *Gammer Gurton's Needle* there is reason to believe that the play was licensed as early as 1562, and that a reference (p. 66, v, 2, 236) to 'the kings name' pushes the date of its composition before Edward's death in 1553. In any event we have but small concern with this play, as its author made little use of proverbial material other than proverbial phrases, and even with them he is not especially adept. Hodge's indignation because Gammer has lost her needle at what may well be a crucial hour in his amatory experiences is expressed in two proverbs:

Fooles will be fooles styll. (p. 10, i, 4, 7)

By gogs soule I thenk you wold loes your ars, and it were loose.
(p. 11, i, 4, 16)

Gammer is slow to cast aside her suspicion of Dame Chat. Why hadn't she denied the matter outright in the first place? It wouldn't have been difficult, and

Ye know she could do litle, and she cold not say nay.
(p. 62, v, 2, 163)

Dame Chat, too, clings to her belief that Hodge paid a felonious visit to her henhouse which, she remarks complacently, turned out to be in

Greater hast then speede. (p. 62, v, 2, 175)

At the very end of the play Diccon, who completely lacks the proverb-mongering which we expect in a

Vice-like character, uses his only proverb, but that sufficiently fitting:

> As proude coms behinde they say, as any goes before.
> (p. 70, v, 2, 331)

Each of the three sententious remarks is used by a different person. Gammer demands her property from Dame Chat with vehemence and an appeal to general justice:

> Pore folks must haue right. (p. 35, iii, 3, 10)

Master Bailie is inclined to believe that Dame Chat was justified in resisting an unlawful entry into her dwelling. Would Dr. Rat assist a thief in at his window, he asks, and he replies to the Doctor's indignant statement that he is 'no thief, but an honest learned clerk' with this sage observation:

> Yea but a man in the darke, if chaunces do wincke,
> As soone he smites his father, as any other man.
> (p. 52, v, 1, 22 f.)

In the end Dr. Rat comes to realize that his fate was the not uncommon one which is likely to fall upon those honest souls who cannot resist a desire to straighten out the affairs of others:

> Such is the lucke that some men gets, while they begin to mel
> In setting at one such as were out, minding to make al wel.
> (p. 63, v, 2, 194 f.)

70

THE BUGBEARS (1564–1565)

[Ed. R. Warwick Bond in *Early Plays from the Italian*, Oxford, 1911, pp. 77 ff. See pp. lxx, lxxviii for lists of proverbs and phrases]

1773 lines: 26; 7; 58; 11

The Bugbears, which Mr. Bond 'assigns to 1564 or 1565' (p. 83), is an adaptation of Antonfrancesco Grazzini's

La Spiritata (1560). If Mr. Bond is correct in the date, the play would seem to antedate Gascoigne's *Supposes* by a year or two. We find a somewhat similar treatment of the original in each case, and the free introduction of proverbial material is even more marked in the present play than in the *Supposes*. The small number of comparisons and sententious remarks in contrast to the proverbs and miscellaneous proverbial phrases is especially striking. The theme of the play is familiar: old people try to force young people to marry against their own wishes. The choice of Brancatius for the hand of his daughter Rosimunda is Cantalupo, and it is Cantalupo's servant Squartacantino (Phoebus! what a name!) who is characterized as a proverb-monger. He uses nine of the twenty-six proverbs and a flock of proverbial phrases. Squartacantino thinks, with justice, that his master is an old fool, especially for wanting to marry a young woman. He is 'al sure to be cornuted,' Squartacantino tells him, whereupon the old gentleman counters with one of his three proverbs, and one more apposite than seemly:

> He shall never pise in medow that fearethe every grasse.
> (p. 95, i, 3, 14)

Squartacantino says that if he must woo he had better modernize his garb and when Cantalupo asks indignantly if he expects him to dress like a tosspot, the servant replies:

> Thers a meane twene starring & starke blinde.
> (p. 97, i, 3, 48)

He opens the third act by singing one of the proverb songs with which we are familiar:

> I feare myne old master shall syng thys new note
> No foole to the old foole when he gynes to dote

He needes must be perfumed brave with powdrs prowd of pryce
With musk with civet & with trickes of new & rare devyce
With amber grece he must be grymed & such lycke costly geare
Wher I suppose a fyer warme for hym far fytter weare
    And therefore I feare hele sing this new note

Hys white beard & his golden teeth which shyver in hys head
With her whyt teeth & golden lokes are even as fytt to wead
As march with lusty may shuld match, wherfore I feare me much
Hys wooyng wil to woeyng turne yf that hys chaunce be such
    I feare myn old etc

And he with martch from fysh to flesh shall march in march hys sygne
And she with may, may taurus make to gemini resygne
Or playne my mynd to tell when she by bearyng one to manye
May pearce my master to the hart, and gyve hys head eveny
    I fear myn old mr etc (p. 111, iii, 1, 1 ff.)

Squartacantino discloses to Cantalupo the sad news that his darling, his Rosimunda, is with child; Cantalupo remarks ruefully:

> Then if I have the Cow I must have the Calf too. (p. 132, iv, 5, 7)

The varlet changes his tactics and tries, insincerely enough, to prove that Rosimunda is a good match. Should Cantalupo be afraid of the cuckold's horn? No indeed, it's invisible and

> That we see not nor fele not, cannot greve vs a whitte. (p. 132, iv, 5, 26)

All Cantalupo needs to do is expect the best:

> Hope well & have well. (p. 132, iv, 5, 28)

Cantalupo tries to persuade himself that perhaps the story isn't true at all. Was there ever such a saint-like lass? But here again Squartacantino has a proverb:

> Young Saint & old devell. (p. 132, iv, 5, 29)

To Cantalupo's insistent and repetitious queries about Rosimunda's state, Squartacantino suggests that perhaps she has eaten ratsbane, and then (p. 133, iv, 5, 39 ff.) reels off a string of proverbial phrases all pointing to, and some explaining, the heroine's interesting condition. Cantalupo decides to make further inquiries elsewhere. His servant warns him against too much talk:

> No more words then nede.
> Lyttle sayd, sone amended. (p. 133, iv, 5, 57 f.)

Cantalupo has confidence in his own discretion and judgment:

> As I trye so will I trust. (p. 134, iv, 5, 62)

After the old man's departure we learn the real reason for Squartacantino's aversion to a mistress. She is likely to interfere with the present household economy:

> New brome clean work doth make
> All is to litle for her, shee wilbe good with a rake.
> (p. 134, iv, 5, 70 f.)

The remaining proverbs are divided among eight characters. Amedeus, discovered when the play opens considerably frightened by the 'old rumbling' in his house, decides to consult his neighbor Cantalupo as well as the famed astronomer:

> Allwaies it is good to have ij⁰ stringes to ones bow.
> (p. 87, i, 1, 46)

Biondello, servant to Amedeus but the ally of his son Formosus, explains his master's greed to the 'astronomer' Trappola:

> He loves not longe barefote for dead menes showes to stand
> Rather wold he one birde redy cawght in his hand
> Then two in the bushe. (p. 91, i, 2, 63 ff.)

Trappola is by no means sure that it will be possible to convince Amedeus that spirits have taken his gold:

> Lett formosus be advised
> For doubt lest he pull an old howse vpon his head.
> (p. 93, i, 2, 123 f.)

Formosus himself is determined not to desert Rosimunda for Cantalupo's daughter Iphigenia. If his father thinks to force him,

> He recons with out his host.
> (p. 103, ii, 3, 93)

Iphigenia is betrothed to Manutius, and he is in such despair that even the two proverbs which his friend Carolino addresses to him fail to comfort:

> There are more maydes then malkyn
> Youe know weddyng & hanging by Desteny are brought in.
> (p. 107, ii, 5, 12 f.)

Iphigenia herself refuses to change Manutius for another:

> I will haue none but him the end shall trulye try.
> (p. 108, ii, 5, 34)

Amedeus finds none to trust to but himself, for even Cantalupo is too concerned with Rosimunda to be of assistance, and he laments that

> Love is blynd. (p. 113, iii, 2, 9)

Amedeus invites his two cronies in to see Trappola, now known as Doctor Nostradamo, expel the spirits. Brancatius, Rosimunda's father, expresses his assent concisely:

> Content is agreed. (p. 125, iv, 2, 20)

Biondello is willing to wait and see how well his master's feast turns out:

> The end maketh all. (p. 127, iv, 2, 64)

Piccinino, a servant of the usual complaining type, confesses that he dare not disregard orders:

> For feare of afterclappes. (p. 131, iv, 4, 7)

But hurry never pays, for his master's vehemence has driven out of his head the very name of the man to whom he was sent:

Haste makes waste. (p. 131, iv, 4, 9)

When his gold is gone and its loss has been explained as supernatural, Amedeus wonders that the spirits don't steal everything from everyone, but Trappola explains that he has disposed of them effectively:

Every thing hathe an end & so have they.
(p. 145, v, 7, 31)

The eleven sententious remarks are divided among seven characters. Biondello warns Amedeus not to tell too many people about the mysterious disturbances in his house:

The ffewer know your case the lesse they shall clatter.
(p. 87, i, 1, 47)

Cantalupo asks his 'horsone elfe' Squartacantino, when the latter chides him for his elderly calf's love, if he has never heard that

Amor vincit omnia. (p. 96, i, 3, 27)

Rosimunda has been told that Formosus's love for her has grown cold. He denies the accusation:

Can I forsake her? Can the fyshe live on land?
Can men live without breathe? Can the heavens rolling stand?
Can the flaming fyer freese? Can the Chilly ryvers burn?
(p. 103, ii, 3, 77 ff.)

Iphigenia tells her lover, Manutius, that Formosus is to marry her. Manutius decides, futile though it may seem, to appeal to the other's better nature:

It is wysdome ere one perrishe to seke all helpes to fynde.
(p. 109, ii, 5, 53)

When Formosus's constancy is revealed, Iphigenia recognizes how foolish it is to believe every bad report:

I see it ys not good to be suspicius over much
They breede ther bane & hatch there harme whos fryghtfull feares are such. (p. 120, iii, 4, 3 f.)

Her maid Catella suggests that Formosus may be lying even under oath:

In perjured lovers othes & wordes ofte tymes lyke truth ys founed. (p. 121, iii, 4, 30)

And she replies to her mistress's natural query about what one can believe if one can't believe an oath with

I have hard that god on hye
Doth lawgh when lovers breake there vowes, & from ther fayth doth flye. (p. 121, iii, 4, 31 f.)

The three remaining sententious remarks are used by that learned charlatan Trappola. His excuse for not talking freely in the house of Amedeus is an unworthy and unprovoked insinuation:

Youe know womens Clackes will walke with euery wynde. (p. 135, v, 2, 2)

Again he refuses fully to explain his dark forebodings in regard to Rosimunda's health:

All we Astronomers amonge vs haue a lawe
Not to vtter all we know, but where it shold be vtteryd. (p. 140, v, 2, 118 f.)

He tries to quiet Amedeus's loud outcries over the loss of his money:

Yf you crie never so muche, it is quite past all remedie. (p. 144, v, 7, 7)

71

MISOGONUS (1560–1577)

[Ed. R. Warwick Bond in *Early Plays from the Italian*,
Oxford, 1911, pp. 161 ff. See pp. cxiv f. for a
list of proverbs and phrases]

2168 lines: 22; 15; 66; 9

Misogonus, composition or revision of which has been dated from 1560 to 1577, shows a use of proverbial material similar to that in *The Bugbears*. As in it the large number of miscellaneous proverbial phrases indicate a desire on the author's part to give a racy, homely flavor to his dialogue, and we find that one character, here the Vice-like Fool Cacurgus, uses eight of the twenty-two proverbs, while the remaining fourteen are divided among nine characters.

The play opens with Philogonus, father of the prodigal Misogonus, recounting his paternal anguish to his friend Eupelas. He was too gentle with Misogonus in his youth,

> Wherof like a foole to late I repente.
> (p. 178, i, 1, 64)

Education was unnecessary for such a promising lad. His kin were all honest and gentle, and the boy would naturally take after them, for

> The like bredes the like. (p. 178, i, 1, 79)

But all has gone askew. Eupelas tries to console him. The boy can't be bad always:

> He goeth farr that never tournes agayne as folke say.
> (p. 179, i, 1, 109)

Philogonus sees the hand of God in the discovery of another son, but he refuses to be too optimistic:

> I ioy likewise but vnder hope my chickings are not hatcht
> I nil to counte of him as yet for so presume I mighte.
> (p. 242, iv, 1, 15 f.)

Eupelas advances proverbial support for believing Cacurgus:

> Children & fooles they say can not l[y].
> (p. 182, i, 1, 185)

The Fool enters, and having talked nonsense to the old men for a few minutes, is left with the stage to himself, and then his tone changes and he explains his tactics:

> A foole yow knowe can kepe no measure.
> (p. 184, i, 2, 16)

Later he sings a song 'to the tune of hartes ease' in which we find two proverbs:

> And takt as god doth send it. (p. 198, ii, 2, 82)

> The merye man, with cupp & cann
> Liues longer then doth twentye.
> (p. 198, ii, 2, 89 f.)

Liturgus, Philogonus's faithful servant, and his master are discussing Misogonus; Cacurgus, who is eavesdropping, keeps up a running fire of satiric comment, as when Liturgus suggests that Misogonus has not yet sown all his wild oats, Cacurgus says, No, he'll cuckold you yet:

> In space commeth grace. (p. 200, ii, 3, 40)

This shocking misapplication of a good proverb is sufficient indication of the depth of Cacurgus's duplicity and rascality. Again when Philogonus mournfully recites the means he'd use if he had his son to bring up again, Cacurgus quotes:

> A curste cowe hath shorte hornes.
> (p. 201, ii, 3, 65)

During the long, scandalous, yet amusing gaming scene Cacurgus makes a shrewd comment on Sir John's bad luck:

> Has the Marchant a shillinge so sone to nine pence brought.
> (p. 211, ii, 4, 206)

As has been pointed out, the following remark made by Cacurgus to the rustic Codrus is a garbled version of 'It's a good horse that never stumbles':

> [Its] a good stumble near horst I ame sure then they w[ere gel].
> (p. 222, iii, 1, 30)

When he has finally been exposed as a rogue and dismissed, Cacurgus pities himself far beyond his deserts and finds proverbial explanation for his mistreatment:

> Poores alwayes thrust toth wall.
> (p. 255, iv, 3, 71)

Melissa, described not unjustly in the list of 'speakers' as 'meretrix,' uses a true gambler's proverb:

> One good stake in an houre is worth a meny driblinges.
> (p. 210, ii, 4, 176)

Sir John, who if not a hedge-priest bids fair to become one, seeks learned authority for his none too decorous behaviour:

> Its good to fetch a friske once a day I fynde it in my texte.
> (p. 213, ii, 4, 267)

Orgelus, one of the servants of Misogonus, finds in a Wellerism the best way to describe the dancing:

> Now closse quod curyer come alofte Jacke with a wim wam.
> (p. 213, ii, 4, 277)

It is this same Orgelus who deserts Misogonus when things look black and the elder twin appears destined to win the inheritance. Orgelus is willing to fight up to a point, but after that his advice is:

Holde your handes when year well.
(p. 252, iv, 2, 29)

Liturgus, the good servant, has little use for Sir John:

Thers no mischeife as they say commonly but a preist at one end.
(p. 217, ii, 5, 73)

We might expect to find the speeches of Codrus, the rustic, and his wife, Alison, abounding in proverbs, but that is not the case. Each directs one at the other. In their very natural excitement both try at once to tell the story of the double birth and Alison calls her husband a liar. His reply is prompt:

And thou saist I lye thou liest as thou bakst so shat brewe.
(p. 229, iii, 1, 197)

She in her turn enlists Philogonus's aid to silence her spouse:

Ile tell one Mr if ye can make him kepe in his fooles boulte.
(p. 230, iii, 1, 212)

Codrus does his best to discredit Madge:

Thou wert nether oth court nor oth counsaile.
(p. 248, iv, 1, 135)

Eupelas, who has tried to be a peacemaker throughout the action, endeavors toward the end to bring Misogonus to repentance:

Shame the devill rather & repent the of thy wickednes.
(p. 251, iv, 2, 14)

Philogonus uses five of the nine sententious remarks. He knows well why he consults Eupelas in his hour of need:

Good counsayle yow knowe to a minde with care oppreste
Is like to holsome medicine taken at nede,

> Which helpeth the stomacke evell humoures to digest
> Lest therof at any tyme some malledey may brede.
> (p. 176, i, 1, 9 ff.)

Eupelas's sage advice strengthens his conviction in the value of friends:

> Nothinge I see well to a frende may be counted.
> (p. 180, i, 1, 118)

> All treasures trwe frendshipp I perceve fare sermounted.
> (p. 180, i, 1, 120)

He is afraid, however, that it is too late to accomplish anything with his wretched son:

> Can you bende a bigge tree which is sappy & sound?
> (p. 181, i, 1, 158)

His later conclusion grows inevitably out of his experience:

> He that spares the rode hates the childe as Salamon writes.
> (p. 201, ii, 3, 69)

Eupelas agrees with him in his praise of Liturgus:

> A good servaunt is worth great rich[es].
> (p. 182, i, 1, 179)

Cacurgus states his own case sententiously:

> A foole in laughture puttethe all his pleasure.
> (p. 184, i, 2, 18)

He also waxes unexpectedly philosophical on the differences between one country and another:

> Good Lord what great diversite & alteratione
> Is that in the manner of diverse people and cuntries.
> (p. 236, iii, 3, 25 f.)

The remaining sententious remark is found in Philogonus's song:

> God gaue and he may take away.
> (p. 220, ii, 5, 150)

The play, it is worth noting, is imperfect, the fourth act being incomplete. The action, however, seems nearly finished and we must wonder what the contents of the fifth act would have been.

72

Richard Edwards's *DAMON AND PITHIAS* (1563–1564)

[Tudor Facsimile Texts, 1908]
1823 lines: 26; 8; 23; 25

Richard Edwards was lavish with proverbial material, saving only comparisons, in his 'tragicall commedie' *Damon and Pithias*. Aristippus the time-serving philosopher is, on the whole, the chief proverb-monger of the play, although his predominance is less evident in proverbs than in proverbial phrases and sententious remarks. After having sworn hypocritical friendship with Carisophus, whose place in the favor of Dionysius he has usurped, he hies him off to the court to make what profit a new courtier may:

> For wot ye what? a new Broome sweepes cleane.
> (sig. B ii[v])

His servant, Will, reports that the ladies of the court are not over pleased with his way of making jokes at their expense. The philosopher resolves to do so no more:

> I know the galde horse will soonest winche.
> (sig. B iv[v])

He feels that he is making very genuine progress on his way up the courtier's ladder:

> I haue plied the Haruest, and stroke when the Yron was hotte.
> (sig. C iii[v])

He has received money from the king, and as it came so will he spend it:

> Money is currant men say. (sig. C iii[v])

When Damon's supposed espionage becomes known, Aristippus finds that a tyrant's favor can change suddenly. His jests are no longer laughed at; he determines once more to alter his course:

> It is very good to be mery and wise. (sig. D ii)

Pithias appeals to him for aid, but receives the answer:

> I am of the Court in deede, but none of the Counsell.
> (sig. D ii[v])

Next to Aristippus in number of proverbs is his lackey, Will, with four. He taunts Jack, who has the misfortune to work for Carisophus, about his master:

> These barking whelpes were neuer good biters,
> Ne yet great crakers were euer great fighters.
> (sig. E iv[v])

Jack threatens him with violence and Will calls to his attention that some do well to boast of victory before the fight:

> Prayse well your winning. (sig. E iv[v])

The two rascals join together against Grim the collier, of whom Will says:

> I see now there is no knaue to the olde knaue.
> (sig. F iii[v])

The remaining proverbs are divided among nine characters, and since no one speaker employs more than two, we may well consider them in the order of their occurrence. Carisophus bemoans his loss of royal and general favor:

> It is a true saying that oft hath bin spoken,
> The pitcher goeth so longe to the water, that he commeth home broken. (sig. B iii)

He has sworn fellowship with Aristippus, but his boy Jack fears that this will be of little avail:

> I haue heard say, there is falshod in felowshippe,
> In the Court somtimes. (sig. B iii[v])

Stephano, Damon's faithful servant, enters saying:

> Oftetimes I haue heard, before I came hether,
> That no man can serue two maisters together.
> (sig. B iii[v])

He then proceeds to disprove the proverb on the ground that he serves both Damon and Pithias. Dinner is a thing that Stephano dearly loves, and his master's philosophical abstinence does not appeal to him. A philosopher's meal lasts but a short time and is mostly words at that:

> A shorte horse soone curried. (sig. C ii)

Carisophus, to regain Dionysius's good will, or at very least, his victim's clothing, accuses Damon of being a spy, and the Greek is arrested and speedily condemned to death. Pithias tries to be resigned:

> Let vs make Vertue our frend, of meare necessytie.
> (sig. D i)

Dionysius's reason for Damon's death, be the sentence just or unjust, is a blunt one:

> A dead dogge can not bite. (sig. D iii[v])

Grim the collier, is introduced solely that he may be cajoled, shaved, and robbed by Jack and Will. They lead him on to boast of his money, and Jack asks

> Can goulde make men mery? they say who can singe so mery a note,
> As he that is not able to change a grote?
> (sig. F iii)

Grim replies:

> I know for my parte,
> That a heauy pouch with goulde makes a light harte.
> (sig. F iii)

They ask him just how he made so much money out of coals, but there he refuses to go into details:

> Nay, ther bate me an ace (quod Boulon).
> (sig. F iii[v])

The form 'Boulon' rather than the familiar 'Bolton' is perhaps worth notice, but it is probably only a misprint. The proverb 'A friend in need is a friend in deed' is too fitting to the plot not to appear, and we find it, in one form or another, used by Carisophus, Dionysius, Pithias, and in the final song:

> A friende ought to shonne no payne, to stand his friend in stead.
> (sig. G ii[v])

> But now I see there is no garde vnto a faithfull friend:
> Which wyll not spare his lyfe at time of present neede.
> (sig. H ii[v])

> Within whose Realme at time of need, no faithful friends are founde.
> (sig. H ii[v])

> True friends are present, and help at each neede. (sig. H iv)

Eubulus, the king's upright counselor, tries to save Pithias when the hour for Damon's return seems about to pass, but all his efforts are fruitless:

> Against the wind and striuinge streame I sayle.
> (sig. G iii[v])

He recognizes the apparent inevitability of the execution:

> Neede hath no law. (sig. G iv)

The only person sure to profit, in his own opinion, is Gronno, the hangman, among whose perquisites are the victim's garments:

> It is an euyll wynde that bloweth no man good.
> (sig. H i)

Aristippus, true to his rôle of philosopher, uses exactly half of the sententious remarks. Seven of these are in Latin:

> Frustra sapit, qui non sapit sibi. (sig. B i)
>
> Quid cum tanto Asino, talis Philosophus? (sig. B ii)
>
> They say, Morum similitudo consultat amicitias. (sig. B ii)
>
> Dictum sapienti sat est. (sig. C iv)
>
> I folow the prouerbe: Amicus Vsque ad auras. (sig. G ii)
>
> Quia prudentis est multum dissimularit.
> To speake more playner, as the prouerbe doth go,
> In faith Carisophus, Cum cretence cretiso. (sig. G iii)

He soon perceives that an angry and fearful Dionysius is not responsive to jests, no matter how clever:

> I perceyue it is no safe playing with Lyons, but when it please them,
> If you claw where it itch not, you shall disease them. (sig. D ii)

He pities Damon but sees no way to help him:

> Nought auayleth perswasion, where frowarde opinion taketh place. (sig. D ii)

He tries to make Pithias think that there is some comfort in the very certainty of Damon's fate:

> Best to content your selfe, when there is no remedie,
> He is well reliued that forknoweth his miserie. (sig. D ii[v])

The courtiers lament for Damon and thus hate Carisophus, whose unpopularity leads Aristippus to reflect:

> By mine owne experience, I proue true that many men tell,
> To liue in Courte not beloued, better be in Hell. (sig. E iv)

He himself seizes the first opportunity to break with his former sworn friend:

> A false knaue I found thee, a false knaue I leaue thee. (sig. G iii)

Damon employs four sententious remarks, two of them in Latin:

Omnis solum fortis patria: A wise man may lyue euery wheare.
(sig. C i[v])

What then? An nescis longas Regibus esse manus?
It is no safe talkynge of them that strykes a farre off. (sig. C iii)

Stephano's only weakness in his master's eyes is his thralldom to his belly, but even so Damon can say,

I would not chaunge him for no new.
(sig. C ii[v])

He expounds the theme of friendship in what he believes to be his last speech before Dionysius:

That you may safely raigne, by loue get friends, whose constant faith
Wyll neuer fayle, this counsell geues poore Damon at his death:
Friendes are the surest garde, for Kinges golden time doo wear away,
And other precious thinges doo fade, frindship wyll neuer decay:
Haue friendes in store therfore, so shall you safely sleape,
Haue friendes at home of forraine foes, so neede you take no keepe:
Abandon flatring tounges, whose clackes truth neuer tels,
Abase the yll, aduance the good, in whome dame vertue dwels:
Let them your play felowes be, but O you earthly kinges,
Your sure defence and strongest garde, standes chifely in faithfull friends.
Then get you friends by liberall deedes, and here I make an ende,
Accept this counsell mightie Kinge of Damon Pithias friende.
(sig. H ii)

Pithias has learned from Dionysius that a good king makes a fortunate people:

As thynges by their contraryes are alwayes best prooued.
(sig. C i)

He never expects to disagree with Damon:

It is said: Amicus alter ipse. (sig. C i[v])

The Prologue desires the audience to be understanding and

Take thinges as they be ment. (sig. A ii[v])

Stephano's hunger comes to the fore again:

> I neuer heard that a man with wordes could fill his belly.
> (sig. C ii)

Outraged at Carisophus for having betrayed his master, he gives him a sound thrashing and declares that all courtiers are not like him:

> In a trope of honest men, some knaues may stand ye know.
> (sig. E iii)

Carisophus feels no remorse for the plight of Damon:

> He is but a stranger, by his fall let others be wise.
> (sig. C iv[v])

Fortune, viewed in two ways, is the subject of an interchange between Dionysius and Eubalus:

> Dyonysius.
> Fortune maketh all thinges subiect to my power.
> Evbvlvs.
> Beleue her not she is a light Goddesse, she can laugh & lowre.
> (sig. D iii[v])

After a drink or two Grim talks freely, and Will comments:

> In Vino Veritas. (sig. F ii[v])

Grim proceeds to read the boys a drunken lecture but one not without some grains of truth:

> Friendship is dead in Courte, Hipocrisie doth raigne,
> Who is in fauour now, to morow is out agayne. (sig. F iii)

73

John Phillip's *PATIENT GRISSELL* (1565)

[Ed. R. B. McKerrow and W. W. Greg,
Malone Society Reprints, 1910]
2141 lines: 11; 10; 17; 8

John Phillip's *Patient Grissell,* whatever we may think of the way the plot is treated, affords a prime example of the preponderant rôle played by the Vice as proverb-monger. Politic Persuasion uses ten out of eleven proverbs, seven out of ten comparisons, eleven out of seventeen other proverbial phrases, and two out of eight sententious remarks. He disapproves of Gautier's approaching marriage and makes unpleasant prophecies:

> But who so euer intendeth of that misterie to be tastar,
> Findeth oft times the graie mare better maister.
> (sig. B iii, ll. 168 f.)

Later he has the same proverb in his mind:

> God send the graie mare good footinge and to amble apace.
> (sig. C ii[v], l. 414)

He has an answer for Fidence's argument in favor of an heir for the marquis:

> Baw waws is no weddinge the prouerbe doth tell.
> (sig. B iii, l. 182)

Gautier's praise of Grissell disgusts him, but he affects admiration:

> I can not blame him thoughe he comend his owne.
> (sig. C ii, l. 356)

It will soon be determined if the glowing account is correct:

> Time the thinge shall trye. (sig. C ii, l. 368)

After the wedding he plans to encompass Grissell's ruin, but to go about it privily:

> For vnder Honnie the prouerbe saith poyson maye lurke.
> (sig. E i, l. 898)

The news of the approaching birth of an heir serves only to increase his spite:

> Let them laffe in the end that the victorye doth winne.
> (sig. E ii, l. 957)

He produces two Wellerisms, one of them not very reverent:

> Whop quoth I to my sheep, and had neuer a one.
> (sig. F i[v], l. 1223)

> Bones quod ioyner who made God all mightie.
> (sig. G i[v], l. 1542)

He is unwearying in his campaign against the hapless wife and mother:

> I am kyn to a womman in all poynts ile haue my will.
> (sig. F i[v], l. 1230)

The other proverb serves Diligence as an argument in favor of his own slowness:

> Soft fyre the common Prouerbe saith, sweete Malt doth make.
> (sig. E ii[v], l. 1014)

Politic Persuasion levels the battery of his two sententious remarks against marriage, the first of them probably an ironical misstatement of a common proverb.

> And some men neuer fall to thriuinge,
> Before they be spoused. (sig. B iii, ll. 166 f.)

> I hard many a one saye,
> That the first daie for weddinge all other doth excell.
> (sig. B iii, ll. 183 f.)

Old Janicle expresses regret that 'blinded Cupids dart' (sig. D ii, l. 651) should wound the marquis, and when his daughter comes home in poverty and disgrace he puts the blame on Fortune:

> Oh froward Fortune, all together disceaueable,
> Full of Gerishe flatterye, all together varyable:
> The chaunges of thy hawtie wheele, to Luna I may compare,
> Who so trusteth thee hath often cause of care:
> From prosperytie to aduersitie the simple thou doste throe,
> Phie on thee Fortune, which art cause of my woe.
> (sig. G iv[v], ll. 1756 ff.)

Rumor shortly before this had also spoken, though with less partiality, of Fortune as the source of Grissell's woe:

> Fortune is fickle, although shee do smyle,
> Her chaunges vnstable, full of mutabylitie,
> Her wheele is full glyding, and of no sertaintie,
> Her freshe vissage, full soone chaungeth cheare,
> As nowe by Lady Grissill, doth playnly appeare,
> For shee is nowe throwne, from the top of prosperytie,
> And with old Jannickle, must suffer paynfull pouertie.
> (sig. G iii[v], ll. 1679 ff.)

Grissell's mother had given good advice before her lamented demise:

> For a Damsell to haue manie wordes it is vnfyttie.
> (sig. C i[v], l. 315)

Janicle has sound ideas on the bringing up of children and providently shares these with Gautier as soon as the marquis has proposed for his daughter's hand. Both Gautier and Reason agree with the wise ancient, the latter remarking:

> In deede a man maye bowe a Twigge which way he liste,
> So in Infancie a Childe with good manners furnished,
> In aige in Vertue will willingly persist. (sig. D iv, ll. 812 ff.)

Gautier's sister, the Countess of Pango, receives the charge of bringing up the children. When she makes her first appearance she is bewailing the death of her husband, and her maid tries to convince her of the folly of such laments:

> It is longe time since that he died therfore your teares do cease
> Can teares giue life, or him restore to former life againe?
> (sig. F ii, ll. 1246 f.)

74

George Gascoigne's *SUPPOSES* (1566)

[Ed. R. Warwick Bond in *Early Plays from the Italian*, Oxford, 1911, pp. 1 ff. See pp. lx f., for a list of proverbs and phrases]

1859 lines: 12; 7; 21; 10

George Gascoigne's *Supposes* is a translation from Ariosto's *I Suppositi*, which was later to appear in the subplot of *The Taming* of both *a* and *the Shrew*. As Bond points out (pp. lv, lx f.), Gascoigne introduced many 'racy English phrases and proverbs,' and so original is he in his respect that there would be little point in going behind, or even reproducing, the footnotes of Bond's edition. Gascoigne, however, used far fewer proverbs and miscellaneous proverbial phrases than had the authors of *The Bugbears* and *Misogonus*. The proverbs are evenly apportioned, although Pasiphilo, the parasite, uses four. The play opens with a proverb spoken by Balia, Polynesta's nurse, who, considering the nature of her young mistress's intrigue, cannot be too careful:

> Within the house the tables, the plankes, the beds, the portals, yea and the cupbords them selues haue eares. (p. 13, i, 1, 3)

We see but little of Pasiphilo before we are introduced to his monstrous appetite, and in his statement that he

> Hath no pastures to passe in than one,
> (p. 21, i, 3, 19 f.)

we are doubtless to find a reference to the proverb 'Change of pasture makes fat calves.' His disgust with Doctor Cleander's poor table and cold invitations makes him almost ready to renounce his patronage:

> He thinkes that I may feede vpon his fauour and faire wordes.
> (p. 21, i, 3, 17 f.)

In the same scene the supposed Dulipo uses this saying in reference to Damon's unwillingness to listen longer to the supposed Erostrato:

> Determined to be fed no longer with faire wordes.
> (p. 23, i, 3, 97 f.)

The 'supposes' are troublesome enough to us and are equally so to the supposed Erostrato, who wants to call his master by his right name. He is rebuked, however, and told never to fall out of part:

> So long the Parat vseth to crie knappe in sporte, that at the last she calleth hir maister knaue in earnest. (p. 25, ii, 1, 13 f.)

'Erostrato' tries to dispel his master's despair at the apparently inevitable wedding of his sweetheart to old Cleander:

> There is a salue for euery sore.
> (p. 26, ii, 1, 63 f.)

Again he chides him for impatience:

> You would fayne leape ouer the stile, before you come at the hedge.
> (p. 28, ii, 1, 123 f.)

One of the Erostrato's father's motives in coming to Ferrara was fear lest his son be studying himself into a frenzy. Erostrato hasn't been available to his visiting countrymen for some time. Such application to books is going too far, and the innkeeper to whom the tale is told, sagely agrees:

> Enough were as good as a feast.
> (p. 49, iv, 3, 66)

Litio, servant to the Erostrato's father, declares that all the people in Ferrara, native or not, are equally bad:

> There is neuer a barrell better herring, beetwene you both.
> (p. 53, iv, 6, 7 f.)

Pasiphilo reports to the supposed Erostrato the sad news that the supposed Dulipo has been discovered and that Damon has confined both Dulipo and the nurse Balia:

> They shall haue sowre soppes too their sweete meates.
> (p. 60, v, 2, 44; cf. note, p. 271)

A little later when Cleander assails him verbally the parasite remembers part, at least, of a proverb:

> What softe and faire sir. (p. 63, v, 5, 23)

The real Dulipo's identity now comes to light: he is evidently Cleander's long lost son, but Litio, who has his doubts of everyone in Ferrara, accuses Cleander of lying, and when the latter replies that he is not used to lie, Litio has a retort ready:

> Euery thing hath a beginning.
> (p. 65, v, 5, 104)

The sententious remarks, like the proverbs, are scattered throughout the play without special regard to the speaker. Cleander shows the modesty which many men express just before they boast most shamelessly:

> It becommeth not a man to praise him selfe.
> (p. 18, i, 2, 49)

When the supposed Dulipo believes that he is to lose his love he can get no pleasure from recollecting his two years of happiness:

> I fare like the couetous man, that hauing all the world at will, is neuer yet content. (p. 23, i, 3, 75 f.)

The feigned Erostrato makes a traveler from Sienna believe that disguise holds his only safety in Ferrara and he further persuades him that the best disguise is that of a respectable Sicilian, Philogano by name, who has a son named Erostrato. The real Erostrato, as deep in the dumps as mortal can be, keeps finding flaws and weaknesses in the plan until at last his servant asks:

When we haue done as muche as we can, how can we doe any more?
(p. 29, ii, 1, 174 f.)

The Sienese, for his part, recognizes clearly the dangers that beset a man who leaves his own fireside:

He that trauaileth in this worlde passeth by many perilles.
(p. 30, ii, 2, 1)

Even when the scheme bids fair to work in the lover's favor, poor Erostrato cannot bring himself to trust in it. His fate has been crossed often:

Thus haue I beene tossed nowe ouer, nowe vnder, euen as fortune list to whirle the wheele, neither sure to winne nor certayne to loose the wager. (p. 39, iii, 2, 16 f.)

Damon is told of the affair between his daughter and his servant and, not unnaturally, feels betrayed:

O fooles that trust any man but themselues now adaies.
(p. 40, iii, 3, 11 f.)

Philogano's anger, sorrow, and fear rise in equal proportions when he not only finds his son's servant masquerading as his son, but resolutely facing him down about the imposture. He pictures his son with his throat cut and decides to seek the law's aid. His servant, Litio, has his own notion of how to advance a case in the law courts:

He that wil goe to the lawe, must be sure of foure things: first, a right and a iust cause: then a righteous aduocate to pleade: nexte, fauour *coram Iudice*: and aboue all, a good purse to procure it.
(p. 56, iv, 8, 42 f.)

The matter is at last cleared up and the proper identities are restored, as well as the children to their parents and the lovers to each other, whereupon Philogano shows that he possesses a consoling philosophy which had been notably absent in his hour of need:

I think that not so much as a leafe falleth from the tree, without the ordinance of god. (p. 70, v, 8, 14 f.; cf. note, p. 274)

75

George Gascoigne's *GLASS OF GOVERNMENT* (1575)

[*The Complete Works of G. Gascoigne*, ed. J. W. Cunliffe, Cambridge, 1910, II, 1 ff.]

2888 lines (poetry and prose): 9; 6; 18; 27

Gascoigne's *Glass of Government* is a sufficiently uninspired and thoroughly Calvinistic example of the drama of the Prodigal Son but, none the less, fairly rich in proverbial material. Echo, the pimp, albeit not a completely unattractive fellow, is the Vice-like character in the play, and is characterized by his fondness for sayings. He speaks four of the nine proverbs, four of the six comparisons, and eight of the eighteen other phrases. He lures Philosarchus, eldest son of Philocalus, with the far from false statement that Lamia may well be available:

All thinges have a beginning, shee is a woman, and nothing is unpossible. (p. 37, ii, 3)

Lamia begins to show a month's mind to the young scholar, or so Echo declares, and delays are dangerous:

Strike the Iron whiles it is hot. (p. 40, ii, 5)

Once Echo has brought Philosarchus and Lamia together he is confident of success, and assures Dick Droom that if the present dupe escape another will take his place, and perhaps for the better:

Hast thou not often heard, that change of pasture maketh fatte calves? (p. 63, iv, 3)

Lamia's beauty may not last, and he hopes to find several such establishments as hers, so that if trade is poor at one he can move on to another:

Store is no sore as the proverbe saith.
(p. 66, iv, 5)

Philopæs, one of the two fathers, declares that if Gnomaticus is really an excellent schoolmaster he had better be engaged at once; it isn't likely that he'll have to wait long for business:

> Now a dayes the good wyne needeth none Ivye garland.
> (p. 10, i, 1)

Philopæs's eldest son, Philautus, is as worthless as Philosarchus, both being sharply contrasted with their slower but more faithful younger brothers. He finds Gnomaticus's long lectures on the manifold duties of man a far different way of instruction from any he had been subjected to before:

> I see wel the olde proverbe is true, which saith: so many men so many mindes. (p. 34, ii, 2)

Dick Droom, thinking on the noble old girls of Antwerp, admires women of spirit:

> It is an olde saying, one shrew is worth two sheep.
> (p. 44, iii, 1)

Gnomaticus, for all his deadly prosing, has some good ideas about the indiscriminate use of punishment, and admonishes the anxious parents accordingly:

> There is time for all thinges. (p. 60, iv, 1)

The final proverb is outside the action, being found in the fourth chorus:

> The fox can preach somtimes, but then beware the geese.
> (p. 71, fourth chorus)

Many of the sententious remarks are likewise in those parts of the play which can be called the author's own. The Prologue announces proudly that there will be no nonsense in the play:

> I have best wares, what neede I then shewe woorse?
> (p. 6)

There are five sententious remarks in the third and fourth choruses:

> For even as weedes, which fast by flowres do growe,
> (Although they be with comely collors clad:)
> Yet are they found, but seldome sweete of smell.
> (p. 59, third chorus)

> Yet inward stuffe, (of vertue) doth excell:
> For like a stone, most worthy to esteeme,
> It loves to be, much better then to seeme.
> (p. 59, third chorus)

> The toiling man which tilles, his ground with greatest paine,
> Hath not alway such crops theron, as yeeld him greatest gain.
> Nor he the fairest house, which laies thereon most cost,
> Since many chips of chance may fall, to prove such labours lost.
> In vaine men build their fortes, with stone with lyme and sand,
> Unlesse the same be founded first, with Gods owne mighty hand
> (p. 70, fourth chorus)

> The heediest hen that is, the puttocke oft beguiles,
> Such wolves do walke in wethers felles, that Lambes mistrust no wiles. (p. 71, fourth chorus)

> But all too late the water comes, when house is burned quite.
> (p. 71, fourth chorus)

There are also three in the Epilogue:

> We live to learne, for so Sainct Paul doth teach. (p. 88)

> But thinges sone got, are lost againe as fast. (p. 88)

> And in meane while, their Brethren rose as fast,
> Much like the snaile, which clymes the Castle wall,
> With easie steppes, when souldiers downe be cast,
> With furious force, and many a hedlong fall.
> Assaults are hotte, but yet if there withall,
> Some temperance, and polycye be used,
> They winne those fortes, which hotter heads refused.
> (p. 89)

Of the individual characters, Gnomaticus, true to his position and name, uses the largest proportion of sententious remarks:

If the sensual apetite of man be such as engendreth affection towardes thehandmaide bicause she is of familiar conversation with the Mistris. (p. 22, i, 4)

Tyme is the greatest treasure which man may here on earth receive. (p. 27, ii, 1)

The quickest wits prove not alwayes best. (p. 38, ii, 4)

Idlenesse is the cause of many evils in youth. (p. 53, iii, 5)

An old saying hath beene *Chi tropo abraccia niente tiene.* (p. 65, iv, 4)

No herbe so cleane but may be hindred by stinking weeds that grow by it. (p. 80, v, 5)

One of the two fathers, Philopæs, comes second to the master. He believes in taking action before it is too late and expresses that belief twice:

Greatest wounds are at the firste more easily cured, than if they continue untill some aboundance of humour or other accident doe hinder the benefite of nature. (p. 51, iii, 5)

Every mischief is most easely cured and redressed in the beginning. (p. 75, v, 2)

He upbraids himself for not being content with having one virtuous and successful son:

Thou ar[t] like unto a covetous man, which having aboundance is yet never contented. (p. 83, v, 8)

He anticipates misfortunes, and again takes himself to task:

Thou maist be compared to the patient which crieth out before the Chirurgions instrument do touch him. (p. 83, v, 8)

Next in numbers comes Lamia's aunt, the old bawd Pandarina, who is sagely solemn in advising her niece to make the best of a world from which the young lady is already getting as much as she can:

> It were now but folly to spend time in bootelesse complaints, nor to lament the thing which may not be remedied. (p. 24, i, 5)

Lamia must not delay her life of pleasure and profit:

> Beauty will not alwayes last. (p. 24, i, 5)

Lovers are fun, but good ones don't come empty handed:

> Lyberall gyfts are the glewe of everduring love. (p. 25, i, 5)

This wise old lady may have taken more than her name from Cressida's uncle. She uses as an expression of derisive emphasis, 'yea hassilwood' (p. 25), which is exactly what Pandarus thought [2] when he heard Troilus audibly hoping to see Cressida soon back from the Greek Camp. There is a similarity, too, between her 'beauty will not alwayes last,' and his reasons why Cressida ought not to reject love.[3]

Echo wishes more than one string to his bow and gives ironic advice to Dick:

> Hee were wyse enough that would leane altogether unto one bough in these dayes. (p. 63, iv, 3)

The idea obsesses him and a little later he phrases it differently:

> Now adayes the broker which hath but one bargaine in hand, may chaunce to weare a thred bare coate. (p. 66, iv, 5)

Fidus, servant to Philopæs, realizes that there is something to be gained from his humble station:

> I am a servant, and shall sometimes heare of thinges before my Maister. (p. 10, i, 1)

Lamia thinks it unwise to discuss her plans in the open street:

> It is not meete that every dancer heare our musike before the maskers be ready. (p. 25, i, 5)

Education in time will make impress on the studious minds of even the less brilliant students, or so hopes Philopæs's younger and better son, Philomusus:

We see the hardest stones are pearced with soft droppes of water.
(p. 48, iii, 4)

76

COMMON CONDITIONS (*c.* 1576)

[Ed. Tucker Brooke, Elizabethan Club Reprints, No. 1, New Haven, 1915]

1904 lines: 8; 15; 15; 21

The title of this curious play, whose inept and hasty conclusion seems to alter comedy to tragedy, *An excellent and pleasant Comedie, termed after the name of the Vice, Common Condicions,* draws attention to a salient feature (see Brooke, p. xiv), namely, that the Vice, darling of author and audience alike, has for once been given his meed of fame. The title character uses six of the eight proverbs, five of the fifteen comparisons, ten of the fifteen other proverbial phrases, and six of the twenty-one sententious remarks. The number of proverbs credited to Common Conditions is swollen by a favorite phrase, certainly proverbial in the first two instances, by means of which the guileless, though unscrupulous rogue celebrates his own cleverness at times of dire threatening:

Welfare olde shift at a neede. (sig. B iv, l. 428)

Welfare a craftie knaue at a time of neede.
(sig. C ii[v], l. 611)

Well fare at a pinche euermore. (sig. C iv, l. 725)

Welfare a head that can bryng sutch things in minde.
(sig. E iii[v], l. 1270)

He is not averse to contesting with a powerful opponent, but even then his fearful sense comes to the fore:

> Tis good to be mery and wise the truth to say.
> (sig. F iv, l. 1580)

His ever present feeling for self preservation is summed up in a single saying:

> It is good to saue one, as far as I can see.
> (sig. G ii[v], l. 1779)

The master of the pirate ship, once he has been granted life by the irate and overwhelming Lamphedon, reflects that probably fate had not intended him to die by the sword:

> I thinke it be my desteny to be hanged or dround.
> (sig. E ii[v], l. 1193)

Sedmond (appearing as Nomides) falls in love with his own sister Clarisia (now, alas, known as Metrea), and bethinks himself of a proverb fit to spur his suit:

> Experience showes faint harted knights wins neuer fayre ladies loue.
> (sig. F ii[v], l. 1499)

Sententious remarks are numerous and heavy, and of them Common Conditions uses six. In the first he expresses at length his opinion of the fair sex:

> It is geuen to weemen to be obscure & ful of simpriety by the way
> Proffer them the thing they most desier they wold it denay.
> They are so full of sleights and fetches that scarce the Fox hee,
> In euery poinct with weemen may scarce compared bee,
> For when men pray they will denay, or when men most desire:
> Then marke me a woman she is sonest stirred vnto ire.
> Their heds are fantasticall and full of variety strange,
> Like to the Moone whose operation it is often times to change.
> And by your leaue howsoeuer it goes the mastery they must haue,
> In euery respect or in ought that they seeme for to craue.
> (sigs. B ii[v],–B iii, ll. 346 ff.)

After he has privily listened to part of Lamphedon's lament over his love for the unknown Clarisia, he, like a perverse off-stage echo, gives him, in stichomythia, the benefit of four pieces of wisdom:

It is hard winning of the city without skaling the fort.
(sig. C i[v], l. 551)

Hee that is by Cupid possest of force must sorrow try.
(sig. C i[v], l. 555)

Hee that trusts to a broken bough, may hap to fall from the tree.
(sig. C i[v], l. 557)

In vaine tis when the dogs are wery to wish after the deare.
(sig. C i[v], l. 559)

He is as aware of his own weakness as he is of his mental agility, and evades undue odds:

Tis not for the weake hart with the Lion for to play.
(sig. F iv, l. 1581)

Sir Nomides, first introduced to a bewildered audience as Sedmond, brother to Clarisia, rejects the forth-putting Sabia's love on the plausible grounds that

The hart that once is fixt or set and hath that likes him best
What needs it for to seeke for more tobreede his more vnrest?
(sig. D ii, ll. 872 f.)

She had earlier alluded to the fact that 'Loue is blind' in speaking of 'blinde Cupido' (sig. C iv, l. 747), and he worked the notion well nigh to death:

Blinde Cupid. (sig. D ii, l. 877)
Blinde Cupidos dart. (sig. F i, l. 1370)

Nomides is not displeased when Lomia, the natural, proclaims him a fit love for the lady of his choice, in point of fact his own sister, and applauds the fool's opinion:

I perceue though fooles want discression yet their meaning are trew.
(sig. F ii, l. 1429)

He does not accept his subsequent rejection very gracefully:

And weemen are of nature such, they alwayes do requier,
That men should seeke and also creep to gayne that they desier.
(sigs. F ii[v]–F iii, ll. 1500 f.)

Lamphedon, prince of Phrygia, overhears Clarisia's declaration of love for him and responds with three sententious remarks in rapid succession:

What needeth further trial then, when Judge hath heard the tale?
What needs there further plee in case, when agreements doth assaile
What needs the Turtell with her mate, & shee in place doth stande?
(sig. C iii, ll. 644 ff.)

Subsequently, before his fight with the pirate boatswain, he reproves his opponent for over-confidence:

He that doth trust to much his strength may chance to lose.
(sig. E ii, l. 1171)

During the preliminaries to his contest with Cardolus, oppressor of women, he develops the same idea:

Let him that doth subdew his fo vaunt of the victory wone.
For why, the wight that reckeneth before that hee obtaine,
May chance to recken twice, and then his reckning is in vaine.
So thou to vaunt of victory before thou gaine the same.
Maist chaunce to haue thy Pecoks tail brought low vnto thy shame
And therfore let vs first begin, and when that wee haue doone.
Let him triumphe with victorie that hath the conquest woone.
(sigs. E iv[r-v], ll. 1314 ff.)

Clarisia is overwhelmed by the vicissitudes to which she falls a prey, suddenly made the victim of three graceless tinkers:

Ah cruell luckles chaunce alas, ah fortune thou vnsure,
That canst in turning of thy wheele still cause vs to endure
Sutch changed heaps of woes (alas) as tongue cannot expresse.
(sig. B iii, ll. 371 ff.)

Things change rapidly for her, and ere long she has fallen in love with an unknown knight, confessed her passion to the heavens, had the knight overhear her and respond appropriately, and been able to reply with modest complacence:

> The silly fish that once is tayne, must yeeld vnto the bayght.
> (sig. C iii, l. 655)

Her remarks on Fortune prepare us, in an odd way, for her exiled father's paean of praise to the same unstable goddess:

> Who can but smyle and laugh to see the state of Fortune shee?
> Who can deuise in rightist wise, to yeelde dew praise to thee?
> Ha Goddisse thou whose countnance straunge doth eb & flow eche day,
> Sometimes thou doest restore to wealth, and sometime to decay.
> As proofe is playnly seene by mee, though banisht wight I was,
> Thou hast restorde to wealth agayne, far better in eche case.
> Though kynge Arbaccus hee, withall his courtly trayne,
> And eke his route of Parasites, did holde mee in disdayne:
> Yet through thy turnyng wheel, and variable chaynge,
> Hast mee restord to wealth agayne in forayne countreis straynge.
> How should I duly lawd your names O heauenly powers for this?
> How should wee giue you half the prayse that you deserue Iwis?
> (sig. B iv[v], ll. 478 ff.)

On the suggested connection between this play, *Sir Clyomon and Sir Clamydes* and Thomas Preston's *Cambyses*, see pp. 292 ff. below.

77

George Whetstone's *PROMOS AND CASSANDRA* (1578)

[Tudor Facsimile Texts, 1910]
2445 lines: 33; 9; 31; 32

Except in the field of comparisons George Whetstone's long and moderately interesting play *Promos and Cassandra* contains as much proverbial material as one could desire. When Shakespeare took over the plot of

Whetstone's play he gave his own vastly improved and purified version a proverbial title, *Measure for Measure*, but he retained very few of the proverbs and failed to add a commensurate number of his own.[4] Approximately half of the characters in Whetstone's play are comic, or, at all events, non-serious. Aside from the usual number of minor characters, these consist of a corrupt confidant of Promos, named Phallax, and the household of Lamia, a courtesan under his august protection. If we examine the distribution of proverbs and sententious remarks between the serious and non-serious groups, we find a nearly equal proportion except that the serious use a few more sententious remarks and the non-serious a few more proverbs. The situation is quite different in the proverbial phrases where, out of forty in all, the comic figures employ thirty-four. Once more we find low, humorous dialogue given raciness by a liberal use of proverbial phrases.

When we turn to individuals we discover Phallax and Rosko, Lamia's servant, almost tied, Phallax having nineteen and Rosko twenty items; Cassandra third with thirteen. No other single character uses an appreciable amount, with the possible exceptions of Promos, with seven, and Lamia with five items.

The most common proverb is 'might masters right,' which is inserted in the margin once, is uttered once exultantly by Promos, and twice reprovingly by the King:

> Might masters right. (sig. C iv[v])
>
> My might, commaundeth right. (sig. E ii)
>
> The poore mans ryght is ouercome by might. (sig. H ii)
>
> I see by proofe, that true the prouerbe is,
> Myght maisters right. (sig. I iv[v])

Rosko, despite his rascality, is an amusing fellow and shrewd enough. He doubts that his mistress can reform:

> Kytte wyll to kinde, of custome, or by chaunce.
> (sig. B ii[v])

This same proverb is quoted by Phallax to suggest that Cassandra, being Andrugio's sister, will be no more averse to wantonness than her brother, who is about to lose his head for that sweet sin, had been:

> The prouerbe sayth, that kyt wyll vnto kinde.
> (sig. C ii[v])

When his mistress is brought before Phallax and charged with leading an immoral life, Rosko refutes the charge with a remark which shows his familiarity with a somewhat shady proverb:

> *Byll.* In deede she is knowne for an ydle huswife.
> *Rosko.* He lyes, she is occupied day and night.
> (sig. D iv)

Phallax takes a fancy to Lamia and makes certain proposals of which Rosko bids his mistress be wary:

> He is a craftie childe, dally, but do not.
> (sig. D iv[v])

He reflects further on the integrity of Phallax:

> A holie Hoode, makes not a Frier deuoute.
> (sig. D iv[v])

After the successful termination of his scene with Grimball, to which we shall return, his victim thanks him, whereupon Rosko retorts:

> I see sometime, the blinde man hits a Crowe,
> He maye thanke me, that he is plagued soe.
> (sig. F iv[v])

His financial economy is based on the motto 'Easy come, easy go':

> Who gets a pace as meryly may spend.
> (sig. I i[v])

Phallax sends out his two officers, Gripax and Ripax, with the exhortation:

Byrds of a fether, best flye together. (sig. C i[v])

His own philosophy is simple:

Each shyft for one, (sig. C i[v])

and shared by Lamia's handmaiden, Dalia:

Euery man shyft for one. (sig. E iv)

Phallax has no trouble in divining the true inwardness of his patron's grief:

Feare not my Lorde, the olde Prouerbe doth saye,
Faynt harts doth steale fayre Ladyes seld away.
(sig. C ii)

Cassandra uses four proverbs, one of them twice. The unhappy lady is forced on two occasions to plead for the life of a loved one, first to Promos for her brother, and second to the king for that same Promos; each time she spurs herself to action in the same way:

Least grace come short, when starued is the steede.
(sig. B iv[v])

Whylst grasse, doth growe ofte sterues the seely steede.
(sig. L iv)

In the first instance one may suspect a printer's corruption rather than a wretched pun. She is given every reason to believe that Andrugio is dead and her honor lost without recompense. At first she thinks of suicide but then reflects:

That hast, weare more then speede. (sig. E iii)

Far better first to gain revenge. Her final proverb is a borrowing. Andrugio, in urging her to sacrifice her honor for his life, had said:

Here are two euyls, the best harde to digest,
But where as things are driuen vnto necessity,
There are we byd, of both euyls choose the least.
(sig. D ii)

In her formal complaint to the king she uses the same words to describe her predicament:

Two euils here were, one must I chuse, though bad were very best.
(sig. K i[v])

Andrugio employs two other proverbs. His approaching execution brings forth a proverb of resignation:

In vayne is hadywist. (sig. B iv)

Free, almost by a miracle, he hesitates to take another chance with death, for

Lyfe is sweete. (sig. L iv)

Lamia, thanks to the favor of Phallax, finds the ban on prostitutes a boon to her:

The match goes harde, which rayseth no mans gainc.
(sig. H iii)

After boasting of her good fortune she makes a remark the ambiguity of which is soon to be resolved:

But let them laugh, that wynneth in the ende.
(sig. H iii[v])

We have already mentioned Grimball, who is none other than our doubly old acquaintance Grim the Collier, borrowed by Whetstone from *Damon and Pithias* in order to gain for his own play the choice humor of the shaving scene. He brings with him a proverb from Edwards's play, this time with the proper name in better shape:

Bate me an ase, quoth *Boulton*. (sig. E iv[v])

He also has a new one:

> Ich haue hearde my great Grandsier saye:
> Maide will saye naye, and take it. (sig. F i)

While he was rummaging in *Damon and Pithias* Whetstone snapped up another unconsidered trifle, the Hangman, who, as in the earlier play, appears remarking:

> The wynd is yl, blowes no mans gaine. (sig. C iii)

Six other characters use one proverb each. Andrugio's jailer, having saved his life, urges him for both their sakes to escape at once:

> The prouerbe sayth, two may keepe counsell if that one be gone. (sig. E iii[v])

Polina, Andrugio's mistress, takes a vow to wash his tomb daily with her tears and is determined to fulfill her lachrymose obligation:

> Promise is debt. (sig. G iii)

The king orders a trusted courtier to investigate the city government. Ulrico feels that the king is wise in appointing him for the task; the king sees much,

> But as at Cheastes, though skylfull players play,
> Skyllesse vewers, may see, what they omyt. (sig. I ii)

One of the suitors for justice is a clown who has hitherto taken a cynical view of the courts:

> He that is rytch, as my dame sayth, goes away with the Hare. (sig. K iii)

When we consider the nature of the charge previously made against Andrugio there is a double edge to John Adroynes's remark to him:

> Kissyng and lying, ich see is all one. (sig. L i)

John Adroynes (John a Droyne) himself seems to be a proverbial figure, turning up as he does in Heywood.[5]

As Promos is being led to execution, Cassandra stops the procession for a fond farewell. The Marshall tries to comfort her and expedite matters:

Wherefore make vertue of necessity. (sig. M i)

Phallax uses eight sententious remarks. His high regard for his own ability is well expressed:

Well fare a head can take his tyme, nay watch for time I trow.
(sig. C i[v])

He tells Promos not to be surprised that Love should overcomc him:

Amor omnia vincit. (sig. C ii[v])

A fondness for Latin saws is one of his more amiable weaknesses, and appears on two other occasions:

Non bonus est, ludere cum sanctis.
The quietest, and the thryftiest course they say,
Is, not to checke, but prayse great mens amys.
(sig. D iii)

But O, O, *quid non pecunia?* (sig. H i)

He himself falls under the sway of the artful Lamia and begs her to return his affection:

And loue with loue ought to be answered styll.
(sig. D iv)

News comes of the king's impending visit, and Phallax directs preparations for a pageant in his honor. He suggests that the merchant tailors exhibit their show of Hercules, monsters, huge great giants, and added attractions such as lions, bears, bayards, and brocks (sig. G iv[v]) at the end of Duck Alley. The beadle of the tailors expostulates mildly that there will be many beggars there. Phallax's reply is calculated to impress any one who wants a large audience:

O, most attendaunce is, where beggers are.
(sig. H i)

He is exiled for his evil deeds and goes off philosophically:

> If thou can not where thou wouldst, lyue where thou maye.
> (sig. L iii)

He has new mischief in mind, one fears, for he says that he well knows where to go and his last words are:

> As the Deuilles lykes, the company of Friers,
> So flattrers loues as lyfe, to ioyne with lyers.
> (sig. L iii)

Cassandra reflects sadly on the misdemeanor which has lodged her brother in jail:

> O blynde affectes in loue, whose tormentes none can tell,
> Yet wantons wyll byde fyre, and frost, yea hassard death, nay hell:
> To taste thy sowre sweete frutes. (sig. B iii[v])

When Promos makes his wicked suggestion that she exchange her honor for her brother's life, she rejects it:

> Honor farre dearer is then life, which passeth price of golde.
> (sig. D i)

It is her fatal beauty which has brought her to this sorry pass:

> I meane my beautie breedes my bale, which many hold so deere.
> (sig. D i[v])

Andrugio takes, as is perhaps natural, a somewhat different view of the situation. He argues that this one unwilling lapse from virtue will not be held against her, but she replies:

> The Prouerbe saies, that tenne good turnes lye dead,
> And one yll deede, tenne tymes beyonde pretence,
> By enuious tongues, report abrode doth spread.
> (sig. D ii[v])

Won over at last she goes to Promos attired as a page, forcing herself to do something very distasteful to her:

No daunger feares the wight, prickt foorth by neede.
(sig. E i[v])

The sordid affair completed, she leaves Promos, wondering whether or not she can believe his oaths:

For louers feare not how they sweare, to wyn a Lady fayre,
And hauing wonne what they did wish, for othes nor Lady care.
(sig. E ii[v])

Oddly enough her conclusions are not unlike those being reached by Promos at about the same time:

And rage of Loue, for thousande oathes nyll spare,
More then are kept, when gotten is the game. (sig. E ii)

Promos employs four other sententious remarks. He finds that it is impossible to conceal his passion for Cassandra:

Doe what one can, fyre wyll breake forth I see.
(sig. C ii)

He fights in vain against what he terms 'blinde affected loue' (sig. C iv), but once conquered he woos, or threatens, Cassandra eagerly. He won't free her brother without some return:

In doubtfull warre, one prisoner still, doth set another free.
(sig. D i)

His only decent qualities appear in the speech he makes on his way to execution in which he expresses the hope that others may take warning from him:

Fresh harmes, they say, the viewers so apall,
As ofte they win, the wicked to amend. (sig. L iv[v])

Rosko is grieved when his mistress decides to discharge him:

They rewarde fayre (their haruest in the stacke),
When winter coms, that byd their seruaunts packe.
(sig. B ii[v])

She offers to give him a passport stating that he had been her servant, but he doubts the value of such a recommendation:

> O the Iudge, sylde showes the fauour,
> To let one theefe, bayle another. (sig. B ii[v])

He sympathizes not at all with Phallax when that worthy has fallen into Lamia's clutches:

> Who others doth deceyue,
> Deserues himselfe, lyke measure to receyue.
> (sig. F ii[v])

Those who enjoy the hospitality of his mistress's house fill their bodies at the expense of their purses:

> Each pleasure hath his payne. (sig. H i[v])

Andrugio warns Cassandra against rejecting Promos:

> Syster, that wise men loue we often see,
> And where loue rules, gainst thornes doth reason spurne.
> But who so loues, if he reiected be,
> His passing loue, to peeuish hate will turne. (sig. D ii)

We cannot feel that Andrugio shines in the early scenes, but he proves himself a man when he decides to risk death rather than see his sister suffer:

> Death, is but death, and all in fyne shall dye.
> (sig. L iv)

Polina pitifully suggests that other maidens learn from her:

> So that (fayre dames) from such consent, my accydents of harme,
> Forewarneth you, to keepe aloofe. (sig. F ii)

Like Cassandra she believes that Andrugio is really dead, and she daily weeps and prays before his cenotaph. She finds it hard to understand how she can continue to live:

> But as the reede doth bow at euery blast.
> To breake the same, when rowghest stormes lackes might,

So wretched I, with euery woe doe waste,
Yet care wants force, to kyll my hart out ryght. (sig. G iii)

Early in the play we see some prisoners led off to execution. They speak conventional warnings to the crowd. A hackster, or bully, confesses to murder:

Blood, axeth blood. (sig. C iii[v])

A female prisoner advises all others to

Shun pride, & sloth, the rootes of euery vice.
(sig. C iii[v])

Dalia goes to market for her mistress and is highly pleased with her ability to get credit:

Well fare credit when mony runneth low.
(sig. E iv)

Ulrico is shocked to find that all are not equal in the eyes or practice of the law:

These cunning Theeues, with lawe, can Lordships steale,
When for a sheepe, the ignoraunt are trust. (sig. I ii)

Phallax asks time before replying to the charges made against him. The king demands to know if he requires the respite to devise a cloak to hide a knave, and states that

Veritas non querit angulos. (sig. K i)

78

SIR CLYOMON AND SIR CLAMYDES
(*c.* 1578)

[Ed. W. W. Greg, Malone Society Reprints, 1913]
2238 lines: 8; 16; 8; 7

Suggestions relating to the authorship of *Sir Clyomon and Sir Clamydes* will be taken up in the discussion of Thomas Preston's *Cambyses* (see pp. 292 ff. below).

Subtle Shift, the Vice, speaks four of the eight proverbs, but his other proverbial material is negligible. When Clyomon invites him to enter his service he accepts the offer with an inappropriate proverb:

> I am like to a woman, say nay and take it.
> (sig. B i, l. 147)

Like most Vices he acknowledges his trickery to the audience, and finds two related proverbs to strengthen him in duplicity:

> But as the prouerbe saith, good fortune euer hapneth to the veryest knaue. (sig. B iv, l. 351)

> A sirra, the craftier knaue, the better lucke, thats plaine.
> (sig. D iv[v], l. 984)

A certain unwilling good nature leads him to offer himself as champion for the widowed queen of the Strange Marshes, but he speedily retreats:

> Of sufferance commeth ease.
> (sig. G iii, l. 1727)

The craven Bryan Sans Foy, a greater coward than Subtle Shift himself, hopes audibly that his disguise will enable him to outwit a proverb:

> Well, yet the old prouerbe to disproue, I purpose to begin,
> Which alwayes sayth, that cowardly hearts, faire Ladies neuer win.
> (sig. D ii[v], ll. 839 f.)

The shepherd Corin is glad that his own daughter is not like to be as speedily fruitful as neighbor Hodge's maid, of whose condition he remarks:

> Well let them laugh that win.
> (sig. F i, l. 1298)

Neronis, daughter to the king of the Strange Marshes, who has just escaped in male attire from the wicked king of Norway, meets with Corin and is taken into his service with such homely words that she philosophizes:

> Alas poore simple Shepheard, by this Princes may see,
> That like man, like talke, in euery degree.
> (sig. F i[v], ll. 1334 f.)

When Neronis's father dies in vain pursuit of his kidnapped daughter, his bereaved queen finds herself confronted with the danger of losing the kingdom to her brother-in-law Mustantius. Alexander the Great, conveniently present, arranges a compromise, which Mustantius accepts on the principle that:

> Well better half then nought at all.
> (sig. G iii[v], l. 1773)

The sententious remarks are not very distinguished. Clamydes, as his vicissitudes demand, attacks Fortune twice:

> Fye on fell fortune she,
> Which hath her wheele of froward chance, thus whirled back on me.
> (sig. D iii[v], ll. 886 f.)

> Ah cruell Fortune why shouldst thou thus wrest my chance amis:
> Knowing I do but honour seeke, and thou doest me defame,
> In that contrary mine exspect, thou all things seekes to frame.
> (sigs. D iii[v]–D iv, ll. 921 ff.)

Clyomon has a like complaint against that cruel and uncertain goddess:

> Ah fortune fickle dame,
> That canst make glad and so soone sad, a Knight of worthie fame.
> (sig. E iv, ll. 1217 f.)

Clyomon dashes into one of his least promising, and, we may add, least sensible, adventures with the remark that

> The bolder the attempt is, more fame it doth bring.
> (sig. C i[v], l. 461)

One of King Alexander's lords advises him to place his faith in God:

> For vaine is trust, that in himselfe, man doth repose we see.
> (sig. B iv[v], l. 389)

Subtle Shift, passing himself off as Knowledge, does not hesitate to speak better of his actions than they deserve:

> A true seruant you may see will deceiue his maister neuer.
> (sig. D iii[v], l. 913)

Neronis favors us with a long passage, of which the first lines are a sufficient quotation, to the general effect that love is little help to a lady whose knight must leave her:

> How can that tree but withered be
> That wanteth sap to moist the roote?
> (sig. D iv[v], ll. 992 f.)

79

THE RARE TRIUMPHS OF LOVE AND FORTUNE (1582–1583)

[Ed. W. W. Greg, Malone Society Reprints, 1930]
1857 lines: 7; 11; 7; 13

The Rare Triumphs of Love and Fortune in which two lovers, Hermione and Fidelia, suffer much distress to illustrate the opposing powers of Love and Fortune, is by no means devoid of proverbial material, but we do not find it brought in for any definite purpose. There are very few proverbial phrases, and the proverbs are not used in such a way as to point up any characters. The two lovers are separated by Fidelia's envious brother Armenio, and she flees her father's palace determined

> In case extreame [to] make vertue of a neede.
> (sig. D i, l. 781)

She meets the aged Bomelio, her lover's father, also in exile, and in due course they are joined by Hermione himself. Now she is happy indeed and says that even Ulysses, who, in all his troubles, was

> Prouiding still for afterclaps,
> (sig. F iii[v], l. 1478)

could be no more exultant, when safe at last, than she is.

Venus employs two proverbs, the first of which suggests that even in love a certain decorum is essential:

> But such as clime before they crale, must drink the sweet with sower.
> (sig. A iii[v], l. 132)

Again she speaks with what for her must be great restraint:

> A woman must a little haue her will.
> (sig. F iv[v], l. 1557)

Armenio brings about Hermione's banishment and gloats over his success but the hero rebukes him for his unfeeling scorn:

> Loosers they say may easily be forborne.
> (sig. B iv[v], l. 466)

The comedy, for what it is worth, is furnished by Lentulo, Bomelio's servant, and Penulo the parasite. Lentulo and Penulo meet and the servant succeeds in tricking the parasite, whereupon the latter loftily remarks:

> I perceiue a wise man of a foole ouertaken may be.
> (sig. C iv[v], l. 726)

Lentulo gets a verbal revenge late in the play when he is able to silence Penulo with the proverb:

> A fooles bolte is soone enough shot.
> (sig. G iii[v], l. 1778)

Hermione discovers that his father is an adept in magic and determines to destroy his books, wondering piously how one can have such awful secrets and still preserve an outward serenity:

> O Gods that deepest greefes are felt in closest smart,
> That in the smiling countenance may lurk the wounded hart.
> I see the noble minde can counterfaite a blisse,
> When ouerwhelmed with a care his soule perplexed is.
> (sig. F i, ll. 1334 ff.)

After his reunion with Fidelia he carries on in two sententious passages:

> How doubtfull are the lets of loyall loue,
> Great be the dangers that true louers proue.
> But when the Sunne after a shower of raine,
> Breakes through the Clowdes, and shoes his might againe.
> More comfortable to his glory then,
> Because it was a while withheld of men.
> Peace after warre is pleasenter we finde,
> A ioy differd is sweeter to the minde.
> So I. (sig. F iii, ll. 1465 ff.)

> Then as the Turtle that hath found her mate,
> Forgets her former woes and wretched state.
> Renewing now her drowping hart againe,
> Because her pleasure ouercomes her paine.
> The same of thy desired sight I make,
> Whereon thy faith, thy hart and hand I take.
> (sig. F iii[v], ll. 1485 ff.)

Before any sorrow comes upon them Hermione and Fidelia argue in stichomythia about love, and she expresses fear

> Least change of ayre should change the absent minde.
> (sig. B ii, l. 290)

Fear, as she confesses to Bomelio in the forest, is an integral part of her nature as it is of any woman's:

> O Father still I feare mishap behinde,
> Suspect is naturall vnto our kinde.

> And perils that import a mans decay,
> Can neuer be estewed too soone they say.
> (sig. F iii, ll. 1444 ff.)

King Phizantius does not share his son's unreasoning hate for Hermione but does consider him too low for the hand of a princess:

> Unequall loue is enemie to rest.
> (sig. B iv[v], l. 451)

He sends him away unharmed and, subsequent events causing him to repent his clemency, when he captures the lovers again, he declares:

> Sometime pardon breedes a second ill.
> (sig. G ii[v], l. 1701)

At once, however, Venus and Fortune, as *deae ex machina*, appear and tell the awe-struck king that Hermione is really of noble birth, son of the falsely exiled and good Bomelio. The case is promptly altered.

Penulo says of the strife between Fidelia and Armenio:

> I haue heard it saide there is no hate,
> Like to a brother or a sisters if they fall at debate.
> (sig. E iii[v], ll. 1202 f.)

He contrasts her love for Hermione with her hate for her brother:

> A right woman, either loue like an Angell,
> Or hate like a Deuill, in extreames so to dwell.
> (sig. E iv, ll. 1267 f.)

Venus compares herself to Fortune. Fortune pulls down those who have been happy; surely it is less unkind for Venus to refrain from making some happy:

> For they that neuer tasted blisse, mislike not their anoye.
> (sig. A iii[v], l. 112)

Fortune is impressed by the transitoriness of created things:

> Is not the wonder of the World a woork that soon decayes:
> Therfore ye see all earthly thinges, are wearing out alwaies.
> (sig. A iv, ll. 165 f.)

When Bomelio meets Fidelia he hopes to be able to cheer her with his sad tale:

> O, I haue heard it saide our sorrowes are the lesse,
> If in our anguish we may finde a partner in distresse.
> (sig. D ii, ll. 823 f.)

Armenio is able to close the play in a proper state of repentance:

> See what proceedeth from vnstable youth,
> Shame to him selfe, and to his freendes a cause of ruthe.
> (sig. G iv, ll. 1803 f.)

80

FEDELE AND FORTUNIO, THE TWO ITALIAN GENTLEMEN (1584)

[Ed. Percy Simpson, Malone Society Reprint, 1909 and Supplement, 1933]
1900 lines: 26; 21; 36; 23

Fedele and Fortunio, now at last available in its entirety, may or may not be the work of Anthony Munday, but it is certainly the product of a proverb-loving author. The character employing the most proverbs is the cowardly Captain Crackstone, one of whose attractions is his cheerful misuse of words: 'This is as excrement for my proposition as can be desirde' (sig. B ii[v], l. 125); 'my learning with my reparrell goes off and on' (sig. D iv, l. 815); 'that victorious Prince of battaile god Marche-beere' (sig. F iii[v], l. 1393); 'I am not strong Sampier' (sig. F iii[v], l. 1397); 'Maister Pediculus, or

Pedantonie, I am not very prospect in your namc' (to Pedante) (sig. G i[v], l. 1524). He is no less free with his proverbs:

> I am as wearie of my cariage as a Dogge of his day.
> (sig. F iv[v], l. 1448)

> Thou knowest the paruerbe, no body taries for the tide.
> (sig. G i, l. 1486)

We also find a proverbial phrase and a sententious remark in Crackstonian disguise:

> When two bones are at strife for a dog, it is commonly seen:
> That the third comes and takes it, and wipes their mouthes cleen.
> (sig. B i[v], ll. 53 f.)

> I thought some strawes were in the pad. (sig. B ii, l. 70)

His remaining proverbs are in more orthodox form. He tries to persuade Fortunio to disclose his secret:

> Nothing venture nothing haue. (sig. B i, l. 17)

He plans treacherously to woo the fair Victoria for himself:

> First come, first seru'd.
> (sig. B ii[v], l. 127)

He is constant in self-admonition:

> And therefore while time serues me to take the same I were best,
> (sig. D iv, l. 819)

and he has all the confidence of one who has been wrapped in his mother's smock:

> Giue me good luck and throw mee into the Seas.
> (sig. D iv[v], l. 859)

Even capture and the disgrace of being led captive in a net cannot diminish the ebullience of his hopeful spirits:

> T'is the Fortune of warre, lucke runnes not euer to one side.
> (sig. F iii[v], l. 1395)

He vows to win Victoria's complacence or give her a good thrashing:

You know loue is a fire, and they say fire and water hath no mercy.
(sig. G i[v], l. 1536)

Finally convinced that he cannot succeed, he takes his customary refuge in proverbial philosophy:

He that eats with the deuil without a long spoone, his fare wil be ill.
(sig. G iv, l. 1730)

Pedante, Fedele's tutor, is not far behind the gallant captain in the employment of proverbs. He encourages Fedele to prosecute his suit:

Faint hart neuer wun faire Lady they say.
(sig. C ii[v], l. 419)

To harp on one string is obnoxious to him:

It is too Cuckolike they say, one song continually to sing.
(sig. E i[v], l. 948)

He devises a plan whereby Fortunio is to be deceived into thinking that Victoria has granted her favors somewhat too freely:

Pedante. See what an olde Fox these rotten ragges shrowds,
I can play the knaue and conuay it in the clowdes.
But heare you Sir?
Fedele. What saist thou?
Pedante. Hould fast Master Fortunio, til I be out of his reach,
Lest he cut me in peeces when he heares me preach.
(sig. E ii[v], ll. 1005 ff.)

This is beyond doubt a reference to the proverb 'When the fox preaches beware the geese.' As his scheme begins to go a little amiss he bolsters his courage with two proverbs:

Witte bought at this rate is an excellent treasure.
Beginnings are harde, this prouerbe is olde.
(sig. E iii, ll. 1049 f.)

For his own purposes he calls Crackstone a courageous captain and gallant gentleman and asks for his confidence:

True me & trust me.
(sig. G i[v], l. 1529)

The next proverb which he directs at the Captain is not so agreeable:

As you brew, so bake.
(sig. G iv[v], l. 1762)

He is willing to take the sorceress Medusa in marriage:

Like vnto like, and learning to skill.
(sig. H i, l. 1788)

Victoria has fallen out of love with Fedele and, characteristically feminine, accuses him of remaining too long in Spain:

Delay breeds losse. (sig. B iv[v], l. 260)

She was afraid that he would cease to love her:

And absence put me out of minde, that shut me out of sight.
(sig. B iv[v], l. 262)

She tries by sorcery to win Fortunio's love. When this is discovered by Fedele she declares brazenly that she has loved Fedele all the time and, poor innocent, is being asked to endure a great deal:

But pacience is a vertue, as the woorthiest wits doo say.
(sig. D ii[v], l. 723)

She expects that Time will vindicate her:

More you shall know when time hath tried, my truth by perfect tuch.
(sig. D iii, l. 738)

Four other characters use one proverb each. Attilia, maid to Victoria, does not yield readily to Pedante's blandishments:

Great barkers are none of the greatest biters.
(sig. B ii[v], l. 111)

Fedele explains his long absence to Victoria:

Need hathe no lawe. (sig. B iv[v], l. 266)

The same proverb is spoken by Virginia's father, Ottaviano, when circumstances make him all too certain that his daughter would do well to marry:

Neede hath no lawe.
(sig. G iii[v], l. 1664)

Medusa has no patience with lovers who do not have foresight:

But swimme against the tide, and then repent when tis too late.
(sig. C i, l. 303)

When we come to the sententious remarks we find Pedante with twelve out of twenty-three, all coming, curiously enough, in the first half of the play. Seven of these are Latin sentences exhibiting the learning of which he is proud:

In via virtutis non progredi, regredi est. (sig. B iii, l. 142)

Quod iuuat exiguum est, plus est quod lædit amantes.
(sig. B iii, l. 165)

Degeneres animos timor arguit. (sig. C ii[v], l. 418)

Amor odit inertes. (sig. C ii[v], l. 420)

Ridetur chorda qui semper aberrat eadem.
(sig. E i[v], l. 946)

Littore quot conchæ, tot sunt in amore dolores.
(sig. E ii, l. 968)

Accidit in puncto, quod non contingit in anno.
(sig. E ii, l. 980)

Love of women, he tells Fedele, has no sound basis:

A beautifull face,
Which no otherwise vanisheth, and away dooth goe:
Then water, that neuer returnes to the spring,
From whence it did flowe. (sig. B iii, ll. 156 ff.)

At one point he is almost tempted to remove the strength of his counsel from Fedele,

> And let you alone till you are beaten with your owne rod.
> (sig. B iii, l. 175)

His tune changes, however, and he bids his master not to take repulses to heart:

> Did I neuer teach you: That a woman denies that in showe,
> Which in deed shee desires. (sig. C iii, ll. 467 f.)

In a moment he is forced to urge restraint:

> You are to hasty a Soldier, too the battaile to goe,
> If you will be reuenged ere your enemy you knowe.
> (sig. C iii[v], ll. 477 f.)

His feigned love for Attilia seems at one time to be changing into something real:

> For loue is a Fox, he beginneth at first by dalliance and play:
> Then encreaseth his gettings euery day. (sig. D iii, ll. 763 f.)

Captain Crackstone admonishes Fortunio to get counsel while he can:

> For when the Cooke is out of the way, you must goe supperlesse to bed. (sig. B i, l. 22)

He thinks himself a great favorite with the ladies:

> Where women take a pitch, it is easy to please.
> (sig. D iv[v], l. 860)

He finds that the force of love operates strangely in him, bringing him, indeed, to assume a beggar's gown:

> See the force of loue, how it is able for a neede,
> To shrowde a braue minde in a base kinde of weede.
> (sig. G i[v], ll. 1522 f.)

Ere long the scene shifts and he finds himself betrayed and rejected:

> I haue heard it often, and nowe I do proue,
> That women are suttle wormes for the conuariance of loue.
> (sig. G iv, ll. 1706 f.)

Fedele levels three sentences at women:

> Constant in naught, but in inconstancie. (sig. D ii, l. 664)
>
> He plowghes the seas, and fishes in the lande,
> And loseth all the labour of them both,
> He fondly reares his fortresse on the sande.
> That buildes his trust vpon a womans troth.
> (sig. D ii, ll. 683 ff.)
>
> Busie they are with pen to write our vices in our face,
> But negligent to knowe the blemish of their owne disgrace.
> (sig. E i[v], ll. 938 f.)

At the end, which is brought about with a rare lack of probability, Fedele renews his suit to Victoria and begs for peace:

> T'is seldome seen but warres haue end, when foes are ouerthrown.
> (sig. G iv, l. 1726)

Fortunio opens the play with a long sententious remark:

> He that discloseth to a freend the secrets of his minde:
> Dooth rob him selfe of libertie, besides we dayly finde,
> That others councels wil by such in euery eare be blowen:
> As haue no power when time requires, to smother all their owne.
> (sig. B i, ll. 1 ff.)

Attilia sums up the whole plot:

> Loe heer the common fault of looue, to followe her that flyes:
> And flye from her that makes persuite, with loud lamenting cryes.
> (sig. C i, ll. 298 f.)

The large number of miscellaneous proverbial phrases bears witness to a raciness of language which helps to redeem the artificiality and absurdity of the plot and chief characters. Another point worthy of mention is Fedele's eighteen line description of Victoria (sig. B iv, ll. 224 ff.), which contains approximately a comparison to a line, most of them very inept; it seems like a parody but probably is not.

81

Robert Wilson's *THE COBBLER'S PROPHECY* (before 1594)

[Ed. A. C. Wood and W. W. Greg, Malone Society Reprints, 1914]
1696 lines (poetry and prose): 1; 22; 4; 8

Robert Wilson's confused and uninteresting play *The Cobbler's Prophecy*, printed in 1594 but doubtless written much earlier, makes a weak note on which to close our chapter on early English comedy, but its very deficiencies are revealing. This play of medium length contains but a single proverb, four miscellaneous proverbial phrases, and eight sententious remarks, and yet there are more comparisons, most of them stereotyped rather than proverbial, than in any other comedy which we have considered. The proverb is directed at Venus by her paramour Contempt — surely as curious a union as heart could wish! — when the goddess objects to a spittle as the safest place for her lying-in. Why, gentle Venus, he remonstrates, don't be so fastidious:

> What thinke ye as the Prouerb goes that beggers haue no lice?
> (sig. D iii, l. 836)

This saying, of which I know no other instance, has been connected [6] with 'Sue a beggar and catch a louse,' but this association is not completely justified.

The sententious remarks are nearly all used by Ralph, the cobbler turned prophet, and Venus. Ralph hears the scholar speak Latin and comments, no doubt with a reference to the story of Apelles and the shoemaker:

> Nay and you speake Latin, reach me my laste.
> (sig. B iii[v], l. 307)

He's by no means sure that the scholar is what he seems:

For all are not sober that goes in blacke.
(sig. B iii[v], l. 313)

When he declares that

All men are but morter,
(sig. D ii[v], l. 812)

only the need for a rime with 'porter' seems to have kept the last word from being 'mortal.' Once his prophetship is over he returns to his humble station:

I, I, and great folke doo amisse,
Poore folke must hold their peace.
(sig. G iii, ll. 1660 f.)

Venus is in an unhappy mood throughout the play. To Contempt she says:

So shall our pleasures haue a bitter end.
(sig. D ii[v], l. 822)

When Mars, with more reason than he knows, chides her, she asks him:

And know you not, vnkindnes kills a woman?
(sig. E i, l. 984)

Even in song she is unable to throw off her gloom:

Yet in cheefe sweetes lies hid a secret snare.
(sig. E i, l. 1004)

The remaining sententious remark is used by the scholar, who is determined not to say too much:

They are fooles that in secret affaires are too familiar.
(sig. B iv, ll. 368 f.)

CHAPTER V

EARLY ENGLISH TRAGEDIES

THE PLAYS which we are considering as specimens of early tragedy in English are easily divided into two groups: first, those which, like *Ferrex and Porrex*, *Gismond of Salerne*, and *Arthur* are purely classical, that is, Senecan in form; and, second, those like *Apius and Virginia*, *Horestes*, and *Cambyses* which contain native English material mainly in the shape of comic scenes centered around the Vice. Our previous investigations would have been vain if we did not approach these plays with the lively expectation of discovering a considerable amount of proverbial material in any play which has humorous scenes and which numbers a Vice among its characters. This is precisely what we do find in the plays of the second group while those of the first are utterly devoid of popular proverbial material though they do contain many sententious passages spread with an ample and dismal Senecan hand.

Thomas Sackville and Thomas Norton's *FERREX AND PORREX* (1561)

[Tudor Facsimile Texts, 1908]
1794 lines: 0; 3; 0; 19

Ferrex and Porrex, better known as *Gorboduc*, in which Thomas Sackville and Thomas Norton drew on Geoffrey of Monmouth and Seneca to hold a monitory mirror up to Queen Elizabeth, is a sufficiently typical English Senecan play, and an absence of proverbial material is among its typical features. There are no proverbs, none of the miscellaneous proverbial phrases which can add some life to the dullest tirade, and only three comparisons. There are, to be sure, nineteen sententious remarks, but they are used without regard to character and with but little regard to situation. The only person of importance who does not contribute at least one sententious remark is the queen and the greatest number, four, are used by the Chorus, while Gorboduc, Eubulus, and Arostos come next with three each. Under the circumstances it does not seem worth while to do more than to list the passages in order of occurrence and to indicate the various speakers.

And often ouerkindly tendernesse
Is mother of vnkindly stubbornenesse.
(Philander, sig. B iii[v])

Good is I graunt of all to hope the best,
But not to liue still dreadlesse of the worst.
(Eubulus, sig. C i)

The stickes, that sondred brake so soone in twaine,
In faggot bounde attempted were in vaine.
(Chorus, sig. C ii [in allusion to first dumb show])

Ah loue, my frendes? loue wrongs not whom he loues.
(Ferrex, sig. C iii[v])

Was this not wrong, yea yll aduised wrong,
To giue so mad a man so sharpe a sworde.
(Hermon, sig. C iii[v])

Know ye, that lust of kingdomes hath no law.
(Hermon, sig. D i)

Mischiefe for mischiefe is a due reward.
(Porrex, sig. D iii)

Oh no man happie, till his ende be seene.
(Gorboduc, sig. D iv)

But timely knowledge may bring timely helpe.
(Arostus, sig. D iv[v])

The fire not quenched, but kept in close restraint,
Fedde still within, breakes forth with double flame.
(Gorboduc, sig. E i[v])

The lust of kingdome knowes no sacred faith,
No rule of reason, no regarde of right,
No kindely loue, no feare of heauens wrath.
(Chorus, sig. E ii[v])

Your grace should now in these graue yeres of yours
Haue found ere this the price of mortall ioyes,
How short they be, how fading here in earth,
How full of chaunge, how brittle our estate,
Of nothing sure, saue onely of the death,
To whom both man and all the world doth owe
Their end at last. (Arostus, sig. F ii[v])

Many can yelde right sage and graue aduise
Of pacient sprite to others wrapped in woe,
And can in speche both rule and conquere kinde,
Who if by proofe they might feele natures force,
Would shew them selues men as they are in deede.
(Gorboduc, sig. F iii)

Blood asketh blood, and death must death requite.
(Chorus, sig. F iv[v])

And happy he that can in time beware
By others harmes and turne it to his good.
(Chorus, sig. G i)

These violent thinges may haue no lasting long.
(Eubulus, sig. G ii[v])

Yet doubtfull is the chaunce of battailles ioyned.
(Fergus, sig. G iii[v])

For right will last, and wrong can not endure.
(Arostus, sig. H ii)

For right will alwayes liue, and rise at length,
But wrong can neuer take deepe roote to last.
(Eubulus, sig. H iii[v])

83

John Pickering's *THE HISTORY OF HORESTES* (1567)

[Tudor Facsimile Texts, 1910]

1206 lines: 13; 5; 17; 15

John Pickering's *History of Horestes* must be considered a tragedy, despite the fact that all ends well for the titular hero. As in the other early English tragedies of the native type, the Vice plays a prominent part and minor comic characters, such as a pair of rustics and the soldiers Haltersick and Hempstring, are not wanting. The distribution of proverbial material is exactly what we expect. The Vice, who is not named in the list of players, but who calls himself variously Patience (sig. A iii), Courage (sig. B i), and Revenge (sig. C iv), employs ten of the thirteen proverbs, three of the five comparisons, eight of the seventeen other proverbial phrases, and three of the fifteen sententious remarks. He becomes needlessly indignant with Rusticus and Hodge and would gladly fight them, even were it to jeopardize a joint:

> But two is to meyney, the prouerbe douth tell.
> (sig. A iii)

He declares that his name is Patience and Hodge understands 'Past Shame,' which has just enough truth to evoke a coarse proverb from the Vice:

> Tell a mare a tall, and shyell gerd out a fart.
> (sig. A iii)

Again he becomes angry but again decides that discretion is the better part:

> It is best to be styll,
> Good slepinge in a hole skynne, ould foulkes do saye.
> (sig. A iii[v])

With due regard for that same skin he starts a quarrel between Rusticus and Hodge, urging the former to pay no heed to Hodge's expostulations:

> These wordes be but wynd.
> (sig. A iv)

He presses Orestes to ask Idumeus's aid without delay, and emphasizes the point by means of three proverbs:

> Faull to it then and slacke no time, for tyme once past away,
> Doth cause repentence, but to late to com old foulks do say.
> When stede is stolen, to late it is to shyt the stable dore.
> Take time I say, while time doth giue a leasure good therfore.
> (sig. B i)

The proverb about the stolen steed and stable door is a favorite with him, and he uses it twice more, once to Clytemnestra and again when he announces that Orestes, having killed his mother, is beginning to rue the deed:

> It is to late,
> When stede is stollen for you in south, to shut the stable gate.
> (sig. D i[v])

> Nowe ites to late;
> To shut the gate;
> Horestes gines to rew. (sig. D iii[v])

Hodge seems to allude to the proverb 'Each look out for one' when he declares that in case of war he'll

> Zaue one I tro. (sig. A ii)

There would also appear to be a hint of a familiar proverb in the counsel which Idumeus gives to Orestes:

> Take them forth with, & forward go, let slyp no time ne tyd,
> For chaunce to leasure to be bound, I tell you can not byd.
> (sig. B ii)

Hempstring taunts Haltersick with 'boy,' which angers the hero, and he replies that size does not count:

> A hart is worth all. (sig. B iii)

Orestes uses one of his sententious remarks twice:

For this is true that bloud for bloud, my fathers deth doth craue. (sig. B iv[v])

Blud for blud my fathers deth doth craue. (sig. D ii)

When Menelaus charges him with undue severity in his invasion, he replies:

It is no iest when sodyares ioyne, to fight within a felde. (sig. E i)

His people present him with a glowing account of their prosperity under his beneficent rule, and he brings the meeting to a close with the remark that

Time wil haue an end. (sig. E iii[v])

Idumeus laments the murder of Agamemnon in his own home, especially since he might have expected better things once

He . . . had past the fate of war, where chaunce was equall set. (sig. B i[v])

He issues a warning against self-confidence and lack of deliberation:

For ouer rashe in doinge ought, doth often damage bringe,
Therfore take councell first before, thou dost anye thinge. (sig. C i[v])

When Menelaus waxes emotional over the sad fate of Clytemnestra, Idumeus strives to sooth him:

Sease of syr kyng leaue morning, lo, nought can it you auaylle. (sig. E i [v])

The Vice determines to meet Menelaus in Athens as soon as possible and he shows himself a man of learning:

Auxilia humilia firma, consensus facit, this allwayes prouided
That consent maketh suckers more sure for to be. (sig. D iv)

The marriage of Orestes reduces him to beggary but fails to crush his spirit:

> Who is meryer, then the pooryste sort? (sig. E ii)

He confesses that in his rôle of Revenge he finds most favor with the women; he tells the sad story of Socrates, Xantippe, and the water jug and concludes by advising the audience not to try to keep women from talking:

> Remembar my wordes, and beare it in mynde;
> What suffer the myll, a whyle to be clackinge,
> Yf that you intend, aney ease for to fynde. (sig. E iii)

Fame utters two allied sayings:

> *Ab alio expectes, alteri quod feceris.*
> For loke what mesure thou dost meate, the same againe shalbe,
> At other tyme at others hand, repayde againe to the. (sig. D iv)

> Therefore I wyshe eache wight to do, to others as he would,
> That they in lyke occasion, vnto him offer should. (sig. D iv)

Truth commends herself in proper style:

> Yée Truth, the daughter of Tyme, wyll it seke,
> And so in a tyme, it wyll be diseryde. (sig. E iv)

Haltersick threatens Hempstring with dire consequences if he continues to move him to ire:

> Colles neauer bourne, tyll they be set one fyare.
> (sig. B iii)

84

GISMOND OF SALERNE IN LOVE (1567–1568)

[Ed. J. W. Cunliffe in *Early English Classical Tragedies*, Oxford, 1912, pp. 163 ff.)
1551 lines: 1; 8; 0; 26

The tragedy of *Gismond of Salerne in Love*, in which five gentlemen of the Inner Temple showed themselves capable of spoiling one of the more moving tales in the *Decameron*, is as devoid of popular proverbial material as was *Ferrex and Porrex*. It is possible that the following lines, spoken by Lucrece to Tancred, allude clumsily enough to the proverb 'Youth will have ruth':

> Such stern hardnesse ne ought ye to require
> In her, whoes gentle hart and tender yeres
> Yet flouring in her chefest lust of youth
> Is led of force to feele the whote desires
> That fall vnto that age, and asketh ruthe
> Of your wonted fatherly tendre Loue.
> (p. 178, ll. 24 ff.)

For the rest we have a handful of comparisons and a considerable number of heavy sententious passages which I list in the order of their occurrence:

> Loe I . . .
> Am that great god of loue that with my might
> Do rule the world, and euerie liuing thing.
> This one hand beares vain hope, short ioyfull state,
> With faire semblance the louer to allure:
> This other holdes repentance all to late,
> Warr, fiër, blood, and paines without recure.
> (Cupid, p. 167, ll. 1 ff.)

> Loue rules the world, Loue onely is the Lorde.
> (Cupid, p. 169, l. 68)

> Oh vaine vnstedfast state of mortall thinges!
> Who trustes the world doeth leane to brittle stay.
> Such fickle frute his flattering blome forth bringes;
> Ere it be ripe it falleth to decaye.
> (Gismond, p. 169, ll. 1 ff.)

> Such bootelesse plaint as hath no timely end
> Doeth but heape grefe to geue new cause to waile.
> (Tancred, p. 171, ll. 3 f.)

> The more yow ar with hard misshappe besett,
> The more your patience shewes a constant hart.
> (Tancred, p. 171, ll. 23 f.)

> A noble hart eche happ can well endure.
> (Tancred, p. 172, l. 44)

Let reason work in yow which time doeth bring
To meanest wittes, whome time doeth teache to beare
The greatest illes. (Tancred, p. 173, ll. 62 ff.)

The diuerse happes which allwayes work our care,
Our ioy so farr, our woe so nere at hand,
Haue long ere this and dayly do declare
The fickle fote on which our state doeth stand.
Whoe plantes his pleasures here to gather roote,
And hopes his happy life will still endure,
Let him behold how death with stealing fote
Steppes in when he shall think his ioyes most sure.
No raunsom serues for to redeme our dayes.
(Chorus, p. 173, ll. 1 ff.)

Our life is but a floure,
Though it be decked with honor and renoune,
Which growes to day in fauor of the heuen,
Nursed with the sonne, and with the showers swete,
Plucked with the hand it withereth yet ere euen.
(Chorus, pp. 173 f., ll. 15 ff.)

Here fortune rules, whoe, when she list to play,
Whirleth her whele and bringes the hye full lowe,
To morrow takes what she hath geuen to day,
To shew she can aduaunce and ouerthrowe.
Not Euripus vnquiet flood so oft
Ebbes in a day, and floweth to and froe,
As fortunes change pluckes down that was aloft,
And minges our mortall ioy with mortall woe.

Whoes case is such, that from his coate he may
Behold afarre the change that chaunceth here,
How sone they rise, how sone they do decay
That leane their states on fortunes slipper sphere,
Whoe liues alôwe, and feleth not the strokes
Of stormes with which the hyëst toures do fall,
Nc blustring windes with which the stoutest okes
Stoupen full lowe, his life is surest of all.
For he may scorne fortune, that hath no power
On him that is content with his estate.
He seketh not her swete, ne feares her sower,
But liues alône within his bounded rate,
And marking how these worldly thinges do wade,
Reioseth to him self, and laughes to see

The follie of mortal men, how they haue made
Fortune a god, and placed her in the skye.
(Chorus, pp. 174 f., ll. 37 ff.)

Of gladsome youth how fleting is the course,
How sone the fading floure of beautie dyes,
How time ones past may neuer haue recourse,
No more than may the running streames reuert
To climbe the hilles when they ben ones downrolled
Amidde the hollow vales. There is no art,
No worldly power, no not the goddes can hold
The swey of flëing time, nor him reuoke
When he is past: all thinges vnto his might
Parforce must bend, and yeld vnto the stroke
Of time. (Gismond, p. 175, ll. 10 ff.)

Scarce can yow now among a thowsand finde
One stedfast hart: we all delight in new.
(Chorus, p. 182, ll. 39 f.)

From sparkes encreasced by blast a blasing flame
Shall showe, how Loue can kindle hartes with heate,
And wast the oken brest to cinder dust.
(Cupid, pp. 182 f., ll. 4 ff.)

So shall they ioy in tasting of the swete,
To make them iudge more felingly the grefe
That bitter bringes, and, when their ioy shall flete,
Endure redobled dole without relefe.
(Cupid, p. 183, ll. 17 ff.)

Pitie, that moueth euerie gentle hart
To rue their grefe which be distressed in paine,
Enforceth me to waile my ladies smart.
(Claudia, p. 183, ll. 1 ff.)

For nedes the louer must esteme that well
Which cometh from her with whom his hart doth dwell.
(Guishard, p. 186, ll. 39 f.)

Cupide ne sought him not: for he is blinde.
(Chorus, p. 188, l. 27)

Loue that blinded boy. (Megera, p. 190, l. 19)

Ease him . . . whom frowning fortunes whele
Hath throwen in depe distresse of farr more pinching paine.
(Tancred, p. 191, ll. 14 f.)

But greater lord is loue, and larger reigne
He hath vpon eche god and mortal wight,
Than yow vpon your subiectes haue, or I
Vpon my self. (Guishard, p. 200, ll. 36 ff.)

Blind Cupide. (Chorus, p. 202, l. 17)

For drede of thinges vnknowen doeth allway cause
Man drede the worst, till he the better know.
(Chorus, p. 204, ll. 35 f.)

For violent is death when he deuoures
Yongmen or virgins while their youth is grene.
(Renuchio, p. 207, ll. 131 f.)

But inust fortune, that so seld vpheaues
The worthy man, hath blindly turned her whele:
The whurle wherof bothe life and honor reaues
From him, on whome she did so lately smile.
(Renuchio, p. 207, ll. 133 ff.)

But date of death that fixed is so fast,
Beyond his course there may no wight extend.
(Renuchio, p. 207, ll. 145 f.)

But what auaileth plaint? it is but breath
Forwasted all in vain. (Renuchio, p. 209, ll. 211 f.)

In 1591 Robert Wilmot, who had written the last act, issued the play 'newly reuiued and polished according to the decorum of these daies.' Wilmot made additions and revisions throughout and although he tampered, usually to its betterment, with the sententious matter, there is nothing in his revision to make it valuable or interesting for our present purpose.

85

Thomas Preston's *CAMBYSES KING OF PERSIA* (1569–1570)

[Tudor Facsimile Texts, 1910, from edition of *c.* 1584]
1254 lines: 4; 6; 11; 7

Thomas Preston's play *Cambyses* was licensed between July, 1569 and July, 1570. A passage in the play, hitherto apparently unnoticed in this connection, suggests that it was composed shortly after September 5, 1569. After Cambyses has added the murder of his wife to his crimes, even Ambidexter inveighs against him with what seems like honest indignation:

> What a King was he that hath vsed such tiranny?
> He was akin to Bishop Bonner, I think verily.
> For both their delights was to shed blood:
> But neuer intended to doo any good. (sig. F iii[v])

Of course this reference to Bonner could have been written at any time after his fall from power, but it seems more likely that it was his death, early in September, 1569, which brought him so strongly to Preston's mind.

The play is not especially rich in proverbs but three of the four are spoken by the Vice, Ambidexter. He also uses three of the eleven miscellaneous proverbial phrases and two of the seven sententious remarks. He runs away when Meretrix beats Snuf and Ruf, later remarking:

> It is wisdome (quoth I) by the masse to saue one.
> (sig. B iv)

He helps turn the wavering viceroy, Sisamnes, to bribery and evil ways:

> Ye are vnwise if ye take not time while ye may:
> If ye wil not now when ye would ye shall haue nay.
> (sig. B iv)

He is not beyond a moral verdict of his own, and, forgetting that he himself was the only begetter of the crime, is a little shocked when Cambyses orders his brother's murder:

> The proverbe olde is verified, soone ripe and soone rotten.
> (sig. D iii[v])

Sisamnes, as soon as he has been delegated royal power, begins to play with the idea of turning it to evil uses. He uses the proverbial phrase 'my mouth I wil vp make' (sig. A iv[v]), calling it an old proverb, and goes on:

But oftentimes the birds be gone, while one for nest doth grope.
(sig. A iv[v])

Ambidexter's two sententious remarks are both directed at the king. He has approved of his execution of Sisamnes, but feels that it was done more or less accidentally and not out of virtue:

The most euill disposed person that euer was,
All the state of his life he would not let passe.
Some good deeds he will doo, though they be but few.
(sig. D i[v])

After the queen's death he begins to think that Cambyses himself must be fated to die a violent death:

He hath shed so much blood, that his will be shed.
(sig. F iii[v])

The Prologue had spoken of the king's fate in similar vein:

But what mesure the king did meat, the same did loue commence
To bring to end with shame his race. (sig. A ii[v])

The king's council warns him that 'uncertain is the event of wars,' and that Death may not hold even his royal person sacred:

Your grace doth meane for to attempt of war the manly art,
Your grace therein may hap receiue with others for your part,
The dent of death in those affaires, all persons are alike.
(sig. A iii)

Returning triumphant he executes the unfaithful Sisamnes and elevates the latter's son Otian, who laments his father's death and reviles Fortune:

O false and fickle frowning dame, that turneth as the winde.
(sig. C ii[v])

Cupid, about to obey his mother's behest and transfix Cambyses, refers to his own blindness and the king alludes to the same thing:

> I am blinde and cannot see, but stil doo shoot by gesse.
> (Cupid, sig. E ii[v])
>
> Cupid he that eylesse boy. (King, sig. E iii)

Scholars have observed that the three plays *Cambyses*, *Common Conditions* (see pp. 249 ff. above), and *Sir Clyomon and Sir Clamydes* (see pp. 263 ff. above) exhibit varying degrees of likeness in plot and phraseology, and the possibility of Preston's authorship of one or both of the other plays, or a common authorship of *Common Conditions* and *Sir Clyomon* has been suggested, though never categorically.[1] There are certainly notable echoes in phraseology and sentiment and, without attempting an exhaustive investigation, we may perhaps profit to a slight degree by re-examining the proverbial material in the three plays. First let us repeat our statistics, remembering here as elsewhere that figures of this sort are relatively rather than mathematically accurate:

Cambyses	1254 ll.	4	6	11	7
Common Conditions	1904 ll.	8	15	15	21
Sir Clyomon	2238 ll.	8	16	8	7

When we take into consideration the shorter length of *Cambyses*, the only striking things indicated by the tables are the large number of sententious remarks in *Common Conditions* and the scarcity of miscellaneous proverbial phrases in *Sir Clyomon*. There is some duplication of specific pieces of proverbial material, the most noticeable being that Ambidexter says, 'It is wisdome (quoth I) by the masse to saue one' (sig. B iv), and Common Conditions echoes him, 'It is good to saue one, as far as I can see' (sig. G ii[v], l. 1779). Again Sir Nomides in *Common Conditions* remarks 'Experience showes faint harted knights wins neuer fayre ladies loue' (sig. F ii[v], l. 1499) and the proverb which the cowardly Bryan Sans Foy in *Sir Clyomon* hopes to disprove is 'Cowardly hearts faire Ladies neuer win' (sig. D ii[v], l. 840). Among the comparisons the following things are used: in *Cambyses*, line, rivers, rose, ship, silk, wind; in *Common Conditions*, bone, deer, flower, fountain, gown, house, howlet, merlin, moon, owl, rat, tiger, Troilus, turtle-dove, wind, wolf; and in *Sir Clyomon*, buzzard, dog, flint, flower, fowls (and falcons, two), gold, grass, hogs, hare, lamb (and lion), lamb (and wolf), owl, post, stock, swine, wolf. It will be seen that several of the same objects occur in both *Common Conditions* and *Sir Clyomon* but the wordings of the comparisons are seldom strikingly similar. Common Conditions remarks 'which waies so euer the winde blowes it is for my commoditie' (sig. C ii, l. 577), and Shift, in *Sir Clyomon*, says 'And who so hath knowledge, what needs he to care Which way the wind blowe, his way to prepare' (sig. B i, ll. 136 f.). Apart from this the miscellaneous proverbial phrases in the three plays have nothing in common, nor is there a marked tendency to use similar types of phrases. Except for attacks on Fortune, most frequent and lengthy in *Common Conditions* and but scantily represented in *Cambyses*, and references to the blindness of Cupid, in *Cambyses* and *Common Conditions*, the sententious remarks of each play are quite distinct.

When we turn to the amount of proverbial material allotted to the Vice we find:

Cambyses	Ambidexter	3	0	3	2
Common Conditions	Common Conditions	6	5	10	6
Sir Clyomon	Subtle Shift	4	1	2	1

Each Vice does reasonably well with proverbs, especially if we remember that Common Conditions uses one three times, but he, it will be noted, is the only one to use many proverbial phrases and sententious remarks.

The evidence of the proverbial material is not very convincing, but when we observe that Common Conditions, in what is usually considered the second in composition of the three plays, displays the typical Vice's spread and use of proverbial phrases, we may doubt if there is any consistent technique running through the three plays. That the author of *Common Conditions* knew *Cambyses* and that the author of *Sir Clyomon* knew both earlier plays is likely enough, but that all three plays were written by Preston seems less likely than that the two later productions were the work of a school of which he was founder.

86

APIUS AND VIRGINIA (1575)

[Ed. R. B. McKerrow and W. W. Greg, Malone Society Reprints, 1911]

1216 lines: 6; 14; 18; 13

In *Apius and Virginia*, as in *Horestes*, we have a classical story told in the manner of the native plays, all complete with Vice, comic servants, and songs. The amount and distribution of the proverbial material is also typical. Haphazard, the Vice, uses five of the six proverbs, twelve of the fourteen comparisons, eleven of the eighteen other proverbial phrases, and three of the thirteen sententious remarks. His opening speech has a proverb in the first few lines:

> Who dippes with the Diuel, he had neede haue a long spoone,
> Or els full smale will be his fare. (sig. A iv[v], ll. 206 f.)

Hap, hazard, and, not least, Haphazard play a large part in the fortunes of men. Under their beneficent rule all things can happen:

> If hap the skie fall, we hap may haue Larkes.
> (sig. B iii[v], l. 407)

Haphazard it is who persuades Apius to his evil plot, and prevents him from paying heed to Conscience and Justice. Having done this good deed, he departs with a Wellerism probably directed at a common element in the audience:

> At hand (quoth picke purse).
> (sig. C i[v], l. 531)

Even after Apius has been condemned by Justice, Haphazard hopes for at least part of his reward:

> And well this prouerb commeth in my head,
> Birlady halfe a loafe is better then nere a whit of bread.
> (sig. E ii, ll. 1109 f.)

He is outraged when Claudius is exiled and he himself is condemned to hang. That's not equity:

> Plaine dealing is best.
> (sig. E ii[v], l. 1164)

The other proverb is employed by Subseruus, who has so far succeeded in deceiving his master:

> But hazard it is, least time will truth tell.
> (sig. D i, l. 772)

Virginius, his wife and daughter sing a song the refrain of which is sententious:

> Then friendly, and kindly, let measure be mixed
> With reason, in season, where friendship is fixed.
> (sig. A iv, ll. 163 f.)

Virginius repeats the idea:

> Let measure beare the ground.
> (sig. A iv[v], l. 197)

His summons to Apius is accompanied by personal ill-omens and a lively sense of impending disaster which he tries to throw off:

> Nothing neede misdoubted be, where grounded cause is none.
> (sig. D i[v], l. 813)

He agrees to kill Virginia:

> And better it is to dye with good fame,
> Then longer to liue to reape vs but shame.
> (sig. D iii[v], ll. 943 f.)

Haphazard has a great respect for the conversational ability of women:

> Nay sure I haue done when women do speake.
> (sig. B ii, l. 301)

He urges all to put their trust in hap and hope:

> Let hope be your helper.
> (sig. B ii[v], l. 327)

His feeling for hope is shared by Subseruus who expresses it in song:

> Let hope holde the Helmet, till brunt it be past.
> (sig. B iii, l. 366)

Haphazard's desire for his reward leads him to the gallows, an end which he had hardly anticipated when he pressed forward ready, as always, to take a chance:

> The worst that can hap is but a noo.
> (sig. E ii, l. 1106)

The Prologue speaks of

> The blinded God of Loue, as Poets tearme him.
> (sig. A ii, l. 26)

Neither physical nor verbal punishment hold terror for Subseruus:

> For bloes are but buffits and words but a blast.
> (sig. B iii, l. 367)

Apius recognizes, much against his will, the power of love and impotently asks:

> Then what is it that loue cannot?
> (sig. B iv, l. 445)

Virginia prefers death to dishonor but has a little maidenly timidity for all that and first binds her wimple about her eyes:

> Fleash to death is fraile.
> (sig. D iii[v], l. 968)

Senecan notes are few in the play but the Epilogue may be said to contain at least a hint of one:

> As earthly life is graunted none for euermore to raigne,
> But denting death wil cause them al to grant this world as vain
> Right worshipfull sith sure it is that mortall life must vade,
> Do practise then to winne his loue that al in all hath made.
> (sig. E iii[v], ll. 1205 ff.)

87

Thomas Hughes's *THE MISFORTUNES OF ARTHUR* (1587)

[Ed. J. W. Cunliffe in *Early English Classical Tragedies*, Oxford, 1912, pp. 218 ff.]

2022 lines: 0; 2; 1; 52

There is a slight touch of humor in the prefatory material to Thomas Hughes's *The Misfortunes of Arthur*. He remarks of his text that it is printed as it was written and presented 'excepting certaine wordes and lines, where some of the Actors either helped their memories by brief omission: or fitted their acting by some alteration' (p. 224). Slight as this is, it is the only humor connected with a play of which one can only say that it is the most sententious, and possibly the dullest, document which we have had occasion to examine in the course of this volume. Many of these sententious sayings are the original lucubrations of the author, but many others, as Professor Cunliffe's notes indicate, are posies plucked from the flowering garden of Seneca. As in the case of the other tragedies of classical type, there would be little merit in doing more than list the sententious remarks, with the warning that their number might easily have been doubled.

And that the shame thou suffredst for his lusts,
Reboundeth backe, and stifeleth in his stocke.
(Gorlois, p. 227, ll. 13 f.)

And let not will vsurpe, where wit should rule.
(Fronia, p. 229, l. 18)

The wrath, that breatheth bloode, doth loath to lurke.
(Gueneuora, p. 229, l. 19)

Great harmes cannot be hidde, the griefe is small,
That can receaue aduise, or rule it selfe.
(Gueneuora, p. 230, ll. 52 f.)

Hatred concealde doth often happe to hurte,
But once profest, it oftner failes reuenge.
(Fronia, p. 230, ll. 54 f.)

The greater flame must needes delay the lesse.
(Gueneuora, p. 231, l. 72)

Whom Gods doe presse, they bende: whom man annoyes,
He breakes. (Gueneuora, p. 231, ll. 84 f.)

The loue, that for his rage will not be rulde,
Must be restrainde. (Gueneuora, p. 232, ll. 1 f.)

They spoile, that bootelesse spare. (Gueneuora, p. 233, l. 30)

Ech where is death: that, fates haue well ordainde,
That ech man may bereaue himselfe of life,
But none of death: death is so sure a doome:
A thousand wayes doe guide vs to our graues.
(Angharat, p. 233, ll. 33 ff.)

When guiltie mindes torment them selues, they heale:
Whiles woundes be cur'd, griefe is a salue for griefe.
(Gueneuora, pp. 233 f., ll. 57 f.)

He safely stands, that stands beyond his harmes.
(Mordred, p. 235, l. 11)

His waies be blinde, that maketh Chaunce his guide.
(Conan, p. 237, l. 74)

Extremest cures must not be vsed first. (Conan, p. 237, l. 82)

In desperate times, the headlong way is best.
(Mordred, p. 237, l. 83)

Dame Flatterie flitteth oft: she loues and hates
With time, a present friend an absent foe.
(Conan, p. 237, ll. 89 f.)

Who sowes in sinne, in sinne shall reape his paine.
(Chorus, p. 239, l. 11)

Let courage worke: what can he not that dares?
(Nuntius, p. 241, l. 26)

Whose breast is free from rage may soone b'aduisde.
(Mordred, p. 243, l. 13)

He that amongst so many, so vniust,
Seekes to be iust, seekes perill to him selfe.
(Mordred, p. 244, ll. 22 f.)

Whom *Fates* constrayne, let him forgoe his blisse:
But he that needlesse yeldes vnto his bane,
When he may shunne, doth well deserue to loose
The good he cannot vse: who woulde sustaine
A baser life, that may maintaine the best?
(Mordred, p. 244, ll. 45 ff.)

But hope
May misse, where hap doth hurle. (Conan, p. 246, l. 98 f.)
The first and last doe sielde agree. (Conan, p. 246, l. 102)
Whom *chaunce* hath often mist, *chaunce* hits at length.
(Mordred, p. 248, l. 42)

Death must be once: how soone, I lest respect.
He best prouides that can beware in time,
Not why, nor when: but whence, and where he fals.
(Mordred, p. 249, ll. 74 ff.)

No lucke can last, nowe here, now their it lights:
No state alike, *Chaunce* blindly snatcheth all,
And *Fortune* maketh guiltie whom she listes.
(Gawin, p. 249, ll. 93 ff.)

The smallest axe may fell the hugest oake.
(Mordred, p. 249, l. 103)

He falleth well, that falling fells his foe.
(Mordred, p. 249, l. 105)

Yea worse than warre it selfe, is feare of warre.
(Mordred, p. 250, l. 117)

Warre seemeth sweete to such as haue not tried:
But wisedome wils we should forecast the worst.
The end allowes the act: that plot is wise,
That knowes his meanes, and least relies on *Chance*.
(Gawin, p. 250, ll. 118 ff.)

Striue not aboue your strength. (Gawin, p. 250, l. 124)

Ye Princely Peeres extold to seates of State,
Seeke not the faire, that soone will turne to fowle:
Oft is the fall of high and houering *Fate*,
And rare the roome, which time doth not controwle.
The safest seate is not on highest hill,
Where windes, and stormes, and thunders thumpe their ill.
Farre safer were to follow sound aduise,
Then for such pride to pay so deare a price.

The mounting minde that climes the hauty cliftes,
And soaring seekes the tip of lofty type,
Intoxicats the braine with guiddy drifts,
Then rowles, and reeles, and falles at length plum ripe.
Loe: heauing hie is of so small forecast,
To totter first, and tumble downe at last.

(Chorus, p. 254, ll. 1 ff.)

He teaches how to sinne, that winkes at sinnes,
And bids offend, that suffereth an offence.
The onely hope of leaue increaseth crimes,
And he that pardoneth one, emboldneth all
To breake the Lawes. Each patience fostereth wrongs.

(Cador, p. 258, ll. 64 ff.)

Lawes must not lowre. Rule oft admitteth ruthe.

(Arthur, p. 258, l. 86)

Where *Cato* first had saued a theefe from death,
And after was himselfe condemnd to die:
When else not one would execute the doome,
Who but the theefe did vndertake the taske?

(Howell, p. 259, ll. 93 ff.)

Attonement sield defeates, but oft deferres
Reuenge: beware a reconciled foe. (Cador, p. 259, ll. 119 f.)

Experience tels me plaine that *Chance* is fraile,
And oft, the better past, the worse to come.

(Arthur, p. 260, ll. 142 f.)

A causelesse courage giues repentance place.

(Arthur, p. 260, l. 147)

Trust me, bad things haue often glorious names.

(Arthur, p. 261, l. 163)

March on: delaie no *Fates* whiles *Fortune* fawnes,
The greatest praise of warres consists in speed.

(Arthur, p. 267, ll. 129 f.)

The deeper guilt descends, the more it rootes:
The younger imps affect the huger crimes.

(Arthur, p. 268, ll. 26 f.)

O base, yet happy Boores! O giftes of Gods
Scant yet perceau'd: when poudred Ermine roabes
With secrete sighes mistrusting their extreames,
In bailefull breast forecast their foultring *Fates*,
And stirre, and striue, and storme, and all in vaine:
Behold, the Peasant poore with tattered coate,
Whose eyes a meaner *Fortune* feedes with sleepe,
How safe and sound the carelesse Snudge doth snore.
Low rooffed lurkes the house of slender hap,
Costlesse, not gay without, scant cleane within:
Yet safe: and oftner shroudes the hoary haires,
Then haughty Turrets rearde with curious art,
To harbour heads that wield the golden Crest.
With endlesse carke in glorious Courts and Townes,
The troubled hopes and trembling feares doe dwell.
(Chorus, p. 270, ll. 46 ff.)

Who forbiddeth not offence,
If well he may, is cause of such offence. (Gildas, p. 271, ll. 4 f.)
Small griefes can speake: the great astonisht stand.
(Nuntius, p. 273, l. 14)

Thus *Fortune* gibes:
She hoyseth vp to hurle the deeper downe.
(Cador, p. 284, ll. 11 f.)

The wickeds death is safety to the iust.
To spare the Traitors, was to spoile the true.
Of force he hurtes the good, that helpes the bad.
(Chorus, p. 286, ll. 57 ff.)

Good is the frend, that seekes to do vs good:
A mighty frend, that doth preuent our harmes.
(Chorus, p. 286, ll. 62 f.)

Lo here the end that *Fortune* sends at last
To him, whom first she heau'd to highest happe.
The flattering looke wherewith he long was led:
The smiling *Fates*, that oft had fedde his *Fame*:
The many warres and Conquests, which he gaind,
Are dasht at once: one day inferres that foile,
Whereof so many yeares of yore were free.
(Chorus, p. 289, ll. 179 ff.)

Yea *Fortunes* selfe in this afflicted case,
Exacts a paine for long continued pompe.
She vrgeth now the blisse of woonted weale,
And beares him downe with waight of former *Fame*,
His prayses past be present shame: O tickle trust:
Whiles *Fortune* chops and chaungeth euery *Chaunce*,

What certaine blisse can we enioy a liue,
Vnlesse, whiles yet our blisse endures, we die?
  Yea: since before his last and outmost gaspe,
None can be deemde a happy man or blest,
Who dares commit him selfe to prosperous *Fates*,
Whose death preparde attends not hard at hand?
That sithence death must once determine all,
His life may sooner flie, then *Fortune* flitte.

(Chorus, pp. 289 f., ll. 194 ff.)

Pride hath his pay:
Murther his price: Adult'rie his desert:
Treason his meede: Disloyaltie his doome:
Wrong hath his wreake: and Guilt his guerdon beares.

(Gorlois, p. 290, ll. 1 ff.)

See heere by this the tickle trust of tyme:
The false affiance of each mortall force,
The wauering waight of *Fates*: the fickell trace,
That *Fortune* trips: the many mockes of life:
The cheerelesse change: the easelesse brunts and broyles,
That man abides: the restlesse race he runnes.

(Epilogue, p. 291, ll. 1 ff.)

Him, whom the Morning found both stout and strong,
The Euening left all groueling on the ground.
  This breath and heate wherewith mans life is fedde
Is but a flash, or flame, that shines a while,
And once extinct, is as it ne'r had bene.
Corruption hourely frets the bodies frame,
Youth tends to age, and age to death by kinde.
Short is the race, prefixed is the end,
Swift is the tyme, wherein mans life doth run.

(Epilogue, p. 292, ll. 40 ff.)

CHAPTER VI

PROVERBIAL PHRASES

I HAVE divided the proverbial phrases which are found in the English plays considered in the preceding chapters into two groups: comparisons, some of which are certainly not popular, and other proverbial phrases. Each group is alphabetized under the modern spelling of the most important word in each phrase, save that by errors discovered too late to be rectified, threc of earth's most intransigent creatures, the urchin (182), the hyena (170), and the Lombard (696), are forever out of place. In the references each play or, as in the case of the cycles, each group of plays, is identified by the number given to it in the earlier discussions. Thus 3: p. 391, xxxi, 147 and 79: sig. C iv[v], l. 774 indicate that the phrases are from the Towneley cycle and *The Rare Triumphs of Love and Fortune* respectively. Numbers have been given to the proverbial phrases for convenience of reference; sayings put under one number whilc connected, are not necessarily identical.

COMPARISONS

1 As valyant, as euer was achylles. (30: p. 12, l. 236)
2 [*I mend*] as zoure ale in sommer, that is still wurse & wurse. (34: p. 32, iv, 2, 991)
3 With grace indewid in fredome as alexandre. (61: sig. C i)
Strenger than Alexander. (7: p. 68, l. 352)
4 Thow sweiter nor the Lamber. (28: p. 395, l. 531)
5 Ye shall here them syng as swetly
As they were angelles clere. (22: sig. E iii)
6 More ranke they are than antes. (29: sig. B viii)
7 But she wyll go a gaddyng very myche
Lyke an Anthony pyg with an olde wyche. (59: sig. A i)

8 And made hym as bare, as an ape is behynde. (64: sig. F iii[v])
As iumpe as Apes, in vewe of Nuttes to daunce.
(77: sig. B ii[v])
He lokis lurkand like an nape. (2: p. 258, xxix, 107)
And make them to lye and mowe like an ape.
(8a: p. 12, l. 296)
He rowles in his Retorike as an Ape in his tayle.
(80: sig. F iv[v], l. 1442)
As wise as an Ape. (36: sig. C iii)
9 My body tir-trymmelyth as þe aspen leffe. (18: p. 27, l. 727)
10 Like an asse as you be. (63: p. 18, l. 652)
They droue me to lernynge lyke a dull asse.
(25: p. 43, l. 1386)
Thou drugst on like an Asse. (44: sig. A iv[v], l. 46)
As dull as euer were asses. (29: sig. D iii[v])
With long eares lyke an asse. (30: p. 34, l. 697)
Naked as an asse. (25: p. 59, l. 1893)
And not Roune on heade, like . . . an asse.
(34: p. 12, i, 4, 362)
11 Hee . . . blusheth like the backe side of a chimney.
(50: sig. C i[v])
12 Lyke backes [*bats*] in þe darke, you alweys take yowr flyght.
(30: p. 18, l. 367)
13 They would hang her vp like Bacon in a chimney to drie.
(50: sig. Di])
14 Swettere þan bawmys breth. (4: pp. 58, vii, 18, 147, xvi, 47)
There is no bawme . . .
More delectable than your langage to me.
(25: p. 73, ll. 2347 f.)
15 Hys browes as brode as barne durres. (58: sig. D iii[v)
16 Breeches as big as good barrels. (39: sig. A iii)
17 As bolde as blinde bayerd. (86: sig. B i, l. 225)
Boulde blinde bayarde. (86: sigs. C iii[v], ll. 690, 696, C iv, ll. 704, 712)
18 Yet is shee curster then the Beare by kinde.
(80: sig. B iv, l. 236)
19 Then sholde ye daunce as a bere. (23: sig. C iii)
And flye as fast as a bere in a cage.
(66: p. 37, l. 840, cf. note, p. 64)
He grones like a beare. (39: sig. C i[v])
And as a sauage beare when her whelps taken are would rage.
(10: p. 211, l. 370)
Tumbling by the eares,
As oftentimes you doo like a couple of great beares.
(39: sig. A iii)

20 As a beast is to be abiected. (15: sig. D i[v])
He shall beare me one cuff yet more like a beast.
(63: p. 18, l. 659)
I account hym neuer better than a best.
(22: sigs. A vi, A vii[v])
For he is boune as beeste in bande. (2: p. 348, xxxiv, 342)
Doo not like a beast decay. (37: sig. F iii[v])
Without abstinence like a beast alway to eate. (15: sig. B iv)
But foloweth thappetytes of hys sensuall affeccyon
As a brute best that lakketh reson. (20: sig. E i)
Fowll as a best. (19: p. 40, l. 158)
Þou fonnyst as a best. (4: p. 32, iii, 117)
They shuld lyff lyke bestes all rudely. (61: sig. B iii[v])
Who no time forbeareth to take his pray:
Most like the greedy or sauadge beast,
Who in creuelty rageth both night and day. (47: sig. F i[v])
He regardeth me no more then a best. (62: sig. B iii[v])
And not Roune on heade, like a brute beaste.
(34: p. 12, i, 4, 362)
Farre worse then anye beaste. (1: II, 331, xviii, 316;
27: sig. A ii[v]; 30: p. 10, l. 180;
37: sigs. A iii[v], C iv; 62: sig. A ii[v])

21 Wormes shall in you brede as bees dos in the byke.
(3: p. 391, xxxi, 147)
She is as nimble as a bee. (10: p. 264, l. 33)
These with other in this hed lyke swarmes of bees
Styng in debatyng theyr contraryetees. (55: sig. D i[v])
They come on thicker, then swarmes of Bees.
(64: sig. F iv[v])
The bee haue no so many herbes
Whereout to suck hony,
As I can find shifts whereby to get mony. (46: p. 24)
As fyt for the warre, Jacke hempstringe thou art,
In fayth as a be, is to drawe a carte. (83: sig. B iii[v])

22 I may be as good to thee as two pots of Beere.
(79: sig. C iv[v], l. 744)

23 Thes betyll browyd bycheys. (8c: p. 82, l. 724; 52: sig. G ii)

24 As bigge as a begger. (86: sig. B i, l. 228)

25 Þou devyl bold as a belle. (17: p. 184, l. 3592)
And now in the Kinges eare like a bell he ringes.
(72: sig. G ii)

26 That Preists sall leid ȝow lyke ane bellie blinde.
(28: p. 489, l. 2951)

27 My blyssynge burnyschith ȝow as bryght as berall.
(4: p. 374, xxxiii, 46)

A dwellynge thou shalt purchase,
Brighter than berall. (8a: p. 21, ll. 505 f.)

28 My face as browne as a berry. (33: III, 243, l. 268)

29 We haue now caught him as Birde is in li[m]e. (49: sig. G i)
Yt ys as clen as a byrdis ars. (18: p. 18, l. 482)
But let our thoughtes fro suche thynges be as free
As be the byrdes that in the ayre flee. (57: sig. A i)
For ych man is borne to labour truly
As a byrde is to fle naturally. (60: sig. B iv)
The chyld makys Ioy, as any byrd
That I in body bere. (3: p. 98, xi, 41 f.)
I am als light as birde on bowe. (2: p. 213, xxv, 388)
As mery as þe byrde on bow. (19: p. 56, l. 626)
Shall I now leade my life
All solitarie, as doeth the bird in cage.
(84: p. 214, v, 4, 14 f.)

30 And make them so dull
As euer was a blocke. (42: sig. F iii[v])

31 Þer Criste syttyht, bryth as blode. (17: p. 87, l. 356)
Redde as blood. (7: p. 76, l. 594; 36: sig. C iv[v])

32 If all my blee be as bright
As blossome on brere. (2: p. 220, xxvi, 20; 3: p. 162, xv, 70 f.)
Bryther þanne blossum on brere. (17: p. 174, l. 3247)
In floures I florishe as blosomes in May. (43: sig. A iii)
Swetter then eyuer wasse blossum on brere. (5: p. 46, ii, 399)

33 That like a Bore in a stie, he fed me at last.
(44: sig. F ii, l. 1184)
With bellyes lyke a Bore. (29: sig. C iv)
Never bore so brymme. (68: p. 167, iv, 6, 5)
Fomyng lyke a Bore. (72: sig. C iv)
I mon whett lyke a bore. (3: p. 175, xvi, 318)

34 As brage as a bodylouse. (45: sig. B i, ii, 1; 69: p. 30, ii, 4, 32)
As busy as a body louse. (71: p. 211, ii, 4, 225)

35 And go straight bolt vppright. (46: p. 10)

36 Hard geare to eat, as hard as a bone. (76: sig. F i[v], l. 1425)

37 How goeth the world with thee? Like a bowle very round.
(70: p. 89, i, 2, 9)

38 . . . Lucifer . . .
That burne shall as a Brand. (1: II, 425, xxiii, 689 f.)
I make them to startyll and sparkyll lyke a bronde.
(25: p. 24, l. 741)

39 As rugh as a brere. (3: p. 119, xiii, 101)
40 She is browyd lyke a brystyll. (3: p. 119, xiii, 102)
41 But I lay braikand like ane Brok. (28: p. 398, l. 624)
Wayte nowe, he lokis like a brokke,
Were he in a bande for to bayte. (2: p. 258, xxix, 117 f.)
Thir stewats stinks as they war Broks. (28: p. 471, l. 2489)
42 As much braine as a burbolt. (68: p. 142, iii, 2, 88)
43 As close as a burr. (71: p. 207, ii, 4, 94)
We cleaue as fast as burre. (49: sig. G iii)
Cleve togither like burres. (34: p. 10, i, 3, 285)
Wherby I thought her owne tale lyke a bur
Stack to her owne back. (55: sig. C i)
Hys eares as ruged as burres. (58: sig. D iii[v])
44 Hys yes as rounde as two bushels. (58: sig. D iii[v])
45 His beard like a buske of breeres. (1: I, 153, vii, 509)
46 I goe painted vp like bvtter-flyes. (33: III, 234, l. 113)
47 His face doeth shine as bright as the buttocke of a beare.
(48: sig. C iiii[v])
48 As Buzzard bold. (78: sig. G ii, l. 1653)
49 Your Father mumbled a while as the Cade which cheweth the
Cudde. (75: p. 50, iii, 4)
50 Ah, that drabe, she can cacklel like a cadowe. (46: p. 26)
51 Thou arte wyse as a calfe. (56: sig. C ii[v])
I learnd to make ruffs like Calues chitterlings. (39: sig. A ii[v])
52 It is as vnpossible for thee his company to deny:
As it is for a Cammel to creep through a needles eye.
(39: sig. B ii[v])
53 Wee silly wretches as course as canuas. (74: p. 43, iii, 4, 19)
54 Crowynge lyke a capon. (29: sig. C iii[v])
Ye speake like a Capon that had the cough now.
(68: p. 111, i, 2, 29)
55 Her eyen relucent as carbuncle so clere. (25: p. 49, l. 1556)
56 Hay! as ane brydlit cat, I brank. (28: p. 392, l. 468)
Now þou kewe as a kat. (17: p. 169, l. 3118)
I lye as still as a Cat in a gutter. (86: sig. D iv[v], l. 1020)
I schal hym bynde
In hell, as Catte dothe þe mows. (17: p. 105, ll. 954 f.)
To catche them in our gyn
As the Cat the mouse. (42: sig. C iv[v])
As greedie thereof as cat of a mouse. (48: sig. D iii)
57 Straighter then Cedar. (80: sig. B iv, l. 225)
58 You wilbe as good as a charme. (48: sig. E i)
59 If God make me looke as red as a Cherry.
(33: III, 243, l. 270; 81: sig. A iv, l. 59)

These lips are cherry red. (50: sig. E i[v])
Her lusty lyppes ruddy as the chery. (25: p. 49, l. 1558)
My harte of goulde as swete as a cherye. (71: p. 203, ii, 4, 3)
60 Meker þanne a chylde. (17: p. 141, l. 2128)
61 Clenner cloþyd þanne any clay. (17: p. 99, l. 736)
My hert doth clynge and cleue as clay. (4: p. 48, v, 164)
My hert is colde as clay. (4: p. 213, xxiv, 115)
Myne hand is ded and drye as claye. (4: p. 143, xv, 255)
62 I clynge as a clodde in claye. (21: sig. C v)
63 With a hede lyke a clowde ffelterd his here.
(3: p. 102, xii, 65)
Hir hede as hy as a clowde. (3: p. 375, xxx, 263)
64 As sure as a clubb. (71: pp. 217, ii, 5, 82, 235, iii, 2, 52)
65 Þou bycche blak as kole. (17: p. 140, l. 2117)
Now ar we waxen blak as any coyll. (3: p. 5, i, 136)
The cole-blacke Moore. (81: sig. B ii, l. 200)
She blushes like coles. (15: sig. C iv)
66 I will be as true to thee as thy coate is to thy backe.
(75: p. 62, iv, 3)
67 We must hop and dawnse
As cokys in a croft. (3: p. 239, xxi, 354 f.)
68 Head . . . as bigge as a Codshed. (72: sig. E iii[v])
69 Cham drest like a coult. (69: p. 64, v, 2, 204)
Beelzebub the mayster deuyll as ragged as a colte.
(62: sig. C ii[v])
70 I wyll beate the knaues as flatte as a conger. (62: sig. B iv)
71 No more wytt than a coote. (30: p. 10, l. 178)
Thou blynde balde cote. (55: sig. C ii)
72 That styckyth at my hart as hard as a core.
(7: p. 79, l. 679)
73 And like a greedie cormorant with belly full farced.
(48: sig. E ii)
74 She is hornyd like a kowe. (3: p. 375, xxx, 269)
Even like a cowe
At my foote oute of hande thou shouldst haue bene [s]l[a]yne.
(71: p. 187, i, 3, 19 f.)
Þou soldyst hym us as . . . kow. (4: p. 279, xxvi, 235)
75 Crabtree facst knaues. (73: sig. B i, l. 33)
76 If I say the word, thou mayest beleue as thy creed.
(46: p. 14)
Take it sothe, as mes crede. (17: p. 142, l. 2166)
As sure as is your crede. (69: p. 48, iv, 2, 99)
All that ye say is as trewe as the crede. (25: p. 8, l. 218)
77 Wee'le be as merry as Crickets. (80: sig. H i, l. 1801)

78 A dwellynge thou shalt purchase,
Brighter than . . . clere cristall. (8a: p. 21, ll. 505 f.)
She is as clene as cristall clyfe. (3: p. 95, x, 308; 2: p. 35, vii, 5; 4: p. 375, xxxiii, 47)
And my coloure as cristall is cleere.
(2: p. 308, xxxii, 24; 3: p. 269, xxiii, 361; 27: sig. D iv)
Cryst . . . clerer than crystal clene. (21: sig. C iv[v])
Ale,
As pure as Christall. (39: sig. C ii)
79 Weepe as the Crocodile. (81: sigs. E ii, l. 1061, E iv, l. 1173)
80 Curse the as blacke as a crowe. (30: p. 6, l. 88)
He looketh pretily as narow as a Crowe. (37: sig. B iv)
They are set a sunning like a Crow in a gutter.
(79: sig. B ii, l. 273)
81 He was as fine as the Crusadoe.
(74: p. 43, iii, 4, 18 f., cf. note, p. 268)
82 We shall be as merry as cup and can. (80: sig. E ii[v], l. 993)
83 He bittes like a cur. (71: p. 214, ii, 4, 289)
84 Heyl, swetter þan . . . cypresse! (8c: p. 132, l. 2047)
85 Theis wordes of yours do slytt
My brest like a Dagger. (70: p. 138, v, 2, 74 f.)
86 Tyll my thryfte was gone as quyte as a dally (*die, knucklebone*). (35: sig. C ii[v], l. 558)
87 They differ as darkenes dothe from light. (40: sig. A iv[v])
88 Ye speke lyke a dawe. (25: p. 43, l. 1379)
Singing and bellowing like a dawe. (36: sig. A iii[v])
As wyse as a dawe. (43: sig. B iii[v])
Then fare ye well as wyse as two dawys. (60: sig. C ii[v])
89 Bright starne that shyneth bright as day.
(2: p. 443, xli, 326)
Þat berde is brighter þan þe daye. (2: p. 491, xlvii, 4)
It appereth as cleare as the day. (15: sig. E iv)
90 Am faine like deare through greedy hound from herd for to depart. (76: sig. F ii, l. 1454)
I liue and languish in my lyfe,
As doth the wounded Deare. (86: sig. C ii, ll. 584 f.)
91 As black as the devyll! (31: p. 42)
As craftie as the Deuill of hell. (74: p. 31, ii, 2, 33)
Ye have so fellyd yower bylly with growell,
Þat it growit grett as þe dywll of hell. (8c: p. 99, ll. 1156 f.)
But shurne thy cumpanye,
As I wolde the deuyll of helle.
(29: sig. B ii; 72: sig. B iii)

It stank like the dwill in hell. (3: p. 17, ii, 283)
And wars then the deyle. (3: p. 375, xxx, 268)
More wicked then the Deuill. (42: sig. G i[v])
92 Yet shall his semblaunce as a dyale declare
Howe the clocke goeth. (55: sig. B i[v])
93 As strong as . . . diomedes. (30: p. 12, l. 235)
94 I dawnse doun, as a doo. (17: p. 82, l. 188)
Dumbe and deafe as a doted doe. (1: II, 288, xvi, 195)
For I am swifter then is the doe. (1: I, 202, x, 434)
And then wyll I for fayne trypp lyke a doo.
(5: p. 28, i, 816; 66: p. 10, l. 229)
95 That many one shall barke,
Lyke dogges agaynst the truth. (29: sig. D v[v])
Lyke a dogge, with a Cudgell I shalbe beaten. (64: sig. E iv[v])
I do come but lyke a dogg that goes to hanginge.
(10: p. 291, l. 839)
I shall make the slaues couche as lowe as dog to bow.
(14: sig. F iii, v, 3)
My hart for fere lyke a dog is couchyd. (61: sig. B iv[v])
He xal dye lyke a dogge whelpe. (4: p. 203, xxiii, 112)
As dogges vnresonable, on most vyle carren fede,
So wyll we cause them, seke ydolles in their nede.
(29: sig. D iii)
Hee has a face like a blacke Dogge. (50: sig. C i[v])
Lyand in dennis, lyke idill doggis. (28: p. 476, l. 2621)
He wyll lye lyke a dogge. (77: sig. I iii)
You haue euen asmuch maners as hath a Dog. (37: sig. C iii)
Touching vertue, as a dogge that is museled. (36: sig. F iii)
I should shake him euen as a dog that lulleth a sow.
(14: sig. C ii, ii, 2)
And when it comes snap at it as my fathers dogge wod doe at a liuer. (50: sig. D iii[v])
Looke how greedie they be, like dogs that fall a snatching.
(50: sig. E iv)
Stynke as dog in dyke. (3: p. 391, xxxi, 146; 23: sig. C v)
As weary as a dog. (44: sig. E iii, l. 982)
96 Bot domme as a dore gon he dwell. (2: p. 322, xxxiii, 65)
97 He is as loving a worme againe as a dove.
(68: p. 140, iii, 2, 48)
She dooth shine as siluer Dooue. (51: sig. B i)
My body full of holys, as a dove-hows. (19: p. 72, l. 1110)
98 As softe as downe my hand. (10: p. 12, l. 209)
99 As deuyl dowty, in draf as a drake. (17: p. 83, l. 197)
As wyse as a drake. (38: p. 27)

100 I knaw my dayis induris bot as ane dreame.
(28: p. 380, l. 98)
101 Thou goest like a Dromeldory dreaming & drousy.
(43: sig. A iii[v])
102 Al þi doynge, as dros is drye. (17: p. 125, l. 1607)
103 Why thou cowardely knaue, no stronger then a ducke.
(62: sig. C ii[v])
104 Why were I not dead as is the donge? (1: II, 435, xxiv, 235)
105 Davy drydust. (4: p. 123, xiv, 21)
106 Ye and as high as an Eagle can fle for a neade.
(66: p. 10, l. 237)
Euen as the Eagle soares against the sunne,
And spite of Phœbus shine, pries in his face.
(81: sig. D i, ll. 698 f.)
107 Fall downe agayne,
Lyke earthen pottes, that breaketh sodaynly. (64: sig. H ii)
108 As fresh as an eyll. (3: p. 127, xiii, 356)
And coryd tyll he be slyke as an ele. (55: sig. E ii)
As trusty as is a quicke ele by the tayle. (43: sig. D iii)
109 Thou art as full of knaverie as an egge is full of meate.
(71: p. 187, i, 3, 26)
An egge is not so ful of meate, as she is ful of lyes.
(69: p. 56, v, 2, 57)
110 As fayne as fawcon wold flye. (1: I, 194, x, 206)
I have a favorows fode, and fresse as the fakown.
(8c: p. 90, l. 942)
As gentell as a faulcon. (46: p. 14)
111 Thy wordes hange togyder as fethers in the wynde.
(25: p. 57, l. 1818)
It hangeth together like fethers in the winde. (36: sig. D ii)
But my woords as fethers in the winde you haue waid.
(37: sig. A iv)
For they place the scriptures as fethers in the winde.
(37: sig. F ii)
He settes me as light as a fether in the wynde.
(71: p. 179, i, 1, 92)
112 As feathers, light of minde. (44: sig. A iiii, l. 9; 46: p. 14)
Except God make me lichter nor ane fedder.
(28: p. 509, l. 3527; 52: sigs. G i[v], G ii)
Softer then feathers of the fairest Swan. (80: sig. B iv, l. 231)
113 The smell of my son is lyke
To a feld with flouris, or hony bike. (3: p. 49, v, 3 f.)
More pleasant then the Feeld of flowring Grasse.
(80: sig. B iv, l. 227)

114 One scab on my narse, as brode as thy fingers end.
(69: p. 59, v, 2, 107)

115 A starne as bright as fyre. (3: p. 149, xiv, 287)
The kyng of Ioy . . . as bryth as fyrys blase!
(8c: p. 91, l. 967)
But yet I burne as doth the fyre.
(1: I, 191, x, 134; 77: sig. C iv)
My hart burnes as hott as fier. (1: I, 89, v[BWh], 6)
Seke to dystroye, as doth the flaming fier. (83: sig. B ii)
My visage flammand as the fyre. (28: p. 386, l. 281)
My bodie . . .
. . . is hait as fyre. (28: p. 389, ll. 371 f.)
With-in I fare as fyre. (3: p. 169, xvi, 101)
My troubled hart with guiltynesse agreu'd,
Lyke fyre doth make my eares and cheekes to glow.
(77: sig. I ii[v])
Ryche rubyys, red as ony fyr. (8c: p. 60, l. 153)
Brennyng in flamys . as fyre out of flynt.
(4: p. 287, xxvi, 469)

116 Whome through deceite, as fysh to bayte,
We made their thrift forth gad. (47: sig. D iiii[v])
Faylyth & fadyth, as fysch in flode. (17: p. 87, l. 354)
As whole as a fish. (63: p. 19, l. 672)

117 Their loue is like a flame,
Quiuering in th'Ayre betweene too blastes of wynde.
(80: sig. D i[v], ll. 651 f.)

118 He hath broken
The two new cords lyke flaxe burnt in the fyre.
(10: p. 143, l. 233 f.)

119 I clefe
You small as flesh to pott. (3: p. 169, xvi, 98 f.)
Twentye suche could I hewe as small as fleshe to pote.
(66: p. 14, l. 335)
As smale as flesh to pott I would hys carcase teare & rende.
(10: p. 177, l. 820)

120 Whyche kepeth our myldams as drye as a flynt.
(56: sig. B iii[v])
Heart more hard then flint. (78: sig. E iv[v], l. 1256)

121 This day stremyt owt lik a floode. (8d: p. 172, l. 26)
Werldlys lay,
þat fadyth as a flode. (17: p. 102, ll. 837 f.)

122 The tylthe of oure landys lyys falow as the floore.
(3: p. 117, xiii, 13)

123 Floure more fresh then floure de lyce! (3: p. 203, xix, 258)
Freshe and flourishyng as the floures in May. (15: sig. B i)
My flesh as flowr, that all to-flaw,
Now tydes a fearly fitt. (1: II, 437, xxiv, 295 f.)
My flesh that as flower can flee. (1: II, 432, xxiv, 145)
And as the flowrs now springes,
Falleth, fadeth, and hings,
So thy ioy now it raignes,
That shall from thee be rafte. (1: II, 415, xxiii, 414 ff.)
As a flour, fadyth my face. (17: p. 166, l. 3001)
Wyll vade from the as floure in maye. (27: sig. A ii)
I fade as doth the flower in sommers day.
(76: sig. C iv, l. 740)
Mine is the heart which vades away, as doth the flower.
(78: sig. E i, l. 1007)
Thi face . . .
Was fare as floure in feylde. (3: p. 268, xxiii, 323 f.)
A lyuelye younge gentilman, as freshe as any flower.
(45: sig. B iii[v], ii, 2)
I am as fresshe as flourys in maye. (21: sig. A iii[v])
124 As light as a fly. (44: sig. B iii, l. 214; 63: p. 3, l. 112)
As the flie playeth with the flame till at last she is cause of hir owne decay, so the louer *etc.* (74: p. 22, i, 3, 64 f.)
125 Tatyrd as a ſoyll (*foal*). (3: p. 5, i, 137)
126 As fat as a foole. (86: sig. B i, l. 228)
127 The blood like fountaines droppeth hot.
(76: sig. F ii, l. 1453)
128 I am ryght glad as foule on flyte. (8b: p. 40, l. 332)
They feare as Fowles that houering flie, from out the Fawcons way. (78: sigs. B iv, l. 378, E iv[v], ll. 1255 f.)
129 Came like a false Foxe. (69: p. 56, v, 2, 51)
I am feller þanne a fox. (17: p. 97, l. 672)
As flat as fox, I falle before your face. (8c: p. 82, l. 730)
Envye flet as a fox. (17: p. 105, l. 936)
Ay lurkeand lyke ane wylie Fox. (28: p. 434, l. 1559)
Yet as the Fox doth win the Kid,
So are his secret treasons hid. (81: sig. E iii, ll. 1104 f.)
130 And thou were as tale a man as frier tucke. (62: sig. C i)
131 Thise fryggys as froggys. (3: p. 377, xxx, 316)
132 Feares follow hopes, as fumes doe flames. (87: p. 237, l. 92)
Haue perished like Fume that flies from fire.
(81: sig. G iii[v], l. 1683)
133 Drawe togither like furres. (34: p. 10, i, 3, 286)
134 Symper lyke a fyrmentie pot. (73: sig. C iii, l. 429)

135 My mowth is bytter as galle.
(4: p. 220, xxiv, 323; 39: sig. D ii[v])
More bytter than gall. (11: p. 46, l. 1174)
He is byttyrer þanne gall. (17: p. 147, l. 2342)
Thys sorow is beytterar þan ony galle. (8c: p. 92, l. 997)
More sour than gal. (74: p. 23, i, 3, 85)
136 And I fall away like a gammon of Bacon.
(79: sig. D iv[v], l. 992)
137 He is as wise as a Gander. (63: p. 23, l. 840)
138 Ye loke now as yt were a gost. (20: sig. G ii)
139 Her face as pale as a carnation gilofloure. (75: p. 61, iv, 2)
140 Þey [*gates of brass*] brast as ony glase. (8c: p. 91, l. 969)
Brighter then the Glasse. (80: sig. B iv, l. 225)
As brittle as the glasse.
(79: sig. A iv, l. 167; 3: p. 120, xiii,121)
As cleare as glasse. (74: p. 38, iii, 1, 30)
As cleyn as that she was beforn,
As . . . shynand glas. (3: p. 221, xx, 542 f.)
Your eyes are gray as glasse. (15: sig. D iii[v])
His face
When that it shoyn as any glas. (3: p. 281, xxiv, 82 f.)
The way is . . . sleeke as any glasse. (81: sig. D ii, l. 776)
The hills too steepe and slipperie all as glass.
(81: sig. D ii, l. 791)
141 Als þe gleme in þe glasse gladly þow glade.
(2: p. 135, xvii, 272)
And myne eyne þei glittir like þe gleme in þe glasse.
(2: p. 308, xxxii, 20)
142 And stuck to them as Glue to the water dooth cleaue.
(37: sig. A iv)
143 You haue a hart like a Gnat. (37: sig. F i)
144 For Esau is rough of heare as any goate. (14: sig. F i, iv, 9)
145 As sekyr as Gode ys in hewyn. (18: p. 24, l. 653)
146 That us hath made gaier then gould.
(1: I, 12, i, 83; 2: p. 124, xvi, 19)
As golde I glyster in gere. (21: sig. A v[v])
Balme more preciose than golde!
(8d: p. 183, l. 363; 24: sig. B i[v], ll. 227 f.; 73: sig. D iii, l. 746)
But to try the as gold is tryed in the fyer.
(9: p. 17, l. 128; 37: sig. G ii)
O words more worth then gold. (78: sig. I i[v], l. 2203)
The haire of your head shyneth as the pure gold.
(15: sig. D iii[v])

And then yt [*hair*] cryspeth and shyneth as bryght
As any pyrled gold. (20: sig. C ii[v])
I can make it [*hair*] shine like golde. (33: III, 244, l. 283)
Her herr . . .
Farr shynyng beyond fyne gold of araby. (61: sig. A iii[v])
Hir owne haire . . . yellow is as gold. (81: sig. D iii, l. 858)
Youre haire me thynke is as yelow as any gold.
(15: sig. C iii[v])
And þe hore þat hillis my heed
Is even like to þe golde wyre.
(2: p. 308, xxxii, 21 f.; 28: p. 388, l. 342)

147 For and I had ones as moche wytte as a gose. (23: sig. C iii)
Nay all ys open that they do there
As open as a gose eye. (20: sig. E iv[v])

148 That is as trewe as the gospell. (22: sig. E ii; 37: sig. D iii; 67: sig. C v[v]; 71: p. 228, iii, l. 181)
More true than the Gospel. (29: sig. E iv)
His wordes are trewer then the Gospell. (36: sig. E iii[v])
Most true alas, I do them fynde,
As thoughe they were written in the Gospell. (64: sig. G ii)

149 Sweeter then swelling grape of ripest wine.
(80: sig. B iv, l. 230)

150 The people fall before them as the flowring grasse
The mower with his syth cuts in the meade.
(81: sig. F iii, ll. 1376 f.)
Mine is the heart which vades away, as doth the . . . grasse.
(78: sig. E i, l. 1007)

151 He saide my seede shulde multyplye,
Lyke to þe gravell of þe see.
(2: p. 56, x, 15 f.; 6: pp. 34, ll. 298 f., 51, ll. 395 f.)

152 Þe gredy devyl xal grone grysly as a gryse (4: p. 149, xvi, 95)

153 There is no . . . gumme of Arabe
More delectable than your langage to me.
(25: p. 73, ll. 2347 f.)

154 I byde, as a brod brustun gutte. (17: p. 84, l. 235)

155 Your body laboreth as doth an hakney. (20: sig. F iv[v])

156 As wytte as a haddocke. (23: sig. C iii)

157 Let them throwe mylstones at the as thick as haile.
(62: sig. A iii[v])
In numbre they are more then the hayle stones.
(42: sig. E ii)
Salt teares from myne eyes lyke hayle stones . . . tricle.
(10: p. 20, l. 456)

158 For like as on both sydys the Iren the hamer makith playn,
So do I. (3: p. 243, xxii, 14 f.)
159 We will make them so bare
As euer was the Hare. (42: sig. D i)
They wyll fle fro thy face
As doth an Hare from the dogges in a chase.
(62: sig. A iv[v]; 78: sig. E iv[v], ll. 1255 f.)
Ye by my trowth as made as an hare. (67: sig. G ii)
160 Myn hed hangyth as an harpe. (17: p. 143, l. 2224)
Ffor swerdys sharpe
As An harpe
Quenys xul karpe. (4: p. 171, xix, 65 ff.)
161 As mad as a harte. (41: p. 67)
Thou ran'st like a Hart. (52: sig. C iv[v])
162 My body plyaunt as a hasel styck. (26: sig. A ii)
163 To gnaw theron, as gredy famine doeth constraine
The egre empty hauk pecemeale to pluck her pray.
(84: p. 193, ll. 78 f.)
As a hawke, I hoppe in my hende hale. (17: p. 91, l. 460)
164 My Venus is as bright as heauen. (81: sig. E i, l. 978)
165 As strong, as hector. (30: p. 12, l. 235; 61: sig. C i)
166 For beautie I to Hellin maie, aptly the maid compare.
(73: sigs. C ii, l. 362, H i[v], l. 1824)
167 As hard as hell. (1: II, 430, xxiv, 78)
168 Thoughe he be stronger then Hercules. (62: sig. A iv[v])
169 Lusty like a herringe, with a bell about his necke.
(45: sig. B i, ii, 1)
170 You laugh Hiena like. (81: sigs. E ii, l. 1061, E iv, l. 1172)
171 I them compair to weil fed hoggis. (28: p. 476, l. 2622)
As fat as a hogge. (44: sig. E iii, l. 983)
His hede is like a stowke hurlyd as hoggys.
(3: p. 377, xxx, 315)
So longe to kepe me, and lye like a hogge.
(45: sig. C iii, iv, 1)
Leaste they perysh
Lyke Hogges swynysh. (42: sig. H iv)
And we are serued with all, like a many of Hogges.
(37: sig. E i[v])
We may sleep with our vaces against the zone, an were hogs.
(78: sig. F i, l. 1295)
172 The other is plyaunt as euer was holly. (47: sig. F i)
173 My Husbande, as pleasaunte as Honnye. (64: sig. D iv[v])
Custance is as sweete as honey. (68: p. 186, song, ll. 13, 14)
O! yowur louely workis, to my soull are swetere þen hony.
(18: p. 9, l. 218)

Sweter then enie honey (*money*). (34: p. 10, i, 3, 288)
More swete than honye, are your thre exhortacyons.
(29: sig. F viii)
More swetter is þi name þan hony be kynd!
(8c: p. 58, l. 94; 48: sig. A iv)

174 Here is a chinne,
As softe as the hoofe of an horse. (72: sig. F iv)

175 And cuts my comb, like a hop on my thomb.
(63: p. 9, l. 304)

176 Making some thinke their heads as big as horses.
(52: sig. B iv)
And as an . . . hors we trewly þe bowth.
(4: p. 275, xxvi, 105)
Þou soldyst hym us as hors. (4: p. 279, xxvi, 235)

177 Hyȝe ouer holtis, as hound aftyr hare. (17: p. 105, l. 924)
But I will not cease huntinge, as a Hound doth for his praye.
(73: sig. B ii, l. 107)
Yet he regardeth me, nomore than doth an hounde.
(13a: sig. C ii)
Lyke a masterles hownde
Wandryng all abowt, seakyng his master. (31: pp. 31 f.)
Werse þan an hownde. (4: p. 67, viii, 126)

178 Hang me as hy as the house. (76: sig. C iv, l. 723)

179 Shee hath a face like a howlet. (76: sig. G i[v], l. 1702)
With toodlcloodlc poopc
As the howlet out of an yvie bushe should hoope.
(68: p. 131, ii, 1, 23 f.)

180 Clearer then . . .
. . . Ysie cruste of Christalles frosen stream.
(80: sig. B iv, ll. 234 f.)

181 Your face like an Incorne, now shineth so gay. (72: sig. G i)

182 Myn hed I wolde hyde
As an Irchoun þat were schent. (17: p. 148, ll. 2395 f.)

183 With balde crownes lyke Iacke dawes. (30: p. 128, l. 2525)
No, but styll cogeld in like Jacke daw that cries ka kob.
(14: sig. C iii[v], ii, 3)

184 To kicke,
Like a iade when hee feleth the spurre for to pricke.
(40: sig. B iii[v])

185 Þei chateryn And chateryn As they jays were.
(4: p. 353, xxxi, 19; 20: sig. B i[v])
I am as gentyll as Jay on tre. (21: sig. A vi[v])
He jangelis like a jay. (2: p. 357, xxxv, 265)
And iet it ioly as a iay. (25: p. 15, l. 465)
I am jolyere than þe jay. (4: p. 154, xvii, 77)

186 Smoother then Iet. (80: sig. B iv, l. 232)
187 As bare as Job. (29: sig. D i[v]; 65: sig. B i)
188 Thocht ȝe cry lyke ane Ke all day. (28: p. 539, l. 4397)
189 Stretch out our legs ant were a cennell of dogs.
(78: sig. F i, l. 1296)
190 See that all shine . . .
. . . as doth a key newly come from the Smiths forge.
(68: p. 160, iv, 3, 18 f.)
191 When like the tender Kid new weaned from the teat:
In euery plesant springing Mead, I took my choice of meat.
(79: sig. C ii[v], ll. 584 f.)
192 They maye lyue as mery as ony kynge. (23: C iii[v])
I wyll make as mery as a kinge. (26: sig. A iv[v])
So that contentation makes me as rich as a king.
(48: sig. C i)
193 And what can courage doe without helpe,
As much as a kitling. (47: sig. A iv[v])
194 Bot nowe my cares aren keen as knyffe.
(2: pp. 45, ix, 7, 52, ix, 223)
Your wordes do slay my hart, as if the knife
In cruell wise forthwith shold perce the same.
(84: p. 178, ii, 2, 36 f.)
195 Chill squease hym as drie as a kyxe. (34: p. 62, v, 10, 1907)
196 Ladys, whyt as lak[e]. (17: p. 132, l. 1849)
197 More humble then a Lambe. (80: sig. C ii, l. 381)
He lokis like a lambe. (2: p. 281, xxx, 273)
Bot as a lam meke was he ay. (3: p. 327, xxvii, 52;
4: p. 274, xxvi, 90;
8b: p. 35, ll. 217 f.)
And after, mekely as a lamb,
Vpon the crose there dyd he dye. (5: p. 71, ll. 7 f.)
And as still as the lambe, which lyeth before the sheerer
He was scourged. (12: p. 30, ll. 904 f.)
As Lambe the Lyon, so my power, the stowtest do obey.
(78: sig. B iv, l. 379)
As Lambe the Wolfe . . .
So do I flie from tyrant he. (78: sig. E iv[v], ll. 1255 f.)
198 And their iust sauer, as a lampe extende hys lyght.
(13a: sig. D iv[v])
199 Myne eyen do shyne as lanterne bryght. (21: sig. A v)
200 She is buxum and whyte as laue. (4: p. 91, x, 275, cf. note, p. 403)
201 Bett as blo as lede. (3: p. 268, xxiii, 327)

My banes er heuy als lede. (2: pp. 103, xiii, 15, 139, xviii, 20 f., 367, xxxvi, 262; 3: pp. 42, iv, 82, 346, xxviii, 210; 4: pp. 13, i, 421, 317, xxvi, 1332; 8d: pp. 179, l. 225, 192, l. 617; 30: p. 108, l. 2138; 71: p. 188, i, 3, 53; 80: sigs. B i, l. 10, D iv, l. 818)
Myne harte is heuy as any lede. (2: pp. 166, xx, 207, 241, xxviii, 21; 3: pp. 192, xviii, 195, 389, xxxi, 71; 5: p. 64, ii, 1015)
The dent of deth is hevyar þan led. (8c: p. 64, l. 272; 17: p. 164, l. 2924)
Myn hede is hevy as lympe of leede. (4: p. 160, xvii, 273)
As heavie as lead lumpes. (68: p. 131, ii, 122)
Wan as led. (3: p. 391, xxxi, 146)
Ther ys to moche cloth, yt weys as ony lede.
(18: p. 25, l. 692)
No greater dyfference betwene lede and golde
Then betwene the rest and her. (55: sig. B iii[v])
My wyl as farre therin out weyth my power
As a sow of led out weyth a saforne flowre. (55: sig. C iv[v])

202 Nowe am I light as leyf on tree. (2: p. 444, xli, 346; 3: pp. 127, xiii, 357 f., 325, xxvi, 623)
Mankynde,
Lyter þanne lef is on lynde. (17: p. 184, ll. 3595 f.)
Mi flesh it quakys as lefe on lynde. (3: p. 365, xxix, 360)
Swifte so lefe on lynde. (16: p. 96, l. 264)
And as a Leafe in a stormye weather,
So is mannes lyfe blowen cleane a waye. (64: sig. H ii[v])

203 Choppe thee as a leeke. (36: sig. E ii)

204 With angylles brygth as þe lewyn. (8c: p. 132, l. 2043)
With gold & syluer, lyth as leuene. (17: p. 104, l. 893)
Myne aungellis louely of late, lighter þan þe levene.
(2: p. 479, xlv, 175; 17: p. 181, l. 3499)

205 I make a fer in mans towte,
Þat launcyth up as any leye. (17: p. 145, ll. 2290 f.)

206 I love hym as my liffe. (2: p. 58, x, 63; 6: p. 39, l. 81; 28: p. 387, l. 317; 80: sig. G i, l. 1508)

207 Hir heid wan heiar than the lift. (53: p. 171, l. 50)

208 Moore cleere then light. (44: sig. B iiii, l. 278)

209 I sawe one like lightnynge. (12: p. 8, l. 248)

210 þis lady is to þe lilly lyke.
(2: p. 96, xii, 97; 3: p. 391, xxxi, 145)
Bere one and forthe brynge,
Als þe lelly floure full faire of hewe. (2: p. 96, xii, 90 f.)
As whyte as a lylly. (64: sig. F ii)
Lely whyte. (4: pp. 90, x, 243, 145, xv, 304; 25: p. 49, l. 1555; 28: p. 386, l. 280)
211 My fingers are as good as a liue (*lime*) twig. (46: p. 24)
212 Now, Jason, as jentyll as euer was the lynde.
(7: p. 67, l. 309)
I am light as lynde. (3: p. 97, x, 368)
Licht as the lynd. (53: p. 171, l. 16)
213 I sall holde þis as euen as a lyne. (2: p. 328, xxxiii, 245)
As right as a line his hart I haue hit. (85: sig. C iv[v])
214 And as a lyon in his weale,
Christ shalbe haunsed hye. (1: I, 96, v, 251 f.)
Ffor thei be as fers as a lyon in a cage. (8a: p. 10, l. 231)
Who lyke a Lyon most commonly frowned. (64: sig. A iv[v])
I lepe as a lyon. (17: p. 105, l. 938)
Thou as a Lyon lye, & as a Lyonesse. (10: p. 38, l. 974)
Whan I loke on þis lady, I am lofty as the lyon.
(8c: p. 91, l. 944)
215 Lyke Locusts they do swarme. (10: p. 118, l. 113)
216 Comende
Youre lawe and youre lordshippe as lodsterne on hight.
(2: p. 124, xvi, 23 f.)
217 þou comaundis lightly as a lorde. (2: p. 352, xxxv, 115)
He will make it as prowde a lord as he were.
(3: p. 102, xii, 64)
218 As mery as a Marche hare. (25: p. 30, l. 922)
219 You are as ful of honesty,
As a mary bone is ful of hoony. (32: sig. D ii)
220 It standys vp lyke a mast. (3: p. 265, xxiii, 232)
I am for þe pope, as for þe shyppe þe mast. (30: p. 36, l. 751)
221 Thi loue is swetter þanne þe mede.
(2: p. 424, xxxix, 89; 3: p. 341, xxviii, 111; 17: p. 100, l. 776)
222 As meeke as a mecocke. (86: sig. B i, l. 227)
223 I pine as doth the Merline shee that could not win her pray.
(76: sig. C iv, l. 741)
224 Olde rotten witche,
As white as midnightes arsehole. (14: sig. G i, v, 6)
225 And as whyte as any mylk. (20: sig. D ii; 30: p. 87, l. 1708; 40: sig. C i[v])

Tent well youre twyfyls youre nek abowte as mylke.
(3: p. 377, xxx, 324)

226 Where lyke a mill horse he grinds corne. (10: p. 147, l. 348)

227 [*Women are*] Like to the Moone whose operation it is often times to change. (76: sig. B iii, l. 353)
A serkyll as rownde as a moyn. (3: p. 125, xiii, 278)
For so much as all yong men for this my Beautie,
As the Moone, the starres, I do farre excell. (64: sig. B ii[v])

228 Þou schalt lye drenkelyd as a movs. (17: p. 168, l. 3080)
As drunk as a mouse. (39: sig. D i[v]; 63: p. 9, l. 300; 64: sigs. D ii, E iii)
Liue like a mouse in a mill and haue another to grinde my meale for me. (51: sig. B iiii[v])
Mute like a mouse (50: sig. E i)
They perceyue as lyttell as doth the Mowse.
(64: sig. D iii[v])
How haue you two liued? . . . Faith euen like two mice in an amberie that eat vp all the meat, and when they haue done, gnaw holes in the cupbord. (51: sig. D i)

229 As muk apon mold
I widder away. (3: p. 25, iii, 62 f.)

230 Thay sould haue luggis als lang as Muillis.
(28: p. 545, l. 4559)

231 For lyke as mustarde is sharpe of taste,
Ryght so a sharpe Fansy must be founde.
(25: p. 18, ll. 552 f.)

232 I am as bare as my naile. (39: sig. E i)
Thou myghtest go as naked as my nayle. (56: sig. D i[v])
As whyte as my nayle. (30: p. 104, l. 2039, cf. p. 84, l. *134)

233 Your wordes be more swetcr than ony precyous narde.
(25: p. 73, l. 2345)

234 Dark as nyght. (3: p. 352, xxviii, 345)
Goe wend thy wayes, obscurer then the night.
(79: sig. C i, l. 487)

235 A tent . . . as big as thy nose. (39: sig. A iii)

236 Nutbrowne Ale. (64: sig. D ii; 69: p. 16, ii, 17; 81: sig. A iv, l. 58)
Their litell buttons, no bygger than twoo Nuttes.
(34: p. 26, iii, 4, 772)

237 To see vs bend like Oakes with his vain breath.
(51: sig. F ii[v])
Harder harted then the aged Oke. (80: sig. B iv, l. 237)
The horson knaue wayeth, & yt were a Croked oke.
(30: p. 38, l. 797)

238 More glib then Oyle. (80: sig. B iv, l. 238)
239 A mouth lyke an Ouen. (72: sig. F iv)
240 Shall I stand crouching like an owle. (32: sig. D iv[v])
The slaue lookes like an owle in a tree.
(76: sig. B iii[v], l. 419)
Loke lyke an owle. (30: p. 11, l. 198)
I loke lyke an howle. (17: p. 149, l. 2410)
Or ellis like an nowele in a stok,
Full preualy his pray for to wayte. (2: p. 258, xxix, 119 f.)
And then as Owle that flies abroad when other fowles do rest,
I creepe out. (78: sig. G ii, ll. 1657 f.)
As riche as an Owle. (86: sig. B i, l. 229)
241 And as an ox . . . we trewly þe bowth. (4: p. 275, xxvi, 105)
And my selfe they can destroie,
As Ox that gnawes biselie
The grasse right to the roote. (1: I, 89, v, 110 ff.)
242 My fo is ded and prendyd as a padde. (4: p. 175, xix, 211)
243 And speaketh like a parat Poppagaye. (66: p. 10, l. 235)
Then wolde we get the stretes trym as a parate.
(56: sig. C iv[v])
244 It was lyke a pawe
Of a whytynge. (35: sig. C ii[v], ll. 555 f.)
245 Here cometh Pryde
As crank as a pecok. (20: sig. H i)
And maydens coy strange:
As Pecockes sit perking, by chaunce in the plomtree.
(86: sig. B iii[v], ll. 403 f.)
Prowde as pacok. (3: p. 344, xxviii, 168; 86: sig. B i, l. 226)
A swane / as prowde as a po. (3: p. 117, xiii, 37)
She prankith and getteth with out faylle
As a pecocke that hath spred, and sheweth hir gaye taile.
(66: p. 10, ll. 226 f.)
246 And see the spitte be scoured as cleane as any pearle.
(14: sig. E ii, iv, 3)
247 A bon grace,
Which like a penthouse may com farre ouer your face.
(15: sig. C iv[v])
248 Her cheekes are become as leane as a pestill of porke.
(75: p. 61, iv, 2)
You shine lyke a pestle of Porke. (72: sig. G i)
249 As fine as phippence (*five pence*). (86: sig. B i, l. 226)
250 Brighter than phebus for al his fervent hete. (8a: p. 20, l. 492)
251 He soiourneth within a mans brest
Lyke the burnynge Fenix in her owne nest. (38: p. 3)

252 That one chatreth lyke a pye.
(20: sig. B i[v]; 66: p. 10, l. 234)
He patris like a py. (2: p. 357, xxxv, 266)
Up as pie he piped. (1: I, 150, vii, 428)
Thou preachest as a pie. (1: I, 96, v, 273)
253 The wyld bore of Rome . . .
Lyke pygges they folow. (30: p. 5, ll. 71 f.)
254 Thou lookest like a poore pidgeon puld of late.
(50: sig. D ii)
255 Straight as any pyller. (69: p. 20, ii, 1, 44)
256 Not one sparke, so byg as a pyns head. (69: p. 13, i, 5, 13)
257 More stately then the Pine. (80: sig. B iv, l. 232)
258 Olde rotten witche,
As white as . . . virgin pitche. (14: sig. G i, v, 6)
259 I sprange as a plante mannes mysse to amende.
(23: sig. A ii)
260 My Venus is . . .
. . . firmer than the poles that hold vp heauen.
(81: sig. E i, ll. 979 f.)
I kyst it as strayght as ony pole. (67: sig. E iv)
Ye say that ye kyst it euyn in the hole
Of the holow ashe as strayte as a pole. (67: sig. E iv)
261 She shall stynke lyke a pole kat. (59: sig. A ii)
262 Fresher then Poplar. (80: sig. B iv, l. 233)
263 And her voyce is as doucett
And as swete as resty porke. (67: sig. C iii[v])
264 I heare no more then a post. (52: sig. G iii[v])
I am as wise as a post. (78: sig. B ii, l. 216)
265 In comparyson bycause they be so small
No more than the prikkes do that be on a gall.
(22: sig. A vi[v])
266 As whot as a black pudding. (39: sig. B i[v])
One as fit for you as a pudding for a friers mouth.
(39: sig. B i[v])
Your answeare then in sooth,
Fyts me as iumpe as a pudding a Friars mouth.
(77: sig. D iv)
Hyt me as pat, as a pudding *Pope Ione*. (77: sig. E iv)
Stuft like a Poddinge bagge full vp to the throat.
(73: sig. F iii, l. 1358)
267 It schal þee weyen, as peys in punder.
(17: p. 155, l. 2629)
268 Heile come as round as a purr. (71: p. 207, ii, 4, 96)
269 I lite on the dunghill like a puttock! (46: p. 34)

270 Bot thay, lyke rams, rudlie in thair rage,
Vnpysalt, rinnis amang the sillie ȝowis.
(28: p. 481, ll. 2764 f.)
Speake out like a ramme. (68: p. 111, i, 2, 28)
271 And ranke as a ratte. (29: sig. C iv)
Like as the Rat that once hath tast of Rosalgar or bayne,
Runnes presently to some moist place to coole her poisned pain.
(76: sig. C iv, ll. 732 f.)
272 As sharpe as a racer. (71: p. 247, iv, 1, 125)
That worde is to me sharper than a rasers blade.
(14: sig. F iv, v, 4)
Nay lyke a rasor, some of their nayles are whet.
(83: sig. E iii)
273 So passe our dayes euen as the riuers flete. (84: p. 174, l. 20)
This day stremyt owt lik . . .
. . . a ryvere grete. (8d: p. 172, ll. 26 f.)
Their thoughtes as streaming riuers swiftly passe.
(80: sig. D ii, l. 559)
Thou makes my eyes to run as riuers doo by streame.
(85: sig. C iii)
274 Theyr heades . . .
. . . be as harde as rocke. (41: p. 64)
Like as the craggy rocke,
Resists the streames, and flings the waltering waues
A loofe, so he reiects and scornes my words.
(87: p. 251, ii, 3, 152 ff.)
275 Now þan am I light as a roo.
(2: p. 281, xxx, 262; 4: p. 327, xxvi, 1640 f.)
Ren so þe ro. (16: p. 96, l. 268)
Swifter then the Roe. (80: sig. B iv, l. 226)
276 Fayr and fresch as rose on thorn. (4: p. 145, xv, 303)
Rubu rody as þe rose! (8c: p. 91, l. 959)
Your lyps as ruddy as the redde Rose. (15: sig. D iv)
Here's water as sweete as a Rose. (77: sig. F iii[v])
Hys laws to pursew,
Ys swetter to me þan sawoure of þe rose.
(19: p. 48, ll. 387 f.)
Oh lylly Babe whose feature fayre surmountes the ruddie rose.
(73: sig. F ii, l. 1281)
She is a Queene whose goodly hue, excelles the royall Rose.
(85: sig. F ii[v])
277 She lookys like a saynt. (3: p. 375, xxx, 267)
278 See that all shine as bright as sainct George.
(68: p. 160, iv, 3, 18)

279 And consumeth a way
As the salt in the water. (70: p. 123, iv, 1, 9 f.)
280 As mighty as Sampson the strong. (43: sig. A iv)
Thoughe he be stronger then . . . Sampson.
(62: sigs. A iv[v], C i[v])
281 Eschewe a hore as ye woud a scorpian. (71: p. 258, iv, 4, 36)
282 As gret as þe se. (4: p. 98, xi, 29)
But as the waving seas doe flowe & ebbe by course,
So all thinges else do chaunge. (34: p. 15, ii, 1, 443 f.)
As sond in þe se doth ebbe and flowe
Hath cheselys many vnnumerabyll
So xal þi sede þou mayst me trowe
Encres. (4: p. 50, v, 221 ff.; 1: I, 82, iv, 450 f.; 10: pp. 18, ll. 385 f., 110, l. 440, 212, ll. 379 f.)
283 Paramourys, swetter þanne sens. (17: p. 137, l. 2026)
284 Flee from euill company as from Serpent ye would flee.
(39: sig. E iiii)
Never was serpent more stinging than ye be. (13b: p. 140)
285 Proues foule, deformd, and like a shadow glides.
(81: sig. G i[v], l. 1551)
Euen as a shadowe it passeth awaye. (64: sig. H ii)
To wayt on me, as shadow in the shining day.
(84: p. 194, l. 111)
286 Euen as rich as a newe shorne sheepe. (45: sig. B i, ii, 1)
But glad to runne away like a new shorne sheepe.
(44: sig. D iii[v], l. 740)
{ Lyke schepe that were scharid
A-way schall ȝe schake. (2: p. 246, xxviii, 141)
287 Swyfter þanne schyp with rodyr. (17: p. 129, l. 1741)
The people and the land,
Which now remaine as ship without a sterne. (82: sig. H i)
But as the ship against the rocks, sustaine and bide the wracke. (85: sig. A iii)
288 I . . . am like a Shittle-cock betwixt two Battledores.
(52: sig. B iv[v])
289 Wyser þan euer was Syble sage. (7: p. 68, l. 351)
290 A shyrt as soft as sylk.
(20: sig. D ii; 28: p. 388, l. 341; 85: sig. D i[v])
Your fleshe was soft os tender silke. (8d: p. 197, l. 774)
291 The temple of Salamon as sylver bryght. (4: p. 198, xxii, 167)
As bright as any syller. (69: p. 20, ii, 1, 43)
As good siluer shall be aye,
Stidfast men and trew. (1: II, 391, xxii, 87 f.)

As cleyn as that she was beforne,
As puryd syluer. (3: p. 221, xx, 542 f.)

292 As denty and nice, as a halpeny worth of siluer spoons. (66: p. 9, l. 218)

293 Lyke as þe smyth trieth ern in þe feer. (18: p. 11, l. 280)

294 Vanishe as the smoke. (48: sig. A ii; 81: sig. E ii, l. 1051)

295 Go and hye the as fast as a snayle. (59: sig. B i[v])
Ffor If I went þus A-way and shrynkyd as a snayle. (4: p. 198, xxii, 148)
Nowe certis þat schall I doo,
Full suerly as a snayle. (2: p. 353, xxxv, 117 f.)

296 And flie their societie as . . . a snake. (40: sig. D iii)
Base minded men I know there are in field,
That doe delight in murder, rape and blood,
As there are . . .
. . . enuious snakes among the fleeting fish. (81: sig. C i, ll. 436 ff.)

297 You are both as constant as snowe in the sunne,
Which from snow to water through melting doth run. (43: sig. D iv[v])
And consumeth a way
As . . . the snow in Somers day. (70: p. 123, iv, 1, 9 f.)
It flyet a-wey, as any snow. (17: p. 156, l. 2642)
Yt's infec't with Leprosie,
Lyke snow. (10: pp. 51, ll. 255 f., 49, ll. 197 f.)
His clothyng is white as snowe. (2: pp. 188, xxiii, 97, 377, xxxvii, 89; 3: p. 295, xxv, 81; 10: p. 82, l. 1150; 12: p. 8, l. 249; 50: sig. E i[v]; 56: sig. A ii[v])
A Mistres whiter then the snowe. (80: sig. B iv, l. 224)

298 As heuy as a sod. (3: p. 101, xii, 21)
In erth, as any sod liffyd with grete grevance. (3: p. 24, iii, 58)

299 As wyse as Solomon. (1: II, 382, xxi, 276)

300 He will be drunkin lyke ane sow. (28: p. 425, l. 1313)
Thou knowest no more to sell wood, then doth the sowe. (64: sig. F i)
I am as wise as my mothers sowe! (46: p. 16)

301 They shold not run & lackie
Like spaniells at my stirrop. (70: p. 99, ii, 1, 19 f.)

302 As a sparke of fyre in þe se,
My mercy is synne quenchande. (17: p. 185, ll. 3603 f.)

303 Dyrectly to myne harte
Percyth his wordys euyn lyke as many sperys. (55: sig. A iii[v])
Thai ar sharp as a spere. (3: p. 372, xxx, 163)

304 In my syght he is, more venym than the spyder. (13a: sig. B iii[v])

305 That he maie bee pressed as men doo presse a spounge. (34: p. 62, v, 10, 1904)

306 He hath rebelled
Agaynst holy churche, vsynge it wurse than a stable. (30: p. 46, ll. 973 f.)

307 As styffe as a stake. (41: p. 61)
As still as a stake
He standith. (83: sig. A iii)

308 And als þe sternes wer strewed wyde,
So saide he þat my seede shuld be. (2: p. 56, x, 17 f.; 1: I, 82, iv, 451 f.; 4: p. 50, x, 217 f.; 6: p. 51, ll. 392 f.; 10: p. 79, ll. 1063 f.; 13a: sig. C i[v])

309 My hart is harde as stele. (3: pp. 347, xxviii, 225, 348, xxviii, 258)
Thou art stabyll as any steyll. (3: p. 197, xix, 70)
Oure knyghtis
That is stedfast as stele. (2: p. 247, xxviii, 166)
Stiffer then Steele. (80: sig. B iv, l. 239)
He is so swre as stele. (30: p. 14, l. 271)
Trew as stele. (3: pp. 26, iii, 120, 123, xiii, 226, 138, xiii, 699; 8c: p. 116, l. 1637; 17: p. 96, l. 618; 26: sig. C iii; 34: p. 49, v, 6, 1493; 69: pp. 33, iii, 2, 4, 66, v, 2, 246; 71: p. 228, iii, 1, 179)
As true as any stele. (14: sig. E iii, iv, 4)
As trusty as steele. (80: sig. B i[v], l. 47)

310 Styff as a stykke. (4: p. 144, xv, 260)

311 Ile beate thee like a stocke. (78: sig. F ii[v], l. 1393)

312 As stout as a Stockefish. (86: sig. B i, l. 227)

313 Beate lyke a stone. (64: sig. A iv)
I was are blynde as any stone. (2: p. 212, xxv, 356; 3: p. 360, xxix, 206)
His hearte as could grew as a stone. (10: pp. 192, l. 1272, 296, l. 987; 80: sig. E iii, l. 1061)
Stark stone dead. (70: p. 136, v, 2, 17)
A hert hard as ston. (4: p. 268, xxv, 1054; 8d: p. 207, l. 1046; 41: p. 64)

Hartes harder then stone. (8d: p. 217, l. 1392)
þe cors þat nere knewe of care,
No more þen stone in weye. (16: p. 91, ll. 101 f.)
Naked as a stone. (2: p. 347, xxxiv, 313)
See thou bee a stone . . .
I ment thou shouldest nothing saye. (14: sig. E iii[v], iv, 6)
As a senslesse stone,
I neither wit nor tong could vse t'expresse my mone.
(84: p. 193, iv, 2, 73 f.)
She spareth no more my flesshe and bone,
Than if my bodye were made of Stone. (64: sig. G ii)
Stande as any stones. (2: p. 356, xxxv, 217)
I woll be as stedfast as ston. (8c: p. 104, l. 1291)
Petra is a ston full of stabilitee,
Alway stedfaste. (8d: p. 210, ll. 1164 f.)
Stiffe as stonne. (1: II, 380, xxi, 213; 3: p. 270, xxiii, 399)
But halde þe stille als stane. (2: pp. 108, xiii, 194, 146, xix, 4; 3: pp. 35, iii, 406, 78, ix, 6; 17: pp. 87, l. 345, 127, l. 1700)
Stande still as a stone. (2: pp. 286, xxx, 372, 303, xxxi, 311; 3: p. 39, iii, 525)
Stand as styll as any stone. (3: p. 222, xx, 561)
Stone stille. (2: pp. 127, xvii, 28, 248, xxviii, 175, 294, xxxi, 65, 300, xxxi, 243, 307, xxxii, 2, 337, xxxiv, 2; 3: pp. 78, ix, 12, 123, xiii, 232, 125, xiii, 280)
As still as stones in the streite. (69: p. 6, i, 2, 25)
Stand as styll as stone in Wall.
(3: pp. 258, xxiii, 2, 327, xxvii, 60 f.)
Stur them self like stoones. (45: sig. E iii[v], v, 3)
True as any stone. (3: p. 356, xxix, 106)
Thou art trew for to trist as ston in the wall.
(3: p. 38, iii, 515)
Truly as stone. (3: p. 246, xxii, 99)

314 And as the streame that rowleth downe the hyll,
So will they headlong ronne with raging thoughtes.
(82: sig. G ii)

315 Heyl, swetter þan sugur.
(8c: p. 132, l. 2047; 34: p. 10, i, 3, 287 f.)

316 His face was like the son for bright.
(3: pp. 295, xxv, 82, 352, xxviii, 347; 4: p. 109, xii, 15 f.)

Behold my contenance and my colur,
Bryghtur then the sun in the meddis of the dey.
(5: p. 18, i, 507 f.)

As bright
As seven tymes the Sonne is light. (1: II, 389, xxii, 41 f.)
I am a thowsand fold
Brighter then is the son. (3: p. 4, i, 88 f.)
Oh cristall cleare as sun. (49: sig. G ii[v], iv, 3)
His face schynes as þe sonne. (2: p. 188, xxiii, 98; 3: p. 269, xxiii, 361; 62: sig. D ii[v])
He lyth in here as sunne in glas. (4: pp. 328, xxvii, 18, 181, xx, 97 ff.; 3: p. 87, x, 35 ff.)

317 As bryght As þe sonnbem.
(4: p. 269, xxvi, 18; 13a: sig. D iv[v])
Bryghtere than þe sunne beem. (4: p. 162, xvii, 317)

318 Like to a faire sunshine day ouercast with Clowds of raine.
(79: sig. A iv, l. 162)

319 Thou fotys it lyke a swanne. (25: p. 25, l. 765)
Whyte as swan. (4: p. 56, vi, 166; 17: p. 99, l. 720)

320 All be-mased in a sowne,
As we had bene sticked swyne. (1: II, 341, xviii, 265)
But die in their filthines like swine. (36: sig. G ii)
As drunke as a swyne. (10: p. 289, l. 797)
I schuld be stekyd as a swyne. (17: p. 110, l. 1111)
He walloweth without measure,
As a beastly swine doth in his filthie stye. (36: sig. F iii[v])
To a filthy Swyne, such mysers are comparable.
(49: sig. C ii, ii, 3)

321 Let this defend thee like a trusty Swoord.
(79: sig. A iv, l. 143)
Swych a sorwe bothe sharpe and smerte
Þat as a swerd perce it xalle. (4: p. 165, xviii, 88 f.)

322 Euen as the swordfish meetes the mighty Whale,
And puts the hugie monster to disgrace.
(81: sig. D i, ll. 700 f.)

323 Base minded men I know there are in field,
That doe delight in murder, rape and blood,
As there are tares in corne. (81: sig. C i, ll. 436 ff.)

324 Tost,
Like to a tennis ball. (44: sig. C iii, ll. 470 f.)

325 Her naylys sharpe as tenter hokys. (25: p. 32, l. 1002)

326 Mesure is lyke a tetter
That ouergroweth a mannes face. (25: p. 18, ll. 543 f.)

327 Hyngis as a theffe.
(2: p. 363, xxxvi, 142; 4: p. 303, xxvi, 901)
þei spared me nomore þan a theffe. (2: p. 507, xlviii, 262)
{ Euen like a theffe heneusly
Hurle ȝe me here. (2: p. 253, xxviii, 294)
328 As sharp as a thystyll. (3: p. 119, xiii, 101)
329 Showres sharper then thorne. (3: p. 365, xxix, 361)
330 I am as whyt as thought. (4: p. 279, xxvi, 214)
331 And speaketh . . .
. . . as fine, as a small silken threede. (66: p. 10, ll. 235 f.)
I can go to hir as streight as a threde. (14: sig. D ii, ii, 4)
The very way and path that shall them lede
Euen to heuen gatys as strayght as any threde. (57: sig. A iv)
He the bands agayne hath broken lyke threeds of lynnen cloth.
(10: p. 145, l. 291)
He the cordes hath broken as a man would breake a threede
Of tow. (10: p. 144, ll. 279 f.)
332 Excomminycacyons, as thonder boltes cam downe.
(30: p. 61, l. 1290)
333 Euen as the . . . tyger fierce doth seeke the lambe to kill:
So seekest thou. (76: sig. A iii[v], ll. 141 f.)
334 Sea and water all shall Brenne
Agaynst kynd, that mon may ken,
Tinder as though it wear. (1: II, 397, xxii, 282 ff.)
335 As true as a Tinker. (86: sig. B i, l. 229)
336 And flie their societie, as a tode. (40: sig. D iii)
337 As hot as a tost. (70: p. 106, ii, 4, 27)
Never . . . tost so hot. (68: p. 167, iv, 6, 5)
338 I remember since it [*his leg*] was no greater then a tree.
(43: sig. B i[v])
339 As trimme as a trencher, as tricke, as swete, as cleane.
(14: sig. E ii, iv, 4; 30: p. 128, l. 2514)
340 Take good hart like Troyelus in strength.
(76: sig. E iii[v], l. 1281)
341 I am forthwith as hole as a troute. (25: p. 51, l. 1624)
342 A Horse which . . .
Was . . . bellied like a Tonne. (73: sig. B i, ll. 22 f.)
My chest bigge as a tunne. (26: sig. A ii)
þanne was his toumbe tome as a tonne. (2: p. 430, xl, 127)
343 My colour is tawny, colouryd as a turffe. (25: p. 61, l. 1959)
344 He is lyke of them, to haue nomore grace than a turke.
(29: sig. F ii; 30: pp. 37, l. 767, 59,
l. 1241, 78, ll. *5 f., 114, l. 2262,
p. 118, l. 2357)

345 He loued a while even like a turtle dove.
(68: p. 176, iv, 8, 37)
I am as the Turkel hath lost her make. (76: sig. G i, l. 1669)
The dowfe is more gentill her trust I vntew,
Like vnto the turtill for she is ay trew. (3: p. 38, iii, 505 f.)
The ladie, that so late lamented here
Her princes death, and thought to liue alone,
As doeth the turtle true without her feere.
(84: p. 182, ii, 3, 41 ff.)
Her turtles truthe. (84: p. 183, iii, 1, 8)
346 As þe fane þat turnyth with þe wynde, so þou art conuertyble.
(18: p. 27, l. 742)
347 There's a Musterd-maker lookes as keene as Viniger.
(52: sig. D iii)
348 I florysh as the vine tre. (26: sig. A i[v])
349 His luddokkys thai lowke like walk-mylne cloggys.
(3: p. 377, xxx, 314)
350 For as a wall both night & day they vs & them defended.
(10: p. 191, l. 1235)
The sea strucke with his rodd, & as a wall yt stoode diuided.
(10: p. 72, l. 856)
Þe see sall stande,
Tille we be wente, right as a wall.
(2: p. 90, xi, 379 f.; 3: p. 76, viii, 390 f.)
351 In the wast I wil haue ye as small as a wand. (15: sig. D i)
I waxe wayke as any wande. (2: p. 138, xviii, 17)
352 Angry as a waspe. (45: sig. B ii, ii, 1)
353 For it liked hir as well to tell you no lies,
As water in hir shyppe, or salt cast in hir eyes.
(68: p. 139, iii, 2, 15 f.)
We were as welcome as water into the ship. (75: p. 46, iii, 3)
Flytte,
As doth the water to and fro. (64: sig. D i)
Thou art pour'd out as water. (10: p. 38, l. 964)
For as water quencheth fier and the flame dooth suppres,
So vertue hateth vice. (39: sig. D i)
But as the water troubled with the mudde
Shewes not the face which els the eye should see,
Euen so your irefull minde. (82: sig. F i)
And as to waters from on head, and fountayne oft do spring,
So vyce and vertue oft do flo, from pallace of a kinge.
(83: sig. C ii)
354 A! In woo I waltyr, as wawys In þe wynd!
(8c: p. 86, l. 819)

355 Her harte doth melt lyke waxe. (77: sig. G iv)
I will worke this geare lyke wax. (75: p. 36, ii, 3)
Money, or faire Women, workes him as waxe.
(77: sig. D iv[v])
356 Lust ys now comun as þe way. (19: p. 57, l. 655)
357 That old lyzarde has no more witt then the wethercocke of poles. (71: p. 233, iii, 2, 3)
I am as very a turncote as the wethercoke of Poles.
(46: p. 24)
358 Base minded men I know there are in field,
That doe delight in murder, rape and blood,
As there are . . . weeds with flowers. (81: sig. C i, ll. 436 ff.)
359 She is as greatt as a whall. (3: p. 119, xiii, 105)
Your teeth as white as euer was the whales bone.
(15: sig. D iv)
360 Thir bony armis . . .
Ar evin als wantoun as any wilk (*whelk*).
(28: p. 540, ll. 4418 f.)
361 Lyke a whelpe he woulde waugh. (30: p. 87, l. 1716)
And what can courage doe without helpe,
As much as a . . . suckling whelpe. (47: sig. A iv[v])
He regardyth no more, þe pope, than he dothe a whelpe.
(30: p. 32, l. 657)
362 As the whyte a boute the yolke of an egg doth lye.
(22: sig. A vi[v])
363 Ye lye lyke a whoore. (65: sig. B i)
364 Husbandes as good,
As wigges made of wood. (47: sig. A iii)
365 As wylde fyre and thondyr blast
He cam cryeng on to me. (4: p. 289, xxvi, 531 f.)
366 Chaungable as the wynde. (26: sig. A iv[v])
More fickle then the winde. (80: sig. B iv, l. 238)
Now fast, now lose, now hot, now cold, unconstant as that wind. (45: sig. A ii, i, 1)
Roome for a turne coate, that will turne as the wynde.
(76: sig. C ii[v], l. 622; 85: sig. C ii[v])
My heart as light as the wynde. (26: sig. A iv)
Words, let them passe like wind. (74: p. 70, v, 8, 2 f.)
Sharp as the wind. (63: p. 4, l. 119)
And swift as winde. (28: p. 500, l. 3240)
Þir wise wordis ware noght wroght in waste,
To waffe and wende away als wynde. (2: p. 95, xii, 53 f.)
I trowe oure wittis be waste as wynde. (2: p. 157, xx, 16)
I . . . take thy wordes but as wynde. (13c: sig. E iii)

As wynde in watyr I wave. (17: p. 88, l. 380)
As wauering as the winde. (79: sig. A iv, l. 168)
And Loue so welcome to euery towne,
As winde that blowes the houses downe. (50: sig. D iii[v])
As wroth as wynde
Is kyng herownde. (4: pp. 7, i, 217 f., 315, xxvi, 1280 f.)
367 Hir arsse gard evin lyke ane wind-mill. (28: p. 538, l. 4358)
His brayne is stedfast as a wyndemyll. (35: sig. B i, l. 200)
368 Nobylyte . . .
Is vanyshed awaye, as it we[*re*] a wynter myste.
(30: p. 71, ll. 9 f.)
369 This waxe is as harde as any wyre. (59: sig. B ii)
I wrynge of the necke lyke a wyre. (25: p. 60, l. 1909)
370 For like a wolfe in lambes skin clad, he commeth with his aide.
(78: sig. E iv[v], l. 1269)
Euen as the wolfe . . . doth seeke the lambe to kill:
So seekest thou. (76: sig. A iii[v], ll. 141 f.)
Lyke rauenouse wolues, poore wydowes ye deuoure.
(29: sig. F.)
371 A Horse which . . .
Was snowted like a wodcoke. (73: sig. B i, ll. 22 f.)
I was as wyse as a woodcock. (23: sig. C iii; 45: sig. B i, ii, 1; 55: sig. B ii; 86: sig. B i, l. 225)
As wyse a Wodcocke, without any wytte. (64: sig. D iv)
It is spoken like a Woodcocke. (51: sig. C i)
372 It is as softe a[s] wulle. (17: p. 149, l. 2401)
373 I walke as werm with-outyn wede. (4: p. 25, ii, 291)

Other Proverbial Phrases

374 He can not goe beyond me one ace. (74: p. 38, iii, 1, 45)
In value I pas you an ace. (58: sig. C iii)
375 A pestell on hym, he comes of the Acyons.
(34: p. 14, i, 4, 409)
376 Heile not care an aglet for him. (71: p. 223, iii, 1, 48)
377 There is not a better dogge for hogges,
Not from Anwyke vnto Aungey. (25: p. 35, ll. 1121 f.)
378 To make her husband her ape. (59: sig. B iii)
379 ȝe ar ane verie Apersie. (28: p. 409, l. 903)
380 If they thinke to beguyle
Or geve me suche a gleke, they must aryse earlye.
(70: p. 134, iv, 5, 63 f.)

381 Beware the arse, breake not thy necke.
(83: sig. C iv[v]; 46: p. 28)
Fo by saynt sauour here is a whot ars
Let me fele your nose, nay fere not man be bolde
Well though this ars be warme and this nose colde.
(55: sig. D i[v])

382 For the honour of Atrebradle (*Arthur Bradley*).
(46: p. 49, cf. Tilly, p. 53)

383 Away the mare. (15: sig. F ii[v]; 25: p. 41, l. 1326)
Tush syr be mery let pas awey the mare. (61: sig. A ii)

384 Resun wyl excusyn us alle:
He helde þe ex be þe helue. (17: p. 153, ll. 2571 f.)

385 My paramours is baith als fat and fair
As ony wench into the toun of Air. (28: p. 505, ll. 3404 f.)

386 Me thinke it were a good sight of your backe. (26: sig. A iv)

387 Nay hoa there, backare, you must stand apart.
(15: sig. C iii)

388 This tinkerly trade wee geue it the bagge.
(76: sig. B i, l. 215)

389 To bakyn þee a byttyr bred. (17: p. 124, l. 1593)

390 You howresun Banbery slaue. (76: sig. B i[v], l. 267)

391 Can ye bark at the mone? (3: p. 137, xiii, 662)

392 All is not worth a beyn. (3: p. 274, xxiii, 527; 61: sig. C i[v])
And saie hym a borowed bene sette I noght be hym.
(2: p. 296, xxxi, 105)

392a Beareth all the world in hand.
(79: sig. A ii[v], l. 40; 34: p. 32, iv, 1, 1)
But yf Reason / tykyll hym in the ere
Or bere hym on hand the kow ys wood. (20: sigs. A iv, H ii)
And beareth vs faire in hande.
(34: pp. 23, iii, 3, 681, 31, iii, 6, 942)

393 Sen ȝe bere . . . þe bell. (2: p. 228, xxvi, 195; 3: pp. 106, xii, 186, 172, xvi, 197; 4: pp. 151, xvii, 5, 178, xx, 2; 25: p. 47, l. 1498; 63: p. 4, l. 114; 64: sig. G iii; 68: p. 107, Prol. l. 20; 73; sigs. E ii[v], l. 991, H iii[v], l. 1989; 75: p. 59; 76: sig. E i[v], l. 1135; 77: sig. E ii[v])
Off all women þou beris þe floure. (2: p. 495, xlvii, 130)

394 And afaith, then, he is in for a berd. (46: p. 14)
Mauger your bearde. (71: p. 216, ii, 5, 46)

395 I have a hive of humble bees swarmynge in my braine.
(34: p. 3, i, 1, 66)

Who so hath suche bees as your maister in hys head.
(68: p. 128, i, 4, 93; 72: sig. B iii[v])

396 Of murdur & man-slawter I haue my bely fyll.
(18: p. 23, l. 632)
Therfore preche hardely thy bely full. (57: sig. B i)

397 It is I that doe guyde the bente of your bowe. (43: sig. B i)

398 Hen to Berewik opon Twede. (16: p. 97, l. 285)

399 I am the best man in the compony,
When there is no more. (46: p. 12, cf. Tilly, p. 94)

400 Indulgence, when thay maried art,
Hath buttur (*better*) pence in store. (46: p. 9, cf. Tilly, p. 46)

401 Then I must pack it
Between the coat and the skin. (63: p. 22, ll. 800 f.)

402 Makynge the people, to beleue he coulde bynde bears.
(30: p. 94, l. 1840; 4: p. 326, xxvi, 1607)
That with the strenth of my hand
Beres may bynd. (53: p. 170, ll. 7 f.)

403 He fryskes abought, as byrdes ware in his breech.
(77: sig. D iii)

404 Thys is as worthye a knyghte
As euer shall brede oute of a bottell byte. (62: sig. B iv[v])

405 She semed to bite on the bridle. (75: p. 40, ii, 5)

406 I can make blacke white, and white blacke againe.
(50: sig. B iiii)
They are no more like:
. . . then blacke to white. (45: sig. E ii, v, i)

407 They never prove stayed untill the blacke oxe hath troden on their toes. (75: p. 81, v, 6)

408 For to blere hys eye. (20: sig. D iv; 4: p. 91, x, 283; 8c: p. 92, l. 985; 28: pp. 382, l. 173, 529, l. 4104; 69: p. 56, v, 2, 56; 70: pp. 92, i, 2, 100 f., 120, iii, 3, 147; 71: p. 187, i, 3, 32; 75: p. 38, ii, 4; 80: sig. G iv, l. 1700)

409 I blysse yow with my lyfte honde: foull yow be-fall!
(18: p. 19, l. 515)
Hold heare
My blessing in a cloute. (46: p. 11, cf. Tilly, p. 47)

410 Bot I com or thay ryse els blawes a cold blast!
(3: p. 127, xiii, 344)

411 A bone in your hoode
I shall put ere it be longe. (65: sigs. A iv[v], A iv)

412 Yai, with the same mesure and weght
That I boro will I qwite. (3: p. 11, ii, 51 f.)

413 All men may me now dyspyse
And seyn olde cokwold þi bow is bent
Newly now after þe frensche gyse.
(4: pp. 110, xii, 54 ff., 128, xiv, 131 f.)

414 Bowle to thy biase. (80: sig. G iv[v], l. 1750)

415 Yt ys not schapyn worth a morsell of brede.
(18: p. 25, l. 691)

416 Ye are as ferce as thowgh, ye had broke yowr nose at þe buttre.
(30: p. 31, l. 641)

417 I make ther commons, agenst them for to be
Twenty Md men, are but a mornyng breckefast
To be slayn for hym, he takyng his repast.
(30: p. 36, ll. 747 ff.)

418 She bredeth yownge boanes. (70: p. 133, iv, 5, 45)

419 Þe knaves are in þe bryers. (30: p. 30, l. 626)
Bryng the, moch farder into þe bryers. (30: p. 73, l. 1582)
He hath left his friend in the briers.
(72: sig. G ii; 75: p. 72, v, 1)
Your owne doubtfulnes tangles you still in the briers.
(80: sig. C iii, l. 466)

420 Ile be with him to bring. (78: sig. C iii[v], l. 632)

421 Sheis none of thes coy dames sheis as good as brown bessye.
(71: p. 206, ii, 4, 76)

422 Out of his
Broune stodie. (46: p. 13)

423 Betweene this and Buckingham. (42: sig. A iii)

424 But why burne we day light?
(70: p. 130, iv, 3, 21; 86: sig. B ii, l. 313)

425 I will get riches throw that rent,
Efter the day of Dume;
Quhen, in the colpots of Tranent,
Butter will grow on brume. (28: p. 443, ll. 1807 ff.)

426 You be not woorth twoo butter flies. (50: sig. D iii)

427 Peace fondelinge, tush a button. (29: sig. B iv[v])

428 By and sell! (54: p. 18)
That were at a conuention heauen to bye and sell.
(62: sig. A ii)
Thus schall þe sothe be bought and solde.
(2: p. 420, xxxviii, 449; 67: sig. B v)

429 Trowis thou, butchour, that I will by blind lambis?
(28: p. 462, l. 2284)

430 His Cake is dow. (63: p. 7, l. 238; 80: sig. G iii, l. 1651)

431 There ys no man hens to cales. (67: sig. D i)

432 Call me cut. (20: sig. B i[v]; 74: p. 63, v, 5, 41, cf. note, p. 273)
Then Call me hardlie Cutt, yf my Arte deceyve me soe. (70: p. 138, v, 2, 79, cf. note, p. 298)
433 For a more vngracious knaue is not euen now
Bytwene this place and Calycow. (66: p. 43, ll. 973 f.)
434 Holde our freendes aloofe at cap and knee. (80: sig. C i, l. 306)
435 Nowe thys is a sure carde. (62: sig. E i)
436 I-wys, fro Carlylle In-to Kent, my carpynge þei take. (17: p. 83, l. 201)
437 Thair is na Monks, from Carrick to Carraill,
That fairs better. (28: p. 505, l. 3396)
438 I am cast out at the cartes arse. (24: sig. B i[v], l. 230)
439 But now how my case is altered suddenly. (44: sig. D iii, l. 731)
The case is altred quight. (77: sig. F ii[v])
440 Of mine office he shall haue a cast. (68: p. 124, i, 4, 4)
441 Se ye not this smoke
In my maisters eyes that they do cast. (61: sig. A vi[v])
442 You haue a castle of comfort brought. (78: sig. E iii, l. 1167)
443 Let the catte wyncke. (21: sig. C ii[v]; 86: sig. E ii, l. 1123)
444 But gyf the Sents war gone, the Cat had eate my mark. (49: sig. D iv[v], iii, 4)
Hem, not to bolde yet, for a mowse the catte wyll gape. (30: p. 90, l. 1768)
I shall kepe ye as well from that,
As my grandame kept her cat,
From lyckynge of her creame. (29: sig. B i[v])
445 They are no more like:
Then chalke to cheese. (45: sig. E ii, v, 1)
He discerneth not cheese from chalke. (36: sig. C iii[v])
Chalke they geue for gold. (13c: sig. E iv[v])
446 I knewe I would make him soone change his note. (48: sig. B iii)
I woll make the chaung that song, ere wee pas this place. (66: p. 21, l. 465)
447 This chayer is chared well. (45: sig. D iv[v])
448 The wight that once, hath tast the fruits of loue,
Untill hir dying daye will long, Sir *Chaucers* iests to proue. (77: sig. B iii)
449 Reason may haue a chek mate. (20: sigs. B iv, H ii)
A little to cheke mate. (24: sig. B iv, l. 398)

To play with me checke mate.
(25: p. 11, l. 307; 67: sig. F iii)
Þou art checke mate. (30: p. 13, l. 254)
Let not hassarde nor riotour, with you be checke mate.
(38: p. 9)
He thinks himself check mate. (49: sig. C iii, ii, 3)
450 I recke not a chery. (26: sig. A ii)
Yt ys but a chery tyme! (18: p. 9, l. 227)
451 Are you with Childe to heare? (34: p. 8, i, 3, 236)
For I am with child, till that I do it heare.
(49: sig. F ii[v], iv, 1)
452 Crafty Conueyaunce is no chyldys game. (25: p. 43, l. 1368)
To speake before a king, it is no childes playe.
(11: p. 12, l. 269)
453 Play choploge. (68: p. 142, iii, 2, 89)
454 Or bere him on hand the kow[*chough*] ys wood.
(20: sig. A iv)
455 Yea, God sped vs well, crystmes songes are mery tales.
(30: p. 27, l. 564)
456 Stope downe a low
And kisse my round rivette while I clawe thine ellbowe.
(70: p. 89, i, 2, 13 f., cf. note, p. 276)
457 And straight (through feare) where he clawes it doth not ytch.
(77: sig. D iii)
458 Thou horson knaue git thee to clout thy shoone.
(42: sig. B iii[v])
459 The coast is cleare. (51: sig. I ii; 49: sig. G ii, iv, 4)
460 Set cock on hoope then.
(44: sig. C i[v], l. 373; 63: p. 18, l. 649; 77: sig. L iii)
Set cocke on the houpe. (29: sig. F ii[v])
Set cocke a whope, and play care away. (36: sig. B ii)
Then faith cock on houpe, al is ours. (14: sig. F ii[v], v, 1)
461 Heis a right cocke oth kinde. (71: p. 214, ii, 4, 288)
462 The mater ys cok sure. (20: sig. C iii; 49: sig. D ii, iii, 3)
463 He that fisheth for him, mighte bee sure to catche a cods heade.
(74: p. 30, ii, 1, 185 f.)
464 She is a collop of my owne flesh.
(74: p. 42, iii, 3, 65 f., cf. note, p. 268)
465 But I bridled a Colt of a contrarie hare. (63: p. 12, l. 414)
Yf hys coltes teeth in his head were yet stiking.
(70: p. 111, iii, 1, 25, 27)
466 I shall with a trice make such meate certain,
As shall say come eate me. (14: sig. E i, iv, 1)
467 A coolyng carde. (70: p. 112, iii, 1, 51; 71: p. 233, iii, 2, 23)

468 All his techynge is not worthe a coost. (21: sig. B iv)
469 I will bringe him to corn. (71: p. 188, i, 3, 58)
Thy words war nather corne nor caiff. (28: p. 509, l. 3531)
Being able twixt Corne and Cockle to discerne.
(49: sig. B ii[v], ii, 1)
But muche good doe it *Domine Doctor*, hee shall be sure to lacke no corne in a deare yere, what soeuer he haue with her else.
(74: pp. 43 f., iii, 4, 47 f.)
470 We will teache maister Doctor to weare a cornerd cappe of a new fashion. (74: p. 62, v, 4, 23 f., cf. note, p. 272)
471 She wyll not fayle
For hys further preferment to send hym in to Corne wayle.
(70: p. 111, iii, 1, 28 f., cf. note, p. 286)
472 To catche *Cornua*. (74: p. 38, iii, 1, 43)
473 Ye are wont to be as bold
As yt were a lyon of cottyswold. (20: sig. G iii)
Now haue at the lyons on cotsolde. (62: sig. A iii[v])
Then will he looke as fierce as a Cotssold lyon.
(68: p. 168, iv, 6, 39)
474 Thou wylte coughe me a dawe for forty pens?
(25: p. 34, l. 1061)
Ye shall coughe me a fole. (25: p. 34, l. 1065)
He shall cough me a mome. (68: p. 142, iii, 2, 86)
475 Farwell cosen cutpursse. (83: sig. E iii)
My cosen cutpursse wyll I truste. (83: sig. C iv[v])
476 The most bawde hens to Couentre. (59: sig. A iii)
477 I am as homlie as the good wife that for loue kist her Cow.
(73: sig. B iii, l. 155)
Thart euen as good a felow as euer kyste a cowe.
(69: p. 32, iii, 1, 2)
I thinke he came lately from riding some Cow.
(85: sig. B i[v])
He is as honest a man as euer spurd Cow. (85: sig. F i)
As fit a sighte it were to see . . . a sadll[e]d cowe.
(40: sig. A iii)
478 Cham scarce woorthe a good cowe taile. (34: p. 34, iv, 3, 1022)
479 We be of one crafte but not of one kynde. (56: sig. C i)
He calleth me knaue by craft. (39: sig. B iii[v])
Thou callest me
Whore by craft. (46: p. 52)
480 My craig will wit quhat weyis my hippis. (28: p. 499, l. 3226)
481 Not a Crosse of money to blesse me haue I.
(39: sig. E i; 46: p. 31, cf. Tilly, p. 56)
With þe crose & þe pyll I xall wrye yt. (19: p. 63, l. 862)

482 Is he crossed than with a chalke? (25: p. 30, l. 951)

483 He is vp day by day before the Crowe pis.
(14: sig. A iii[v], i, 2)
Take hede Sir yow goe not to loe for the crowe.
(71: p. 197, ii, 2, 59)
Say as she sayeth, allthought that she
Doe say the crowe is white.
(46: p. 10; 66: p. 44, l. 1019; 67: sig. A iv[v])

484 When the Crowes feete groweth under her eye.
(75: p. 66, iv, 5)

485 I woulde make the knaues to crye creke.
(62: sig. A iii; 72: sig. F i;
75: p. 66, iv, 5; 85: sig. E i[v])

486 This same is kind cuckolds luck. (46: p. 31)

487 It was a kocko
And men say amonge
He that throwyth stone or stycke
At suche abyrde he is lycke
To synge that byrdes songe. (67: sig. E iii[v])

488 Lyberte was not worthe a cue. (25: p. 2, l. 36)

489 Here I do curse hym, wyth crosse. boke. bell. & candle.
(30: pp. 50, l. 1035, 51, l. 1060,
64, l. 1359, 93, l. 1827, cf. p. 79,
l. *41; 28: pp. 416, l. 1080, 423,
ll. 1258 f., 454, l. 2085, 516, l. 3718)

490 Set my Maister beside the cushin. (80: sig. B ii[v], l. 124)
As cunninge as yeare ye mist cushinge once yet Margerye.
(71: p. 246, iv, 1, 101, cf. note, p. 321)

491 I haue taught them their daddies daunce.
(70: p. 136, v, 2, 23)

492 Þat daunce is done. (2: pp. 81, xi, 225, 149, xix, 96; 3:
p. 72, viii, 238)

493 I know not what will please you, except Darbyes bandes.
(45: sig. D i, iv, 1)

494 Thy purse shall not come home weeping for lose; and as for the,
thou shalt be commist to Dawes crosse. (46: p. 28)

495 Ych thinke, each daye a nowre. (77: sig. L i[v])

496 I shall bryng that hart of hys
To be more howt than yt ys
By a dewys ase. (20: sig. C iv)

497 Þe deuyll and his dame. (2: p. 300, xxxi, 237; 31: p. 17; 44:
sig. E i[v], l. 892; 62: sig. A iv[v];
71: p. 210, ii, 4, 196; 80: sig. C
iv[v], l. 566)

The deuill go with you and his dun dame. (43: sig. C ii[v])
My dame & thou [*addressed to Devil*]. (39: sig. A iii)
The deuyll or hys dam. (29: sig. D i[v]; 69: p. 9, i, 3, 29)
I pray God, nor the devils dame dryte on thy grunȝe!
(28: p. 470, l. 2462)
Charme olde witche in the deuils name
Or I wyll sende the to him, to be his dame. (62: sig. C iv[v])
She would out scold the deuils dame I wene.
(65: sig. B iv[v])

498 Then may we be here the dewill in a bande.
(3: p. 129, xiii, 407)
I wyl make them thinke, the deuyll caryeth them to the wood.
(62: sig. A iv[v])
þe deull may daunce in my purse for ony peny.
(18: p. 18, l. 481)
Qwyst! pesse! þe Deull ys dede! (18: p. 22, l. 586)
The dewill in youre ee. (3: p. 123, xiii, 217)
The deuyll shall haue the tone to fet the tother.
(56: sig. D ii)
I wold gyue the dyuell the tone to cary away the tother.
(59: sig. A iii[v])
To be rid I would giue the Deuill one halfe to fetch the other.
(73: sig. B iii[v], l. 191)
What newse, ist the deuell in hell? (83: sig. B iii)
With wy wyppe: 'Farewell,' quod I; 'þe deuyll ys wppe!'
(19: p. 52, l. 518)
Play the devill in the horologe. (68: p. 142, iii, 2, 91)
Thus can I lerne you, Syrs, to bere the deuyls sacke.
(25: p. 23, l. 721)

499 In the dwillis way. (3: p. 22, ii, 449)
In the devill way. (2: pp. 88, xi, 354, 37, vii, 52, 130, xvii, 121, 269, xxix, 398, 306, xxxi, 406, 313, xxxii, 188, 380, xxxvii, 133; 3: p. 12, ii, 89; 4: p. 296, xxvi, 728; 61: sig. B iv)
Go we hens, a deull wey! (18: pp. 6, l. 153, 19, l. 514)
Come in, wife, in 20 devills waye.
(1: I, 56, iii, 219; 69: p. 10, i, 3, 43)
In twenty dwill way.
(3: pp. 21, ii, 439, 155, xiv, 465, 210, xx, 200)
Walke ye forth in the twenty Devills way!
(1: II, 416, xxiii, 452)
Dryue hym hence therfore in the .xx. deuyll waye.
(57: sig. B ii[v])
Adewe a xx[ti] devyl way. (4: p. 205, xxiii, 143)

What a lobbing makest thou,
With a twenty Deuill! (46: p. 50)

500 Suche lubbers as hath, dysgysed heades in their hoodes. (30: p. 3, l. 36)

501 Oh it is a ioylie wenche to myns and deuyd a fart. (66: p. 10, l. 233)

502 There is nothing with them but in docke out nettle. (68: p. 133, ii, 3, 8)

503 What mayster doctour dotypoll. (23: sig. C i)
Dotty-pols. (3: p. 173, xvi, 231)

504 A life wythall my hart I would not wyshe a dogge. (45: sig. C iii, iv, 1)
Here's a Dogges life. (52: sig. D iv)
What dog pater noster's that which to thy selfe thou there art mumblinge? (10: p. 291, l. 838)
He hath as much neede to bid me do this,
As to make a dogge hold vp his legge when he doth pisse. (48: sig. B i[v])

505 I set not by the worlde two Dauncaster cuttys. (25: p. 10, l. 293)

506 His daughters purse shalbe continually emptie, vnlesse Maister Doctour fill it with double ducke egges. (74: p. 32, ii, 3, 10 ff., cf. note, p. 265)

507 Yea, yt ys a dobyll hood and that a fett. (8b: p. 31, l. 117)

508 For, now ye ar cum, I dare well saye
Betwyn Douyr & Calyce þe ryght wey
Dwellth non so cunnyng, be my fey. (7: p. 73, ll. 509 ff.)

509 Without a cuppe than myght I drynke. (35: sig. B iii[v], l. 353)
Ye will drink without a cup. (68: p. 119, i, 3, 29)

510 And it (*memory*) once lost thou shalt in south, accomptyd lyke to be,
A drope of rayne that faulyth in, the bosom of the see. (83: sigs. D iii[v]–D iv)

511 These fellowes haue giuen me a drie pluck. (46: p. 31)

512 These wold by thare wytt make a shyp be drownde. (3: p. 105, xii, 145)

513 I wait, nane better into Dumbartane. (28: p. 496, l. 3134)

514 Don is in the myre. (3: p. 373, xxx, 205)

515 I will teach him to know the way to Dunmoe. (63: p. 4, l. 122)
But you may now go for bacon to Dunmo. (63: p. 21, l. 760)

516 He that will haue a thing kept secrete, let him tell it to *Pasiphilo*: the people shall knowe it, and as many as haue eares and no mo. (74: p. 68, v, 6, 22 ff.)

517 Quyte ouer the eares in loue and felt no ground.
(55: sig. B iv[v])
Up is he to the harde eares in love. (68: p. 109, i, 1, 40)
518 Set them by the eares. (76: sig. D ii, l. 895)
Sett them to gether by the eares.
(10: p. 295, l. 955; 76: sig. D ii[v], l. 902)
Set a thousand by the eares. (76: sig. D ii[v], l. 909)
Set al the world by the eares. (52: sig. H i)
Tib & her dame hath ben by the eares together.
(69: p. 6, i, 2, 22)
Fall together by the eares. (52: sig. M iii; 64: sig. F iii)
519 Its a good while agoe Codrus since we tow eat a bottell of hay.
(71: p. 222, iii, 1, 24)
520 Then Ile counterfett for counnyng
To have eat a conyes tayle. (70: p. 94 f., i, 2, 157 f.)
521 We haue made Magnyfycence to ete a flye. (25: p. 17, l. 503)
He wyll make the ete a gnat. (25: p. 38, l. 1193)
We haue etyn garlek euerychone. (17: p. 118, l. 1372)
522 I were eten outt of howse and of harbar (3: p. 124, xiii, 245)
523 And nabour *Hodges* maide, meddle not with her, she hath eaten set leekes. (78: sig. F i[v], l. 1326)
524 Ye but he that is so hasty at euery worde
For amedsyn must ete his wyues torde. (67: sig. C vi[v])
525 I can cate tell, I sweate and worke
Tell I am a-cold. (46: p. 12, cf. Tilly, p. 93)
526 Come yow in with your seven egges. (71: p. 215, ii, 5, 23)
527 For he carith not whiche ende goth before. (67: sig. C i)
528 Eyuer the worse yend of the staff to haue,
Att the lattur yend. (5: p. 49, ll. 504 ff.)
Ichc had not, the best end of the staffe. (83: sig. A iv[v])
529 He hathe his arrand with him I warrant him he is sped.
(70: pp. 88, i, 1, 71, 120, iii, 3, 143 f., cf. note, p. 275)
He sayd she had her errand.
(70: p. 132, iv, 5, 6, cf. note, p. 297; 80: sig. C iii, l. 461)
530 To set all your fortune at euen and od. (80: sig. B iii, l. 174)
531 Every man for him selfe. (75: p. 61, iv, 2)
532 She hath an eie behind her. (69: p. 24, ii, 2, 30)
533 Haue an eye to the mayne chaunce. (50: sig. E ii[v])
534 I schal lyue euer mo
For boþe two þin eye.
(16: pp. 94, ll. 193 f., 95, ll. 241 f.)
535 Maugre their faces. (48: sig. C i)
536 Well, fall backe, fall edge. (34: p. 48, v, 5, 1467)
And we sall neuer sleip ane wink,
Till it be back or eadge. (28: p. 390, ll. 403 f.)

537 She hathe falne vpon feathers & hath brused her very sore. (70: p. 133, iv, 5, 43)

538 Farewell frost. (47: sig. E i[v]; 71: p. 190, i, 3, 99)
Farewell gentle Hary. (42: sig. F iii)
Nowe farewell gentyll John. (22: sig. C v)
Farwell, jentyll Jaffrey. (18: p. 6, l. 155)
Now farewell gentell gefferye. (70: p. 88, i, 1, 70, cf. note, p. 275)

539 Mary farewell and be hangd. (50: sig. E iii)
Farewell and be hangde. (80: sig. E iii, l. 1048)
Come away, and be hangd! (46: p. 50, cf. Tilly, p. 91)
Come vp and be hangde. (79: sig. D iv[v], l. 996)

540 A fart for yow all. (71: p. 217, ii, 5, 76)
But for thy displeasure I care not a farte. (66: p. 16, l. 397)
Bi all men set I not a fart. (3: p. 19, ii, 369; 42: sigs. A iii, E i[v]; 67: sig. E iv[v])
Thy speach is not worth a fart. (1: I, 95, v, 234; 17: p. 143, l. 2209)
I will not gif, for al ȝour play, worth a sowis fart. (28: p. 449, l. 1956)

541 At fast or loose, with my *Giptian*, I meane to haue a cast. (77: sig. C iii)

542 The fat is in the fier. (80: sig. D iii, l. 760)

543 Forsoth, for fault of a better,
[*My name*] is Due Disporte. (46: p. 34, cf. Tilly, p. 91)

544 My tonge is with Fauell forked and tyned. (25: p. 24, l. 727)

545 Geve a fether for agooce. (34: p. 27, iii, 5, 797)

546 By cryst I recke not a feder. (23: sig. C iv)
All the grete arguments . . .
Do not preuayle the weyght of a fether. (60: sig. C ii[v])
Thus will ye be turned with waggyng of a fether. (68: p. 171, iv, 7, 47)

547 I fere she wyll make me weare a fether. (59: sig. A ii)
I loue not to weare an other birdes feathers. (14: sig. E iv[v], iv, 8)

548 To feather my neste. (34: pp. 3, i, 1, 88, 30, iii, 6, 916, 60, v, 10, 1847)

549 Canst fede them with honyesoopes. (70: p. 124, iv, 1, 34)

550 The falsehood of *Ferara*. (74: pp. 52, iv, 6, 3, 65, v, 5, 100, cf. note, p. 270)

551 Giue her a Fico out of hande. (80: sig. E iv[v], l. 1179)

552 Nane better into Fyfe. (28: p. 496, l. 3140)

553 A figge for him. (47: sig. A iv; 42: sig. E iv; 50: sig. A iii; 86: sigs. C iii[v], ll. 691, 697, C iv, ll. 705, 713)

554 For this drift ile not giue a fyg. (73: sig. G ii[v], l. 1587)
555 She set the fynger in the eye. (55: sig. C i)
The finger shalbe in there eye. (73: sig. C iii, l. 429)
Eche finger is a thombe to day me thinke.
(68: p. 120, i, 3, 70)
I picke not this geare (hearst thou) out of my fingers endes.
(69: p. 61, v, 2, 153)
556 Ye fysh before the nett. (3: p. 104, xii, 139)
557 Ile giue him his olde fippens. (71: p. 192, ii, 1, 12)
558 He is gon his waie
Withe a flea in his eare. (70: p. 88, i, 1, 69 f., cf. note, p. 275)
559 Which shoulde be but a flea bytinge for hir to lese.
(34: p. 4, i, 1, 106)
560 The flower
Of the frying-pan. (46: p. 13, cf. Tilley, p. 89; 67: sig. D ii[v]; 76: sig. G i[v], l. 1700)
Oh frying pan of my head vplandish now.
(79: sig. E ii, l. 1100)
561 I care not a Flie. (63: p. 2, l. 49; 65: sig. B iv)
And tell you fables dere inoughe a flye. (57: sig. B ii)
But I wol not giue for that boye a flye. (66: p. 13, l. 314)
I wald nocht gif ane sillie flie
For ȝour treasure. (28: p. 383, ll. 212 f.)
To matche my sonne with such I past not of a flye.
(48: sig. E i[v])
I set not by hym a fly. (25: pp. 14, l. 412, 59, l. 1889; 42: sig. F i[v]; 62: sig. A iii[v]; 65: sig. A iii[v])
Counterfet Reason is not worth a flye.
(25: p. 16, l. 470; 60: sig. A iii[v])
He settys not a fle wyng bi sir cesar. (3: p. 231, xxi, 94)
562 He dare scarce looke a flye in the face.
(80: sig. F ii[v], l. 1320)
To bring Fedele to the Counter, is but to fight with a flie.
(80: sig. F iii, l. 1344)
Than vsurped power, maye goo a birdynge for flyes.
(30: p. 120, l. 2396)
563 He wold goe wood, by my faye,
And fly out of his skin. (1: I, 165, viii, 135 f.)
564 To bringe me, to some foolishe paradice. (12: p. 39, l. 1209)
565 Lett vs ryn fote hote. (3: p. 178, xvi, 398)
566 She opened a wyndow and put forth her hed
Hens .xl.d (*forty pence*) quod she. Jack noble is abed.
(20: sig. F ii)

567 What, Lob, I say, come away with a foule euill!
(46: p. 50, cf. Tilley, p. 54)

568 Thou haste the four quarters of a knaue.
(25: pp. 37, l. 1166, 70, l. 2252; 38: p. 26)
Thou shalt beare .iiii. quarters of a foole. (36: sig. D ii)

569 I gaue hym a blowe with a Foxe tayle. (42: sig. B i[v])
And hym wyth a Foxtayle wee wyll flappe. (42: sig. B ii[v])

570 As proper a praunce
As any I know between this and Fraunce. (39: sig. C i[v])

571 And wolde haue made me Freer Tucke,
To preche out of the pylery hole
Without an antetyme or a stole. (25: p. 12, ll. 357 ff.)

572 And yet three Frogs out of a bush, my heart did so affright,
That I fell dead almost therewith. (78: sig. D ii[v], ll. 844 f.)

573 Giue her not the bridle for a yeare or twayne.
(45: sig. B ii[v], ii, 1)

574 She is as mete for him, as a glove for a horses nose.
(70: p. 91, i, 2, 69)

575 So they haue money they care not for vs a gnate.
(48: sig. A iii[v])
I wolde not set a gnat
By Magnyfycence. (25: p. 53, ll. 1704 f.)
Al is not worth a gnat. (69: p. 58, v, 2, 93)

576 And gnawe vpon the bytte. (29: sig. A vii[v])

577 Go to the dwill, and say I bad! (3: p. 12, ii, 94)
And go with a vengeance & say thou art prayde. (59: sig. B ii)

578 But to the Pot, he is sure to goe.
(49: sig. D ii, iii, 2; 77: sig. K iii[v])

579 He wyll say that God is a good man. (32: sig. C iv)

580 One of them is left with as many crosses as God hath brethren.
(74: p. 39, iii, 2, 12 f.)

581 God a mercy horse! (46: p. 27)
Mary god a mercy John for that now. (60: sig. A i[v])
But if you wil needs be chiefe, God speed wel the plough.
(49: sig. C iv)

582 None but *goddigod eve*, & *goddigod spede* youe.
(34: p. 53, v, 8, 1636)

583 Cham vaine to take an hatte of godsgood on my heade.
(34: p. 34, iv, 3, 1028)

584 Ye ar worth thy weyght of gold. (20: sigs. C iv[v], F iii)
Such a girle is worth golde in a deare yeere.
(80: sig. G iv, l. 1703)

585 But if the kynge once frowne on him, then good night Tomaline. (72: sig. C iv[v])

586 Hold thi tong, yit I say,
Euen ther the good wife strokid the hay. (3: p. 12, ii, 87 f.)
587 As fit a sighte it were to see a goose shodde. (40: sig. A iii)
588 I thinke thy wittes be gone goslings to kepe.
(73: sig. F i[v], l. 1222)
589 Sagh I neuer none so fare bot the foles of gotham.
(3: p. 106, xii, 180)
The wise men of gotum. (71: p. 199, ii, 3, 10)
590 The nonnes . . .
Wolde take . . .
The grace of God vnder *benedicite*. (25: p. 16, ll. 488 ff.)
591 Ad græcas calendas. (52: sig. D ii)
592 There hath grown no grasse on my heele since I went hence.
(68: pp. 148, iii, 3, 150, 165, iv, 5, 10;
34: p. 31, iii, 6, 947)
593 Wyth golde and grotes they grese my hande.
(25: p. 15, l. 432; 23: sig. A vi; 44: sig. C iii[v], l. 486; 47: sig. C i; 49: sig. D ii[v], iii, 3; 77: sig. I iii[v])
594 This geare is Greeke to me. (74: p. 15, i, 1, 62)
595 I ne ȝeue a gres. (17: p. 142, l. 2170)
596 Now Ile haue my ten shillings in spite of your guts.
(51: sig. I iii)
597 Eche kys of her mouth called you to gybbes fest.
(55: sig. D ii)
598 Their all hab or nabes. (71: p. 210, ii, 4, 195)
599 Not the prowdest of them all can hurte me a heare.
(34: p. 54, v, 8, 1650)
But the loue that in thee doth appere
Is not worthe the valour of a heare. (42: sig. A iv)
600 Me thynke hys hayre groweth thorow his hode.
(38: p. 29; 34: p. 34, iv, 3, 1036; 39: sig. B iv; 64: sig. E iii; 65: sig. A iv)
601 Your myndes were all on your haulfe penie.
(34: p. 12, i, 4, 360)
I thought my halfe-peny good silver. (75: p. 24, i, 5)
602 Is the preist hande ith honye pott yet? (71: p. 210, ii, 4, 180)
The preistes handes ith mustardpott the knave throwe at ninch. (71: p. 209, ii, 4, 169)
603 He feareth nothing he thinketh the hangman is dead.
(49: sig. B iv, ii, 2)
604 Hap what hap may. (20: sig. C iii; 86: sig. E ii, l. 1111)
Well hap as can hap, or no. (86: sig. D iv, l. 999)
605 Happy man be his dole. (72: sig. B ii[v])

606 There went the hare away. (20: sig. G ii; 40: sig. D i, ii, 3)
þe hare fro þe fforme we xal a-rere. (4: p. 202, xxiii, 80)
Nai, now youe zai zouth een þieke same waie goeth the hare. (34: p. 23, iii, 3, 675)
I haue the Hare on foot. (80: sig. C i, l. 292)
So how, I say, the hare is squat! (25: p. 41, l. 1300)
607 Yow harpe all of one stringe. (71: p. 257, iv, 4, 17; 80: sig. E i[v], l. 947)
You harpt before vpon to bad a stryng. (70: p. 122, iii, 4, 34)
These .ii. folk harp both on refrayte. (20: sig. B iii[v])
Thou strik'st too much vpon one string. (52: sig. A iii)
608 All is out of har. (3: p. 234, xxi, 210; 25: pp. 29, l. 913, 65, l. 2095)
609 These women are all of the hastinges. (70: p. 96, i, 3, 37, cf. note, p. 278)
Yow are none of the hastlinges. (71: p. 190, i, 4, 9)
610 I ȝyf not þer of An hawe. (4: pp. 29, iii, 22, 272, xxvi, 13; 17: p. 91, l. 481)
I rekke [not] an hawe. (17: p. 112, l. 1169)
Is non to us wurthe An hawe. (4: p. 179, xx, 27; 25: p. 65, l. 2089; 67: sig. C v)
611 He hawketh, me thynke, for a butterflye. (25: p. 19, l. 575)
612 Yea hassilwood. (75: p. 25, i, 5)
613 Magre þin heed. (4: p. 134, xiv, 327)
614 I finde neither head nor foote in it. (74: p. 28, ii, 1, 107 f.; 75: p. 34, ii, 2)
615 I fere no man that bereth an hed. (20: sig. G iii)
Eate my meat I can thanke God, with him that Beares a head. (73: sig. F iii[v], l. 1361)
616 Spyte of my hart. (59: sig. B iv[v]; 62: sig. C iv[v]; 83: sig. E ii[v])
Mavgre ther hertes. (8a: p. 5, l. 94; 30: p. 6, l. 98)
617 What saie you hart of gold? (62: sig. B i[v]; 71: p. 203, ii, 4, 3)
He weepes on the other side, that it would pearce an hart of stone with pitie. (74: p. 45, iii, 5, 32 ff.)
Take harte of grace. (71: p. 257, iv, 4, 10; 45: sig. E iv, v, 4; 63: p. 15, l. 550)
618 Thy hart is in thy hose. (3: p. 113, xii, 424; 30: p. 42, l. 880; 62: sig. B iv)
My stomack so swelles that I am driuen to lay out my heart in my hose. (80: sig. E iii[v], l. 1077)
And who lustith to feale
Shall find his hart creping out at his heele. (66: p. 14, ll. 348 f.)

I might feele
Your soule departing within an inche of your heele.
(68: p. 146, iii, 3, 97 f.)

619 There is neuer a wyfe betwene heuen and hell. (59: sig. A i)

620 But her hed so gydy and her helys so shorte. (58: sig. Di)
I haue no fault but one, I am somwhat short in the heele.
(80: sig. B i[v], l. 48)

621 I haue founde a helpe at a dead lyfte. (77: sig. F ii[v])

622 For vndoubtedly it is as hard as they say,
To get the scepter out of the hand of Hercules.
(36: sig. G iii)

623 Here ys the dore, her ys the wey! (18: p. 6, l. 154)

624 I will haue youe on the hyppe. (34: p. 25, iii, 3, 743)

625 Yet may you say vpon the hed
The very naile is hit! (46: p. 63; 71: p. 240, iii, 3, 132)
Now be myn trowth ȝe hytte þe pynne.
(4: p. 129, xiv, 189; 76: sig. C i[v], l. 553)

626 Who is that hob-ouer-the-wall? (3: p. 17, ii, 297)

627 Were thou borne in trumpyngton
And brought vp at Hoggesnorton? (26: sig. C ii)

628 The quest of Holborn cum in-to þis placis.
(19: p. 59, ll. 724, 734)

629 Go with a ryffen hood. (3: p. 13, ii, 141)

630 I hauc scne as wyse a man as you, wear a hood and a coloe.
(73: sig. C iv[v], l. 540)
I will vye slepes with him that lookes oute of a hood.
(70: p. 106, ii, 4, 39)

631 By hooke or by crooke. (34: p. 6, i, 3, 169; 37: sig. E iv[v])

632 But there is a towne cald Hopshort;
Thay haue me not yet! (46: p. 39)

633 Horns of cuckold (*simple references*).
(23: sig. C i; 35: sig. B i, l. 211; 63: p. 22, l. 784; 70: pp. 111, iii, 1, 28, 132, iv, 5, 8, 24; 74: p. 37, iii, 1, 13, 15, cf. note, p. 266; 77: sig. C i[v]; 81: sig. A iii[v], l. 27; 86: sig. B i, l. 217)
Sagh I ncucr in a crcdyll
A hornyd lad or now. (3: p. 135, xiii, 600 f.)
I beseech God send you with her, as manye hornes as a Bucke.
(73: sig. B iii[v], l. 208; 76: sig. C iii[v], l. 695)
But who maketh al these hornes your self or your wife.
(56: sig. B i)
I wyll rappe you on the costarde with my horne.
(23: sig. B i)

For womens hornes sounde more in a mannys nose.
(56: sig. A iv[v])
Why? wylte not thou thy hornes in holde
Thinkest thou that I am a cocklode. (62: sig. C i)
I can weare a horne & blow it not. (72: sig. F iii[v])
Mayster horner. (56: sig. B i)
To waxe horne wood
On a girle at these yeres. (70: p. 95, i, 3, 8 f.)
[See also numbers 411, 469, 470, 471, 472, 748, 814]

634 He was a good man that made yt, I warant yow;
He was nother horse ne mare, nor yet yokyd sow.
(8b: p. 31, ll. 118 f.)

635 And here again I trow, ere an horse licke his eare.
(14: sig. E ii[v], iv, 4)
We wil be heer again or a Horse can lick his eare.
(37: sig. F i)

636 That samin hors is my awin Mair. (28: p. 400, l. 698)

637 Euery houre til I come they think a day. (37: sig. B ii[v])

638 Welcome syr huddy peke. (29: sig. A vii)
Hodypeake wretche. (14: sig. C ii, ii, 2)

639 As men dare speke it hugger mugger.
(25: p. 13, l. 387; 71: p. 233, iii, 2, 9)

640 The hunt is vp. (80: sig. F iv, l. 1413)

641 And when there is no more inke in the pen,
I wyll make a shift as well as other men. (32: sig. E ii)

642 Of all Swyne for to be skaithles,
Betuix this toun and Invernes. (28: p. 537, ll. 4339 f.)

643 þow þer come both jakke and gylle. (4: p. 314, xxvi, 1237)
Sir, for Iak nor for gill will I turne my face.
(3: p. 33, iii, 336)
With care and with thought howe Jacke shall haue Gyl?
(25: p. 10, l. 287)

644 Its no tale of Jacke a male. (71: p. 231, iii, 1, 253)

645 Packe hence away, Jacke Drums intertainement, she will none of thee. (50: sigs. D ii[v]–D iii)

646 We are as like in condicions, as Jacke Fletcher and his Bowlte.
(72: sig. B ii)

647 Heares more a do with Jacke Napes, then twenty Beares.
(73: sig. C iv[v], l. 543)

648 Some iangelynge Jacke of the Vale. (25: p. 9, l. 258)
And that he can as finely doe as Iacke Raker.
(68: p. 132, ii, 1, 28)

649 Ye may fly vp toth roust with Jacksons hens.
(71: p. 252, iv, 2, 31)

650 Haue with ye to Jerico. (86: sig. D i, l. 787)
651 And so manye great estates,
From hens to Hierusalem.
(29: sig. C ii; 66: p. 43, l. 976)
652 Youde be in iocundare cum amicis an yow had all toulde.
(71: p. 224, iii, 1, 85)
653 Lo, John a Bonam, where is thy brayne? (25: p. 38, l. 1205)
I would teach him John come kisse me. (63: p. 5, l. 166)
654 A false Iudas kysse. (30: p. 106, l. 2096; 33: III, 235, l. 134)
655 Oh oh quod ha, keepe againe the sow. (32: sig. B iii[v])
656 He wenes he kennes more then he knowes.
(1: I, 213, xi, 242; 2: p. 159, xx, 90; 3: p. 188, xviii, 64)
657 They be the craftiest cattell in Cristendome or kent.
(73: sig. C iii, l. 433)
658 A, whorsonne! thou callest me
Whore by craft;
Thou art a Kentish man, I trow. (46: p. 52)
B. Mary canst thou syng
A. Ye that I can
As well as ony man in kent. (67: sig. D i[v])
659 Ites hard for me to kycke,
Syth gods commaund as on would say, in fayth against the prick. (83: sig. E i; 42: sig. H iv[v])
660 With kindnes my her ye do kyll. (24: sig. D i[v], l. 735)
661 Kyng copyn in oure game thus shall I indew the.
(3: p. 233, xxi, 166)
662 Wherfore we counsaile you
This cuppe sauerly for to kisse. (2: p. 257, xxix, 79 f.)
She shall rather kysse, wher as it doth not ytche.
(30: p. 6, l. 96)
663 You are two as dronken knaues
As are betwene this & your owne skyns.
(42: sig. B iii; 43: sig. B ii[v])
Goe and a knaue with thee. (77: sig. C i[v])
The king . . . wyll spye a knaue in your face. (77: sig. I ii[v])
Now a knave put on thie cote? (70: p. 94, i, 2, 145)
664 Ffor yf I xulde sle my wyff
I sclow my self with-owtyn knyff. (4: p. 28, ii, 400 f.)
It consumyth natur, the body sleyth with-owt knyf.
(8b: p. 48, l. 555)
For gloton kyllyth with-owtyn knyf. (17: p. 125, l. 1620)
Kyll hym a-non, with-owtyn knyve,
And speke hym sum schame were þou go.
(17: p. 111, ll. 1127 f.)

665 To be made knyght of the colere. (26: sig. B i)
And knyght of the halter my fader ware an horne.
(23: sig. C i; 37: sig. B iii)
666 Shee is such a pestilent woman
As is not hence to our Lady of Basan. (42: sig. F iv)
667 Yett at last lady lucke cane fourd you some good hap.
(70: p. 151, v, 9, 23)
668 Take the ther a langett
To type vp thi hose! (3: p. 29, iii, 224 f.)
669 Faith youer Marsship will thrive att the latter Lammas.
(34: p. 27, iii, 5, 814)
670 Laugh in my sleeue. (47: sig. F iii[v]; 71: p. 199, ii, 3, 9)
671 There lay a strawe.
(70: p. 140, v, 2, 117, cf. note, p. 299; 80: sig. B ii, l. 93)
Naye there stoppe and laye a strawe. (38: p. 34)
But lay there a strawe I began to be wery.
(49: sig. E i[v], iii, 4)
What, M[r] Idelnes! lay a straw vnder your feete. (46: p. 14)
672 But yet this repulse of myne, they wyll lay in my dishe.
(45: D iii[v], iv, 3)
673 My thryfte is laid on soake. (70: p. 134, iv, 5, 72)
674 Wherfore any thing that is here done or sayd,
Shalbe layd vnder foote, and go no further.
(15: sigs. H i[v], I i[v])
675 I promes yow I haue no lede on my helys. (18: p. 21, l. 548)
Runne with leaden heeles. (45: sig. E iii[v])
Some leden heeled
Lubber. (46: p. 58; 52: sig. F i[v])
676 You lead the worlde in a string. (50: sig. E i)
677 Some of vs erelong maie happe leape at a daisie.
(34: p. 43, v, 2, 1322)
To make ye leape at a Dasye. (69: p. 66, v, 2, 235)
678 That is the lest care I haue of nyne. (59: sig. B i)
Nay that is the leest though[t]e that they haue of fyftene.
(23: sig. A iiii; 67: sig. D ii[v])
679 Now, therof a leke what rekys vs? (3: p. 5, i, 129)
This is not worth oone leke.
(3: p. 17, ii, 285; 24: sig. A iv, l. 134; 28: p. 396, l. 564)
680 If one paire of legs had not bene worth two paire of hands
He had had his bearde shauen. (69: p. 47, iv, 2, 77 f.)
681 He wold teache mee my lerrypoope. (70: p. 106, ii, 4, 28)
I taught them thier lerrie & thier poop. (70: p. 145, v, 7, 28)
682 He wyll licke all the fatte from my lippes. (72: sig. B iii)
683 Thou hast sene nothinge yet, to that thou shalt see.
For yet it lies & bledes. (70: p. 130, iv, 3, 36 f.)

684 But what should I light a Candle to the bright Sunneshine of my glorious renowne. (52: sig. D i[r–v])

685 But my lyppes hange in my lyght. (26: sig. A iv[v])
Thy lyppes hange in thyne eye. (25: p. 33, l. 1050)
Ye purblinded fooles, doo your lyps blinde your eyes? (49: sig. C ii[v], ii, 3)

686 I saue some lypp labour. (70: p. 106, ii, 4, 26)

687 This leysy lout, who ys as lither as longe. (10: p. 290, l. 816)

688 Yowur wytt ys lytyll, yowur hede ys mekyll. (18: p. 3, l. 47)

689 Farewell, three false knaues, as betweene this and London. (49: sig. E i[v], iii, 4)
Here is the trimmest Hogges flesh from London to Yorke. (72: sig. G i)

690 The lenger I lyue the more knaue you. (56: sig. D ii[v])

691 If we should chance to looke through an hemp Windowe, and our arse brake our necke. (46: p. 28)

692 Some one or other lookt babies in here eie. (70: p. 133, iv, 5, 40)

693 I care not a louse. (68: p. 133, ii, 2, 21)
Þis werldys wysdom ȝeuyth no[t] a louse
Of God, nyn of hye heuene. (17: pp. 92, ll. 491 f., 100, ll. 772 f.)
There was no man that did set by him a Louse. (37: sig. A iii[v]; 37a: I, 4, 320, l. 78; 66: p. 14, l. 345)
It is not worth a louse. (43: sig. A iii; 67: sig. C v)

694 It was love in a cloake bagge that brought this ffeat to passe. (70: p. 132, iv, 5, 22)

695 We are no such sucklings to take lubun lawe. (71: p. 210, ii, 4, 194)

696 If he haue not one Lumbardes touche, my lucke is bad. (68: p. 133, ii, 2, 23)

697 I am the most shrew in all myn kyn,
That is from this towne vnto lyn. (3: p. 283, xxiv, 154 f.)

698 Neare an M by your girdle? (68: p. 148, iii, 3, 135)

699 A man or a mouse. (71: p. 211, ii, 4, 223, cf. note, p. 313; 86: sig. C i, l. 497)
A man of your handes, to matche wyth a mouse. (45: sig. B i, ii, 1)

700 Can I remember a longe tale of a man in the moone. (45: sig. B i, ii, 1)
Alas good silly soule has toulde me a tale here oth mann ith moone. (71: p. 225, iii, 1, 102)
But he wolde here no more than the man in the mone. (57: sig. B iii[v])

701 A fare mayde marion. (71: p. 206, ii, 4, 75)
702 And woonne Townes, nourse, as fast as thou canst make Apples. (68: p. 127, i, 4, 82)
703 Might I thaym haue spyde,
I had made thaym a berd. (3: p. 171, xvi, 188 f.)
704 I pray the good Mulciber make no mo bones. (62: sig. A ii[v])
705 His arse makith buttens now. (66: p. 14, l. 348)
My buttocks made buttons of the new fashion. (39: sig. B i[v])
706 According to the prouerbe old, my mouth I wil vp make,
Now it doth lie all in my hand, to leaue or els to take. (85: sig. A iv[v]; 34: p. 3, i, 1, 88)
707 Take ye this to make vp thy mouth. (69: p. 33, ii, 3, 49; 70: p. 130, iv, 3, 22, cf. note, p. 296; 72: sig. C iv)
708 Ites a good mery greke. (71: p. 208, ii, 4, 123)
709 To set hys hart on a mery pyn. (20: sig. C iv; 22: sig. E iv; 34: p. 20, ii, 3, 594; 65: sig. A ii[v])
Mon coeur iocunde is sette on a mery pynne. (38: p. 21)
Thys wyll set hym on a mery pyn. (20: sig. D ii[v])
Let us set in, on a merrie pin. (63: p. 19, l. 683)
I woll sett my soule a mery pynne. (19: p. 51, l. 492)
710 Were you borne in a myll, curtole? you prate so hye. (77: sig. B iii[v])
711 Who wolde be a myller as good be a thefe. (56: sig. B iv[v])
Or ane Millair that hes na falt,
That will nather steill meall nor malt. (28: p. 530, ll. 4109 f.)
712 I haue eyes, will looke into a Mylstone. (77: sig. C i[v])
713 I shall thinke ereye minnit seven yeare. (71: p. 207, ii, 4, 102)
714 All youre mutyng amendis not a myte. (2: p. 303, xxxi, 322)
I care not a myght. (8a: p. 6, l. 142)
Count ȝe nocht that ane myte. (28: p. 529, l. 4105)
I ȝeue not a myth. (17: p. 84, l. 247)
I set not a myte by thy checking. (32: sig. E ii)
Other matter not worth a myte. (22: sig. A ii[v])
I forse for no man the worth of a myte. (55: sig. B ii[v])
715 She hath a monethes minde unto *Phylosarchus*. (75: p. 40, ii, 5)
716 Made you beeleve the Moone was a grene chese. (34: p. 58, v, 9, 1780)
To beliue and saye the moune is made of a grene chese. (66: p. 44, l. 1005)

717 He must euer be extolled aboue the Moone.
(14: sig. G iii, v, 10; 24: sig. A ii, l. 21)
That all is without Measure and fer beyonde the mone.
(25: p. 8, l. 224)
His dawghter whom formosus
Dothe love beyonde the moone. (70: p. 90, i, 2, 31 f.)

718 I am so lasy, the mosse groweth an
Inch thick on the top of my finger!
(46: p. 13, cf. Tilley, p. 89)
He is not worthe a handfull of mosse. (38: p. 27)

719 Our mother tounge. (71: p. 246, iv, 1, 98)

720 No mo wordes but mum. (24: sig. C i, l. 461; 39: sigs. A iii, A iv, E iii; 47: sig. B ii)
I dare say nothinge but mum.
(11: p. 20, l. 481; 69: p. 27, ii, 3, 6)
You know what meaneth mum. (69: p. 48, iv, 2, 105)
But mum, no words of it. (51: sig. I ii)
Whiste, scilence! not aworde Mum.
(34: p. 8, i, 3, 235, cf. ll. 246, 248)
Stande and play mum. (55: sig. D iv[v])
But mumbouget for Carisophus I espie. (72: sig. C iii[v])

721 What wylt thu fall to mutton?
(29: sig. B iv[v]; 25: p. 70, ll. 2265 ff.)
Ledges (*legs*) of
Mutton stufte with heare. (46: p. 27)
He lou'd lase mutton well. (77: sig. B iii)
Russhe vp mutton, for beefe is deare. (38: p. 23)

722 The see doth ebbe and flowe,
And varyeth not a nayle. (29: sig. A viii)

723 Or else my neck verse cun. (77: sig. E iii)

724 Your synnes in youre nekkys. (3: p. 384, xxx, 555)

725 I haue bene seeking ye, as a man should seek a load of hay in a needles eie. (51: sig. I i[v])

726 Then was myne not worth a neld. (3: p. 13, ii, 123)

727 These young gallants are caught without a net.
(75: p. 43, iii, 1)

728 I loke fast and neuer the nere. (5: p. 49, l. 514)

729 That shall be at neuermas. (62: sig. D iv)

730 I wyll geue the somewhat for the gifte of a newe yeare.
(62: sig. C i[v])

731 Tom tospot . . .
Hath incresed a Noble iust vnto nine pence. (39: sig. D iiii)

732 Is not this a pang trow ye beyonde the nock.
(55: sigs. E i, B iii[v])

733 I xall spare master Woode of Fullburn;
He ys a 'noli me tangere!' (18: p. 19, ll. 504 f.)

734 Ȝe must speke to þe schryue for a 'cepe coppus,'
Ellys ȝe must be fayn to retorn with 'non est inventus.'
(18: p. 29, ll. 773 f.)

735 My nose is ioynted. (80: sig. G iv, l. 1729)
I haue a good nose to be a pore mans sowe. (46: p. 27)

736 Within a while they would not be worth a couple of nuts.
(15: sig. B i)

737 Will ye haue a nutmugge to grate? (71: p. 206, ii, 4, 79)

738 And to have an ore in everye bodies bote?
(34: p. 38, iv, 4, 1152)
Beholde the devill, whose ministers are prest:
To stir an ore, in every forward boate.
(75: p. 43, second chorus)

739 And after the Prouerbe, we put oyle to the fyre.
(64: sig. B iv)

740 I am both old and colde. (1: I 110, vi, 134)

741 Old morell wold have a new bridell I suppose.
(70: p. 91, i, 2, 70)

742 Go! teach thy old shoes! (13b: p. 140)

743 Old wiues tales. (52: sig. E iv; 70: p. 115, iii, 2, 70; 86: sig. D i[v], l. 804)

744 By honest men he setteth not an Oynion. (36: sig. F iv[v])
He shall see it not worth an onyon. (55: sig. C ii)

745 Gyuen me the ouer hand. (20: sig. A iv[v])
Had of me the ouer hande. (20: sig. B iv; 30: p. 108, l. 2123)

746 He may chaunce to ouersee the best poynt in his tables sometimes. (74: p. 17, i, 2, 5 f., cf. note, p. 262; 70: p. 133, iv, 5, 41)

747 I am not worthe so much as an Oyestershyll.
(37a: I, 4, 320, l. 96; 66: p. 4, l. 61, cf. note, p. 48)

748 Your wyfe tolde me you were an Oxe. (72: sig. G i)

749 Rafe roister . . .
Hath brought a pack of wul to a faire paire of hosen.
(39: sig. D iiii)

750 There is a pad in the straw. (69: p. 57, v, 2, 83; 80: sig. B ii, l. 70)

751 I hope well to bring hir in such a paradise
That hirselfe shall sue me to haue my service.
(34: p. 9, i, 3, 253 f.)

752 I am spoken of more than they all
Hens to parys gatys. (20: sig. C ii)

753 You looke like an honest man in the Parrishe.
(79: sig. B i[v], l. 251)

754 Thou art sibbe to a parrot, thou canst chatter with a wittnesse. (70: p. 149, v, 8, 24)

755 To say nay one Pater noster whyle. (55: sig. C iii[v])

And wald nocht let me bide sa lang
To say my Pater noster. (28: p. 423, ll. 1262 f.)

756 Your tongue can renne on patins. (68: p. 118, i, 3, 24)

The tonge it went on patins. (69: p. 31, ii, 4, 35)

757 That lye, ere this, is flowen as ferre hens as Polle steple. (34: p. 33, iv, 3, 1010)

I had thought as soone to have mette here Paules steeple. (34: p. 22, iii, 2, 636)

758 Ile pay thee thy fortypence, thou brawling slaue. (86: sig. B i[v], l. 251)

759 For he was moste like for the pottage to paye. (43: sig. B i[v])

760 This is the olde prouerbe, to cast perles to an hogge. (40: sig. A iii; 81: sig. B iv[v], l. 396)

He thinks, as frustrate all his toile,
As peereles taste [cast?] to filthy Swine, which in the mire doth moile. (78: sig. A ii[v], ll. 16 f.)

761 I had not cared a pease. (85: sig. E ii)

He is not the better one Pease. (36: sig. C i)

Whan they haue not to eate,
The substaunce of a pease. (29: sig. C viii)

It is not worth a pease. (11: p. 17, l. 391)

762 Pitie nor pencion, peny nor pater noster shoulde euer haue made Nurse once to open hir mouth in the cause. (74: p. 14, i, 1, 43 ff., cf. note, p. 261)

763 Hee is such a felow
As is not hence to Peterborow. (42: sig. B ii)

764 Nowe to thee, Avarice; have att thye petticote. (34: p. 61, v, 10, 1893)

765 Blere myn ey and pyke out a mote. (4: p. 91, x, 283)

766 Then I may
Goe pyke strawes and take me rest. (24: sig. B i, ll. 211 f.)

Ye wolde make vs pycke strawes. (30: p. 22, l. 463)

Poore I maie picke strawes these hungri dogges will snatch all. (34: p. 11, i, 3, 314)

767 Bring me in credyte that my hande be in the pye. (34: p. 9, i, 3, 257)

768 And take hede Sir yow goe not to hye for the pye. (71: p. 197, ii, 2, 60)

Then shall I haue her in spight of the pye. (80: sig. D i[v], l. 626)

769 This is euyn a pyg of our own sow. (60: sig. A i[v])
Then had I a pyg in the woyrs panyer. (59: sig. B iv[v])
770 [A]re yow in year pilats voyce. (71: p. 252, iv, 2, 37)
771 From piller to post.
(44: sig. C iii, l. 471; 86: sig. E i[v], l. 1091)
From post to piller. (44: sig. D iii[v], l. 734)
772 A pinn for his layinge. (71: p. 181, i, 1, 161)
For her mother she cares not a pin.
(47: sig. D iii; 49: sigs. C ii[v], ii, 3;
71: pp. 216, ii, 5, 45, 235, iii, 2, 64)
For the preaching I passe not a pin. (47: sig. E ii[v])
Thi felowship,
Set I not at a pyn. (3: p. 34, iii, 363 f.; 14: sigs. F iii,
v, 2, G i, v, 6; 15: sig. F ii[v];
83: sigs. A ii[v], C iii[v], D i)
But without councell, I am not worth a pyn.
(15: sig. B ii[v]; 37: sig. E iii;
50: sig. F ii; 56: sig. C iii[v])
Or els all is not worth a Brasse pynne. (64: sig. C iv[v])
Thou hadst not ben worth a Flaunders pyn. (32: sig. B iv)
Then care not for consience, the worth of a pin.
(86: sig. C i, l. 516)
773 Pipe what I list yet he'l daunce what doth his humour please.
(10: p. 279, l. 489)
He is now full glad, as our pype goeth to daunce.
(30: p. 98, l. 1938, cf. p. 81, l. *74)
774 I pist on a nettell. (46: p. 30)
Truce for a pissing while or twaine. (68: p. 176, iv, 8, 33)
775 I am plaine Dunstable. (73: sig. B iii, l. 154)
776 But *piers piekpurse* plaieth att organes vnder my gowne.
(34: p. 41, v, 2, 1246)
777 He will playe at small game, or he sitte out.
(77: sig. D iv[v])
778 Playe boo pepe. (30: p. 126, l. 2478; 76: sig. B i, l. 240)
Thay play bo-keik, evin as I war ane skar.
(28: p. 437, l. 1633)
And he and I sall play cap'out.
(28: pp. 395, l. 539, 424, ll. 1295, 1296)
What canest thou do but play Cocke Wat?
(25: p. 37, l. 1192)
Howe I haue made the knaues for to play cowch quaile.
(62: sig. A i[v])
779 She hathe playd false at tabelles, & berne a man too manie.
(70: p. 133, iv, 5, 41, cf. note, p. 297)

780 Howe we schall play papse for þe pages prowe.
(2: p. 267, xxix, 358)
And playe euer styll the old boy. (20: sig. D i[v])
It is time now to playe the man, and not a symple sheepe.
(73: sig. G ii, l. 1583)
Can you not play with both hands & turn with the winde?
(85: sig. B iv)
781 I haue played with his beard. (72: sig. B ii[v])
782 Throwe the knave downe & with him plucke a crowe.
(71: p. 191, i, 4, 39)
I woulde topple with ye,
And plucke a good crowe ere ye brake your fast with me.
(14: sig. C i[v], ii, 2)
Na, na, abide, we haue a craw to pull. (3: p. 18, ii, 311)
783 I, Policie, have made hym to plucke in his hornes.
(34: p. 49, v, 6, 1523)
It will make yow plucke in your hornes.
(71: pp. 233 f., iii, 2, 24, 25)
784 I care not a poynt.
(50: sig. B i; 83: sigs. A iii, A iv[*bis*], B iv)
785 Yt ys grawntyde of Pope Pokett. (18: p. 6, l. 139)
786 But Lust is lusty and full of porridge. (43: sig. C i[v])
787 I set not by the prowdest of them a prane.
(25: p. 47, l. 1489)
Set ȝe nocht by twa preinis. (28: p. 531, l. 4169)
Thocht I ane seruand lang haif bene,
My purchais is nocht worth ane preine.
(28: p. 382, ll. 154 f.)
788 I trowd it drew nere the prik. (3: p. 378, xxx, 370)
I gyue the pryk and pryse. (20: sig. F ii[v])
For this I care not a puddyng prycke. (41: p. 63)
And pynche at the payment of a poddynge prycke.
(25: p. 66, l. 2122)
789 I haue more to yow to say
Than as þe sayeng is, þe prist dyd speke a sonday.
(30: p. 18, ll. 344 f.)
790 His preest wyll I be by cockes body.
(23: sig. A viii[v]; 71: p. 187, i, 3, 21)
791 Fleming commeth euen in pudding time. (39: sig. C ii)
792 That theif is hangit by the purs. (28: p. 477, l. 2656)
793 I care not a quinche. (72: sig. B iv[v])
794 You shall not haue her at rack and maunger.
(80: sig. B i[v], l. 51)

795 Here a roll of ragman of the rownde tabill.
(3: p. 374, xxx, 224)
To publysh his ragman rolles with lyes. (57: sig. B iii[v])
796 Wold he have me kepe nothyng agaynst a raynye day?
(70: p. 113, iii, 2, 23)
797 Rawhead, & bloudibone the ouglie. (70: p. 117, iii, 3, 72)
798 [Make] him tast of the rodde & ride byard rather.
(71: p. 188, i, 3, 61, cf. note, p. 307)
And ryde the horse with foure eeres. (35: sig. C i[v], l. 509)
But I thynke he rydyth ouer þe galous, to lern for to daunce.
(18: p. 22, l. 591)
799 Beyonde all reason or rime.
(14: sig. C iv, ii, 3; 43: Hazlitt's Dodsley, III, 296)
It forseth not of the reason, so it kepe ryme.
(25: p. 36, l. 1151)
Wit. A verie prettie one, I would it were in rime.
Wealth. In rime Wit, why so?
Wit. Because it wantes reason. (51: sig. B ii[v])
All this is out of season, and nothing done by reason,
Nor yet by good ryme. (11: pp. 20 f., ll. 484 f.)
800 I rose on my lift side to day. (46: p. 30)
801 You tell vs a tale of a rosted horse. (45: sig. C ii[v], iv, 1)
802 They are as much a kynne to the Markegrave, as Robyn Fletcher and the sweet Roode of Chester. (75: p. 39, ii, 4)
803 Telling a tale of Robin hoode. (50: sig. B iiii[v])
Why sir do ye thinke to doe any good,
If ye stande in a corner like Roben hood.
(45: sig. C iii[v], iv, 1)
804 Than wyll I playe Robsons part. (29: sig. C v[v])
805 But we have Roddes in pysse for them everye chone.
(34: p. 27, iii, 5, 820)
806 She is the erranst baud betwene this and Rome.
(59: sig. B ii[v])
Would God I hadd bene in Rome,
When I the way hither nome. (1: II, 298, xvi, 418 f.)
I had leuer go to rome / yei thryse, on my fete [*than meet Jesus*]. (3: p. 371, xxx, 128)
It were better go to *Rome* on my head then so.
(68: p. 133, ii, 2, 19)
For yf ony of vs thre be mayre of london
Iwys ywys I wyll ryde to rome on my thom. (23: sig. B i)
807 But I had rather haue your rome as your componie.
(46: p. 27)
808 I woll no more row a-geyn þe floode. (19: p. 51, l. 491)

809 I kyndell in her suche a lyther sparke
That rubbed she must be on the gall
Bytwene the tappet and the wall. (25: p. 39, ll. 1232 ff.)
And on the gall ye rubbe. (29: sig. A viii)
810 Rule the roste. (25: p. 26, ll. 805, 804; 34: pp. 5, i, 2, 136, 23, iii, 3, 690; 50: sig. A ii [v]; 58: sig. C i; 72: sig. B iii[v])
811 That they set theyr chyldren to rynne on the brydyll. (25: p. 66, l. 2136)
812 Not a rush for the I do not care. (73: sig. C iv[v], l. 547)
No man the Gospell will esteeme then a rushe. (40: sig. D i[v])
Esteeme the other, as light as a rush. (49: sig. F iv)
Thats no matter a rush. (71: p. 226, iii, 1, 140)
Yet I set not by you both a rysshe. (38: p. 6)
Þi wytt is not wurth a rosch. (4: p. 28, ii, 391)
813 And came saling in a sowes yeare (*ear*) ouer sea into Kent. (46: p. 13)
814 I doubt your younge wife will mark you I wott how
With Saint Cornelius badge. (70: p. 95, i, 3, 11 f., note, p. 278)
815 The vickar of S. fooles. (71: p. 213, ii, 4, 270, cf. note, p. 314)
816 Would it not anger a saynt at the hart? (83: sig. A iii)
It would grieve any Saint. (63: p. 23, l. 809)
817 Thou shalt find her moning
Her piteous case with a saint Johns face. (63: p. 13, ll. 447 f.)
818 And be a fellow amongst good fellowes to be held by S. Lukes horne. (50: sig. B iiii)
819 As he that from sterlyng, goth to sent thomas watryng. (11: p. 23, l. 542)
And after that saint thomas watring there to rest a tide. (11: p. 33, l. 804)
For at saynt thomas of watrynge & they styke a sayle. (23: sig. C iii[v])
820 They haue sawce bothe swet & sowr. (30: p. 12, l. 240)
821 So that yt was vnto the people into a prouerbe turned
What's Saul also amongst the prophets? (10: pp. 162, ll. 385 f., 181, ll. 936 f.)
822 Or eles it may chaunce you, to seke a new houd. (83: sig. A ii)
823 O gall in hunnie, serpent in the grasse. (51: sig. D iii[v])
824 Gods blessing on their heart that sette suche a brouche on my cappe. (74: p. 13, i, 1, 15 f.)

825 To cast the warld in seuen. (3: p. 101, xii, 38)

826 My son that I neuen,
Rewarde you this day as he sett all on seuen.
(3: pp. 115, xii, 487 f., 140, xiii, 737 f.)

827 Seaven yeare. (1: I, 120, vi, 406, II, 312, xvi, 756, 776; 4: p. 172, xix, 102; 8b: p. 31, l. 107; 10: pp. 16, ll. 330, 332, 17, l. 338, 18, ll. 381, 388, 389, 65, l. 674, 111, l. 477, 118, l. 111, 135, l. 18, 219, l. 569; 13a: sigs. D i, D ii; 21: sigs. A iii[*bis*], A iii[v], C iii[v]; 22: sig. E vii; 25: p. 34, l. 1079; 28: p. 527, l. 4024; 30: pp. 52, l. 1087, 96, l. 1894, cf. p. 80, l. *54; 34: p. 25, iii, 3, l. 733; 46: p. 33; 56: sig. C ii; 57: sig. B iv; 58: sig. D i[v]; 59: sig. B iii; 60: sig. C ii[v]; 61: sig. C i; 62: sig. C iv; 66: pp. 6, l. 104, 13, l. 310, 15, l. 364; 69: pp. 6, i, 2, 30, 18, ii, 1, 26, 65, v, 2, 223; 71: pp. 221, iii, 1, 23, 233, iii, 2, 10; 75: p. 70, iv, 7; 78: sig. F ii[v], l. 1410; 81: sig. D iii, l. 864)

828 He neuer learned his manners in Siuill.
(86: sig. E i[v], l. 1098)

829 For they are not worth, þe shakyng of a pertre
Whan the peres are gon. (30: pp. 8 f., ll. 158 f.)
I sett not by yowr curssys, þe shakyng of a rod.
(30: p. 65, l. 1383)

830 I had rather haue shakinge oth shetes. (71: p. 213, ii, 4, 272)

831 What tell you me of shame, it is shame to steale a horse.
(45: sig. C iii[v], iv, 1)

832 To shake the goodman, and sometime shaue his beard.
(39: sig. B iiii; 69: p. 47, iv, 2, 78)

833 Cast a sheeps eye. (63: p. 4, l. 124)

834 Nor nought coulde ye wynne that way wurth an old sho.
(55: sig. B iv[v])
Go meddle thu with olde shone. (29: sig. E vii)
Ouer the shooes . . . yn loue. (77: sig. G iv)

835 One might showe the gouse an all were gone.
(71: p. 223, iii, 1, 69, cf. note, p. 317)
I may goe shoe the Gosling now if I will.
(80: sig. G iv, l. 1729)

836 I am shorne in the neck. (70: p. 140, v, 3, 1)

837 We wyll short ther hornys, yf god send tyme & space.
(30: p. 12, l. 229)

838 Princes giue to many bred
Which wish them shorter by the head.
(81: sig. E ii[v], ll. 1094 f.)

839 He made is purgacyon vpon a boke
Or els redemed wyth the syluer hoke. (38: p. 34)

840 Sincke or swyme. (10: p. 279, l. 482; 14: sig. C iv, ii, 3; 36: sig. C iv; 55: sig. E iii; 68: p. 120, i, 3, 71; 86: sig. C iii[v], l. 669)
Here is none forsyth whether you flete or synke. (25: p. 9, l. 254)

841 His sange ful sone sall be, 'allas!' (2: p. 75, xi, 128; 3: pp. 68, viii, 141, 270, xxiii, 406; 8d: p. 195, l. 720)
Of care may thou syng! (3: pp. 232, xxi, 129, 244, xxii, 55)
Then sorow and care wolde be his songe. (24: sig. B i[v], l. 255)
With sorrow I may sing my sang. (28: p. 498, l. 3203)
Of Sorrow now may I singe. (1: II, 436, xxiv, 240; 4: p. 171, xix, 67 f.)
Of sadde sorwe now may I synge. (17: p. 168, l. 3062)
Of sorowes sere schal be my sang. (2: p. 157, xx, 43)
He shall singe a sory song. (1: II, 322, xvii, 118)
A sorrowfull songe, in fayth, shall he singe. (1: II, 426, xxiii, 702)
Of woful wo, man may synge. (17: p. 87, l. 328)
Sore syghyng is my sang. (3: p. 271, xxiii, 429)
I may syng ylla-hayll. (3: p. 240, xxi, 375)

842 My song may be 'well awaye!' (1: I, 78, iv, 350; 4: pp. 176, xix, 245, 225, xxv, 8, 374, xxxiii, 29; 6: p. 45, l. 234; 17: p. 143, l. 2218; 26: sig. A iv)

843 Nay eueryman I synge a nother songe. (27: sig. B ii[v]; 57: sig. B iv; 63: p. 7, l. 236; 70: p. 126, iv, 2, 62; 80: sig. F iv[v], l. 1458)
I must make you sing another note. (75: p. 78, v, 4)

844 Make the singe the cuccolds notes. (71: p. 200, ii, 3, 39)

845 All in Irons was my songe. (23: sig. A v)
And I were a mayde agayne, nowe maye be here songe. (62: sig. B ii)

846 To ioy my chaunce to syng old care away. (70: p. 122, iii, 4, 42)
I in his rage (poore wretch) shall sing *Peccaui*. (77: sigs. D ii, I i, K i)
And cry peccaui too. (45: sig. B ii)

847 They are syngyng of placebo. (30: p. 36, l. 761)
I may syng
With purs penneles. (3: p. 101, xii, 32 f.)
I will teache you to sing sol fa. (74: p. 46, iv, 2, 19 f.)
Sursum corda for hym to synge. (35: sig. A ii[v], l. 60)
Thou art sure shortly to play sursome corda. (48: sig. D ii)
What ye dolt ye be euer in one songe. (65: sig. A ii)

848 Hee'le doo nothing all day long but sit on his arse, as my mother did when she made powtes. (79: sig. C iii, ll. 647 f.)

849 I syt on thornes tyll I come ther. (38: p. 26; 70: p. 114, iii, 2, 45, cf. note, p. 286)

850 I shall, and that in hy set all on sex and seuen. (3: p. 169, xvi, 128)

851 When you haue their skin sir, what wil you doo with the case? (79: sig. G ii, l. 1665)

852 As prowde as pennyles his slefe has no poket. (3: p. 374, xxx, 236)

853 Here is a sleeueles aunswer. (80: sig. C iii, l. 460)

854 Small wyttam be your spede. (29: sig. B ii)

855 I can smell an appell seuen mill in a haye mowe. (46: p. 27)
We have smelled a ratte. (34: p. 6, i, 3, 162)

856 I smiled in my sleue. (72: sig. E iv; 78: sig. G ii[v], l. 1681)

857 I come of the smiters. (80: sig. B ii[v], l. 110)

858 Their talke is nothing but soft and fayre and tary. (45: sigs. C ii[v], D i; 67: sig. D iii)

859 The sooner the better in ende you will say. (49: sig. G i, iv, 1)

860 These maters that ye moue are but soppys in ale. (25: p. 69, l. 2233)

861 Alas Lucar I am sorie for thee, but I cannot weepe. (50: sig. D ii)

862 He hath as much landes I warrant you
As lyeth betwene thys & southhampton. (42: sig. E i)

863 Now take outt that sothren tothe,
And sett in a torde! (3: p. 123, xiii, 215 f.)

864 It is not for Idlenis that men
Sowe beanes in the wind. (46: p. 45)

865 He hath not yet sowne all his wilde otes. (71: p. 200, ii, 3, 37)

866 For is it not as good to say playnly
Gyf me a spade
As gyf me a spa ve va ve va ve vade? (22: sig. E vii[v])

867 Speke parot. (55: sig. E i)

868 Forsoth then were it a faire threedc that I had sponne. (14: sig. C iii, ii, 2)
Lo, Mary, haue ye not sponne a fayre threde? (15: sig. E iv[v])
The Courte is changed, a good thread hath bin sponne
Of Dogges woll heretofore. (72: sig. B i[v])
869 Of a spyndell I wyll make a sparre. (25: p. 33, l. 1036)
870 Yet is he farre out of square. (72: sig. E iv)
871 Stand to thy tackling stout. (46: p. 11, cf. Tilley, pp. 48, 93; 45: sig. F i; 76: sig. D iii[v], l. 993)
872 My feete do stande vpon a thorne. (64: sig. C i[v])
873 A man myght as wele stere a stokke as a stone. (2: p. 301, xxxi, 267)
874 She is stung with a lizart. (70: p. 133, iv, 5, 44)
875 It is time to stir Coles. (37: sig. B iii[v])
876 Strawe for the patches
Of worldly mucke! (31: p. 2; 60: sigs. A v[v], A vi)
A straw, all this geare wyll quickly be doone. (15: sig. G iv)
By his woundes, not a strawe. (34: p. 5, i, 2, 130)
Tushe, a strawe! (25: pp. 18, l. 549, 19, l. 564; 37: sigs. F iii, G i)
A straw for þi tale. (4: p. 222, xiv, 377; 7: p. 61, l. 125; 14: sig. E iii, iv, 5; 67: sig. C iv [v]; 68: pp. 152, iii, 4, 105, 162, iv, 3, 92)
He'l not care for vs all a straw. (10: p. 142, l. 215; 63: p. 12, l. 444)
I wolde not gyue a strawe for his techynge. (21: sig. C ii[v]; 59: sig. A iv[v])
But a matter of a strawe, and a thing of nought. (14: sig. D i[v], ii, 4)
I set not a strawe by you. (14: sig. G i, v, 6; 27: sig. A v[v]; 42: sig. E i[v]; 62: sig. A iv[v]; 65: sig. B ii[v])
And varyee not a strawe. (29: sig. A viii)
I weigh the not a straw. (10: p. 46, l. 110)
For thy wytt ys not worthe a strawe. (5: p. 61, ii, 896; 21: sig. B i; 25: p. 43, l. 1378; 38: p. 4; 42: sigs. A iv[v], C ii; 44: sig. C iv, l. 517; 50: sig. B iii[v]; 85: sig. E ii[v])
And a wreke his malyce for valew of strawe. (24: sig. A iv, l. 149; 71: p. 178, i, 1, 84)

And all was not worthe a newe strawe.
(35: sig. C ii[v], l. 550)

I care nat for the an olde straw. (57: sig. B i)

His worde is no more regarded than a vile strawe.
(15: sig. B iv[v])

I care not twoo strawes. (50: sigs. D i, E iii)

As for this king, I cure him nocht twa strais.
(28: p. 440, l. 1729)

Haue babelyd what they can no force of .ii. strawis.
(22: sig. A iii)

Thy news are not worth two straws.
(13b: p. 140; 29: sig. D iii)

Pike a quarell . . .
. . . for a cople of straues. (66: p. 45, ll. 1044 f.)

That is not worth .iii. strawes. (22: sig. E i)

877 I stryue agaynst the streame.
(10: p. 275, l. 380; 34: p. 47, v, 5, 1443)

878 From Stroude to Kent. (25: p. 31, l. 983)

879 I began to loue her in iest,
And may chaunce to swallow a Gudgion in earnest.
(80: sig. D iii, ll. 761 f.)

880 Yet ere I go, as Swans sing at their ende,
In solemne Song, I meane my knell to ryng.
(77: sigs. G i, M i[v])

881 I thought thy talke was too sweete to be true. (77: sig. B iii)

882 As lewde personnes, tagge, and ragge. (77: sig. K iii[v])

883 He waieth neither the time, person nor place:
Neither (as they say) the taile nor the face.
(37: sig. C ii)

884 Of hire tayle ofte tyme be lyght
And rygh tekyl vndyr þe too. (4: p. 126, xiv, 63 f.)

885 Ye haue eten sauce, I trowe, at the Taylers Hall.
(25: p. 44, l. 1404)

886 So you may if you please, take your eyes in your hande.
(80: sig. G iv[v], l. 1760)

887 I did but ieste Ile to take vp the rost. (71: p. 190, i, 3, 101)

888 Will you take snuffe so soone? (49: sig. C ii[v])

889 Of pleasaunt conceiptes, ten busshells to the pecke.
(45: sig. B i, ii, 1)

890 Thy wyfes .x. commaundements may serch thy .v. wittes.
(58: sig. E i[v])

Her ten commaundements are sene in the goodmans face.
(73: sig. C ii[v], l. 415)

891 Thars not within this land
A muryner Cat then Gyb is, betwixt the tems and Tyne.
(69: p. 40, iii, 4, 6 f.)
892 Thorow thyn and thycke. (41: p. 63; 45: sig. A iii[v])
893 And euery man sette at a thost [*bit of dung*].
(17: pp. 109, l. 1067, 149, l. 2413)
894 Or els for the sporte I wyll not geue two threades.
(37a: I, 4, 318, l. 63)
895 Yow haue geuen them a threde which theil never vntwist.
(71: p. 217, ii, 5, 78)
896 Naye thre knaues in a lease is good at nale.
(23: sig. A viii[v])
897 And in eueri thing as iust as .iii. pens to a grot.
(66: p. 39, l. 886, cf. note, p. 65)
898 I am afraid it is a
Timpany with two legges! (46: p. 15)
899 Þer is no lord lyke on lyve to me wurth a toost.
(4: p. 173, xix, 133)
900 Come toste me a fig. (68: p. 135, ii, 3, 48)
901 Why this is like to Tom turners doule.
Hang one man, and saue all the rest.
(86: sig. E ii[v], ll. 1162 f.)
902 Sir, we myght als wele talke
Tille a tome tonne! (2: p. 264, xxix, 249)
903 Ye may now put your toong in your purs. (54: p. 11)
904 For your tooth she ys too dayntie a dishe. (70: p. 107, ii, 5, 9)
Derided him to his teth. (71: p. 256, iv, 4, 6)
Thou canst not loue but from the teeth forward.
(50: sig. E ii[v])
Here is a prelate, euen for myne owne touth. (29: sig. D i)
Mawger our Teeth. (1: II, 323, xvii, 143; 20: sig. B i[v])
Spyte of hys tethe. (38: p. 6; 52: sig. C iii; 46: p. 27)
In despite of the teeth of them. (50: sig. F ii[v])
905 Assuring of friendship both with tooth and nayle.
(72: sig. B ii)
He lieth on my maister continually, as it were with tooth and naile for a straunger. (74: p. 35, ii, 4, 85 f.)
906 No nyghar (I saye) for there ye touche fre holde.
(13c: sig. E i)
907 I haue tow on my rok more then euer I had.
(3: p. 128, xiii, 389)
I haue more tow on my dystaffe than I can well spyn.
(57: sig. B iv[v])

908 All is . . .
. . . out of trace. (25: p. 29, ll. 913 f.)
909 As vp right a fellowe as ere trod on netes lether. (71: p. 249, iv, 1, 158)
910 She hath troade her shoe awrye. (70: p. 139, v, 2, 107)
She hath trode her slipper a wrie. (70: p. 133, iv, 5, 39)
He wyll not tread on thornes for none. (72: sig. F ii[v])
And trading (*treading*) vertues trace. (46: p. 7, cf. Tilley, p. 46)
911 And may noȝt wele tryne over two strase! (2: p. 103, xiii, 13)
912 Were thou borne in trumpyngton? (26: sig. C ii)
913 A tale of a tubbe. (29: sig. A viii; 45: sig. B i, ii, 1; 71: p. 235, iii, 2, 50)
914 Care not a tourde. (71: p. 191, i, 4, 28)
I pas not a turd for thee. (76: sig. B i[v], l. 278
I set not a torde
By none of them al. (62: sig. A iv)
It is not worth a torde. (13c: sig. E ii; 17: p. 144, l. 2227)
Nay, for my head, care not a Tinkers torde. (77: sig. F i)
The deuyls torde for thy brayne! (25: p. 34, l. 1087)
What canst thou tel me, tel me of a turd. (79: sig. F iii[v], l. 1506)
915 Marry that in dede, wolde make a Turke to grone. (29: sig. C v)
916 They maye go turne a socke. (29: sig. C viii[v])
Turne the catt in the pane. (46: p. 24, cf. p. 70)
Tourne Cat in the panne. (72: sig. C iv[v])
917 I chaunge all in the turning of a hand. (36: sig. D iv)
918 It is twenty pound to a goose turd. (69: p. 25, ii, 2, 61)
919 In the twinkling of an eye. (44: sig. E i, l. 849; 58: sig. D i; 64: sig. H ii)
In twinkling of an hower. (79: sig. A iv, l. 170)
920 Jorowur, in on hoode berith to facis. (19: p. 59, l. 721; 25: p. 23, l. 710; 50: sig. F i[v])
921 Playes the two legged foxe. (69: p. 58, v, 2, 86)
The land of the two legged mare. (39: sigs. C iiii, D iiii[v], E iii[v])
922 She is sick of two left heeles. (70: p. 112, iii, 1, 53, cf. note, p. 286)
923 A Tyborne checke
Shall breke his necke. (25: p. 29, ll. 910 f.)
Ye but wente ye neuer to tyburne a pylgrymage. (23: sig. A vi)
To preche at Tybrone. (26: sig. B i)

924 From Tyne to Trent. (25: p. 31, l. 982)

925 She helde me with a tale of a tytemary tally.
(35: sig. C ii[v], l. 557)

926 Gotten the vpper hand. (32: sig. E ii; 52: sig. G iv[v]; 57: sig. B iv[v]; 64: sigs. A ii, F iv; 74: p. 39, iii, 2, 14; 85: sig. A iv)

927 Ye seeme a man to be borne in the vale. (62: sig. B i[v])

928 Nowe by wades myll. (11: p. 24, l. 566, cf. note, p. 55)

929 Somtyme I laughe at waggynge of a straw.
(25: p. 32, l. 1015)

930 My master is waltum and I waltumes calfe.
(71: p. 184, i, 2, 17, cf. note, p. 305)

931 Þat is not worth a rottyn wardon. (30: p. 48, l. 989)

932 Þou beryst wattes pakke. (8c: p. 99, l. 1154)

933 Water in the one hande and fyre in the other.
(25: p. 23, l. 711)

934 Sonne Salomon into the way of all flesh I do enter.
(10: p. 223, l. 665)

935 Gentylmen ye gentyl men Jak heryng
Put your shone in your bosome for weryng. (60: sig. A iii)
A gentleman nay a iack hearinge,
As honest as he that caries his hose on his neck for feare of wering. (86: sig. E i[v], ll. 1099 f.)

936 He is in by the weke, we shall haue sport anon.
(68: p. 110, i, 2, 4)

937 Goes home by the weepinge crosse. (10: p. 295, l. 957)

938 Thou mayest be
More welcome and more bolde. (46: p. 10, cf. Tilley, p. 93)

939 In þe wanyand. (2: p. 124, xvi, 37; 3: p. 15, ii, 226)
Step furth, in the wenyande! (3: p. 227, xx, 748)
Walk in the Wenyand.
(3: p. 129, xiii, 405; 2: p. 319, xxxii, 389)
Whistyll ye in the wenyande! (3: p. 290, xxiv, 339)
Furth in þe wylde wanyand be walkand.
(2: p. 336, xxxiii, 485)
We! Whythir now in wilde waneand. (2: p. 36, vii, 45)
With a wannion to my master. (71: p. 245, iv, 1, 86)
Now a wild wannion on it. (70: p. 131, iv, 4, 11)
Up with a wilde wenyon. (14: sig. A ii, i, 1)

940 Had She oones Wett Hyr Whystyll. (3: p. 119, xiii, 103)

941 Lett all go a wheles. (71: p. 190, i, 4, 13)
Runnes your heades a wheeles? (77: sig. K iii[v])
The right course of the world, now he runnes vpon wheeles.
(80: sig. B iii, l. 171)

All the world me thought did runne on wheeles.
(80: sig. D i[v], l. 637)

942 He lyes for the quetstone. (3: p. 230, xxi, 80)
I must borrow thy Whetstone (*to Mendacio*).
(52: sig. C iv[v])

943 To haue whipping cheere. (40: sig. A iv, i, 1; 77: sig. E i[v])

944 Told a long round about not worth a whistle.
(70: p. 113, iii, 2, 16)
Cham afraid che may goe whistle now for money.
(44: sig. C i[v], l. 364)
The senses might haue whistled for the victory.
(52: sig. C iii[v])
He shall go whystle in a mary bone. (41: p. 61)

945 Like white liver Jakes to flye. (71: p. 252, iv, 2, 46)

946 Thou wast once a white sonne. (39: sig. C i[v])
Holde up his yea and nay, be his nowne white sonne.
(68: p. 110, i, 1, 49)

947 If I be a whore, thou art a knaue then it is quit.
(85: sig. B ii[v])
Adieu like a whore. . . .
Farwell like a knaue. (85: sigs. B ii[v]–B iii)

948 Will he, nyll he.
(48: sig. E i; 49: sig. H ii, v, 4; 87: p. 245, l. 79)

949 Naye sure, I will eyther wynne it, or take the foyle.
(45: sig. C iii, iv, 1)

950 I trow I haue now wonne my spurres for euer.
(14: sig. F iii, v, 3)

951 Let him winne it and weare it.
(45: sig. C iii, iv, 1; 51: sig. C iv)

952 What wynd hath you downe hither blowne? (10: p. 142, l. 218)
What wind brought you hether. (46: p. 14)
Which waies so euer the winde blowes it is for my commoditie.
(76: sig. C ii, l. 577)

953 And who so hath knowledge, what needs he to care
Which way the wind blowe, his way to prepare.
(78: sig. B i, ll. 136 f.)

954 Is the wynd in that dore.
(70: p. 131, iv, 5, 1; 74: p. 37, iii, 1, 14)
Do not set your mynde
To fyghte with the wynde. (62: sig. B iii[v])
Aha standeth the wynd so cold quod I? (20: sig. F ii[v])
There is sumwhat in the winde. (72: sig. B iii[v])
Somewhat hanges in the winde, that makes her to lower.
(80: sig. D iii[v], l. 767)

Trifle owt the tyme and tel a tale to the winde.
(70: p. 131, iv, 4, 15)

I doe but wast my winde. (48: sig. A iiii[v])

Thou hast winde at wyll, but in thy eyes no water.
(77: sig. L ii)

955 Let wiues were the Codpeece. (86: sig. B iii[v], l. 403)

956 Jacke shall cry wo the pye. (72: sig. B iii[v])

957 Ther ys a wolffe in a lombys skyn. (19: p. 51, l. 490)

Ane wolfe cled in ane wedders skin. (28: p. 534, l. 4264)

958 And Loe where Avarice comth, a woulff in the tale!
(As the proverbe saithe) what dothe he after hym hale?
(34: p. 25, iii, 3, 750 f.)

Lupus est in fabula, no more woords. (37: sig. C iii[v])

959 I am a very wodcok. (59: sig. B ii[v])

Mayster woodcock.
(55: sig. B i[v], cf. sigs. B ii, C ii, D iv[v], E i)

960 Let there be but a worde and a blow.
(36: sig. D i; 45: sig. A iv[v], i, 1; 73: sig. E iv[v], l. 1156)

961 How so euer the world goeth. (72: sig. G ii)

962 It is a worlde to se her whyrle. (22: sig. C v[v])

963 Wee two will live howe soever the world wagge.
(75: p. 63, iv, 3)

Let the worlde wag. (43: sig. B ii[v]; 60: sig. C ii[v]; 71: p. 217, ii, 5, 82; 76: sig. B i, l. 213)

To see the world wag. (39: sig. F i)

964 The wylde worm ys come into hys hed.
(20: sig. F ii[v]; 80: sig. B ii, l. 67)

965 I was neuer worth a pottfull a wortis. (18: p. 10, l. 265)

966 This was my fathers craft, for he euer made my Mother to wrap mee in her smocke. (80: sig. D iv[v], l. 857)

967 Ther is garn on the reyll other, my dame. (3: p. 32, iii, 298)

968 There is no vatter between this and Yorke. (85: sig. D iv[v])

But for all that she hath no felow
In syngynge hens to yorke. (67: sig. C iii[v])

APPENDIX

Proverbs from French Plays

In the Appendix is brought together the proverbial material from the various French plays or groups of plays which have been discussed from time to time in the body of this book. These plays fall into seven groups, some consisting of a single play and others of several plays printed together in a modern edition. For purposes of reference these groups are designated by the letters A to G. References are given as follows: designating letter, volume number (B is printed in one volume), page, number of the individual play in the collection (B and C are without subdivisions), and line (C, E and F are without line numbers). Of the collections A, D, and G are published by the Société des Anciens Textes français and B and F are almost equally accessible. E, on the other hand, is printed in a small and, it may be added, exasperating edition, in which each play is paged separately. One or two pieces from E and F are also in G and have been quoted from that source.

The alphabetization of the proverbs and, especially, of the sententious remarks is, in many places, as unsatisfactory to me as it can possibly be to anyone.

A *Le Mistére du Viel Testament*, ed. Baron James de Rothschild (Société des Anciens Textes français), 6 vols. (Paris, 1878–1891).

B Arnoul Greban's *Le Mystère de La Passion*, ed. Gaston Paris and Gaston Raynaud (Paris, 1878).

C [Simon and Arnoul Greban?], [*Le*] *Mystere des Actes des Apostres*, 2 vols. (Paris, 1540).

D *Miracles de Nostre Dame par Personnages*, ed. Gaston Paris and U. Robert (Société des Anciens Textes français), 8 vols. (Paris, 1876–1893).

E Leroux de Lincy and Francisque Michel, *Recueil de Farces, Moralités et Sermons Joyeux*, 4 vols. (Paris, 1837). Each play is paged separately, except that numbers 8 and 9, 12 and 13, 17 and 18 in volume one, and 2 and 3 in volume three, are printed together. The plays are listed only in volume one and there numbered continuously from 1 to 74, but it has seemed advisable here to start the numeration again at the beginning of each volume.

F [E. L. N.] Viollet Le Duc, *Ancien Théatre François*, Vols. I–III (Paris, 1854). The actual editor of these three volumes was A. de Montaiglon (cf. X [1857], v). The glossary (Vol. X) identifies many proverbs. The references to F give volume, number of play, and page.

G Émile Picot, *Recueil Général des Sotties* (Société des Anciens Textes français), 3 vols. (Paris, 1902–1912). Parallels to many proverbs are given in the notes.

PROVERBS

1 Qui bien actend ne suractend. (A: II, 217, xx, ll. 14043, 14049, 14055, III, 197, xxvii, l. 21686; G: I, 214, vii, l. 227)

2 Car en dit en substance
Que vraye amour ne va jamais sans craincte.
(A: V, 1, xxxix, ll. 36544 f.)
Note sur ce point
Qu'amour sans crainte ne vault rien:
Car sache que, s'on ayme bien,
On craint courroucer sa partie
Aussi cher qu'on ayme sa vie. (F: I, 1, 8)

3 On appaise d'une totee
Les petis enfans, quant ilz pleurent. (G: I, 71, iii, ll. 79 f.)

4 Quant l'aquest vient, il le fault prendre.
(A: IV, 352, xxxvii, l. 35188)

5 Gens à l'aulne ne sont vendus:
Au grant fardeau n'est pas l'aquest.
(A: IV, 128, xxxiii, ll. 30017 f.)

6 On congnoyt à l'arbre le fruict. (E: II, 4, 5)

7 Pour argent on apaise toult. (E: II, 5, 20)

8 Il n'est chose qu'argent ne face. (B: p. 398, l. 30379)
Argent faict partout la voyee.
(E: II, 13, 22; G: III, 97, xxii, ll. 287, 290, 293)

Qui cherche argent cherche debat. (E: II, 4, 11)
Car on dict, ou ie l'ay songe,
Qui porte argent porte sa mort. (E: III, 18, 6)
9 On dit qu'argent voulentiers hape. (D: I, 355, viii, l. 11)
10 Sur ma foy, qui d'argent n'a point
Maintenant n'a il de varletz. (G: I, 68, iii, ll. 37 f.)
11 On ne plaide poinct sans argent. (E: II, 4, 7)
12 Mais vella: qui ne peult ne peult,
Car il n'a pas argent qui veult,
Ainsi qu'on dit communement. (A: VI, 194, xlv, ll. 48641 ff.)
13 On taille, on ronge, on baille, on coupe & court
Et tousiours gros asnes ont oreilles. (E: III, 2, 6)
14 C'est follie d'attendre a demain
Ce que au jour d'uy on peult bien faire.
(A: IV, 351, xxxvii, ll. 35169 f.)
15 Tout avient quanqu'avenir doit. (D: I, 81, ii, l. 692)
Tout avient ce qu'avenir doit. (D: I, 160, iv, l. 265)
16 Qui ne s'aventure il n'a rien. (A: IV, 125, xxxiii, l. 29930, VI, 63, xliii, l. 45802; F: II, 27, 69, III, 63, 374)
Il n'a rien qui ne s'auenture
Dict le parmentier bon pilote. (E: II, 5, 5)
Comment! il fault qu'on s'aventure. (F: I, 6, 75)
17 On baille souuent, l'entens tu?
Le baston dont l'on est bastu. (E: III, 12, 17)
18 Vous avez la verge baillye
A voz enfans dont ilz vous batent.
(F: III, 63, 352; A: VI, 178, xliv, ll. 48336 ff.)
19 Car baiser attraict autre chose. (A: V, 142, xli, l. 39994)
20 J'apercoy en ce lieu, de faict,
Que telle baise qui trahist. (A: V, 348, xlii, ll. 44195 f.)
21 On dict bien qu'un barbier raid l'aultre. (E: II, 14, 29)
22 Car tandis que le fer est chault
Il le fault batre. (A: V, 235 f., xlii, ll. 41983 f.)
Bas le fer tandis qu'il est chault. (B: p. 287, l. 21941)
Doncques pense batre le fer
Pendant qu'il est chault. (F: III, 52, 119)
Il le bat trop froid . . .
On ne frapons poinct a l'endroit. (G: I, 34, ii, ll. 268, 270)
23 Scez-tu point que dit un proverbe
Que à battre la maulvaise gerbe
Se pert la peine du villain. (F: I, 10, 150)
24 Beau parler apaise les gens. (E: IV, 8, 25)
25 On voyt beau temps venir apres la pluye. (E: I, 23, 14)

Ne saues vous pas
Qu'apres la pluye vient le beau temps. (E: IV, 13, 5)

26 Sire, au besoing voit on l'ami.
(D: VI, 69, xxxiii, l. 2034; G: III, 262, xxviii, l. 527)
Au grant besoing on congnoist ses amis.
(A: IV, 388, xxxviii, ll. 36006, 36016, 36026)
[Le] seneschal,
Qui m'a esté ami loyal
A mon besoing. (D: VI, 70, xxxiii, ll. 2045 ff.)
Hostes, tout est bon au besoing. (D: V, 305, xxxii, l. 1395)
Et nous sommes monstrés mal fermes
De le laisser a son besoing. (B: p. 250, ll. 19344 f.)
Belle maniere a au besoing
Qui de sa voye a quelque apuy. (G: III, 146, xxiv, ll. 397 f.)

27 Or dit un proverbe approuvé
Que besoing fait (la) vieille trotter. (F: II, 25, 40)
Le pont aux asgnes est tesmoing:
Besoing fait la vieille trotter. (F: II, 25, 49)
Trottez, vieille, trottez, trottez. (F: II, 25, 48, 49)

28 Bien assailly, bien deffendu;
Qui assault n'a pas l'avantaige.
(A: II, 222, xxi, ll. 14155 f., 14161 f.)
Fort assailly, bien deffendu:
C'est leur responce. (A: V, 297, xlii, ll. 43244 f.)

29 Car qui bien ayme bien chastie,
Comme souvent vous l'oyez dire. (F: III, 51, 29)

30 Qui bien se garde, bien se treuve. (A: V, 349, xlii, l. 44220)

31 Car un ver dit, et je l'appreuve,
Que celluy qui bien quiert bien treuve.
(B: p. 70, ll. 5469 f.; C: I, lxxiii)

32 Ung boiteulx se mocque d'ung tort,
Et ung bochu d'ung contrefait. (G: I, 96, iii, ll. 365 f.)
Il cloche devant les boyteux
Et faict le sot devant les sotz. (G: III, 222, xxvii, ll. 201 f.)

33 Qui bon l'achéte, bon le boit. (A: VI, 194, xlv, l. 48633)

34 Mais on dit que mauvaise atente
Ne vault pas une bonne fuyte. (A: I, 347, xvi, ll. 8598 f.)
Vne bonne fuyte
Vault mieulx c'une mauuaise atente. (E: I, 8, 7)

35 Car, mon enfant, il vault miex naistre
De bonne heure que de bons estre,
Selonc m'entente. (D: II, 300 f., xv, ll. 519 ff.,
VII, 20, xxxvii, ll. 429 f.)

36 Qui bon maistre servir entend
Par droit bon loier en attend. (B: p. 230, ll. 17812 f.)

37 Un homme qui le braz a court
N'a mestier de longue chemise. (D: III, 46, xvii, ll. 1430 f.)
38 Tout tel que nous l'avons brassé
Le fault boire. (B: p. 8, ll. 447 f.)
Ce qu'il brasse il le fault boire.
(F: I, 7, 107; A: VI, 178, xliv, l. 48239)
39 Après la brebis vient l'aignel. (F: I, 14, 247)
40 Car on ne sçauroit nullement
D'un busart faire un esprevier. (F: I, 17, 304)
On ne faict poinct d'vn espreuier
Vn busart en ville ne champs. (E: II, 10, 14)
41 La chance n'est qui ne retourne. (G: II, 243, xiii, l. 340)
42 Tousjours ne court pas une chance. (A: V, 62, xl, l. 38085)
43 De grant folye s'entremet
Qui se chastie par aultruy.
(G: III, 146, xxiv, ll. 411 f., 290, xxix, ll. 263 f.)
44 Scays tu point pourquoy boit chat eau
C'est pource quil na point de vin. (C: II, xix)
45 Mais, quant le cheval est perdu,
Bien tard est de clorre l'estable. (A: II, 146, xix, ll. 12280 f.)
46 Car qui n'a bon conmencement
Il ne peut a droit parfiner. (D: IV, 92, xxiv, ll. 537 f.)
47 De court joye grant meschef. (A: V, 350, xlii, l. 44228)
48 En court de roy,
Beaux amis, chacun est pour soy;
Qui ne le fait, il n'est pas sage. (B: p. 87, ll. 6795 ff.)
49 Vous ne sçavez combien
Grace de court a homme dure. (A: VI, 54, xliii, ll. 45614 f.)
David. Mais vous sçavez, pour le jour d'uy,
Qu'on dit ung mot qui partout court.
Isay. Et quel?
David. Que service de court
N'est pas heritage. (A: IV, 119, xxxiii, ll. 29818 ff.)
50 De son cousteau, il s'est couppé,
De ses verges il s'est batu;
Le brassin a beu que a brassé (A: VI, 178, xliv, ll. 48237 ff.)
51 Tant plus croist mal / tant plus constrainct. (C: II, clxxxvii)
52 Plus crye on / plus bruyct le meffaict. (C: II, clxxxvii)
53 Cul de femme et museau de chien
Si sont tousjours froiz comme glace. (G: I, 108, iii, ll. 509 f.)
54 La dame faisois serviteure,
Qui est reprouche de grant gref.
(A: II, 373, xxiii, ll. [G 1734 f.])
C'est grand abus quant on honneure
Mains la dame que serviteure. (A: II, 351, xxiii, ll. [G 1139 f.])

55 C'est un prouuerbe bien commun:
Deuil de vieille n'est pas uny;
L'un veult du blanc, l'aultre du brun,
L'une dict ouy, l'aultre nenny. (E: IV, 1, 15 f.)

56 Tu scez, par ton mesme record,
Que deux coquins ne vallent rien
A un huys. (F: II, 26, 60)

57 Dieu et les saintz sont au *credo*,
Et le diable si est au rendre. (G: I, 109 f., iii, ll. 531 f.)

58 Le dyable l'a bien amené,
Car il vient devant que on le mande.
(G: I, 104, iii, ll. 459 f.)

59 L'eaue benoiste efface tout. (F: I, 10, 157)

60 Tel cuide par trop embrasser
Qui laisse eschaper son fardeau. (F: III, 59, 253)

61 Qui trop emprent
Souvente fois il se repent;
Mais de venteur petit faiseur. (A: V, 338, xlii, ll. 43989 ff.)

62 Qui emprunte, ne choisit mye. (E: IV, 1, 26)
Qui emprunte en la fin fault rendre. (A: V, 18, xxxix, l. 36967)

63 Car enfans ne se sçayvent tayre. (A: II, 304, xxiii, l. 16149)

64 Car il ennuye a qui actent,
Je le sçay bien, c'est chose vraye.
(A: III, 129, xxv, ll. 20222 f.)
Il ennuye trop qui attent. (B: p. 199, l. 15325)
Car trop annuie a qui atent.
Je le sçay bien, n'est pas nouvelle. (D: I, 325, vii, ll. 346 f.)

65 Car, quant on eslongne de l'oeil,
On s'eslongne de la pensée. (A: IV, 173, xxxiv, ll. 31009 f.)

66 Et pour ce dy qu'il avient peu
Qu'estoupes n'ardent près de feu:
Estoupes est homs et feu femme;
Qui tost est espris de tel flame. (D: III, 175, xix, ll. 1050 ff.)

67 D'aultre part vous avez mespris:
Car quant meschant homme s'excuse
Et en s'excusant il s'accuse,
C'est petite excusacion
Bien digne de pugnicion. (B: pp. 403 f., ll. 30771 ff.)
Besoing na de se excuser
Celluy que personne naccuse. (C: II, clxxii[v])

68 Il vault mieulx qu'il soit fait que affaire.
(A: I, 348, xvi, l. 8610)

69 Qui faict ce qu'il peult (,il) est excuse. (F: I, 6, 70)

70 De faulce monnoye faulx coing,
C'est bien entendu le dispos. (G: III, 257, xxviii, ll. 381 f.)

71 Car femme a peine peult celler
Chose qui doit estre cellée. (A: IV, 42, xxxi, ll. 28036 f.)
Quant une femme se taira
Pour son mary, menés la pendre. (G: I, 85, iii, ll. 231 f.)
On scet que femmes scevent dire
Ainsi que leur vouloir les meust. (B: p. 390, ll. 29771 f.)
72 Je ne sçay si rude personne
De femme, pour le faire court,
S'une foys l'oreille abandonne
Qu'on ne gaigne la basse-court. (F: I, 14, 239)
73 Car il n'y a si ferré qui ne glice.
(A: IV, 362, xxxvii, l. 35406, V, 344, xlii, ll. 44123 f.)
74 Oncques feu ne fut sans fumée.
(F: I, 19, 339; G: II, 150, xi, ll. 293 f.)
75 Fin contre fin autre deçoy. (F: I, 16, 288)
76 Au foible on veoyt porter le sort. (E: II, 1, 15)
77 Mais fol ne croyt tant qu'il reçoit. (G: I, 262, ix, l. 387)
78 Fol cuide d'un, et l'autre advient. (G: II, 328, xvii, l. 2)
Point n'est vray tout ce que fol pense. (G: II, 328, xvii, l. 6)
79 Car on ne peust, au fort aller,
Aux folz deffendre le parler. (B: p. 366, ll. 27901 f.)
80 On dit qu'il est fol qui s'oublye. (F: I, 17, 294)
81 C'est voir que j'ay oy nuncier:
'Qui sanz donner a fol promet
De noyent en joie le met.' (D: IV, 265, xxvii, ll. 680 ff.)
82 Bien est fol qui ayme follie. (F: III, 63, 408)
83 De fol juge briefve sentence,
L'en le voit souvent advenir.
(B: p. 153, ll. 11733 f.; E: II, 8, 31)
84 En folle teste folle chose. (G: II, 328, xvii, l. 5)
85 On voit souvent qu'une fortune
Ne vient point seulle, se dict-on. (F: I, 15, 265)
86 Tel ne sairoyt un coup frapper
Qui toutefois se faict bien craindre. (G: III, 58, xxi, ll. 61 f.)
87 Et puis que nous sommes fréres, nous nous devons entreaidier, car l'en dit que deux ou trois fréres valent plus en une bataille que cinc ou six estranges.
(D: IV, 122, cf. p. 121 — Sermon before xxv)
88 Qui rien ne fume, rien ne ceult. (E: III, 14, 6)
89 Tant plus gelle / tant plus estrainct. (C: II, clxxxvii)
90 A grant fiance grant faillance. (A: V, 43, xxxix, l. 37620)
91 Puis qu'après grant mal vient grant bien,
Ainsi qu'on dit en brief langaige,
D'avoir soucy n'est que bagage.
(G: II, 357 f., xviii, ll. 1 ff., 11)

92 Dame, il eschiet souvent grans pertes
Ou l'en cuide grant gaaing avoir. (D: IV, 21, xxiii, ll. 556 f.)
93 Aux grans seigneurs les grans honneurs. (G: I, 247, ix, l. 132)
94 Tant gratte chieure que mal gist.
(C: II, clxxxvii; E: III, 2, 9)
95 De gros boudins larges rouelles. (G: III, 218, xxvii, l. 129)
96 Car ainsi qu'on dit, 'qui a terre
Ne peult vivre sans avoir guerre,'
Le proverbe assez s'entend. (A: IV, 338, xxxvii, ll. 34850 ff.)
97 Car selon l'habit l'homme vault. (G: III, 42, xx, l. 255)
98 Voirement dit on voir: l'abbit
Ne fait pas le religieux. (D: III, 107, xviii, ll. 1036 f.)
99 On dict qu'a hardy demandeur
Y fault hardiment refuser. (E: IV, 8, 27)
100 Les plus hardis sont premiers mors. (B: p. 204, l. 15740)
101 Qui trop se haste,
Souvent pert son bruit et se gaste.
(A: IV, 171, xxxiv, ll. 30976 f.)
102 L'homme propose et Dieu dispose. (G: II, 328, xvii, l. 1)
Mon chier ami, homme propose
Et Diex ordene, c'est tout voir. (D: IV, 90, xxiv, ll. 461 f.)
103 Quant ung homme si est tout seul
Il n'a garde de s'entrebatre. (G: I, 91, iii, ll. 309 f.)
Ung homme seul est peu de chose. (A: I, 247, xi, l. 6360)
104 Qui ne dort, il n'est pas filz d'omme,
Au dire voir. (D: I, 131, iii, ll. 754 f.)
Car il n'est pas, se dit on, homme
Qui ne dort et qui ne prent somme.
(D: V, 113, xxx, ll. 580 f.)
105 Selon la jambe la chausse. (B: p. 301, l. 22969)
106 A jeune prince viel conseil. (G: II, 241, xiii, l. 290)
107 Bon larron est qui larron emble. (G: II, 368, xviii, l. 219)
107a Lieu assailly n'est pas rendu. (A: II, 222, xxi, ll. 14157 f.)
108 On dict bien . . .
. . . qu'une main l'aultre suporte. (E: II, 14, 29)
109 Si le maistre demande un baston,
Le serviteur apporte de la paille. (F: II, 33, 146)
110 Par commun proverbe conclu:
Qui mal y pense, mal luy vient.
(A: VI, 177, xliv, ll. 48226 f.)
Vous sçavez bien:
Qui mal pourchasse mal luy vient.
(A: VI, 178 f., xliv, ll. 48234 f., 48243, 48251, 48259)
111 De malle vie malle fin. (C: II, clii[v])

112 Il n'est point marchand qui ne ment. (F: III, 63, 361)
113 Ung mareschal dedens sa forge
Ne boit nen plus que terre a four. (G: I, 83, iii, ll. 215 f.)
114 Mauvaise herbe croist voulentiers. (A: V, 300, xlii, l. 43296)
115 Ung mauvais maistre avez servy
Dont recevez si dur loyer. (B: pp. 326 f., ll. 25004 f.)
116 Après les maux viennent les biens
Souventes foiz. (D: I, 176, iv, ll. 743 f.)
117 Tel cuide souvent menasser
Qui est frappé de son cousteau.
(F: III, 59, 253; A: VI, 178, xliv, l. 48237)
118 Celuy peut bien menger sans nappe
Qui fust engendré sans lincheul. (G: I, 91, iii, ll. 307 f.)
119 Quay / gens qui ont mange chappons
Mangeroyent voluntiers beuf. (C: I, cxxiii[v])
120 Mais plus tost la merde.
Menges la donc, qu'el ne se perde;
Car qui la mangera, l'aura. (E: IV, 10, 14)
121 Sy vous voyes communement
Que mocqueurs viennent a nyent. (E: IV, 5, 32)
122 Berger de pencee amoureuse,
Ne cherche iamais grand desiun;
On dict en prouuerbe commun
Qui moins a a respondre,
Cela est commun a chascun;
Qui n'a betail y n'a que tondre. (E: IV, 13, 6)
123 Trop hault monté voit on descendre.
(A: VI, 136, xliv, l. 47357)
Pour ce qui s'est par trop hasté
De monter, il est cheu à val. (F: III, 59, 256)
Car l'en dit souvent: 'Quant plus hault
Est li homs montez qu'il ne doit,
De plus hault chiet qu'il ne vouldroit.'
(D: I, 105, iii, ll. 12 ff.)
Qui plus hault monte qu'il ne doit,
Il voit ung clocher de plus loing.
(G: III, 147, xxiv, ll. 421 f.)
124 Y n'est pas mort qui se repose. (E: IV, 13, 4)
Tel n'est mort qui ressucita. (G: II, 147, xi, l. 240)
125 On dit voulentiers que une mouffle
Vault mieulx que gant en ung bisson. (G: I, 97, iii, ll. 379 f.)
126 Necessité n'a loy aucune. (A: I, 293, xiv, l. 7352, III, 185, xxvi, l. 21388, V, 127, xl, l. 39647, 319, xlii, l. 43687)

127 On dit bien vray que nourriture
Passe aage. (A: I, 378, xvi, ll. 9354 f., III, 244, xxvii, ll. 22801 f.)

128 A gens nouveaulx nouvel coustume. (G: I, 119, iv, l. 9)
A nouveaulx gens nouvel estat. (G: I, 121, iv, l. 37)
Nouveau maistre, nouvel argent. (A: III, 208, xxvii, l. 21949)
Vous sçavez que c'est commun dit:
Nouveau prince, nouvel esdit. (A: III, 255, xxvii, ll. 23053 f.)
Nouveau prince, nouvel usaige
Et nouvelles invencions. (G: II, 219, xiii, ll. 69 f.)

129 On ot les nouvelles au four,
Au moulin et chiez les barbiers. (G: I, 67, iii, ll. 25 f.)

130 La nuyct tout bren semble farine. (A: II, 356, xxiii, l. [G 1255])

131 Orgueil paie a la fin son homme. (A: VI, 148, xliv, l. 47594)

132 On congnoist l'ouvrier a l'ouvrage. (B: p. 196, l. 15130)

133 Ung oyseleur et ung coquin,
C'est tout ung a gens qui ont haste (G: I, 107, iii, ll. 503 f.)

134 Le pardon qui donna le chat
A la souris vous soit donné! (G: I, 95, iii, ll. 351 f., cf. E: I, 3, 15)

135 Le parler n'est pas le plus fort. (A: V, 266, xlii, l. 42640)
On dit souvent: 'Trop parler nuyt.' (A: V, 290, xlii, l. 43123)

136 Ha dea! on scet bien quant on part,
Mais on ne scet quant on revient. (A: II, 74, xvii, ll. [F 1605 f.])

137 Passe partout souventes foys s'acroche
Et deschire ce qui est autour soy. (F: III, 59, 256)
Toutes choses il fault passer. (A: III, 30, xxiv, l. 18198)
Riens n'est qu'il ne faille passer:
Nous n'avons cy pas nostre cours
Au monde pour estre tousjours. (B: p. 193, ll. 14862 ff.)

138 Compaignon certes passience
Comme l'on dict passe science. (E: I, 6, 4)

139 Le péché est tout pardonné
Quand on ne le faict que en cachettes. (F: I, 10, 157)
Faisons le tout secretement:
Il sera demy pardonné. (F: II, 29, 92)

140 Pecune faict par tout la voye. (E: III, 16, 8)

141 Qui doit pendre, il ne peust noier
Se le gibet ne va nouant;
Cela c'est ung ver tout truant:
Tout le monde le doit savoir. (B: p. 327, ll. 25006 ff.)

142 Tousiours les perdans sont moques. (E: I, 20, 15)

143 Car qui veult venir aux honneurs
Des pebitz vient on aux grans biens. (C: I, lxiiii[v])
144 De petit don ne peult chaloir. (E: IV, 10, 24)
145 Qui petit parle bien besongne. (A: II, 370, xxiii, l. [G 1658])
Peu parler et bien besongner. (G: III, 13, xix, l. 119)
146 Et pour ce dict on bien souuent
Petite pluye abat grant vent. (E: I, 2, 21)
Petite pluye abat grant vent
Et si fait saulver mainte barge. (G: I, 87, iii, ll. 255 f.)
147 Pour petit proces, peu de plet. (E: IV, 11, 21)
148 A peu besongner bien vanter. (F: II, 43, 331)
149 Bien sçavons que tel l'oyson plume
Qu'au menger n'est pas invité. (G: I, 120, iv, ll. 11 f.)
150 Quant la pomme est meure,
Force est qu'elle chaye. (A: I, 168, viii, ll. 4416 f.)
151 Tant va le pot a leau quil casse. (C: II, clxxxvii)
152 Poulle chantant devant le coq
Auant qui soyt la fin de moy. (E: II, 7, 4)
153 Pourceau blasme pomme paree
Aussi fort que truye espices.
(G: I, 96, iii, ll. 361 f., cf. III, 347)
154 Plus vault avoir pourchas que rentes. (F: II, 49, 433)
Elle vit, sans plus, de sa rente
Ou de son pourchas. (F: III, 51, 33)
155 Voire, qui ne peult ne ne vault. (A: VI, 94, xliv, l. 46438)
156 Ung povre homme n'a point d'amy. (B: p. 183, l. 14094)
Mes povres gens n'ont point d'escout:
Qui a assés, tout bien l'assault,
Et qui n'a riens chacun luy tault. (B: p. 183, ll. 14150 ff.)
157 Voire, car les premiers assis
Ont tousjours les plus gras lopins,
Et s'il y a point de bons vins
Ilz en sont les premiers servis. (B: p. 146, ll. 11184 ff.)
Qui premier y vient, premier solle:
Des premiers sont premier ferus. (B: p. 289, ll. 22124 f.)
158 Qui premier l'a sentu l'a faict. (F: I, 7, 95)
159 On prent voulentiers du convent
Le plus meschant pour estre abbé. (G: I, 67, iii, ll. 31 f.)
160 Mais j'ay oy pour voir retraire
Que de deux folies emprendre
Doit on pour soy la meilleur prendre.
(D: I, 185, iv, ll. 1007 ff.)
Seigneurs, de deux maux le mains pire
Doit on eslire pour le miex. (D: V, 280 f., xxxii, ll. 669 f.)

Si as pris de deux poins le pire,
Qu'aultrement ne m'as frequenté. (B: p. 291, ll. 22246 f.)

161 Mon seigneur, on dit c'on amande
De preudomme servir, c'est voir. (D: I, 290, vi, ll. 1085 f.)

162 Car on dit tout communement
En ung ver que j'ay retenu,
Qu'il vault mieulx au commancement
Prevenir qu'estre prevenu. (B: p. 378, ll. 28842 ff.)

163 Rien n'a en cause qui ne prouue. (E: II, 8, 24)

164 Dangier n'y a que de la fin,
Car j'ay mainte foys oy dire
Que a la queue gist le venin. (G: I, 218, vii, ll. 316 ff.)

165 Oncques femme n'y reculla,
Seurement, que pour mieulx saillir.
(A: V, 327, xlii, ll. 43828 f.)

Y fault qu'on recule
Bien souvent pour saillir plus loing. (G: I, 20, ii, ll. 70 f.)

166 Il faict icy du papelart /
Le vieil regnard faict du deuot. (C: I, cli)

167 Il s'en pourroit bien repentir,
Mais peult estre sera trop tard. (F: III, 51, 46)
Or vient trop tard le repentir. (F: III, 60, 292)

168 Il ne fault point servir de rost
Ou boullu est acoustumé. (A: VI, 74, xliii, ll. 46031 f.)

169 Les plus rouges y sont bien pris. (G: I, 162, v, l. 357)

170 Dict on pas en toute saison
Qu'i ne fault qu'en vne maison
C'vn sage pour la faire riche? (E: I, 5, 8)

171 Mais sanz saint Pierre a la grant Romme
Requerre, ne si loing aler,
Puis qu'est a l'uis. (D: VI, 83, xxxiv, ll. 78 ff.)

172 Il fault payer comptant,
Et faire de sainct Pol sainct Pierre. (G: II, 193, xii, ll. 164 f.)

173 Y nous fault de propos changer
Et conclure, sans alibis,
Qu'on faict reuerence aux abis,
Non pas aux gens siencieulx. (E: III, 9, 19)

174 J'ay ouy dire aulx gens antiens
Que toulx ceulx ne sont pas sciens
Portant habit disimulé. (G: III, 95, xxii, ll. 253 ff.)

175 Chacun appéte son semblable. (A: I, 214, ix, l. 5592)
Toute chose ayme son semblable. (C: I, lxi, lxxiii)
Toute beste ayme son samblable.
(B: p. 301, l. 23018; D: I, 149)

176 Tel seme froment et aveine
Qui n'en mengit jamais d'ung grain. (G: I, 247, ix, ll. 139 f.)

177 On dict en ung commun langaige,
Sept ans acreu et puis pendu. (A: II, 306, xxiii, ll. 16191 f.)
Sept ans acreu et puis fendu
L'arbre qui porte dommage. (The same, version C)

178 Voirement dit bien celi voir
Qui premier dit: 'qui va si leche,'
Et aussi dit: 'qui siet si seche.' (D: VI, 255, xxxvi, ll. 768 ff.)

179 La douleur est bien plus amère,
Mourir de soif emprès le puis. (F: I, 18, 312)

180 De sotes gens sotes raison. (E: III, 15, 31)

181 A ung sourt ne fault point deux messes. (F: III, 63, 359)

182 Nonpourquant a ce je m'assens
Que tant de testes, tant de sens,
Ce dit on souvent en conmun.
(D: VII, 149, xxxviii, ll. 807 ff.)

183 Il vous vault mieulx tart que jamais. (F: III, 51, 19)

184 Sy le prendrons
Et l'amenrons tel feur, tel vente. (B: p. 246, ll. 19023 f.)

185 C'est a tel maistre, tel valet. (E: IV, 5, 13)

186 Elle est a tel pot tel culier
Et selon la jambe la chausse. (B: pp. 301, ll. 22968 f., 327, l. 25023; D: V, 9, xxix, l. 202)

187 Sy dict on souuent qu'a toute heure
Y fault aler auec le temps. (E: IV, 13, 12)
Au temps qui court n'y a fiance:
Maintenant joye et demain pleur. (G: II, 328, xvii, ll. 7 f.)
Il fault penser au temps qui court. (G: III, 229, xxvii, l. 354)
On voit le Temps souvent muer. (G: III, 18, xix, l. 191)
Le Temps se mue d'heure en heure. (G: III, 23, xix, l. 290)
Le Temps n'est pas tousjours egal. (G: III, 18, xix, l. 192)
Le Temps est beau, le Temps est laict;
En ung estat point ne demeure. (G: III, 24, xix, ll. 291 f.)
Ainsi comme le temps viendra
Prendre le fault. (A: II, 108, xviii, ll. 11300 f., 209, xx, l. 13861, III, 49, xxv, l. [G 3246]; C: II, clii; D: IV, 368, xxviii, l. 1461; E: III, 2, 8; F: III, 63, 404)

188 J'aymeroye, par Dieu, mieulx ung *tien*
La moitié que deux *tu l'avras*. (G: I, 69, iii, ll. 59 f.)

189 Sy est vn tiers bien dangereux,
Sy n'est amy. (E: II, 11, 7)

190 Tost gaigne & tost despence,
C'est l'estatu d'entre nos seurs. (E: I, 15, 14)

191 Car je sçay que le touchement
Procéde de l'acouchement. (A: III, 67, xxv, ll. 18749 f.)

192 A tous seigneurs, toutes honneurs. (A: V, 6, xxxix, l. 36659)

193 A trompeur trompeur et demy. (F: I, 15, 270, II, 29, 93; G: III, 23 f., xix, ll. 283, 300)
Trompeurs sont voluntiers trompez. (F: II, 28, 87)
Par trop tromper je suis trompé. (G: III, 22, xix, l. 276)
Par bieu! avant que soit dix ans
Chascun trompeur se trompera. (G: III, 21, xix, ll. 239 f.)
Tel trompe au loing qui es trompé.
Trompeurs sont de trompés trompez,
Trompant trompettez au tromp[é]
L'homme est trompé. (F: II, 33, 157)
Tromperye tousiours retourne
A son maistre. (E: III, 12, 16)
Qu'a trompeur tromperye luy vient. (E: II, 4, 46)

194 Ie n'y veulx aulcun poursuyuant
Car le troysiesme poinct n'y fault. (E: II, 4, 22)
Ouy, le troisieme n'y vault rien. (E: II, 15, 29, 30)

195 Tel va bien souvent au retraict
Qui de chier n'a poinct d'envye. (G: III, 58, xxi, ll. 65 f.)

196 Voirement dit bien celi voir
Qui premier dit: 'qui va si leche,'
Et aussi dit: 'qui siet si seche.' (D: VI, 255, xxxvi, ll. 768 ff.)

197 C'est le dict de chascun quartier:
A la vache est tousjours le veau. (F: I, 14, 248)

198 Par sainct Jehan, qui la veult sengler,
'C'est aultre chose,' dit la vache. (G: I, 66, iii, ll. 17 f.)

199 Mais de venteur petit faiseur. (A: V, 338, xlii, l. 43991)

200 On dit que, qui veult argent prendre,
Il fault souvent vendre et mesvendre.
(A: III, 3, xxiv, ll. 17610 f.)

201 Tel qu'il viendra il le prendra;
Mais il fault vivre toutesfoiz. (A: II, 108, xviii, ll. 11302 f.)

202 On congnoyt . . .
. . . le bon vin a la liceur. (E: II, 4, 5)

203 Fault il pas voir ains que scauoir? (E: III, 6, 8)

Proverbial Phrases

Comparisons

204 Et moy vaillant comme un Achiles. (E: IV, 8, 14)
205 Chacun de vous estoit isnel
Comme aigles. (A: IV, 165, xxxiv, ll. 30823 f.)
206 Qu'il a ung lyon combatu
Et comme ung aigneau abatu. (A: IV, 5, xxxi, ll. 27207 f.)
Doulx et begnin comme l'aigneau.
(A: II, 42, xvii, l. [EF 823])
Et ausy douces c'un aigneau. (G: III, 340, xxxi, 271)
Aussi doulx que petis aigneaulx. (A: III, 290, xxviii, l. 23921)
Plus doulx
Que vng aigneau. (C: I, xciiii[v])
Mieulx fust de les avoir mengées
Aussi bien que fut ung aigneau.
(A: II, 381, xxiii, ll. [G 1933 f.])
Comme laigneau soubz le tondeur
Est muet sans commotion
Ainsi ne fist nostre seigneur
De iuge murmuration. (C: I, xci)
Tu voys le pauvre enfant qui s'offre
Comme l'aigneau. (A: II, 66, xvii, ll. [F 1416 f.])
Et comme vng aigneau blanc ou bis
Deuant le tondant se rend nud. (C: I, xc[v])
Simples comme petis aigneaux. (A: II, 200, xx, l. 13645)
Tu es plus sot qu'agneau qui belle. (E: II, 6, 14)
207 Il est aussy royde c'un ais. (E: II, 15, 19)
208 Vous estes plus blancs
Que nest vne ymage dalbastre. (C: I, clxiii)
209 Est tant friant et tant gourmant
Qu'il mangeroit plus qu'un alemant. (F: II, 34, 160)
210 Il brullera comme allumettes. (A: II, 35, xvii, l. 9955)
211 Ne alose
Mieulx composé . . .
Que estoit Joseph. (A: III, 48, xxv, ll. [G 3224 ff.])
212 Vous lerray je cy assemblées,
Duchesses, si comme alouettes? (A: VI, 14, xliii, ll. 44653 f.)
213 J'ay le corps mieulx faict qu'ung andouille. (F: III, 51, 25)
214 Sans charite sy i'ey parole d'ange
C'est com arain qui rend un son estrange. (E: I, 4, 6)
215 Hardy, vaillant, droict comme un arbre. (E: III, 18, 14)
216 Que son corps comme vng arc tendu. (C: I, xxxiiii[v])

217 Ce sont armeures esmolues,
Aussi cleres que fin argent. (B: p. 364, ll. 27724 f.)
A Saül sont presens honnestes
Qui vallent mieulx que . . . argent.
(A: IV, 140, xxxiii, ll. 30265 f.)
218 Et serez plus soubtil qu'Argus
Se vous eschappez de la feste. (B: p. 316, ll. 24106 f.)
219 Sus donc, alés!
Comme une aronde. (G: II, 309, xvi, l. 36)
220 Et devint son corps aussi noir
Conme arrement. (D: V, 338, xxxii, ll. 2370 f.)
221 Nient plus q'un asne mort feru
Il ne dit mot. (D: VI, 49, xxxiii, ll. 1436 f.)
De ouyr vostre teste glorieuse
Comme un asne ricaner. (F: II, 30, 107)
222 S'y n'est trop plus sot c'une anesse.
(G: III, 187, xxvi, l. 243)
223 Et fust il aussi grant que Athlas. (C: I, cl)
224 Mais si m'atens je estre atampis
De Cerberus, nostre portier,
Comme beaux aux en ung mortier
Par force de lourdes hurtures. (B: p. 437, ll. 33390 ff.)
225 Et fust plus dur que l'ayment. (B: p. 299, l. 22867)
Il fault avoir le cueur plus dur . . .
. . . que dure pierre d'aymant.
(G: III, 265, xxviii, ll. 612, 614)
226 Il a le groing enluminé
Comme le B de *Beatus vir*. (F: II, 36, 198 f.)
227 En peine et dueil et griefve ardure,
Plus ardent que barre de fer. (B: p. 161, ll. 12333 f.)
228 Pour avoir tantost sa poitrine
Plate comme ces gros baris. (B: p. 186, ll. 14358 f.)
229 Son oeil pire que basilique. (A: V, 300, xlii, l. 43293)
Ton regard
Plus tresperçant qu'ung basilique. (B: p. 94, ll. 7315 f.)
230 Doulce fleurante comme basme.
(A: IV, 167, xxxiv, l. 30883)
Elle sent trop plus fort que basme. (C: II, ccxli)
231 Par l'instrument mainct compaignon
En deuient sec comme vn baston. (E: I, 18, 21)
232 Nous tuons, par Dieu! autant d'hommes
Comme ung belistre faict de poulx.
(A: IV, 204, xxxiv, ll. 31702 f.)
233 Hellas! c'est ainsi que une beste. (A: II, 55, xvii, l. 10233)

Mes disans,
Qui vont par mes disans
Des sages, et ne sont que bestes. (F: II, 33, 146)
Sus une roche conme beste
Trois jours entiers, dame, esté ay.
(D: IV, 292, xxvii, ll. 1493 f.)
Je suis icy comme une beste. (F: III, 61, 303)
Battre le fault comme une beste.
(A: II, 385, xxiii, l. [G 2052])
Ne sont comprins ne plus ne moins
Que vne beste mue pourroit. (C: II, ccxxi)
Qu'aussi q'une beste esbahie
Sui ci. (D: V, 290, xxxii, ll. 955 f.)
Et sont tous ceulx plus folx que bestes. (F: III, 63, 372)
Pire es que beste irraisonable. (A: I, 190, viii, l. 4955)
Il n'a ne memoire n'assens
Plus qu'aroit une mue beste. (D: III, 29, xvii, ll. 874 f.)
Et qu'elle soit, comme une beste,
Nue. (G: III, 133 f., xxiv, ll. 153 f.)
Des Egyptiens obstinez
Jusques aux bestes de pasture
Feit mourir tous les premiers nez. (C: I, lxxvi[v])
Car leur petitz filz plaisans . . .
Comme bestes rauissans . . .
Mangeront contre lusage
De dame nature. (C: I, lxxviii[v])
Cayn, vagant et fugitif,
Ainsi que une beste sauvaige. (A: I, 189, viii, ll. 4934 f.)
Et en parolles admonnestes
Aux hommes comme simples bestes. (C: II, cxliii[v])
Les gens me tiendront pour beste. (F: I, 3, 30)
Il est tenu pour une beste. (F: I, 6, 71)
Je me tenroie bien pour beste. (D: IV, 138, xxv, l. 422)
L'ung est vellu comme une beste. (A: II, 130, xix, l. 11867)
Et me pourras conme une beste
Vendre au marchié. (D: VI, 191, xxxv, ll. 625 f.)
Tu as vescu com une beste. (F: III, 51, 79)
Je le veste
De blanc comme une sote beste
Qui n'a ne sens n'entendement. (B: p. 293, ll. 22395 ff.)
Ou tout temps mais que viveras
Conme beste herbe brouteras. (D: II, 179, xiii, ll. 183 f.)
Mais vous, qui estes gent sanz foy
Et qui vivez aussi com bestes. (D: IV, 96, xxiv, ll. 653 f.)

Mais les laisser tels vous reputes
Viure ainsy comme bestes brustes. (E: I, 16, 9)
Ne vivez pas comme les bestes. (F: III, 63, 370)
Vous vivez doncques comme bestes. (G: I, 168, v, l. 487)
Comme beste vivant sans foy. (G: II, 80, x, l. 1113)

234 Tenez, je me tourne aussi court
Qu'ung beuf qui court après la vache.
(G: III, 138, xxiv, ll. 246 f.)
Et voz maulx rongeans mugyrez
Comme vng beuf. (C: II, lxxvi[v])
Et tout mon peuple rongera,
Comme beufz qui l'erbe mangeussent
Jusque a la racine. (A: III, 408, xxx, ll. 26689 ff.)
Et venez tost comme un bœuf de pasture.
(G: II, 287, xv, l. 177)

235 Elle seroit plus tost fondue
Que beurre en vng four de verrier. (C: II, xlviii)

236 Il est aussi ront que une bille. (F: II, 31, 117)

237 Oncques . . . bombarde
Ne sonna plus terriblement. (C: I, x[v])
Ung ton gros comme une bombarde. (C: I, xxvi)

238 Je tue, je jette par terre
Comme fait le boucher ung veau. (F: II, 41, 293 f.)

239 Se on me deuoit comme vng boucler
Pollir les yeulx a laymery. (C: II, xlvi[v])

240 Tu seras batu comme bourre. (C: I, lviii[v])

241 Decepuant comme une bouteille
De vingt & deulx pos. (E: IV, 5, 20)

242 Et fut y grand comme vn boyseau. (E: I, 8, 5)

243 Ce villain,
Qui est plus yvre que un bracquet. (F: II, 25, 39)

244 Mes demandez s'il art:
Comme brandons au vent remus. (B: p. 95, ll. 7393 f.)
Ha! chault brasier de convoitise,
Plus ardant que brandons de fer. (B: p. 277, ll. 21166 f.)

245 L'enneny, la char qui domine
Le monde tost croit et escoute
Comme la branche qui s'encline
Au vent qui le plus fort la boute. (B: p. 33, ll. 2502 ff.)

246 Nous burons gros comme le bras. (E: II, 15, 16)

247 Je suis pis que ung brasier chault.
(A: IV, 180, xxxiv, l. 31181)

248 Ainsi je vous envoie tous
Comme brebis entre les loups. (B: p. 155, ll. 11846 f.)

Mene au lieu doccision
Ainsi que vne poure brebis. (C: I, xc[v])
Mene fut a occision
Comme la brebis debonnaire. (C: I, xci)
Comme brebis a nul nuysante. (G: II, 80, x, l. 1117)

249 Il a les dentz comme vne broche. (C: II, ccvii[v])

250 Amours d'amys je boy et hume
Comme brouet. (A: II, 344, xxiii, l. [G 927 f.])

251 L'avugle
Qui ne veoit rien plus qu'un bugle.
(D: III, 339, xxii, ll. 841 f.)
Qui te tiens icy comme ung bugle. (B: p. 270, l. 20652)

252 Il se mussa comme une caille,
Tant estoit hardy et vaillant. (F: II, 31, 118)

253 Chair doulce comme ung canepin. (G: I, 252, ix, l. 223)

254 Je suis plus blanc que carmes. (F: II, 36, 194)

255 Voyre a gens pirs que Cayfas. (E: III, 16, 19)

256 Aussi com le cerf la fontaine
Desire a trouver d'yaue plaine. (D: I, 62, ii, ll. 86 f.)
Se je ne le vois pasturant
Aussi conme cerf . . .
N'enterra viande en mon corps. (D: V, 117, xxx, ll. 711 ff.)

257 Le cueur froyt plus que chaine en puys.
(A: I, 305, xiv, l. 7642)

258 Je les feray aussi menus
Comme chair en la boucherie. (A: IV, 36, xxxi, ll. 27908 f.)
Nous les ferons aussi menus
Comme la chair de haricoq,
Puis que nous y mettrons le croq.
(A: III, 365, xxix, ll. 25711 ff.,
IV, 186, xxxiv, ll. 31320 ff.)

259 Que des genoulx auez la peau
Comme les genoulx dung chameau. (C: II, clxxxiii[v])

260 Prestz sommes comme chandeliers.
(A: III, 226, xxvii, l. 22388; IV, 204, xxxiv,
l. 31719; B: p. 181, l. 13935)
Moy je suis tousjours aussi prest
Et debout comme ung chandelier. (G: I, 109, iii, ll. 523 f.)

261 Feu qui estincelle
Cler comme chandelle. (A: III, 296, xxviii, ll. 24078 f.)
Corps advenant, plaisant et belle,
Fassonnée comme une chandelle. (F: I, 10, 167)
La matière est bien abregée
Et s'en va comme une chandelle. (F: I, 8, 122)

262 Le garde-cul
Ausy chault que cherbon de forge. (E: II, 5, 18)
Je veil que vous me rotissiez
Aussi rouge comme ung charbon. (B: p. 23, ll. 1650 f.)

263 Ma conscience
Est plus orde que la charongne
Qui est jectée en une fosse. (F: III, 63, 401)
Voz enfans / voz petis dyablotz
Plus puans quoncques fut charongne. (C: I, lxix)

264 Car il est tout cler et certain
Que le chartier, qui a la main
A la charrue et qui regarde
Derriére luy, sans prendre garde
A l'œuvre de devant ses yeulx.
(A: II, 41 f., xvii, ll. [EF 795 ff.])
Rebelles comme charetiers. (A: III, 227, xxvii, l. 22390)

265 Ilz s'entreleschent le morveau
Comme les chatz au moys de may. (F: I, 10, 170)

266 Frere Redymet,
Rouge comme vn beau cherubin. (E: II, 14, 12)

267 Il craint le bas
Plus que cheval de poisonnier. (F: II, 36, 195)
Si femme prent le frein aux dens
Comme un . . . cheval. (G: III, 132, xxiv, ll. 119 f.)

268 Entray, comme un leger cheureau
En la ville. (E: III, 18, 7)

269 Le sens [luy] croist en sa cornette
Comme le sens d'une chevrette.
(A: II, 378, xxiii, ll. [G 1847 f.])

270 Ressemblent les chiens à la lune
Ses sotz icy. (F: II, 37, 213)
Ilz seront batus comme chiens.
(A: V, 57, xl, l. 37980; C: I, xxix)
Bouté en terre comme ung chien. (B: p. 370, l. 28247)
Ione comme beaulx chiens couchans. (E: IV, 13, 21)
Attacher les fault deux a deux
Comme chiens courans. (C: I, xxxi)
Courez
Comme chiens a mont et a val. (B: p. 226, ll. 17461 f.)
Ainsi que chien quon mastine
De mon espee courtine
Aura le col estrene. (C: II, xcviii)
Elle me maudict comme vn chien. (E: I, 5, 4)

Les enmenrez com chiens en laisse.
(D: IV, 200, xxvi, l. 604, 211, xxvi, l. 935, VII, 78, xxxvii, ll. 2152 f.)

Mais, par Dieu, jamais un chien court
Ne fut plus paillard qu'i sont tous. (G: III, 167, xxv, ll. 258 f.)

Il est plus parjure qu'un chien. (F: I, 8, 112)

Plusieurs y a pires que chiens. (A: II, 106, xviii, l. 11264; III, 77, xxv, l. 18990, 232, xxvii, l. 22522, 262, xxviii l. 23224; V, 256, xlii, l. 42394)

Je vail pis q'un chien. (D: VI, 38, xxxiii, l. 1074)

Vous estes pis que chien mastin. (F: I, 4, 44)

Mon maistre est aussi piteux
Comme ung chien mastin enraigé.
(A: IV, 349, xxxvii, ll. 35121 f.)

Et sy ne font que papier,
Comme un chien prins en une bare. (E: I, 3, 6)

Quant ma femme me avroyt baisé,
Je m'en riroye comme un chien vert.
(G: III, 141, xxiv, ll. 298 f.)

Lung urle en chien. (C: II, cxvi)

Ceulx me tiennent plus vilz q'un chien.
(D: VI, 189, xxxv, l. 553)

Conme un chien,
Sire, vivroie. (D: III, 340, xxii, ll. 890 f.)

Il n'est abay que de vieil chien. (F: II, 36, 193)

Aussi esseullé qu'ung vielz chien. (B: p. 282, l. 21543)

Ie suys auec vous si troublee
Et plus martiree c'vn viel chien. (E: I, 11, 11)

Je suys avec vous si troublee
Et plus martiree c'un viel chien. (G: I, 189, vi, ll. 130 f.)

Je suis plus vaincu qu'un viel chien. (B: p. 139, l. 10679)

271 De gens qui sont conme chiennaille.
(D: VII, 29, xxxvii, l. 691)

272 Tous ensemble
En vng mont comme belles chieures. (C: I, lxxi[v])

Ilz ont tant charge lesperit
De mal quilz puent comme chieures. (C: II, xl)

273 Je tiendray mieulx en pays
Que ung chinotoire. (F: II, 30, 110)

274 Il resplendist comme les cieulx. (C: I, lxii)

275 Abbatez boys et clicquettez
Comme vne cygongne qui couue. (C: II, xlvii[v], ccli)

276 Aussi facille comme cire. (A: III, 318, xxviii, l. 24596)
Dieu vos gard, belle au gentil corps,
Mieulx faict que s'il estoit de cire. (F: I, 13, 215)
Et moy, j'en faictz come de cire. (G: III, 54, xxi, ll. 2, 8)
Il est ja jaune conme cire. (D: IV, 193, xxvi, l. 383)
Vous vous en aidez au besoing
Et comme de cire en ouurez. (C: I, xlviii, II, cxlvii[v], clxxxvii, ccvii[v]; E: IV, 3, 12)

277 Vostre langue na de repos
Non plus qung claquet de moulin. (C: I, xxi)

278 Plus que colombe belle. (C: II, li)

279 Qu'en la fin vous viendrez à moy
Aussi droit que compas de lune. (F: III, 56, 210)

280 Ou comme vne vielle compresse
Yl est de moy habandonne. (E: I, 17, 3)

281 Et barbetez comme . . .
. . . vielz corbeaux tous affamés. (B: p. 49, ll. 3846 f.)

282 Il est . . .
. . . faict comme ung corbillon. (F: II, 41, 293)

283 Ilz sont plus drus que corcaillotz
Nouveaulx nez. (G: II, 185, xii, ll. 9 f.)

284 Il est aussi gros q'une corde. (G: III, 224, xxvii, l. 235)
Je men yray par cy dessus
Aussi droict que vne corde darc
A lhostel. (C: I, clv[v])
Quant elle vit son cher enffant, . . .
En ce gros arbrier estendu
Comme une corde en l'arc tendu.
(B: p. 405, ll. 30889–30893)

285 Ilz ont tous les costez plus durs
Que nest le bout de ma cornette. (C: I, xxvii[v])

286 Plus reluysant que nul corps lumineux
Ce que le ciel circuyst. (C: I, lxviii)

287 Vous estes plus blanc que cotton. (C: II, xliii)

288 Armés sommes et adoubés,
Aussi fiers que coulons tubés
Pour faire une grosse hemee. (B: p. 98, ll. 7605 ff.)
Tu as yex conme de coulon. (D: V, 92, sermon before xxx)
Et simples comme les coullons. (B: p. 155, l. 11850)

289 Je courus plus tost que la cource,
En poste. (G: II, 147, xi, ll. 238 f.)

290 Avant, avant, que l'en le frotte
Aussi hault que ung coureur qui trotte!
(A: II, 382, xxiii, ll. [G 1962 f.])

291 N'ayez le cueur dur comme cuyvre.
(A: II, 384, xxiii, l. [G 2026])
292 Si femme prent le frein aux dens,
Comme un courtier. (G: III, 132, xxiv, ll. 119 f.)
293 Sa langue est de telle manière,
Comme est d'ung coutel à tripière,
Car il trenche des deux costez. (F: III, 63, 366)
294 Il me pense tenir estroit
Les mains, comme on fait un coye. (F: I, 11, 187)
295 Je suis tombé a la renverse,
Les piez dessus, comme ung crappault.
(B: p. 437, ll. 33359 f.)
Princes sacerdotaulx
Qui sont plus enfflés que crappaux.
(B: pp. 279, ll. 21329 f., 394, l. 30012; C: I, iv[v])
296 Je voy la mer clere et seraine,
Et nette comme ung beau cristal. (B: p. 416, ll. 31739 f.)
Le faisant transparant ainsi
Que le cristal. (C: I, l[v])
297 Son visage est aussi plaisant
Que le cul de la barbouillée. (F: I, 17, 300)
Je suis contend que lon me tonde
Rasibus comme cul de cynge. (C: I, cxxii)
298 Les Hongres puent comme dains. (G: I, 111, iii, ll. 558 f.)
Ilz saillent, courent comme dains.
(A: V, 8, xxxix, l. 36699)
299 Ie parle gresle
Comme faict vne damoyselle. (E: II, 6, 18)
300 Dessoubz mes grifz trop plus poignans que dardz.
(C: I, iv[v])
301 Car ie croy que oncques dent de chien
Ne fut plus sec que iay la mouse. (C: I, clxxxvi[v])
302 Tu n'y says non plus q'ung dodin. (F: III, 51, 43)
303 Douge
Comme ung dozilh. (G: II, 49, x, l. 566)
304 Sans le menger toute comme un drongart. (F: II, 34, 174)
305 Et feust il cruel comme vng dyable. (C: I, clxii)
Je estudie à tort comme ung dyable. (F: I, 19, 329)
Les Egiptiens sont trouvez
Pires que dyables reprouvez.
(A: III, 268 f., xxviii, ll. 23407 f.)
Car il est pire que le dyable. (C: II, ccxlviii)
Moins piteux que n'est ung grant Dyable.
(A: I, 256, xi, l. 6575)

306 Vertu abolye
Pis qu'eau a bolye
Faict et observe elle. (G: II, 41, x, ll. 413 ff.)
Ainsi en toy habonde
Comme eaue en bonde / vne grace planiere. (C: I, iii[v])
Et feray decourir leur sang
Comme eaue decourt d'une fontaine.
(A: IV, 188, xxxiv, ll. 31357 f.)
Sa poure teste ne repose
Non plus que faict l'eau de la mer. (E: III, 6, 14)
Son sang s'en va, comme eau courant. (F: III, 51, 61)

307 Ces bons sergens,
Qui sont ausy doulx qu'elephans. (E: I, 3, 10)
Et quilz soient fermes comme elephans. (C: II, xxix)
Et fort comme un elephant. (E: III, 18, 14)
Gens hardis comme ellephans. (A: III, 225, xxvii, l. 22344)

308 Se cueur n'est plus dur qu'une enclume.
(B: p. 198, l. 15234; E: III, 15, 20)
Et pesante comme une enclume.
(A: II, 344, xxiii, l. 930; C: I, lx; F: II, 36, 191)
Il est legier comme ung enclume. (F: II, 41, 293)

309 Les autres cifflant
Ainsi comme ung petit enfant. (F: II, 37, 221)
Comme enfant au giron sa mére;
De rien ne vous fault soucier. (A: II, 195, xx, ll. 13522 f.)
Il ne ramonne plus
Non plus qu'un enfant nouveau né. (F: II, 36, 204)
Qu'il ne saiche nom plus parler
Que faict ung enfant nouveau né. (F: II, 31, 121)

310 Elle est basse comme ungz enffers. (B: p. 310, l. 23665)

311 Mes grans botes
Aussi ternyes qu'escarbotes
De ratizier en ces fourneaulx. (B: p. 379, ll. 28899 ff.)

312 La barque va comme vne esclistre. (C: II, clxxxvii)
J'ay du fart,
Qui est plus luissant que esclistre.
(A: IV, 277, xxxvi, ll. 33396 f.)

313 Mes tu poins comme escorpion. (B: p. 316, l. 24152)

314 Ilz sont larrons comm' Escossoys,
Qui vont pillotant les villaiges. (G: II, 364, xviii, ll. 129 f.)

315 Reagal est . . .
. . . jaune comme pié d'escoufle. (G: I, 87, iii, ll. 249 f.)

316 Il me jetta à la renverse
Ny plus ny moins qu'une escrevisse. (F: I, 16, 282)

Il font comment fait l'escrevice
Qui chemine à reculons. (F: III, 51, 27)
Croy qu'ilz ressemblent l'escrevice
Qui va tousjours a reculons. (G: II, 363, xviii, ll. 123 f.)

317 Je suis . . .
. . . faict comme ung esmerillon. (F: II, 41, 293)
Mon compagnon,
Qui est plus fin qu'[un] esmerillon. (F: II, 27, 76)
Et l'œil gay en esmerillon. (E: II, 11, 10)

318 Flagrant trop plus que espice aromaticque. (C: I, lxviii)

319 Fais tes ministres armer
Contre les bons et les poingz comme espine!
(B: p. 368, ll. 28088 f.)

320 Et lair des nues attourner
Pleines dhumeurs comme vng esponge. (C: I, cxvi[v])

321 Alaigre? Comme ung esprevier. (A: IV, 232, xxxv, l. 32344)

322 Corps glorieux plus clair que vne estincelle. (C: II, l[v], li)
Mon pere qui faictes florir
Les iustes comme vne estincelle. (C: II, xxxiiii)

323 Et comme estoilles sont au ciel . . .
Sans nombrer. (A: II, 72, xvii, ll. [F 1553–1555])

324 Sil ne brusle comme vne estoupe. (C: II, cxii[v])

325 Agrippart est plus marmiteux
Que vng estront. (C: II, clxxxii[v])

326 Je le vous monstreray plus noir
Que nest vng Ethiopien. (C: I, cxxxvi)

327 Il est bien voir conme evangille.
(D: VI, 234, xxxvi, l. 113, VII, 93, xxxvii, l. 2589)
Tenez pour vray comme evangille.
(D: V, 329, xxxii, l. 2120; C: I, xxiii; F: II, 25, 37, 31, 120)

328 Ie suys ainsy qu'vn poure exain
Qu'on chasse volant d'arbre en arbre. (E: II, 1, 5)

329 Il est fasonné comme ung fais
De fagotz. (F: II, 36, 197 f.)

330 Quand j'en viens
Tout aussi droit qu'une faucille. (F: II, 24, 26)

331 Vng iambon . . .
Ne monteroit dedans ma panse
Non plus que vne febue en vng puys. (C: I, xxxii[v])
Ne vous chaille cest bien vescu
Ayons entre nous amoureux
Grans ongles & le cul rongneux
La barbe grasse & la maschoire

Car tout cela nempesche a boire
Non plus que vng febue a vng puys.
Si tost que les pastez sont cuys,
Frappez dedans en destrauee
Chascun en prenne sa hauee
Tant quil se brusle le palays.
Songemal
Ces prouerbes ne sont pas laidz
Ilz vallent bien auctoritez. (C: I, clxix[v])

332 Estourdis et opiniatres,
Comme femme qui vent harens. (G: III, 67, xxi, ll. 268 f.)

333 Sy tu ches au las de fortune,
Estat et toy, dame simplesse,
Iamais fer batu sur l'enclume
Ne fut tenu en tel detresse. (E: I, 10, 14)
Si iestois aussi dur que fer. (C: I, xxxvii[v])
S'il estoit plus dur que nul fer. (D: I, 140, iii, l. 1027)
Plus durs a ployer que le fer. (C: II, xlvi[v])
Ilz sont aussi fermes que fer. (A: IV, 203, xxxiv, l. 31699)
Vostre vin est fort comme fer. (C: II, cvii[v])
Vrayement voicy plus fort que fer. (C: I, clx[v])
Lucifer,
Qui est assez plus noir que fer. (F: III, 60, 292)
D'un baston rouge comme vn fer chault. (E: III, 13, 6)

334 Ardant
Comme feu. (A: III, 68, xxv, ll. 18767 f.)
Nous sommes bruyans comme feu. (B: p. 378, l. 28863)
Ilz sont aussi rouges que feus.
(B: p. 429, l. 32706)
Salomon. Et brouit plus tost que en feu l'herbe.
Bananyas. Vella ung notable proverbe.
(A: IV, 401, xxxviii, ll. 36335 f.)
Dictes, ie ne tiens non plus
Que feu feroyt de paille d'orge. (E: IV, 13, 17)
Ma vielle capeline
Plus rouge que le feu d'enffer. (B: p. 230, ll. 17757 f.)
Ung baing
De beau plonc et de beau metal,
Bruyant comme feu infernal. (B: p. 438, ll. 33476 ff.)
Forte fievre quarte
Chaulde comme feu infernal. (B: p. 380, ll. 28982 f.)
Ardant comme feu de fournaise. (B: p. 51, l. 3978)
Vostre museau
Plus ardant que feu de fournaise. (C: I, x[v])

Voicy ung heaulme en bourgeois,
Plus rouge que n'est feu gregeois. (B: p. 225, ll. 17392 f.)
Feu d'enffer
Plus ardant que feu de tempeste. (B: p. 95, ll. 7385 f.)
Gros barreaux,
Ardans comme feu de tonnoirre. (B: p. 14, ll. 936 f.)
Fer
Plus rouge que feu de tonnerre. (C: I, lii[v])
335 Je brusle comme feurre en four. (A: III, 52, xxv, l. 18607)
336 Or ça, si la femme mauldict
Comme une malle fiebvre aygre.
(G: III, 129 f., xxiv, ll. 72 f.)
337 Mais plus amer est que fiel. (A: IV, 402, xxxviii, l. 36368)
338 Qui suis puante comme fiens.
(B: pp. 180, l. 13890, 306, l. 23393)
339 Maistre danceur? Ouy, plus seur
Ou plus hardy que Fierabras. (G: III, 139, xxiv, ll. 250 f.)
Iamais le vailant Fier-a-bras
N'eust tant de charge que tu as. (E: II, 5, 14)
Sy tu estoys un fier a bras. (E: III, 16, 19)
340 S'il ne tient plus que fil d'archault,
J'espère qu'il m'accu[ei]llira. (F: I, 14, 236)
341 Et plus menu la devisa
Que flaméches vollant au vent. (A: V, 146, xli, ll. 40087 f.)
342 Je luy voy une espee avoir
Moult grande et rouge comme flamme. (B: p. 22, ll. 1576 f.)
343 D'un beau filz, gent comme une flour. (B: p. 75, l. 5873)
Qui ne durent terme n'espace
Ne que la fleur du champ qui passe.
(D: IV, 140, xxv, ll. 475 f.)
Tuit sont plus blanc que fleur de lis. (D: II, 195, xiii, l. 619)
Ne fleur de lyz [*mieulx composé*]
Que estoit Joseph. (A: III, 48, xxv, ll. [G 3225 f.])
Ses vestemens . . .
Sont odorans comme la fleur nouuelle. (C: II, li)
344 Simple comme vng fondeur de cyre. (C: II, cv)
345 Piteulx comme un fondeur de cloches. (E: III, 18, 10)
346 J'en suys plus bas qu'au fons du puys. (G: I, 26, ii, l. 150)
347 Et de ce bien cy se desriue
Comme dune fontaine vive. (C: II, xxv)
348 J'ars tout comme rouge fornaise. (B: p. 343, l. 26338)
349 Bruyans comme fouldre et tonnerre. (C: I, liii)
J'eusse destruit et mis comme fouldre
Tout ce qu'il y avoit de damoiselles. (F: II, 43, 329)

G'y veuil entrer plustost que fouldre. (E: III, 16, 17)
Ie cours, ie racours comme fouldre. (E: IV, 5, 11)
Ung jouvenceau
Ayant le vis resplendissant
Comme fouldre du ciel yssant. (B: p. 396, ll. 30183 ff.)
Ce baillif redoubt come fouldre
Qui si s'aire et si s'esfoudre
Contre moy. (D: IV, 213, xxvi, ll. 994 ff.)
Or va que de fouldre deffaict
Tu soys de gresil et tempeste. (C: I, lxxxvi[v])
Et a l'ung la face vermeille
Comme foudre venant du ciel. (B: p. 383, ll. 29253 f.)

350 Nous nauons sur luy de puissance
Non plus comme vng petit fourmy. (C: I, cxli)

351 Il vous les font blans comme fouaches. (E: II, 5, 11)

352 Plus souple que n'est ung fouet. (A: II, 344, xxiii, l. [G 936])

353 Y sentent comme la framboysse. (E: IV, 11, 12)

354 Je tremble tout comme une fueille. (B: p. 381, l. 29089; D: II, 391, xvi, ll. 1317 f.)

355 Ce ne dure ne que fumee
Saillant de la flamme allumee. (B: p. 217, ll. 16736 f.)

356 Il est plus espes que fumiere. (C: II, ccxli)

357 Tandis que la matiere est fresche
Tost tost vng gallant a cheual. (C: II, xlvii[v])

358 O craignent leur partis aduerses
Comme la galle de sainct Iob. (E: II, 5, 7)

359 Or remaint nostre assamblee
Ainsi comme la gallee
Esseullee
Sans gouvernail sur la mer. (B: p. 376, ll. 28726 ff.)

360 Elle est plus tristresse que Ganes. (F: II, 25, 44)
Helas! helas! les rains, le dos!
Au meurdre sur ce trahistre Ganes! (F: II, 25, 48)

361 Ie sens
En quelque lieu dur comme gaulles. (E: I, 5, 18)

362 Souple & droicte comme vne gaule. (E: II, 11, 10)

363 Qu'il sache gaser comme un gay. (E: IV, 3, 13)
Et vos caquettez mieulx que vng geay
En cage. (C: II, lxxi)
Ie parle myeulx qu'vn gay en cage. (E: I, 13, 11)

364 Et suis hardy comme ung gendarme. (F: I, 9, 129)

365 Qui eust pensé gens anymés
Fondre au soleil comme la glace? (G: III, 57, xxi, ll. 51 f.)

Cul de femme et museau de chien
Si sont tousjours froiz comme glace. (G: I, 108, iii, ll. 509 f.)
366 Mais tout est plus froit qu'un glasson. (F: II, 34, 158)
367 Et m'aourez comme ung gobitre. (B: p. 14, l. 915)
368 Et sont plus enfflés qu'une graigne
Qu'ilz n'ont venu a leur dessus. (B: p. 394, ll. 30001 f.)
369 Qui aura du cueur munde
Si gros que vng grain de cinapis
De foy. (C: I, lxxxix)
370 Et, comme . . .
. . . gravier au port de la mer,
Sans nombrer. (A: II, 72, xvii, ll. [F 1553–1555])
Qu'elle seroit plus forte a extimer
Et a nombrer que gravelle de mer,
Dont le nombre est infini par science.
(A: II, 255, xxi, ll. 14992 ff.)
371 O poure coeur, sy n'est plus dur que un gres. (E: III, 5, 9)
372 Toute femme fillant quenoille
Est plus sotte que n'est gribouille. (F: II, 37, 218)
373 Tu n'entens non plus qu'une grive. (B: p. 296, l. 22627)
374 Tu as le museau rechigné
Comme le groing d'un vielz lymier. (B: p. 295, ll. 22620 f.)
375 Quelque fille vilagoise
Refaicte comme vne groiselle. (E: III, 3, 20)
376 Je trouve aussi à mon propos
Une autre quantité de folz
Qui s'en vont de nuyt par les rues,
Estendant les colz comme grues. (F: II, 37, 212)
J'en ay veu tropes comme grus
Qui se faisoyent fraper et bastre
Pour suyvre un povre gentilastre
Qui n'avoit rien au pays de Bray. (G: III, 87, xxii, ll. 51 ff.)
377 Car ilz ont lestomach halle
Comme la gueulle dung four chault. (C: I, lxxix)
378 Coupper leur fault comme a ung haire
La queue près du cul. (G: II, 366, xviii, ll. 185 f.)
379 C'est ung viel pourpre tout troué,
Plus deschiré qu'ung viel haillon. (B: p. 300, ll. 22900 f.)
380 Il n'y a haquenee de barde,
Qui se marche plus proprement. (E: III, 1, 14)
381 Il y pert bien a sa chemise
Elle est plus iaulne que haran. (C: I, cxxii)
382 Il si est ainsi enfume /
Et aussi roux que vng harenc sor. (C: I, liii)

383 Ie suys fort comme un Arcules. (E: IV, 8, 14)
384 Aussi rebours que herissons. (A: III, 227, xxvii, l. 22401)
385 Je suis hardiz comme ung heron. (B: p. 367, ll. 27977, 27983)
Qui plus tost que lheronde
Mes aesles faictz voller pour estandars. (C: I, iv[v])
386 J'ay la conscience aussi large
Que les housseaux d'un Escossais. (G: I, 87, iii, ll. 257 f.)
Aussi noirs que sont mes houseaulx. (C: I, xxxviii[v])
Le vin voire / comme vng houzeau
Jay donc desieune en dormant. (C: I, xxvii)
387 Cerberus tourne cy ton groing
Plus enrouille que vng huys de fer. (C: I, x)
388 Et plus beau cent foys que Iason. (E: IV, 8, 26)
389 Ilz ne sont que douze meschans
Qui sont aussi poures que Job. (C: I, xi[v])
390 El est plus belle que le jour. (A: V, 184, xli, l. 40887)
L'autre est beau comme jour d'esté.
(A: II, 130, xix, l. 11869)
Je seray tousjours franc et quicte,
Comme le jour du mardi gras. (G: III, 63, xxi, ll. 180 f.)
391 Luysant comme en or le joyau. (A: II, 43, xvii, l. [EF 834])
392 Il a le broudier et la pance
Plus pesant que nostre jument. (F: II, 41, 293)
393 Et de mal aussi innocente
Que Judas de la mort Jesus. (F: II, 37, 210)
394 Il est ainsi mollet que laine.
(A: I, 271, xii, l. 6848, II, 151, xix, ll. 12388 f.)
Que tu seras plus mol que layne. (C: I, lii[v]; F: I, 12, 211)
395 Blanche com laict. (C: II, li)
Dens de maniére
Plus blanche que lait.
(A: III, 189, xxvi, ll. 21495 f.; F: I, 16, 288)
Et le me boy doulx comme laict. (C: I, xxv[v]; E: I, 1, 6)
396 Je suis creux com une lanterne. (F: I, 14, 243)
397 Vous seres plus bastu que lard. (E: III, 14, 20)
Car vous estes gras comme lart. (F: II, 36, 191)
Tu seras hachié comme lard
Par menus morceaux à larder. (F: III, 51, 70)
Qui veult bien rimer contre pois,
Au monde ne peult mieulx que lart. (G: I, 77, iii, ll. 153 f.)
398 Chantes vous clair.
Comme laton. (E: II, 11, 23)
399 Gens habilles comme levriers. (A: V, 243, xlii, l. 42144)
Et que je soys cordonnyer mys,
Ausy abille c'un levrier. (G: III, 183, xxvi, ll. 170 f.)

Plus tost leur verrez mettre a fin
Qu'a deux fors levriers un connin.
(D: IV, 110, xxiv, ll. 1088 f.)
Ie suys sage comme vn leurier. (E: I, 5, 18)
On en veult avoir de la race,
Ne plus ne moins que de levriers. (G: III, 66, xxi, ll. 246 f.)
400 Comme leopardz veulz que soyez ardiz. (G: II, 45, x, l. 506)
Plus aspres que liepars. (G: III, 5, xix, l. 9)
Plus enflambez ilz sont que leopardz. (C: I, iv[v])
Oncques vieulx lieppars arrabis
N'orent tel fain de devorer
Que nous avons de labourer. (B: p. 246, ll. 19026 ff.)
Plus fiére la truis que liepart. (D: IV, 265, xxvii, l. 686)
Les apostres peruers
Plus hardis que . . . lyepars. (C: I, cix[v])
Oncq . . . lieppart
Ne porta tel austerité. (B: p. 302, ll. 23050 f.)
401 Je le sçay plus courant qu'ung lievre. (B: p. 81, l. 6345)
Tu es aussi hardy que vng lyeure.
(C: I, xlix, cliii[v]; G: III, 190, xxvi, l. 291)
Mais elle senfuyoit plus viste
Que lieures quant ils sont chasses. (E: II, 11, 15)
402 D'un voyre droict comme vne ligney. (E: III, 14, 12)
403 Il vous mettra bas comme lin
Versé. (A: II, 350, xxiii, ll. [G 1098 f.])
Vos tetins ausy blancs que lin. (E: II, 4, 37)
404 Tetins poinctifz comme linotz. (F: I, 18, 318)
405 Et moy qui suis, beaux doulx amis,
Plus que n'est point un loup famis. (F: II, 27, 76)
Affamez sommes comme loups. (A: III, 226, xxvii, l. 22389)
Il brait comme ung lou forcené. (B: p. 436, l. 33335)
Et chassez sommes comme loups. (A: V, 82, xl, l. 38545)
Ainsi que ung loup a la huee
En m'a chassé et tot et tart. (G: I, 211, vii, ll. 164 f.)
Luy qui auoit de cruaulte . . .
Plus quonques neut loup rauissant. (C: I, xciiii[v])
Il est plus dangereulx c'vn leu. (E: II, 5, 13)
Les apostres peruers
Plus hardis que loups. (C: I, cix[v])
Qui me hayent comme loups les chiens.
(A: IV, 12, xxxi, l. 27374)
Vous hurlez comme ung lou famis. (B: p. 47, l. 3724)
Hurlant comme ung loup forcené. (B: p. 94, l. 7352)
Hurler et braire
Comme ung lou de rage affamé. (B: p. 378, ll. 28882 f.)

Lautre [urle] en loup. (C: II, cxvi)
Monstrez les dentz comme vne looue
Qui veult deffendre ses petitz. (C: II, xlvii[v], ccli)
Mordantz comme loups. (G: III, 132, xxiv, l. 128)
Les Caldiens, pires que loups. (A: V, 34, xxxix, l. 37373)
Tu as de pitie comme vng loup. (C: I, clxxiiii)
C'est pire que chasser aux loups. (E: IV, 1, 24, 25)
Regardez plus suis dessire
Que vng loup. (C: II, cxxvii[v])
Vous venez ainsi comme loups
Qui ravissent les brebiettes. (A: IV, 309, xxxvi, ll. 34151 f.)
On tient
Qu'i sont apres comme vieulx loups.
(G: III, 198, xxvi, ll. 436 f.)
Et hurlez a grande goullee
Comme vielz loups tous affamés. (B: p. 288, l. 22068 f.)

406 Que lyonnesse ne . . .
. . . loupcerue . . .
Neurent rigeur si tresamere. (C: I, lxxiii)

407 Ausy vray qu'i n'est c'vne loy. (E: II, 8, 13)

408 La rend plus que la lune belle. (E: III, 5, 23)
Belle et plaisant comme la pleine lune. (C: II, li)

409 Plus espois que n'est lye de biere. (E: I, 3, 7)

410 Il crye & bruyt comme vng lyon. (C: I, clxxi[v])
Plus cruelle
Que nul leon rauissant. (E: I, 10, 5)
Et sera requis qu'il se dresse
Comme ung lion. (A: III, 421, xxx, ll. 26987 f.)
Car il est fier comme ung lyon. (F: II, 47, 389)
Les Cessars & Sipions
Se monstrant plus fiers que Lions. (E: I, 16, 16)
Il forcene, ce vous puis dire,
Conme un lion bien attené. (D: VII, 217, xxxix, ll. 662 f.)
Chacun de vous estoit . . .
. . . comme lyons fors. (A: IV, 165, xxxiv, ll. 30823 f.)
Mais suis hardy comme ung lyon.
(A: IV, 98, xxxiii, l. 29345, V, 243, xlii, l. 42145)
Fureur humble comme ung lion. (G: II, 83, x, l. 1161)
Propres, promptz, prestz, preulx,
Comme sont lyons. (A: II, 32, xvii, l. [EF 560 f.])
Comme ung lyon tres fort,
De mort vendra casser l'effort. (B: p. 26, ll. 1875 f.)
Et puis comme vng lyon tres fort
Suscita. (C: II, xxvi[v])

411 Oncq leonesse . . .
Ne porta tel austerité. (B: p. 302, ll. 23050 f.)
Le peuple Israel se eslevera
Aussi hault que une lionnesse. (A: III, 421, xxx, ll. 26985 f.)
Dequoy voz cueurs sont plus esprins
Que lyonnesse. (C: I, xxxiiii)
Mort l'est venue soudain querre,
Ainsi que fiére lyonnesse. (A: IV, 274, xxxvi, ll. 33338 f.)
Que lyonnesse ne panthere . . .
Neurent rigueur si tresamere. (C: I, lxxiii)
412 Voire encore qu'il a la pate
Dure comme ung maillet de fer. (B: p. 274, ll. 20920 f.)
413 Cela est vray comme la maisse. (G: III, 38, xx, ll. 184, 190)
414 Comme ces mallardz font ces boures,
Ensemble lavasmes nos foures. (G: II, 195, xii, ll. 212 f.)
415 Et feussent eulx plus durs que marbre. (B: p. 133, l. 10185)
O cueur plus dur que le noir marbre. (B: p. 405, l. 30897)
Me rendant plus froid que marbre. (E: II, 1, 5)
416 Pendu soyt-il comme Margny,
En vn gibet de grand haultesse. (E: II, 8, 5)
417 Je congnoy des menestrieux
Qui sont plus paillars que marmos.
(G: III, 165, xxv, ll. 213 f.)
Et barbetez comme marmotes. (B: p. 49, l. 3846)
Tu barbottes plus que vng marmot. (C: II, cxxii)
Mais vous
Estes plus fort à chastier
Qu'un marmot. (F: I, 16, 280)
418 Les dentz cliquetans à la gorge
Aussi dru que marteau de forge. (F: II, 37, 212)
419 Yl est fleury comme vne mate. (E: I, 12, 8)
420 Ce semble ung vieulx matin famis
Hullant huit jours en ung tenant. (B: p. 225, ll. 17411 f.)
Nient plus qu'un viel matin
N'y congnois rien. (D: V, 12, xxix, ll. 272 f.)
421 Et ceste ci redevient seiche
Aussi conme une vielle mèche. (D: I, 214 f., v, ll. 198 f.)
422 Il sera plus de mengeriez
De povretez et diableriez
Que en Sayne il n'y a de menuise. (G: I, 229, vii, ll. 535 ff.)
423 Et beau sire ne boy pas tout
Cecy est salle comme mer. (C: I, clviii[v])
424 Tu parle ausy droyt c'vn mesle
Qui est en la cage. (E: II, 6, 18)

425 Vng pain aussi gros que vne meulle. (C: I, xxxii[v])
Tournant vite comme vne meulle. (E: III, 14, 17)
426 Il sera plus doux que miel. (F: I, 8, 125; D: II, 339, xv, l. 1697; E: I, 18, 21, IV, 11, 8)
427 Il y en a de toutes pieces
Plus haut que les mons d'Armenie. (B: p. 290, ll. 22156 f.)
Pluye / neige / gresle aussi grosse
Comme la grant montaigne Drosse /
De Pelion ou Caucasus. (C: I, liii)
428 Car c'est pis que des mors. (F: I, 10, 146)
Je ne doubte plus que la mort
Sans cause et sans ocasion. (F: I, 8, 118)
429 Glassons gelez depuis cent ans
Jecterez sur luy tous entiers
Gros et espes comme mortiers. (C: I, liii)
Ou mol ou dur comme un mortier,
C'est le dict de chascun quartier. (F: I, 14, 248)
C'est une vieille besague
Qui poise comme ung vieulx mortier.
(B: p. 378, ll. 28860 f.; C: I, lxxix)
430 Mais tu ressembles le mosnier
Qui se maschure en sa farine. (G: II, 95, x, ll. 1380 f.)
431 Et de cracher gloses et loix
Ausi dru que mouches de boys. (G: III, 72, xxi, ll. 359 f.)
Et ny eust entour
Pour toy faire aucune escarmouche
Que . . . vne mousche. (C: II, cxv[v])
432 Plus royde que volle ung mousquet. (F: III, 61, 301)
433 Je seray plus fin que moustarde. (G: III, 22, xix, l. 271)
434 On ma dict qu'elle est amyable
Comme vn mouton. (E: II, 11, 11 f.)
Ce samble ung mouton qu'on escorche:
La peau s'en vient avec l'abit. (B: p. 313, ll. 23894 f.)
435 Et si courray parmy la plaine
Plus viste qung moyne house. (C: I, cxiii[v])
436 Maiz tu es toy aussi craché
Comme qui t'avroit arraché
D'ung mur. (G: I, 167, v, ll. 456 ff.)
Il fault avoir le cueur plus dur,
Plus ferme et asseuré qu'un mur.
(G: III, 265, xxviii, ll. 612 f.)
437 Entrer la science en ma teste
Grosse comme un museau de veau.
(G: III, 138, xxvi, ll. 174 f.)

438 Faictes moy mon cheual grison
Bondir comme vne grant mytaine. (C: I, xxvii[v])
Plus mol que ne sont mes mytaines. (C: I, xxxi)
439 J'é le cueur aussi froid que nef. (A: III, 68, xxv, l. 18766)
Ses vestements furent tous blancs
Qua neige. (C: I, l[v], II, ccxl[v])
Ses habis ont changé couleur:
Maintenant sont de tel samblance
Qu'oncques nege ne fut plus blanche. (B: p. 172, ll. 13217 ff.)
440 Ie l'ay tenu ainsy que Octouyen. (E: IV, 2, 9)
441 Et m'avoir aussi cher que l'œil. (F: III, 51, 28)
Aussi tost conme oeil euvre et clot. (D: III, 297, xxi, l. 1630)
442 Et sy est blanc comme oeuf. (E: I, 12, 8)
J'en suis net comme ung œuf de poulle. (F: I, 22, 392)
443 Je m'y porte aussi vaillant
Que fist Olivier. (F: II, 23, 15)
444 Alons comme une onde. (G: II, 309, xvi, l. 33)
445 Elle pleure comme vn ongnon. (E: II, 11, 21)
446 De te la garder est descent,
Comme un onguement precieulx. (E: III, 11, 22)
447 O sentence haulte & pesee
Plus claire que fin or de touche. (C: I, clxx)
Auquel raison bien esprouvée,
Mieulx que n'est pas l'or au fourneau.
(A: II, 42, xvii, ll. [EF 832 f.])
Tant qu'estez reclamée
Plus luisante que n'est fin or massis.
(A: IV, 384, xxxviii, ll. 35943 f.)
Ou il resplendy comme l'or. (B: p. 262, l. 20041)
A Saül sont presens honnestes
Qui vallent mieulx que or. (A: IV, 140, xxxiii, ll. 30265 f.)
448 Le faict gras comme vn oueson. (E: II, 6, 25)
Le Monde est plus sot c'un oueson,
Est il privé ou estranger? (G: III, 43, xx, ll. 280 f.)
449 Il dit ainsi: Comme l'oueille
Est mené a l'occision. (B: p. 215, ll. 16557 f.)
A dit de moy: *Sicut ovis*
ad occidendum ducitur. (B: p. 215, ll. 16553 f.)
450 Je danse en ours, et vois en nage
Comme une congnye desmanchee. (G: I, 70, iii, ll. 63 f.)
Dessirez sont plus que vieulx ours. (C: II, lxxi)
Tu nous rens plus vilz que vielz ours
Pour nous et nostre folle vie. (G: I, 266, ix, ll. 463 f.)
Tu n'est qu'ung droit ours de Savoie. (B: p. 324, l. 24732)

Berith / Galath truculent comme lours. (C: I, iii[v])

451 Foulz de Forestz et de Savoye
Sont aussi couars comme une oye. (F: II, 37, 216)
Gras comme vne oyee. (E: II, 8, 9)
Je yray plus doulcement que vne oye
Ne faict quant elle est defferree. (C: I, xxxvii[v])

452 Ay je vollé comme ung oyseau.
(A: III, 208, xxvii, l. 21950; C: II, xvii, cxv[v]; E: II, 15, 20 f.)
Mais que a gripper ma rapine ie voye
Plus leger suis que nest oyseau de proye
Pour trauerser les regions marines. (C: I, iv[v])
Le deduit deust chier avoir,
Et il est conme oisel en mue
Celi qui de cy ne se mue,
Ce m'est advis. (D: V, 98, xxx, ll. 135 ff.)
Et ny eust entour
Pour toy faire aucune escarmouche
Que vng oysillon. (C: II, cxv[v])
Il me tura comme ung oyson. (F: I, 13, 218)
Ils ont moins de sens c'un oyson. (G: III, 66, xxi, l. 234)
Il n'a sens non plus que ung oyson. (F: I, 19, 328)

453 Je assemble tousjours et amasse
De l'argent autant com(me) de paille. (F: III, 63, 388)
Je les tue plus dru que paille.
(B: p. 101, l. 7796; E: III, 9, 13)
De sancté, j'en ay a revendre
Largement, trop plus que de paille. (G: I, 16, ii, ll. 9 f.)
Il est fasonné comme ung fais
De . . . paille d'orge. (F: II, 36, 197 f.)

454 Voz cueurs sont plus esprins
Que . . . panthere. (C: I, xxiiii)
Que lyonnesse ne panthere . . .
Qui sont sans ame raisonnable
Neurent rigueur si tresamere. (C: I, lxxiii)

455 I'ey plus de volunte de bruyre
Qu'un paon qui fait sa queue reluyre. (E: III, 1, 13)

456 Aussy gent comme ung papegay. (F: II, 41, 292)

457 Il est aussi mollet que paste. (A: IV, 326, xxxvii, l. 34561)
Son corps seroit tout depesy,
Comme pastez seroit haché. (A: III, 55, xxv, ll. [G 3366 f.])

458 Tu es subget de la garder
Ainsi comme ung pasteur son ouaille.
(A: IV, 181, xxxiv, ll. 31197 f.)

459 Vous dites voir com patenostre.
(D: I, 84, ii, l. 763, II, 236, xiv, l. 114)
Ausy vray que la patenostre. (E: I, 20, 7; F: I, 5, 53; G: III, 30, xx, l. 3, 162, xxv, l. 169)
460 Je te batray comme peaultre. (F: II, 33, 155)
461 Qui sent souef conme permanche. (D: IV, 53, xxiii, l. 1510)
462 Abismes les ont couvers
En leur fons comme une pieere.
(A: III, 307 f., xxviii, ll. 24342 f.)
Et puys chascune mauldira,
Tout ainsy que pierres ameres. (E: IV, 11, 20)
Faictes moy souffler Boreas
Qui vault autant que vent de Bize
Lequel ainsi que pierre bize. (C: I, liii)
Mais noz cueurs trop plus durs que pierre.
(C: II, iiii, cxxiiii[v], cxxv, ccxxxiiii[v], ccxlvii; G: II, 193, xii, l. 166)
Sainct Pierre,
Qui fut ferme com une pierre. (F: III, 51, 74)
Te remainent a sauvegarde
Plus tost que pierre de bombarde. (B: p. 138, ll. 10562 f.)
Faveur est la en my les sandres
Que adviendroit mieulx que pierre en l'or.
(G: II, 76, x, ll. 1030 f.)
463 Je n'en ay pitié ne pitace
Ne que de la peau d'une vache. (B: p. 256, ll. 19759 f.)
464 El est ferme comme ung pillier. (A: IV, 2, xxxi, l. 27143)
Comme ung pillier qui tremble fermes.
(A: III, 227, xxvii, l. 22400)
Ton ventre . . .
Se me semble ung pillier qui tremble. (F: II, 31, 117)
465 Je truynte
Comment un pinçon ardenoys. (F: II, 44, 356)
Il na pas par dieu de ceruelle
Aussi gros quing petit pinsson. (C: II, xli[v])
466 Et seriez sain comme un piot. (G: I, 32, ii, l. 233)
Dea, je suis plus gay qu'un pyot. (F: I, 5, 52)
467 Et qui vous batist comme plastre. (F: III, 63, 353)
T'ont-ilz batu?
Comme beau plastre. (F: III, 57, 221)
Je vous battray plus que plastre. (F: I, 4, 39)
Se briser devoys comme plastre. (F: I, 14, 237)
Frappez dessus cest estourdy;
Ne l'espergnez non plus que plastre. (F: I, 17, 303)

468 Ie distille
Et fons comme plomb en fournaise. (C: I, lii)
Ilz poisent
Comme plomb. (C: II, xcii)
469 Je suis leger comme vne plume. (C: I, cxxii; A: II, 344, xxiii, l. [G 929]; F: II, 41, 293)
Dont il rendit cinq cens enclumes
Aussi pesantes comme plumes. (C: I, lxxxiiii)
Tremblans comme plume en balance. (F: III, 56, 203)
Ie suys variable & muable
Comme une plume auant le vent. (E: IV, 13, 11)
Qui est plus volage que plume? (B: p. 251, l. 19415)
470 Tousjours troussée comme une poche. (F: II, 43, 331)
471 Lard
Qui soyt gros, gras comme le poing. (E: III, 10, 10)
472 Car par dieu iay vng appetit
Aussi agu comme vng poinsson. (C: I, cxiiii)
473 Aussi drus comme pois en cosse? (A: IV, 349, xxxvii, l. 35119)
Deschargez sur ce pelerin
Torchons plus drus que pois en pot. (B: p. 94, ll. 7311 f.)
Getter dune pierre de poix
Aussi legierement que vng pois. (C: I, lxvi[v])
Sentent plus fort que poix refine. (E: I, 2, 20)
474 Que l'on nous hayt plus que poison. (C: I, clxxiiii[v], cl)
Il meuvent aussi et debatent
Com poisson vif hors de riviére. (D: IV, 259, xxvii, ll. 520 f.)
475 Qui n'ont pas la teste plus grosse
C'une pome de capendu. (G: III, 65, xxi, ll. 228 f.)
Dedens ce beau chapeau de paille
Murir comme . . . pommes. (E: I, 5, 12)
Sain conme une pomme.
(D: III, 326, xxii, l. 485, IV, 145, xxv, ll. 654 f.)
476 El est par le corps bien plus dure
Que n'est le pommeau d'une dague. (E: II, 11, 12)
477 Tu es grant comme vng pommier. (C: I, cxxii[v])
478 J'estoye ainsi comme les porcs,
Qui guettent quant le glan cherra. (F: III, 63, 404)
Mais vous tous ressemblez aux porcs
Du glan viuent & ne lair tient
De regarder dont le fruict vient. (C: I, xcviii[v])
Et tu vivras comme les porcs. (F: III, 63, 392)
Se je ne le vois pasturant
Aussi conme . . . pors,
N'enterra viande en mon corps. (D: V, 117, xxx, ll. 711 ff.)

479 Aussi tost qu'ung poste qui court. (G: II, 360, xviii, l. 49)
480 Il est ausy neuf qu'un viel pot. (G: III, 175, xxvi, l. 11)
481 Tu soyes aussi bien venu
Que vng poul deuant vne marmote. (C: I, lxxi)
482 Vous puissez estre par fouldre
Boutez aussi menu que pouldre. (C: I, xi[v])
Ta semence . . .
Sera comme pouldre estandue.
(A: II, 182, xx, ll. 13211–13213)
483 Rouges comme poules a fleurs. (E: II, 5, 23)
484 Ilz sont roides comme poullains. (A: III, 259, xxviii, l. 23129)
485 Les fesotes de ces filletes
Qui sont ioinctes comme poulletes
Qui n'urent iamais de poucins. (E: II, 15, 9 f.)
486 Et assommer comme pourceaulx.
(A: III, 328, xxix, l. 24844, IV, 72, xxxii, l. 28718)
Tu couches comme les pourceaux. (A: V, 29, xxxix, l. 37253)
Gros et gras et plus detravez
Que sont pourceaulx en la mengeoire.
(G: II, 366, xviii, l. 183 f.)
Ilz dormiront comme pourceaulx.
(A: II, 282, xxii, l. 16616; F: I, 6, 74)
Car ilz sont couchés endormis
Comme pourceaulx a la renverse.
(B: p. 383, ll. 29221 f.; F: II, 41, 294)
Et sont yvres comme pourceaux.
(A: I, 326, xv, l. 8101, III, 364, xxix, l. 25704)
487 Vella la Lune, sans doubtance,
Qui est variable en substance
Comme le pourpoint Jehan Gippon. (G: II, 162, xi, ll. 486 ff.)
488 Dedens ce beau chapeau de paille
Murir comme poyres. (E: I, 5, 12)
489 Qu'il est ausy sot c'vn prunyer
D'aler tant de filles tromper. (E: II, 8, 12)
490 Ilz sont simples comme pucelles. (B: p. 180, l. 13863)
Je suis aussi simple, aussi quoy
Comme une pucelle. (F: II, 43, 335)
491 Je suis plus plat qu'une pugnaise.
(A: VI, 71, xliii, l. 45966; C: I, cxxii[v])
Plus platz que vne vieille punaise. (C: I, cxxiii[v])
492 Jay lestomach creux comme vng puys. (C: I, cii)
493 Tu es si beste
De cerueau ny a en ta teste
Ne quen la queue dung merlus. (C: II, clxxxii[v])

494 La femme folle de costume
A la langue plus fort tranchent
Q'un fin rasouer de Guigant. (A: IV, 403, xxxviii, ll. 36372 ff.)
Jamais les rasseurs de Gingans
N'alist a la sorte qu'i vont.
(G: III, 160, xxv, ll. 132 f., cf. note)
495 Mére, je suis appareillé
Comme ung petit rat esveillé. (A: IV, 50 f., xxxii, ll. 28209 f.)
Tu es aussi enfle
Que vng rat noye dedans vng puys.
(C: I, lxxi; F: II, 36, 198)
N'a celluy qui ne soit plus rogue
Et plus enfflé qu'ung rat pellé. (B: p. 394, ll. 29991 f.)
Et sont plus enflez que vieulx ratz
Qui sont noyez dedans vng puys. (C: I, clviii)
Fust il plus vilain c'un rat mort. (G: III, 36, xx, l. 128)
Il y en a plus que de ratz. (G: III, 9, xix, l. 50)
496 Renome plus fort que Raulet. (E: III, 15, 9)
497 Et toy soys aussi bien venu
Que vng regnard a lhuys dung mastin. (C: I, clviii)
Fouyra comme ung regnard. (G: II, 33, x, [l. 245])
Mordantz comme . . . regnardz. (G: III, 132, xxiv, l. 128)
Iamais vn regnard prins au ny
Ne fust si peneulx qu'i seront. (E: II, 4, 9)
Vous estes mieulx pris a la trappe
Qu'un viel regnard, ort pautonnier. (B: p. 371, ll. 28318 f.)
Vous puisse otroyer telle grace,
Comme . . . fist . . .
. . . le regnard a une oye grace. (E: I, 3, 15)
498 Et plus durs que vne roche bise. (C: II, xlvi[v])
499 Je m'y porte aussi vaillant
Que fist . . . Rollant. (F: II, 23, 15; G: III, 284, xxix, l. 134)
500 Dame plus belle que la rose. (A: IV, 22, xxxi, l. 27606)
Et les tetins plus blancs que roze. (E: IV, 1, 6)
Elle est doulce comme la rose. (A: VI, 18, xliii, l. 44731)
El est plus doulce que une rose. (F: III, 63, 365)
Car oncques roze
Ne fut si vermeil . . .
Que estoit Joseph. (A: III, 48, xxv, ll. [G 3223–3226])
Onc rose vermeille
N'eut la couleur que vous avez.
(A: IV, 175, xxxiv, ll. 31057 f.)
Il a couleur aussi vermeille
Conme belle rose en esté. (D: II, 337, xv, ll. 1621 f.)

Comme la rose porte odeur
Entre les espines pongnantes,
Le filz de la Vierge en honneur
Monstrera ses vertus puissantes.
(A: VI, 219, xlv, ll. 49217 ff.)

Oncques en may de fleur de rose
Ne fut telle senteur yssant. (C: II, xxxvii[v])

501 Plutost elle tourne que ung rouet.
(A: II, 344, xxiii, l. [G 935])

502 Ployant et vacillant souvent
Comme fait le roseau soubz vent.
(A: II, 40, xvii, ll. [EF 743 f.])

503 Ausy riche comme le roy. (E: III, 18, 7)
Mais aussy vray qui n'est q'vn Roy. (E: I, 1, 14)

504 Elle est clere comme un ruby. (F: I, 8, 123)

505 Le sang en court comme ung ruseau
Vermeil. (A: II, 381, xxiii, ll. [G 1941 f.])
Le sang de toutes pars courir
Comme ruisseaux d'une fontaine. (B: p. 405, ll. 30911 f.)
Mais yeulx courent comme ruisseaux.
(A: V, 39, xxxix, l. 37514)

506 Lye comme ung sac de farine. (A: III, 91, xxv, l. 19308)

507 Il est arme comme sainct Gorge. (E: IV, 13, 17)
Ilz sont vaillans comme sainct George. (F: II, 37, 214)

508 Tu seras homme plus martyr
Que sainct Laurens qu'on fit rostir. (F: I, 1,10)

509 D'estat jamais ne se contente,
Et s'estime autant que sainct Pol. (G: III, 43, xx, ll. 289 f.)

510 Tu as les ioues et les lippes
Aussi iaulnes que vne sallade. (C: I, xlix[v])

511 Et fust aussi fort que Sanson. (C: I, lxiiii[v])
Et fust il plus que Sanxon fort. (A: V, 180, xli, l. 40826)

512 Ie seray plus gay que satin. (E: III, 14, 19)

513 Vous le voueres par Dieu! troter
Comme vn sauatier portant cuir. (E: II, 4, 17)

514 Ton ventre est comme une sebille. (F: II, 31, 117)

515 Et la couleur
En est rouge comme sendal. (F: I, 10, 171 f.)

516 Deux clerjons que j'ay manderay
Qui ont doulce voiz con seraine. (D: V, 146, xxx, ll. 1577 f.)

517 Nous en aurons plus de cinquante [*pieces of money*]
Ausy rouges que seraphins. (E: II, 4, 8)

518 Ses langues a demi cliquet
Plus afiles que serpentes. (E: IV, 1, 39)

Je voy enfle plus que vng serpent
Nostre tribun. (C: II, cxxxvi[v])
Et conme un serpent vous fuiray. (D: III, 277, xxi, l. 1025)
Tu mors & pinces . . .
Plus c'vn serpent. (E: I, 10, 6)
De tes dentz pires que serpens. (C: I, clxxxi)
Soiez donc sages et prudens
A la maniere des serpens. (B: p. 155, ll. 11848 f.)

519 Vestus dessus de robes linges
Et emmantelés comme singes. (B: p. 61, ll. 4798 f.)
Ou chascun deulx scait de cautelle
Plus que vng synge de soixante ans. (C: II, lxx[v])
Plus malicieux
Que nest vng cinge de trente ans. (C: I, clxxxvi[v])
Tu es pelu comme ung cinge. (F: III, 63, 384)
Et sy tourneroyent comme un singe.
(G: III, 340, xxxi, l. 270)

520 C'est un vent chault, en verite,
Plus que le soleil en este. (E: I, 2, 14 f.)
Ausi clair est que le soleil
A peu le puis ie regarder. (C: II, ccxxxvii)
Joinct a lesprit plus clair que le soleil. (C: II, li[v])
Que circuyt lestoille scintillant
Plus que soleil clairement rutillant. (C: II, xlix[v])
Mais reluyt ta mundicite
Comme vng soleil qui estincelle. (C: II, xxxv[v] f.)
Plus que soleil lumineuse. (C: I, xlii)
Sa doulce face humaine
Passant le soleil en lueur. (B: p. 172, ll. 13215 f.)
Le visage de sainct Estienne reluisant comme le soleil.
(C: I, lxii)
Car tous resplendissans estoient
Comme ung soleil de grant lueur. (B: p. 438, ll. 33456 f.)
Mes freres, regardez la face
De nostre maistre clarissant:
Onques soleil resplendissant
Plus clerement ne resplendy. (B: p. 172, ll. 13209 ff.)
Sa face . . .
Resplendit comme le soleil. (C: I, l[v])
Resplendissant comme vng soleil rose. (C: II, li)
Comme rose soleil vermeille. (A: VI, 43, xliii, l. 45352)
Mon dire
Ausy vray comme le soleil. (E: II, 8, 10)

521 Vrayment que mon cueur en bavolle
Comment en la mer faict la solle!
(A: III, 160, xxvi, ll. [G 5971 f.])
522 Ie seroys lourd comme une souche. (E: II, 9, 10)
Suys ie poinct plus lourd c'une souche. (E: III, 10, 25)
523 Il est yvre comme une souppe. (F: I, 10, 161, II, 23, 15)
524 Vn instrument naturel
Plus doulx que sucre. (E: I, 18, 20 f.)
Comme sucre fault avaller
Ta poison. (A: VI, 149, xliv, ll. 47614 f.)
525 Je suis plus hardy qu'un suisse. (F: I, 16, 281)
526 Cent foys plus amére que suye. (A: III, 310, xxviii, l. 24413)
Reagal est doulx comme suye. (G: I, 87, iii, l. 249)
527 Je luy ay faict lame sonner
Dedans le corps comme vng tabour. (C: I, lxvii[v])
Quil en a le ventre plus rond
Que vng tabourin. (C: I, cxxii[v])
528 Dragons plus ardans que tempeste. (B: p. 47, l. 3715)
Ma voix
Bruyant, tonnant comme tempeste.
(B: p. 11, ll. 657 f.; C: II, xlvii)
Ilz courent fort comme tempeste. (F: II, 37, 215)
529 Si hault, si doulx, si net que terre. (F: II, 43, 329)
Cecy est ja vielz comme terre. (B: p. 419, l. 31943)
Il est plus vieulx que la Terre. (G: II, 37, x, l. 337)
530 Il est estourdy
Comme la teste dung belier. (C: II, xliii[v])
531 Il a moins d'esp(e)rit qu'ung thoreau. (F: I, 11, 190)
Car Leuyathan quant si mect
Chante plus gros que deux thoreaulx. (C: I, xxvi)
532 Aussi enfle ie suis
Que vng tonneau. (C: II, cxli[v])
533 Nous avons vent de si bonne erre
Que plus tost qu'ung cop de tonnere
Nous serons en Tharse singlés. (B: p. 88, ll. 6833 ff.)
534 Criant plus que sept torterelles. (G: III, 135, xxiv, l. 172)
535 Fondée est ferme conme tour
Ici endroit ceste chappelle. (D: II, 400, xvi, ll. 1581 f.)
536 Y le fault batre comme toylle. (E: II, 6, 11)
537 Ferme de rains, dure comme vne traiste. (E: III, 3, 28)
538 Ma langue va comme ung traquet.
(A: II, 344, xxiii, l. [G 933])
539 Il est aussi dur comme ung tref. (A: II, 374, xxiii, l. [G 1746])

540 Fuyez comme triacle venin. (F: III, 51, 37)
541 Et sy ont l'oreille ausy flache
Et ausy mole c'une trippe. (E: I, 8, 14)
542 Il nous songe icy le moron,
Nos fais ne luy samblent que truffes. (B: p. 274, ll. 20982 f.)
543 Desordre les tient cy en renne
Comme un trupelu. (G: II, 310, xvi, ll. 52 f.)
544 Quant je te regarde au visaige
Se me semble la truye que fille. (F: II, 31, 117)
Je suis, par Dieu, aussi honteux
D'un 'Den bon jour' comme une truye. (G: I, 86, iii, ll. 247 f.)
Il humeroit trop plus d'honneur
Que une truye ne feroit de laict. (A: V, 245, xlii, ll. 42174 f.)
Je suis pied a pied les Apostres
A celle fin que ne les perde
Comme vng truye faict la merde. (C: II, cvi[v])
545 Que je vous jur je seray celle
Qui seray com la turterelle
Qui, quant a perdu son mari,
Elle en a le cuer si marri
Que depuis ne va ne ne ganche
Ne ne s'assiet sur verte branche. (D: VII, 315, xl, ll. 1019 ff.)
546 Que lyonnesse ne
Tygre . . .
Neurent rigueur si tresamere. (C: I, lxxiii)
547 Il a l'entendement ouvert
Comme une belle uistre en l'escaille.
(G: III, 141, xxiv, ll. 300 f.)
548 Et le liez a celle estache
De cordes aussi c'une vache. (D: III, 350, xxii, ll. 1159 f.)
Elle est panchue comme vne vache. (E: II, 15, 15)
Vous parles trop mieulx c'vne vache. (E: I, 5, 13)
Puis vous vous en irez a couple,
Ainsi que une vache et ung beuf.
(G: III, 145, xxiv, ll. 382 f.)
Y n'a que des chiens a bergers
Tous ausy velus c'une vache. (E: I, 8, 14)
549 Noz enfans sont nulz comme veaulx.
(G: III, 133, xxiv, l. 146)
Estre attaché comme un gris veau.
(G: III, 254, xxviii, l. 307)
En te chaboulant comme vn veau. (E: II, 15, 16)
Et moy, un povre maquereau,
Feray la grue ainsi c'vn veau. (E: III, 13, 13)

Mais je fus frappé par le front
Mieulx qu'ung veau n'est d'une massue.
(B: p. 437, ll. 33367 f.)
Et ne suis-je mie aussi gras,
Qu'un veel? doy-je dire un veau? (F: I, 5, 52 f.)
Car il na non plus de memoire
Par mon ame que vng veau de laict. (C: I, clviii[v])
Vous estes plus pesant que vng veau. (C: I, clii[v])
Et on faict des facteurs nouueaulx
Qui ne sauent nom plus que veaulx. (E: II, 17, 8)
Je saulte et trepoye
Comme ung jeune veau. (A: II, p. 33, xvii, ll. [EF 592 f.])
Gens estourdis, qui sont plus sotz que veaulx.
(A: V, 228, xli, l. 41835; G: I, 91, iii, l. 303)
Et les tuerons comme veaulx. (A: II, p. 282, xxii, l. 16617)
Qui ont la teste aussi subtille
Que ung veau natif au mardy gras. (G: III, 9, xix, ll. 51 f.)
550 Je la hayoye comme venin. (F: III, 63, 411)
551 Tantost accourront comme vent. (C: I, x[v])
Aussi chaulde que vent de bise. (G: II, 144, xi, l. 178)
Je cours aussi tost comme vent. (G: III, 227, xxvii, l. 295)
Sy fault il plus tost que le vent
Que ie treuue fason d'aler. (E: II, 4, 15)
Ausy souvent que le vent vente
Du Monde le cerveau s'esvente. (G: III, 44, xx, ll. 308 f.)
Mieulx que le vent vulterne scay voller. (C: I, iv[v])
552 Mon ventre est plus cler que veriere. (E: IV, 10, 7)
On te monstrera sa puissance
Aussi clérement comme verre.
(A: III, 283, xxviii, ll. 23755 f.)
Ton urine,
Qui est clère comme verrine. (F: I, 20, 367)
Il est passé
Autant que d'un voirre cassé. (A: III, 208, xxvii, ll. 21943 f.)
Son ange devers moy se transporte
Devant mes ieulx, aussi cler comme voirre
(A: II, 229, xxi, ll. 14346 f.)
Les vecy cliquans comme ung voirre. (B: p. 14, l. 938)
553 Et fault brancher droict comme vigne. (F: I, 22, 393)
554 Les yeulx plus clers aura
Que vin. (A: III, 189, xxvi, ll. 21494 f.)
555 Que lyonnesse ne . . .
. . . vipere . . .
Neurent rigueur si tresamere. (C: I, lxxiii)

556 Pendent deux lampes vers conme yerre.
(D: I, 357, viii, l. 61)
557 Elle (re)luyroit comme une ymage. (F: I, 8, 123)
558 Et dens de maniére
Plus blanche que . . . yviére. (A: III, 189, xxvi, ll. 21495 f.)

Other Proverbial Phrases

559 Touz jours nous jeue Dieu soubz chappe,
Qui nous fait si d'un *a* un *b*
Que touz jours nous sommes gabé
Et perdons tout. (D: VI, 249, xxxvi, ll. 578 ff.)
560 Sy me croys, tu iouras du croc
Partout ou tu pouras estendre,
Tu prendras d'abac & d'aboc
Partout ou tu les pouras prendre. (E: III, 11, 14 f.)
561 N'a tel, je croy, de cy en Acre. (D: III, 193, xx, l. 116)
562 Je n'y acompte pas ung ail. (B: p. 212, l. 16320)
Nostre vie ne monte vng ail. (C: II, clxxxviii)
Sire, tout ce ne prise un ail. (D: V, 233, xxxi, l. 2339)
Ne retenray qui vaille un ail
De ma terre. (D: IV, 342, xxviii, ll. 694 f.)
Sa sainté ne vaulra un ail.
Je n'y compteroie une alie. (D: III, 5, xvii, l. 76)
Ton faict ne vault pas ung aillot. (B: p. 61, l. 4788)
563 Et qu' alouettes sont grenoulles. (F: II, 25, 37)
564 Voir, s'il aloit de ce en Arle
A coudes nuz. (D: VI, 29, xxxiii, ll. 816 f.)
565 Il n'y a d'icy en Arragon
Ung plus fort yvroigne qu'il est. (F: II, 23, 12)
566 Eusse voulu estre a Arras. (G: II, 196, xii, l. 243)
567 Le plus fort yvroigne parfaict
Qui soit d'icy en Avignon. (F: II, 23, 10)
568 Vrayement, il la baille bien verte. (F: II, 45, 368)
569 Entrez ens, seigneurs:
Le baing est chault, on le vous mande.
(B: p. 394, ll. 30039 f.)
570 (Je) te vouldroye avoir baisé morte. (F: I, 4, 45)
571 Gorier, ie faictz la barbe a tous.
(E: III, 9, 22; F: I, 9, 132; G: I, 203, vii, ll. 33 f.)
572 Maulgre sa barbe. (C: II, cci[v])
573 Le bon vieil asgne craint les bas,
Tout ainsi que fait nostre femme. (F: II, 25, 46)

574 Je cuide que le bas vous blesse
Où vostre dos est eschauffé. (F: I, 9, 143)
575 Il n'y a bon temps qui rien vaille
Ne de quoy donnasse ung baston. (F: I, 6, 70 f.)
576 Les Batards de Caulx. (E: Title of III, 7)
577 Et que je bate(s) et que je vanes. (F: II, 25, 43)
578 Il n'est pas donc si mal aysé
A passer. Quant il pleut en Beausse,
Qui se course si se deschausse. (G: III, 140, xxiv, ll. 294 ff.)
579 Vecy la relique
De l'un des os de sainct Belin.
(A: VI, 138 f., xliv, ll. 47415 f.)
580 On faict bien sa confession
Desoublz le *benedicite*. (E: IV, 1, 35)
581 Je vueil comme euesque des champs
Faire la beneysson du pie. (C: I, li[v])
582 Vous faictes la beste à deulx doulx.
(F: I, 11, 188, 15, 259; G: III, 298, xxix, l. 454)
Se vous aviés une mechine,
Vous sariez vous bien entremettre
De deux ventres sur un dos mettre?
(D: VII, 347, xl, ll. 2002 ff.)
583 Du meilleur endroit de la beste,
Qui s'enfle au pot. (F: II, 50, 446)
584 Il sera jour quand je verray
De beurre frez faire chivieres. (G: I, 65, iii, ll. 5 f.)
585 Il estoit assez bon folastre,
Et se marchoit de bon biès. (F: II, 24, 22)
586 Je n'aconte a li une bille.
(D: IV, 334, xxviii, l. 429, V, 16, xxix, l. 414)
Ne le feri pas d'une bille
Ce jour en l'ueil. (D: IV, 54, xxiii, ll. 1522 f.)
Quanque j'ay perdu ne pris bille. (D: IV, 385, xxviii, l. 1967)
587 Puisqu'elle n'a plus ne pain, ne paste,
Elle n'enrage que de bluster. (F: II, 50, 443)
588 Je suis mis jus de ceste lutte.
Allez luy dire que je blutte
La farine pour ung grant pain. (F: I, 14, 226)
589 Et puis il n'y fault que ung bon coup,
Ainsi qu'on dit communément. (F: I, 5, 55)
590 Si dires vous bon grc mal grey.
(E: II, 4, 44; G: I, 38, ii, l. 325)
Bon gré mau gré. (A: VI, 152, xliv, l. 47689)
Bon gré maulgré. (A: II, 370, xxiii, l. [G 1662])

Bon gré bieu et maulgré ma vie.
(A: III, 65, xxv, l. [G 3689])

591 Bon jour vous doint nostre Seigneur
Et vous met en bonne sepmaine. (F: III, 51, 7)

592 Taisez vous, j'auray bonne bouche.
(A: II, 107, xviii, l. 11291, 171, xx, l. 12889, 386 f., xxiii, ll. [G 2104, 2107, 2112])

593 Je vous requier bouche cousue. (F: II, 25, 44)

594 C'est mal encontre d'un boueteux,
Le grand deable emporte le borgne. (E: III, 12, 16)

595 Par Mahoummet si Godeffroy
Venoit / et Rolland de billon /
Et Oliuier / vng papillon
Nen donneray / bouf / baf / bif / bou.
Qui vive la / ou sont ilz ou. (C: II, clx [misnumbered clf])

596 Maintenant nous sommes au boult. (E: II, 6, 29)

597 Or est-il le plus franc pyon
Qui soit point d'icy en Bourguoigne. (F: II, 23, 6)

598 Ca la bourse ou sont les escus. (C: II, ccxxxiii[v])

599 Paulus vous ne dubuez donner
Vng bouton de tout ce quil chante. (C: I, clxxxiii)
Je ne donne un bouton de haye. (D: III, 235, xx, l. 1428)
Ilz n'y comptent pas deux boutons.
(A: IV, 79, xxxiii, l. 28885)
Nous ne vaurrons pas deux boutons.
(D: IV, 78, xxiv, l. 112)

600 C'est ce faulx prophete Jhesus
Qui nous a brassé ce brassin. (B: pp. 196, ll. 15122 f., 222, ll. 17227 f., 372, l. 28377, 419, ll. 31933 f.)
Que j'ay ce brouet cy brassé
Qui nous tournera a tel perte! (B: p. 327, ll. 25046 f.)
Qu'oncques si tres mauvais brassage
Ne brassates en vostre vie. (B: p. 370, ll. 28260 f.)
Car quelqu'un faulx bruvaige brasse. (G: II, 132, xi, l. 11)

601 Vn poure gentilastre,
Qui n'auoyt rien au pays de Bray. (E: II, 13, 8)

602 Tous ensemble ne valent pas
Les vieilles brayes dung pendu. (C: I, xxxii)

603 Cheminez tant que Brie est belle.
(A: III, 18, xxiv, l. 17934; cf. VI, p. 337, *s. v.* Brie)

604 Il fault mettre au tonneau broche. (F: I, 12, 210)

605 Les brodequins sont de saison
Quant femmes chevauchent les hommes. (F: I, 1, 9)

606 J'ay pris belle caille de puis:
A peu se relever me puis. (B: p. 247, ll. 19140 f.)
607 Ie me souhaicte en Calabre,
Car parler contre toi ie n'ose. (E: II, 1, 6)
608 Adviengne qu'advenir pourra,
Jamais l'homme à Cambray n'ira. (F: III, 61, 319)
609 Messieurs, vous notterez ces mots
Qu'a l'appetit d'un tas de sots,
Comme l'on void bien sans chandelle.
(G: II, 346, xvii, ll. 307 ff.)
610 Nous chantons bien autre leçon. (F: I, 10, 158)
611 La sera ta chançon: helaz! (D: VII, 190, xxxviii, l. 2060)
612 Chanter te fault la chantepleure.
(A: II, 373, xxiii, l. [G 1730])
Pour tous dancer la chantepleure. (G: I, 268, ix, l. 512)
613 Se vous me chantiez la preface
Du grand sanctus ou le credo. (F: I, 14, 242)
614 De ceulx qui, pour avoir cas netz,
Ont esté faictz chardonneretz. (G: III, 243, xxviii, ll. 93 f.)
615 Et faire chasteaux en Espaigne. (E: I, 2, 17)
616 J'entens chat, sans dire minon. (F: I, 12, 204)
Il semble que renouveller
Vueillez la noise et le decort
Pour esveillier le chat que dort. (D: III, 12, xvii, ll. 312 ff.)
Les chatz feront les canars pondre. (F: I, 19, 330)
Sy quelque homme me vient a courage
Que ie ne prenne bien en grey
Laiser aler le chat en fourmage. (E: III, 3, 32)
On n'a point tel chat sans mitaines
D'une fois, de deux ne de quatre. (F: I, 14, 237)
Et souvent, pour femme incogneue,
Prennent bien un chat par la queue.
(G: III, 319, xxx, ll. 319 f.)
Il a bele queue, le chat;
Il ne pourra mais de lait boire. (D: II, 110, xi, ll. 505 f.)
617 Cela n'est pas peller chataignes;
Tu songnes du bec, Narinart.
(B: pp. 97, ll. 7524 f., 347, l. 26595)
618 Attendez moy la
Et chauffez vng petit la cire. (C: I, xxxviii)
Nous luy ferons chauffer la cire. (F: I, 12, 208)
Et son mary chauffe la cire! (F: I, 12, 211)
619 Je croy, par ma foy, qu'on y entre
Assez souvent sans chaussepied. (F: II, 50, 436)

620 Quant un homme est prins aulx cheveulx,
Comme esse qu'il en chevira? (G: III, 76, xxi, l. 453)
621 Tu semble aux sainctz de la paroisse,
Tousjours as la cheville au trou. (F: II, 50, 439)
622 Or, venes ca, se ie vous hare
Ung chien, lequel soyt noir ou blanc,
Me voules vous premier pourtant
Qui soyt vert, ie le vous nye.
A! dea, s'il auyent qu'on fournye,
Et qui se touille a la farine,
N'est il pas tout blanc? or, deuigne:
Y n'est ne iaune, ne bigare,
Et sy n'est ne vert, ne bare,
Comme l'on voit en un prouerbe. (E: I, 3, 14)
623 Les Picquars ilz sont trop eureux;
Et que sont-ilz! foulx amoureux:
Si une chièvre portoit coiffète,
Ilz en feroient leur amyète. (F: II, 37, 215)
Vostre mary est(-il) mort?
Tout mort au paradis des chièvres. (F: II, 36, 204)
624 Au clin de loeil ie passe tout le monde. (C: I, iv[v])
625 Malgre . . . vostre coeur. (E: II, 8, 18)
Il a le cueur à la cuysine. (F: II, 44, 350)
J'en sçay plus par cueur que par lettre. (F: I, 1, 10)
626 Il fault tout faire par compas. (C: I, clxxiiii[v])
Plus ne parle que par compas. (E: II, 2, 4)
627 Il fault qua nostre hoste comptons
Hoste combien vous debuons nous. (C: I, cix)
628 Y fault bien qu'i vienne a Iube
D'estre party sans conge prendre
Du conuent. (E: II, 10, 7)
629 Que mieulx valoit, tant estoit noble
Que tout l'or de Contentinoble.
(D: III, 122, xviii, ll. 1500 f.)
630 J'ay cy encore un grand tas
De coque-grues d'oultre mer. (F: II, 26, 59)
631 Pleust a Dieu qui fust a Coquengne,
En Lombardye ou en Espaigne. (E: IV, 1, 12 f.)
632 Ce n'est pas ceans qu'est la vente
Ou debues vendre vos coquilles. (E: IV, 8, 23; F: I, 19, 350)
Car trestous tes biens je ne prise
Pas la value d'une coquille. (F: III, 63, 410)
633 Il faisoit tant du loricquart,

Du temps qu'il estoit fiancé.
De la corne il avoit assez. (F: I, 2, 19)
634 Vous me la chantes bien cornue. (E: III, 14, 19)
Jalouzie est comme la lune
Qu'en son crescent se faict cornue. (G: II, 95, x, ll. 1390 f.)
635 Mais coupons la broche à ceste heure. (F: I, 5, 60)
636 Quel appetit.
Fringant / fringant
Pour coupper vng clou de charrette. (C: I, cxxi[v])
637 Tu es de finese la crayme. (E: II, 4, 15)
638 Et croix ne pille ne me baille.
(C: II, cxxvii[v]; D: IV, 185, xxvi, l. 155)
639 L'honneur des femmes est mys au croq. (E: II, 7, 4)
640 Si irons croquer ceste pie. (A: VI, 169, xliv, l. 48017; C: I, ci;
F: II, 23, 20, 30, 114, 31, 119, 41,
292, 297)
641 Sy fault il que chascun labeure
Du meileur cuir de son panier. (G: I, 17, ii, ll. 29 f.)
642 C'est trop tiré le cul arriére. (A: III, 417, xxx, l. 26886;
E: IV, 1, 10 f., 25; G: II,
358, xviii, ll. 25 f.)
Je n'y voys plus du cul frotter. (F: II, 25, 40)
C'est mal chante son contrepoinct,
L'honneur sy pres du cul ne pent. (E: II, 14, 7)
Se vous couchez tousjours à dens,
Jamais n'aurez les culz meurtris. (F: I, 18, 306)
Par dieu ie te donne conge
De faire de mon cul mittaines. (C: I, cxxii[v])
Non pas ainsi comme volle oye
Vous auez le cul trop pesant. (C: I, xxi[v])
Je n'auray plus au cul que plume. (F: I, 18, 315)
On m'a faict entendre,
Puis ung peu qu'elle a le cul tendre. (F: I, 10, 150)
Y l'est, il a le cul au vent;
Mais quel vent? au vent de bise,
Il a tant honny sa chemisse,
Qu'il n'a morcel du cul entier. (E: I, 3, 11)
643 Ne la fait-il point dancer
Aulcunes fois la basse note? (F: II, 50, 439)
644 On ne getteroit pas vng de
Que sur testes tant sont espes. (C: I, cxcvi[v])
S'ilz dechéent
Par moy la value d'un dé. (D: I, 390 f., viii, ll. 1081 f.)

645 Que j'en suis clerc jusques aux dens. (G: II, 283, xv, l. 85)
En despit de vos dens. (F: II, 47, 397)
Que nous travaillons roidement
Ou nous avrons bien froid aux dents.
(G: II, 333, xvii, ll. 91 f.)
Il rit!
Voire, du bout du dent:
C'est risee d'ung antenois. (B: p. 264, ll. 20232 f.)
Maulgré nos dens. (B: p. 393, l. 29934; C: I, xxviii [v]; E: II, 8, 18; F: I, 6, 81, II, 43, 326; G: II, 364, xviii, l. 139)
Vous auez menty par les dentz.
(C: I, clxi, II, xliii, xliiii; F: I, 3, 24)
Nous mentirons par my nos dens.
(B: p. 400, l. 30479; E: IV, 11, 12)
646 Ie desiunes souuent de vent. (E: IV, 10, 7; F: I, 10, 162)
647 Quel double mors, quel trenchefille;
El desvide plus qu'el ne fille
De babil sans comparaison. (F: II, 25, 41)
648 Le diable m'a bien chanté messe;
Je n'ay besoing de Dieu prier. (F: I, 5, 55)
Le dyable emporte le dernier! (G: III, 221, xxvii, l. 186)
649 Haro! et plus dit et pis dit. (B: p. 371, l. 28312)
650 Tu ne scez ou en est le duc. (A: II, 213, xx, l. 13950)
651 Entre deux oy. (A: III, 7, xxiv, l. 17694)
652 Plus tenir ne puis
Mon eaue. (C: II, cxli[v])
653 Je vouldroys qu'el fust a l'empire. (G: III, 91, xxii, l. 154)
654 Mais viellesse me tient dessoubz son esle.
(A: I, 338, xvi, l. 8383)
655 Chascun n'entend pas bien latin,
Car il fut faict d'estain trop fin. (F: II, 23, 16)
656 Qui n'a vaillant une estamyne
Quant ses debtes seront payes. (E: IV, 5, 32)
657 Prise suis d'estoc et de taille.
(F: I, 14, 241, II, 41, 294; E: I, 16, 17; G: III, 19, xix, l. 202)
658 Je ne les crains pas d'ung estront. (F: III, 63, 387)
Car il ne donneroit en toy
Ung estronc, se tu estois mort. (F: III, 63, 389)
Je feray ung estront de chien. (A: I, 119, v, l. 3128)
Autant que d'un estront de chien
Je fais compte de ton language. (A: I, 250, xi, ll. 6430 f.)
Autant que d'un estronc de chien! (A: V, 30, xxxix, l. 37282)

Tu ne me peulx ayder ne nuire,
Pas d'un senglant estronc de chien. (F: II, 49, 419)
Mais, ung sanglant estront de chien,
Il resgnera. (A: II, 336, xxiii, ll. 16920 f.)
Table n'avons ne banc tournis,
Qui vaille ung estront de chien chié. (F: I, 14, 228)

659 Grant chose a en 'faire l'esteut.' (D: I, 161, iv, l. 273, 332, vii, l. 548, II, 139, xii, l. 476)

660 Il n'y eust en haye ne buisson
Ou je n'eusse faict la fanfa. (G: II, 188, xii, ll. 73 f.)

661 D'entrer *per fas* ou *nefas*. (E: III, 16, 19)
Que tost vendrons a nostre compte
Soit par *phas* ou soit par *nephas*. (B: p. 401, ll. 30577 f.)

662 Il luy semble que l'en lui tire
Faucille du cul tous les coups. (F: I, 8, 114)

663 Il n'est ne de fer ne d'acier
Ne q'un autre. (D: IV, 329, xxviii, ll. 314 f.)
Les fers au feu vous convient mettre.
(A: IV, 290, xxxvi, l. 33717)

664 Sur ma conscience, je cuide
Qu'il conviendra les oues ferrer. (G: I, 92, iii, ll. 317 f.)

665 Je ne donrray point
Un festu en vostre creance. (D: VI, 213, xxxv, ll. 1291 f.)
Quant a nous,
Et puis? Autant que d'un festu. (A: V, 244, xlii, ll. 42160 f.)
Certes, je ne prise un festu,
Empereur, toutes tes meances.
(D: IV, 108 f., xxiv, ll. 1033 f., VII, 181, xxxviii, l. 1789; E: II, 7, 7; G: I, 249, ix, ll. 163 f.)
Parquoy leurs dictz ne vallet vng festu.
(C: II, xxiii; D: I, 135, iii, l. 887; E: III, 15, 23; F: I, 8, 126, II, 31, 126, 33, 146, 49, 430, III, 61, 318)
Pour moingtz que le tour d'un festu,
Il semble qu'ilz me doyuent menger. (E: III, 1, 21)
Je n'y donne pas deux festus
S'on les chastie. (F: III, 51, 11)
Ne les prisa pas deux festuz. (D: II, 206, xiii, l. 977)

666 Que puis le temps de Fierabras
Homme ne fut mieulx estendu. (C: II, cxlviii)

667 On ne gaigne plus ung figue. (G: III, 160, xxv, l. 112)

668 Bailleray-je du foing à l'oyson,
Que de la fourche sur la teste? (F: I, 11, 182)

669 Ie t'estime moins c'un formy. (E: III, 16, 19)
670 Vous m'aues mys la paste au four. (E: II, 7, 20)
671 Ung moyen suffisant
Pour avoir fourree la pate. (B: p. 402, ll. 30621 f.)
672 El a trouue franc du collier. (E: III, 14, 12)
673 Ales impetier benefices
Soublz l'abaye de Frevaulx. (G: I, 42, ii, ll. 396 f.)
674 Il n'y a plus que frire. (G: I, 261, ix, l. 366)
675 Une femme fait l'empechee
Bien trois jours pour une fusee. (G: I, 70, iii, ll. 71 f.)
676 A! y gaigne le gal qui peult. (G: I, 41, ii, l. 378)
677 Myeulx te vauldroict garder un singe
Sans horeilles, sans nes sans coue,
Que cela de quoy tu te loue. (E: II, 5, 10)
678 Tout m'est ung: Gaultier et Robin.
(A: II, 350, xxiii, l. [G 1095])
Gresse, ce sont les mos Gualtier. (E: IV, 13, 4)
A Gaultier et à Massé. (F: II, 36, 191)
679 Et de Genays jusques a Mante. (D: VI, 15, xxxiii, l. 375)
680 Jaffubleray ceste coeffette
Qui est du bon temps Godeffroy. (C: I, clxv[v])
681 Je ne vous cherche pas un grain. (G: I, 26, ii, l. 152)
Il n'ose grain
Sa gorge du vin arrouser. (G: I, 248, ix, ll. 143 f.)
Il ne se remuoit point un grain. (F: II, 30, 112, III, 63, 412)
682 Faictez vous icy le grosbis? (B: p. 369, l. 28127)
683 Ouy, ouy, c'est a Guillaume;
Vous en irez regner aillieurs. (B: p. 310, ll. 23684 f.)
684 C'est mal entendu sa Guybray,
C'est mal exersé son vacat. (G: III, 87, xxii, ll. 55 f.)
685 Jusques au fleuue de Gyon
Na point de plus faulx ypochrite. (C: I, clx)
686 Trouveron par *hac* ou par *hec*. (A: II, 106, xviii, l. 11257)
687 La harpe sonnera bien bas,
Par le sang bieu, se je ne dance. (G: I, 257, ix, ll. 307 f.)
688 Hazart a tout: argent ou gaige. (A: III, 16, xxiv, l. 17884)
689 Gare le heurt pour les portoires. (F: I, 12, 201)
690 Il ne m'y fault hoe ne besche. (D: II, 322, xv, l. 1170)
691 Je veulx qu'on m'appelle Huet.
(F: II, 31, 126; G: III, 225, xxvii, l. 264)
692 Vous en estes ung fin ouvrier
Pour enchasser huille de mur. (A: VI, 190, xlv, ll. 48519 f.)
693 Non, ce n'est qu'vn Ieanin. (E: II, 7, 19)
Pourroit-il estre vray ou fainte
Que ma femme m'ayt faict Jenin? (F: I, 9, 132)

694 Voyla un bon Iehan de Lagny. (E: III, 13, 37)
695 Touchant de ses sots Angevins,
Ilz ne sont foulx que de bons vins:
Car Jehan des vignes, qui est tant beau,
Incontinant leur gaste le cerveau. (F: II, 37, 215)
696 S'on joue de la sacqueboute. (F: I, 14, 243)
697 La langue tirons par derriére,
Et vella tout ce qu'il en ont. (A: IV, 280, xxxvi, ll. 33459 f.)
La miex tranchant
Qui fust de cy jusqu'a Larchant.
(D: III, 367, xxii, ll. 1649 f.)
699 Ung tel vieillard,
Qui ne vault nom plus que vieil lart. (F: I, 6, 64)
700 Elle entend bien son latin. (E: IV, 1, 18, 19)
Vous perdries vostre latin. (E: IV, 8, 26)
Des hommes qui vont au matin
Aulx tavernes parler latin. (G: III, 296, xxix, ll. 402 f.)
701 Nous disions que plus tost le liege
Sans floter fut fondu dans l'eau
Et que de plomb vng grand fardeau
Plus tost floter on eut peu voyr
Que d'asault ceste vile auoir. (E: I, 6, 6 f.)
702 Quant d'un lion fier et estoux
A fait un aignelet si doux
Et si humble. (D: VI, 34, xxxiii, ll. 951 ff.)
703 Entre vous, qui estes logez
Au Plat d'argent, faictes hommage
A vostre hoste. (G: II, 140 f., xi, ll. 124 ff.)
704 Et laissez les aller
Je les ayme mieulx loing que pres. (C: I, clxxxv[v])
705 Va du long et du le. (C: II, lxxxiiii; E: III, 12, 18)
706 Nous ne procedons que par ditz
Et menaces de longue main. (B: p. 211, ll. 16279 f.)
707 N'avoit de ci jusques Losanne
Plus vaillant dame qu'elle estoit. (D: V, 287, xxxii, ll. 861 f.)
708 Le loup est mue en aigneau. (C: I, xcvii)
Allons après; c'est le loup pris. (F: I, 8, 127)
709 Et si n'aconte je sanz faille
A toute ma perte pas maille. (D: IV, 367, xxviii, ll. 1450 f.)
Il ne m'en chault pas d'une maille. (F: II, 49, 422)
Ie n'y conquesteray pas maille. (E: III, 15, 19)
Je ne vous crains maille. (F: II, 43, 327)
Je nen donneroys vne maille.
(C: II, xcvii[v]; F: I, 19, 329, III, 53, 162)
Nous ne gaignons pas une maille. (E: III, 6, 13)

Vostre pouoir ne prise maille,
Nom pas la feuille d'une ronce. (D: IV, 322, xxviii, ll. 86 f.)
Trestout n'en vault pas une maille.
(B: pp. 378, l. 28821, 404, l. 30790; C: I, clxxviii[v], II, xliii; F: II, 33, 146; III, 51, 44; G: III, 19, xix, l. 204)

710 Belle doctrine prent en luy
Qui de son poing faict un maillet. (G: III, 146, xxiv, ll. 399 f.)

711 Dieu vous donne mal an. (C: II, lxxxviii[v])
A qui Dieu doint sanglant mal an! (B: p. 275, l. 21039)
Paix! que Dieu te mect en mal an!
(E: II, 6, 9; F: I, 5, 53, 16, 283, II, 23, 9, 17, 24, 30, 41, 298, 300, III, 53, 161)
En mal an puisses entrer! (E: I, 20, 13; B: p. 264, ll. 20226 f.; F: II, 25, 37 f., 26, 53)
Jeunesse est en malle année. (F: III, 63, 409)
Que fiche soit en grant mal an
Qui en Cesaree le mena. (C: II, clxi)

712 Dieu le mette en mal sepmaine.
(B: p. 245, l. 18942; C: I, xxvii; F: III, 51, 28)
S'entrera en male sepmaine. (B: pp. 101, l. 7804, 250, l. 19339; C: II, clvi; F: III, 51, 49)
Passez tost en malle sepmaine. (F: III, 51, 67)
S'ilz eschappent male sepmaine. (B: p. 364, l. 27730)
Allons que de malle sepmaine
Puist estre estrene le message. (C: I, xxv[v])

713 Mon cas sen va de mal en pire.
(C: I, cxxxviii; E: III, 1, 18; G: I, 134, iv, l. 317, 136, iv, l. 355, 202, vii, l. 10)

714 Point n'est maladie de prebstre. (F: I, 13, 219)

715 Je croy que je fus en Mars né,
Car j'ayme tousjours à combatre. (F: II, 29, 100)

716 Et si fault, puis qu'on se demente,
Mettre le marteau en la vente,
En despit de luy, ma commère. (F: II, 29, 93)

717 Il fault chanter d'aultre martin. (B: p. 255, l. 19683)
Mais a moy parlerez, Amille,
D'autre Martin. (D: IV, 39, xxiii, ll. 1078 f.)

718 Si elle te triche, voicy
Martin Baton qui en fera
La raison. (F: I, 16, 278)

719 Mettez le me tost math en l'angle. (D: III, 283, xxi, l. 1190)

720 Car mengerent leur blé en herbe.
Il fault croniquer ce proverbe. (G: II, 225, xiii, ll. 155 f.)
721 Voyla que c'est que d'entreprendre
Menger la lune a belles dens. (G: III, 57, xxi, ll. 57 f.)
722 Maulgre . . . son menton. (C: II, cci[v])
723 Est il homme de ça la mer
Si hardy. (B: p. 79, ll. 6152 f.)
724 Que s'il n'a vaillant que deulx miches. (E: III, 18, 6)
725 Et ne luy en chault dune mitte. (C: II, cxvii)
Qui onques vaillant d'une mitte
Ne fist pour vous. (D: I, 196, iv, ll. 1333 f.)
Je n'y aconte pas deux mittes. (D: VI, 24, xxxiii, l. 640)
726 Y se degoisent,
Moitié figues, moitié raisins. (G: I, 41, ii, ll. 366 f.)
727 De ci au Mont
Saint Michel. (D: VI, 14, xxxiii, ll. 330 f., 15, xxxiii, l. 374)
728 Par mon ame, moquin, mocart. (E: IV, 1, 6)
Di, mon pére, en moquin moquas. (D: III, 113, xviii, l. 1247)
729 Tousjours ronge son frain Moreau. (F: I, 14, 249)
730 Ouy vrayment des foys plus de dis
Voyela le mot qui clos la lestre. (E: I, 17, 14)
731 Si en ay-je de tous mestiers,
Se ne sont les loyaulx mouniers. (F: III, 63, 379)
Ses mounyers sont tant amoureulx!
Y n'est finesse qui n'en sorte. (E: II, 4, 38)
Prions pour ces loyaux muniers,
Que tous chascuns disent larons,
Qui puissent aller tous mitres
En paradis a reculons. (E: I, 3, 9)
732 Et qui n'entend ne my ne gourd. (F: II, 35, 178)
733 C'est bien dict, mymin a sonnetes. (G: I, 29, ii, l. 190)
734 As tu poinct veu mon estan?
Ouy ouy les neiges d'auten. (E: I, 8, 9)
735 Tenés, quel nés de saint Poursain,
Enluminé de vin de Beaune! (F: II, 23, 8)
736 Tenez,
Qui luy tordroit ung peu le nez
De vin rendroit une symaise. (F: II, 23, 8)
737 Mais tout ne valoit une nicque. (G: I, 249, ix, l. 176)
738 Et luy faire entendre que noir
Sera blanc. (G: I, 20, ii, ll. 76 f., cf. pp. 28 f., ll. 174 ff.)
739 Je ne te crain pas une nois. (D: VII, 76, xxxvii, l. 2086,
IV, 327 f., xxviii, ll. 257 ff.)
Je te doinray ja une noiz. (D: I, 348, vii, l. 1005)

Il ne m'en chault point d'une noix. (F: II, 32, 135)
Mes mon fait n'y vault une nois. (B: p. 137, l. 10500)
Nostre cas ne vauldra deux noix.
(G: II, 42, x, l. 443, III, 22, xix, l. 275)
Je porte sur moy la valeur
Encor de demy cent de nois. (G: I, 90, iii, ll. 293 f.)
740 De ce ne donne pas ung œuf. (F: III, 51, 53)
Ie n'en donroys pas plus d'un oeuf. (E: III, 10, 21)
Vous ne debues tous trois c'un oeuf. (E: IV, 13, 15)
Que tu naurois plume vng oeuf. (C: II, c)
Il labatra / mais quil ny touche
Six poulles tueroit pour vng oeuf. (C: II, clxxxii[v])
Pas n'y acompteray deux œufz. (F: III, 63, 412)
Ilz jureront Dieu pour deux œufz. (F: III, 63, 361)
Que vaillant deux oeufz je n'ay mye. (F: III, 63, 371)
741 Je ne te crain pas d'ung ongnon. (F: II, 49, 423)
Du chois j'en don(ne)rois un oignon.
(F: I, 15, 269, II, 36, 203)
Aussi ne fais-je pas ung oygnon. (F: II, 33, 146)
Je n'en donroye pas deux ongnons
Si n'y a autre pillerie. (A: V, 280, xlii, ll. 42903 f.)
Mais ses compaignons
On ne prison pas deulx ongnons. (E: IV, 10, 20)
742 Venez vous comparoir soubz l'orme. (F: II, 47, 403)
743 Ne lui vauldra pas une osiere. (B: p. 419, l. 31952)
744 Cela ne vault pas vne paille. (C: I, clxxii[v])
Plus que de paille ne m'en chault
D'or ne d'argent. (F: III, 51, 49)
745 Et voire, voire, i'entens bien
Qui fault faire de tel pain soupe. (E: III, 12, 13)
746 Tu me veulx, ce croy, faire paistre.
(A: VI, 80, xliii, l. 46133, 90, xliii, l. 46343)
747 Veez cy ung aussi faulx garçon
Qui soit de ci a Pampelune. (B: p. 327, ll. 25020 f.)
Le plus ort, le plus rafleux
Qui soyt d'icy a Pampelune. (E: IV, 1, 19)
748 Il a doncques quelque aultre mal.
A il point le panthagruel? (G: III, 223, xxvii, ll. 209 f.)
749 Si est-ce le plus maulvais homme
Qui soit d'icy jusque(s) à Paris. (F: I, 10, 157 f.)
I'ey faict cent mille tours
Depuys Paris iusques a Tours. (E: IV, 8, 6)
750 Dis que tu parles a cheval.
(D: VII, 166, xxxviii, l. 1318, IV, 109, xxiv, l. 1040)

751 Il parle deuant qu'on l'acuse. (E: II, 2, 7)
752 Ouy, parlez-luy d'une forge,
Il respondra une pantoufle. (F: I, 9, 332)
753 De cy jusques au Pas
En Artoys. (D: I, 78, ii, ll. 602 f.)
754 On luy a fait tous ses pastés. (B: p. 263, l. 20184)
755 Plaisir sera au vieil mastin
De trouver son pastis herchié. (F: I, 18, 310)
756 Vous n'avez vaillant ung patart.
(A: II, 388, xxiii, l. [G 2148])
757 Je ne prise point deux patardz
Mon frère Anathoille et sa vie. (F: III, 52, 99)
758 Puis qu'on m'a mys la pate entre les doys,
Je vivray sans reproche *a ceste foys*. (G: II, 261, xiv, ll. 73 f.)
759 Mais tout ne vault pas ung patin. (F: I, 19, 329)
Mais je n'en compte pas ung patain. (F: II, 33, 146)
760 Vrayement, s'il ne se faict reffondre,
Il mourra en la peau d'ung fol. (F: I, 22, 392)
761 Que tu y ferois ung beau peaultre! (A: VI, 83, xliii, l. 46182)
Il est paye au peaultre, au peaultre. (E: III, 12, 11)
Se j'en devois aller en peaultre
Et batue. (F: II, 29, 94, 35, 179)
762 Nous leur ferons tel labouraige
Que *peccavi* trop tart diront. (A: V, 234, xlii, ll. 41942 f.)
763 Je croy qu'il fait meilleur icy
Qu'il ne fait aller peller l'orme. (B: p. 147, ll. 11228 f.)
764 Le roy Pepin
Ne fut honc si subite escheue. (G: II, 45, x, ll. 489 f.)
765 Nous n'aurions pas perdu un chou. (F: I, 16, 283)
766 Et ne respond n'à Pernet n'à Colin. (F: II, 33, 141)
767 Les autres, par beauté de femme,
Souvent peschent en eau infame. (G: III, 320, xxx, ll. 339 f.)
Pescher des tanches. (G: I, 261, ix, l. 367)
768 Je n'y en compte pas un pet. (F: II, 34, 160)
Bren pour vous, vn pet ie n'y donne.
(E: II, 9, 16; F: I, 15, 269)
769 Ce ne vault pas un po de piautre. (D: II, 351, xvi, l. 54)
770 Femme qui se léve matin,
Sans avoir prins son picotin,
Le jour ne fait que rechiner. (G: III, 315, xxx, ll. 213 ff.)
771 Avant que vous eussiez dit picq,
Vous seriez gueri trestost sain. (F: II, 26, 54)
772 Tant qu'auray vaillant une picque,
Sachez, certes, je le tiendray. (F: III, 51, 46)

773 Quoy, tenez vous le pié derriére? (A: V, 241, xlii, l. 42097)
774 M'aist Dieux, quand j'estois de son aage,
Et je trouvoye mon advantage,
Incontinent sur pied sur bille
C'estoit. (F: II, 44, 350)
Je tenoye tousjours pied à boulle. (F: II, 47, 393)
Mais que fain ou soif me traueille
Je ne scay de quel pied danser. (C: I, xxii)
Je suis aussi homme de bien
Que homme qui soit dessus mes piedz. (F: I, 3, 23)
Ou il a sellé son martin,
Il en apporte ou pié ou elle. (A: VI, 77, xliii, ll. 46083 f.)
Puis que la chose m'est commise,
Vous en admenré pied ou elle. (G: III, 214, xxvii, ll. 58 f.)
Quesse que dict Sathan.
Il gronde
Et ne peult piedz en oeuure mettre. (C: II, xxxix)
775 N'a son pareil d'icy à Pise. (F: II, 41, 298)
776 Car je luy eusse faict acroire
Qu'il eust pissé contre le vent. (F: III, 63, 402)
777 Il fust bon avocat en court,
Car il scet trop bien langueter
Et moz de *placebo* jetter
Ou il lui plaist. (D: I, 63, ii, ll. 138 ff.)
778 Il me plante de beaux rosiers. (G: I, 264, ix, l. 422)
779 Vostre tasche
Estoit bien d'ung aultre plumaige. (F: II, 36, 190)
780 Cestuy ne vault mieulx d'une plume. (B: p. 327, l. 25022)
Je ne prise
Toutes les choses de ce monde
La plume d'une povre aronde. (D: II, 212, xiii, ll. 1143 ff.)
781 Je crain autant le poil d'un chien
Conme vous trois. (D: V, 182, xxxi, ll. 774 f.)
782 Elle ne vault mie une poire. (D: I, 48, i, l. 1332)
Y menge des poyres d'engoysse. (E: I, 2, 17)
783 Je ne les prise touz un poys. (D: VI, 23, xxxiii, l. 605)
En ce n'aconte un pois baien. (D: VII, 149, xxxviii, l. 834)
Les crestiens un pois baien
Ne prise. (D: VII, 155, xxxviii, ll. 995 ff.)
Ie n'y aconte pas deux poys. (E: III, 15, 15)
Luy & moy auons desconfis
Deux grans plains platz de pois au lard. (C: I, cxxii[v])
Pendu soys si ie demeure
Je voys ailleurs passer mes pois. (C: I, lxii)

784 Il ne m'en chault pas d'une pomme!
(A: IV, 355, xxxvii, l. 35237)
Je ne craing maishuit homme
Qui nous face assault une pomme.
(D: IV, 327 f., xxviii, ll. 257 f.)
Je n'en donrois pas une pome. (G: I, 8, i, l. 45)
Ne se prise pas une pomme.
(D: IV, 131, xxv, l. 204, 153, xxv, l. 884)
Qui n'avoyt vailant une pomme,
Maintenant est grand gentilhomme.
(G: III, 36, xx, ll. 120 f.)
Je n'y aconte pas deux pommes
En ce que dites. (D: VII, 232, xxxix, ll. 1114 f.)
Ie ne te crains deux pommes. (E: I, 16, 18)
Nous ne vous prisons pas deux pommes.
(D: IV, 332, xxviii, l. 372, VII, 103, xxxvii, l. 2894)
785 Vade, tenés le pont aux asgnes. (F: II, 25, 43, 44, 47)
786 Tu ne vaulx pas deux porions. (F: III, 53, 163)
787 Son caquet ne vault ung porreau. (G: III, 130, xxiv, l. 89)
788 Il fait con celui qui au vent
Porte pouldre. (D: V, 103, xxx, ll. 286 f.)
789 Il fut bien fondé a raison
Le droit de la Porte Baudaiz. (G: I, 80, iii, ll. 181 f.)
Cela est plus commun en France
Qu'a Paris la porte Baudès. (G: III, 35, xx, ll. 108 f.)
790 Bien la faict au pot et au voerre,
Par quoy, pour ceste grand prouesse,
Il se dict extraict de Noblesse. (G: III, 36, xx, ll. 131 ff.)
791 Tu ne vaulx en pot ny en rost. (C: I, xcvi[v])
792 Je luy dresseray du potage. (A: II, 314, xxiii, l. 16366)
Le diable luy forge potaige. (A: III, 65, xxv, l. [G 3681])
Et puys dire pour tout potage
Y n'y a poinct de tesmoignage. (E: I, 22, 5, II, 4, 38)
793 Je m'en vois mettre en beau pourpoint. (F: I, 15, 254)
794 Je vueil prendre le frain aus dens. (D: V, 213, xxxi, l. 1718)
795 Il ne m'en chault pas d'une prune.
(A: IV, 334, xxxvii, l. 34758)
796 Y m'ont mys la puce a l'oreille. (G: I, 188, vi, l. 109)
Mes je leur ay tel pusce mise
En l'oreille. (B: p. 419, ll. 31965 f.)
Mais j'ay tant la puce en l'oreille
De ceste femme. (A: IV, 178, xxxiv, ll. 31125 f.)
797 Et si n'y a ne qua ne si. (A: III, 299, xxviii, l. 24158)
Sans repliquer ne *si* ne *qua*. (A: II, 90, xviii, l. 10856)

798 Cella vault ung *quando celi*
A gens qui redoubtoient le hault.
(A: VI, 74, xliii, ll. 46023 f.)
799 Fust la meilleur en verité
Qui soit de cy jusques au Quaire.
(D: IV, 278, xxvii, ll. 1064 f.)
800 J'ay gouverner les quatre vens
Depuis ung an, encor n'a gueres. (G: I, 89, iii, ll. 283 f.)
801 De chascun de nous que d'ung queu
Ne tient compte. (A: III, 58, xxv, ll. [G 3442 f.])
Vostre seigneur, qui ne vous prise
Pas la queue d'une serise. (D: IV, 344, xxviii, ll. 729 f.)
Le monde, ainsi comme l'en chante,
Ne tient plus que a la queue d'un veau.
(A: II, 187, xx, ll. 13322 f.)
802 Je craing d'avoir ung *quid pro quo*. (B: p. 305, l. 23289)
803 Le mauvais ne prise une quille. (D: III, 154, xix, l. 451, VI, 66, xxxiii, l. 1945, VII, 313, xl, l. 964)
N'en sçay pas qui vaille deux quilles.
(D: V, 197, xxxi, l. 1231)
804 Nous jeues tu d'un tour de quille
Par moquerie? (D: IV, 384, xxviii, ll. 1958 f.)
805 Ne luy ne toute sa famille
N'ont pas vaillant une quoquille. (F: III, 63, 383)
806 Il me fault cy estendre en raine. (F: I, 18, 316)
807 Tendeur se prent bien a sa rais.
(A: V, 349, xlii, l. 44212; cf. VI, 376 *s.v.* tendeur)
808 Dieu ayt l'ame de Raul Flatart! (G: I, 37, ii, l. 303)
809 Renart, je croy, devient hermittes. (D: VI, 31, xxxiii, l. 853)
810 Ilz me rendront compte du lart
Que qui ait mange le iambon. (C: II, lxix[v])
811 Tu parles d'ung tas de fatras
Dont ne es requise ne priee. (G: II, 167, xi, ll. 555 f.)
812 Sans dire ryme ne raison. (A: II, 152, xix, l. 12410, I, 354, xvi, l. 8766; C: I, xxvii[v], xxxiii, clv[v]; E: II, 17, 9)
Parlant sans rithme et sans raison. (C: II, cxviii)
813 Ainsy que Robin danse en tache. (G: I, 26, ii, l. 160)
814 Et il n'y venist roc ne roy. (B: p. 114, l. 8866)
Il ne tient ny a roy, ni a roq.
S'une fois, de hanche ou de croq. (E: IV, 1, 33)
815 Le paillard est vng beau gendarme
Sil neust si roide le iarret. (C: I, clxv[v])

816 Touz li mondes de cy a Romme
Vous tenoit a si saint preudomme.
(D: II, 249, xiv, ll. 497 ff., III, 155, xix, l. 474, IV, 300, xxvii, l. 1754, VII, 82, xxxvii, l. 2260; F: II, 23, 18, 45, 361)
Qui soit dicy iusques a Romme.
(C: I, cxxxi[v]; D: III, 243, xxi, l. 14, VI, 117, xxxiv, l. 1104; F: II, 29, 103, 46, 380, III, 51, 24)
Car il estoit magacien
Le plus grant qui fust iusque a Romme.
(C: I, xvi[v], II, xliii[v])
Je le cuiday au plus preudomme
C'on sceust entre ci et Romme! (D: I, 272, vi, ll. 544 f.)
Il vouldroict bien estre a Rome
Vostre amoureulx dont n'ose dire. (E: III, 13, 24)
Je vouldroy que fussez a Rome! (G: III, 133, xxiv, l. 148)
Il a perdu le plait à Romme,
Il peult bien appeller à Rains. (F: II, 36, 200)
817 Avant! est rompu le festu? (D: III, 177, xix, l. 1113)
818 Pour rien nous rompons bien la teste.
(A: I, 19, i, l. 491, 303, xiv, l. 7595, II, 270, xxii, l. 15326, III, 81, xxv, l. 19083, IV, 40, xxxi, l. 27998, 179, xxxiv, l. 31156, V, 2, xxxix, ll. 36573 f.; F: I, 19, 329; G: I, 159, v, l. 310)
819 Trop long temps on nous fait ronger
Nostre frain. (A: V, 330, xlii, ll. 43866 f.; C: I, cxxxiii; E: III, 9, 19; F: I, 14, 249)
820 Qu'en homme roux peu de fiance,
C'est commune relacion. (A: II, 254, xxi, ll. 14952 f.)
821 En sa mort je ne donne ung sac.
(A: II, 388, xxiii, l. [G 2145])
822 Car, entre cy et Sainct Marceau,
Chascun n'a pas argent qui veult.
(G: III, 291, xxix, ll. 282 f.)
823 I'estoys plus yure que la nee
Lendermain de la sainct Martin. (E: I, 12, 7)
824 C'est ung guippelin,
Et le mal de sainct Mathelin
Le tient au sommet de la teste. (G: III, 222, xxvii, ll. 196 ff.)
825 Perdre aussi bien va son langage
Conme s'il aloit batre Saine. (D: VI, 235, xxxvi, ll. 158 f.)

826 Je luy feroys estrange saulce
Si je sçavois qu'elle eust mesprins. (F: I, 9, 132)

827 Je ne daingneroye resoldre
D'esconmenier ne d'absoldre
Que puissés faire une senelle. (D: III, 13, xvii, ll. 323 ff.)

828 Se sont les plus superlatives
Que soyent d'icy à Senlis. (F: I, 6, 82)

829 Sept ans. (A: II, 197, xx, ll. 13562, 13577, 13582, 200, xx, l. 13652, 204, xx, ll. 13740, 13742, 13745, 13748, 205, xx, l. 13776, 215, xx, l. 14000, 216, xx, ll. 14021, 14033, 14038, 218, xx, l. 14065, III, 98, xxv, ll. 19502, 19505, 99, xxv, l. 19507, 100, xxv, ll. 19547, 19551, 108, xxv, ll. 19720, 19724, 113, xxv, l. 19828, 114, xxv, l. 19867, 120, xxv, l. 19986, 172, xxvi, l. 21078, 322, xxviii, l. 24696; B: pp. 117, l. 9126, 123, l. 9529, 124, l. 9590; C: I, xxviii, cxviii[v], II, iii[v], lxxxv, ciii[v], cxci; D: I, 14, i, ll. 311, 317, 15, l. 355, 16, l. 381, 19, ll. 470, 474, 21, l. 540, 22, l. 553, 32, l. 875, II, 301, xv, l. 544, 406, xvi, l. 1776, III, 114, xviii, l. 1257, 115, l. 1281, 127, l. 1659, 313, xxii, l. 71, IV, 3, xxiii, l. 5, 7, l. 138, V, 83, xxix, l. 2378, 86, l. 2462, 87, l. 2504, 122, xxx, l. 835, 126, l. 974, 135, l. 1246, 144, l. 1535; G: I, 67, iii, l. 22, II, 66, x, l. 843)

830 Bonne estoit sans si et sans mais. (A: II, 291, xxii, l. 15842)

831 Vous estes de ses sieurs d'ais.
(G: III, 60, xxi, l. 97, 63, xxi, l. 173, 74, xxi, l. 399, 76, xxi, ll. 469, 473)

832 On l'a destrossé maintenant
En la forès de Sis et Quatre. (G: I, 9, i, ll. 57 f.)

833 Va t'en coucher, tu es soppé. (G: III, 22, xix, l. 277)

834 Mais n'est tel que souffler la plume. (B: p. 81, l. 6362)

835 J'amasse miex qu'a la Saussoie
M'envoiast ou jusqu'a Saint Brice,
Par Dieu, que faire cest office. (D: I, 93, ii, ll. 1041 ff.)

836 Ne vainqui-ge pas Talebot?
Ouy, par bieu, & son filz ausy. (E: III, 15, 6)
La journee de Tallebot:
S'en fouyrent les plus ligers. (G: II, 254, xiv, ll. 20 f.)

837 Il fauldra partir de bonne heure
Et montrer les tallons aux gens. (F: III, 53, 145)

Tu payes tousiours des tallons. (C: I, xlix)
Alez. J'ay plus chier le talon
Que les visages. (D: VII, 237, xxxix, ll. 1264 f.)

838 Miex ameroie estre en Tarse
Que ce qu'elle fust morte ainsi. (D: I, 187, iv, ll. 1061 f.)
J'ameroie miex estre en Tarse
Seule et esgarée, voire arse,
Que brisasse mon mariage. (D: IV, 263, xxvii, ll. 641 ff.)
Miex amasse en Tarse
Avoir esté prisonnier pris
Que ce qu'eust telle mort pris. (D: V, 22, xxix, ll. 584 ff.)

839 Je sçaray tout en ung tenant
Se son sens vault un porion. (B: p. 274, ll. 20978 f.)

840 Quant a moy, j'en tendray la lice. (G: II, 307, xvi, l. 9)

841 Note bien le texte et la glose.
(A: V, 115, xl, l. 39360, III, 364, xxix, l. 25685; B: p. 107, l. 8259; F: I, 14, 247)
On dit voulentiers que la glose
D'Orleans si destruit le texte. (G: I, 82, iii, ll. 201 f.)

842 Nous sommes tous deux d'ung tinel. (F: III, 63, 373)

843 S'il ne porte encor les cliquettes,
Je suis content d'estre tondu. (F: II, 23, 11)

844 Il semble que ce villain traine
Ung mortier après ses tallons. (F: I, 12, 208)

845 Les bourgoyses de Beauvoisine
Font trois mors en une cerise. (G: I, 98 f., iii, ll. 399 f.)

846 Se Margot estoit attournee,
On l'appelleroit daimoiselle,
Et, s'el mengeoit une groisselle,
Par Dieu ce seroit a trois fois. (G: I, 77, iii, ll. 149 ff.)

847 Quoy, compere, ai vng yuronge,
Regardes, qui faict bonne trongne. (E: II, 7, 8)

848 Vous en dira le *tu autem*. (A: VI, 72, xliii, l. 45974; F: I, 16, 281; G: II, 189, xii, l. 98, III, 313, xxx, ll. 168 f.)

849 Olivier, baille luy ses botes;
Y tura Karesme prenant. (G: III, 285, xxix, ll. 148 f.)

850 On ne sçauroit trouver
De plus fins d'icy (à) Vaulgirart. (F: I, 6, 80)

851 Monsieur, ie me viens prendre a vous
Que les veaux ont menge les loups. (E: II, 10, 3)
Je n'ay pas oreille de veau
Ne sourde, que bien ne l'entende. (B: p. 241, ll. 18647 f.)

852 Quel vent vous boute? (D: V, 311, xxxii, l. 1562)
Ce sont quelques gens voyagiers;
Il fault sçavoir quel vent les maine. (A: I, 296, xiv, ll. 7436 f.)
Besongne tant qu[e l']on l'empoigne,
Car tu as bien le vent a gré. (A: II, 370, xxiii, ll. [G 1659 f.])
Laisson venter le vent qui vente. (A: III, 66, xxv, l. [G 3732])
Qui me baille vent au visaige?
(A: VI, 31, xliii, l. 45038, 151 f., xliv, ll. 47670 f.)
Le tiers est du vent de chemise,
Qui vault pirs que le vent de bise. (E: I, 2, 10)
853 A vous je ne compte une vesse. (F: III, 61, 314)
854 Si n'esse pas preste viande. (A: IV, 308, xxxvi, l. 34129)
855 Diex en cest homme a fait miracle,
Car de venin a fait triacle
Et de mal bien. (D: VI, 34, xxxiii, 947 ff.)
856 Laboureux, pour moy maintenir,
Menger te fault ta vigne en vert. (G: I, 250, ix, ll. 185 f.)
857 Maugre son visage. (C: II, cx)
858 Et vogue la gallee! (G: III, 17, xix, l. 173)
859 Ilz n'auront garde de voller
Avant que de ses mains il parte. (F: III, 51, 47)
J'ay le gallant si bien plumé
Qu'il n'a plus garde de voller. (F: III, 51, 68)
Voler nous fault bas par les branches. (G: I, 261, ix, l. 365)
Voicy friandes et pongnans
Pour faire gens voller sans elles.
(C: II, cxxxv[v]; E: III, 9, 12; G: I, 121, iv, l. 41, III, 44, xx, l. 311)
On dit que nul ne peult voller sans aesles /
Mais ie scay bien quelles luy ont failly. (C: II, ccxx[v])
860 Maugré nos yeulx. (B: p. 437, l. 33376)

Sententious Remarks

861 Quant la chose en est achevée,
Il ne s'en fault plus conseiller. (A: III, 49, xxv, ll. [G 3239 f.])
862 Quant on a achevé sa tache,
Doit on pas prendre son repas? (A: VI, 139, xliv, ll. 47421 f.)
863 Aucunesfois quant on actent
On requeuvre ce qu'on desire. (A: III, 334, xxix, ll. 24991 f.)
864 Nous sommes tous d'Eve et d'Adam. (G: I, 39, ii, l. 328)
Ne desprisez nulz poures hommes
Pour les petis habitz / nous sommes
Tous dung premier pere venus
Et dune mere. (C: II, lxxii[v])

865 Il fault quil aduienne
De moy comme doit aduenir. (C: II, ciiii)
Et ce qui aduiendra aduiendra. (C: II, clxxxvii)

866 Car on ne scet des adventures.
(B: p. 358, l. 27406; C: I, xlvi)

867 Nous voyons par experiences
Cil qu'en plusieurs mestiers s'affiche
A grant peine n'est-il riche.
Qui a pluribus intentus
Major est a singula sensus.
Ce prouerbe si est commun:
Se chascun en sçavoit bien ung,
Il luy debvroit assez suffire. (F: III, 51, 13 f.)

868 On n'a plus d'amour qui ne fonce. (E: IV, 8, 24)
Amour sy est quant argent dure. (E: IV, 8, 25)
Amour rend l'homme tout gaillart
Et sy faict sage le paillart
Le sot sage & le viel honneste. (E: I, 7, 13)
Amours c'est la plus grand folye
La plus diuerse fantasye
En quoy l'homme se puisse mectre.
Amours ont faict les sages pestre
Et affoler. (E: I, 18, 24)
L'homme amoureulx faict maincte folye. (E: II, 4, 45)
Amour qui a sur toutes riens
Dominacion et haultesce.
Et qui les cuers humains aspresce
D'amer si, par son grant pouoir, *etc.* (D: I, 69, ii, ll. 324 ff.)
Iamais amoureux bien n'aura. (E: I, 7, 7)
D'amours, c'est régle de droicture:
Pour une joye cent doulours. (A: V, 350, xlii, ll. 44234 f.)
Quant on a d'amours jouissance
On pert tout son entendement. (A: V, 333, xlii, ll. 43920 f.)
Amer sanz paine riens ne vault,
Et s'aime on trop miex le chaté,
Quant il est plus chier achaté,
Et s'emploie bien cilz sa paine
Quia a perfeccion l'amaine. (D: IV, 255, xxvii, 396 ff.)
Quant si fort est amours que mort. (D: I, 70, ii, l. 356)
Car cuer loyal ne peut mentir
Ou vraie amour est et habite.
(D: VI, 113, xxxiv, ll. 998 f.,
VII, 14, xxxvii, ll. 252 f.)

869 A ses amys rien ne se celle. (E: II, 14, 6)

On doibt tout dire à ses amys
Et à ses amyes aussi. (F: I, 6, 73)
Car on voit souvent advenir
Quand on pert ung amy leal,
Et pour cause qu'il en fait mal,
On le requiert par mainte voye. (B: p. 390, ll. 29701 ff.)
On doict souffrir pour ses amys. (E: II, 2, 16)
Un bon amy pour aultruy veille. (E: IV, 13, 30)

870 S'il est annee de grosses nois,
Se Dieu plaist, nous avrons de l'uylle. (G: I, 68, iii, ll. 47 f.)

871 On ne se peult plus aquicter
Tout en un coup de grosses debtes. (G: III, 55, xxi, ll. 21 f.)

872 Se ung arc n'est bien raide bendé,
Il ne fera ja coup qui vaille. (G: I, 70, iii, ll. 67 f.)

873 Qui a argent, il a des brus. (G: III, 97, xxii, ll. 288, 294)
Par argent Justice s'esmeut. (G: II, 311, xvi, l. 78)
Qui porte argent, il porte joyee,
Autant esbarbés que barbus. (G: III, 97, xxii, ll. 291 f.)
Voulentiers: qui argent reçoit,
Il le doit une foiz compter
Pour savoir qu'ait tout sanz doubter.
(D: VI, 270 f., xxxvi, ll. 1241 ff.)

874 Quand on arrouse ung tantet l'ance,
Elle en pipe plus souplement. (B: p. 55, ll. 4349 f.)

875 Ma chiére cousine, il convient
C'on attende tout son plaisir. (D: I, 177, iv, ll. 777 f.)
Tout vient a lieu qui peult atendre. (E: IV, 5, 7)

876 Aujourd'huy vos verrez monsieur,
Et demain simple maistre Jehan. (G: II, 328, xvii, ll. 9 f.)

877 Fy d'auoir qui n'a son plaisir. (E: III, 13, 10)
Il n'est celle qu'avoir n'effame. (F: I, 14, 241)

878 Il n'ayme pas bien son enfant
Qui ne le chastie de bonne heure. (F: III, 63, 353)

879 On voit souvent homme baillant
Qui n'est pas reppeu de bailler. (G: I, 163, v, ll. 367 f.)

880 Ainsi va de plusieurs batailles [*not always well*].
(A: IV, 207, xxxiv, l. 31769)

881 Beau parler a tousiours vigueur /
Beau parler est tant gracieux
Que les courages furieux
A doulceur et pitie reduyt /
Beau parler est tousiours en bruyt /
Beau parler maint oeuure parfaict. (C: I, liiii)

882 Beaulté souvent retourne a villeté. (A: V, 2, xxxix, l. 36565)

Car biauté sanz bonté poy vault. (D: I, 268, vi, l. 409)

883 Espargner ne fault ne or ne argent:
Au besoing tout est d'avantage. (A: V, 273, xlii, ll. 42770 f.)

884 Homme qui veult fort besongner
Se treuue tout acoup mine. (C: I, xv[v])

885 Il fault dire du bien le bien. (F: II, 47, 394)
Bien dire est tousiours en saison. (C: II, clxxxvii)

886 Je feray bruyt en cest esté
De bien parler et de bien dire. (G: III, 226, xxvii, ll. 267 f.)
Cil qui bien vit a bien mourir apprent. (C: II, ccxx[v])
Le bien mondain se peult soudain lesser.
(A: V, 3, xxxix, l. 36581)
Le bien ne peult tousjours durer:
Il est transitoire et muable.
(A: V, 34, xxxix, ll. 37377 f., 138, xli, l. 39902)
Peu de chose est des bien mondains;
Corps mort ne demande que terre.
(A: IV, 297, xxxvi, ll. 33889 f.)
Ce nest mie le bien mondain
Qui la felicite procure /
Car il est muable & soubdain
Fol est qui trop y met sa cure.
Ceulx qui ont des biens de nature
Quon ne peult rompre ne briser
Sont heureux & moult a priser. (C: I, cxxvii)
Les biens mondains ne sont que vent.
(A: IV, 397, xxxviii, l. 36226)
Bien mondain comme la challeur
Se passe, que l'iver rabesse. (A: V, 24, xxxix, ll. 37108 f.)
Le bien mondain aux gens peu couste;
Il va, il vient, on le sçait bien. (A: V, 26, xxxix, ll. 37165 f.)
Des biens avez habondamment,
Mais ung jour fauldra tout lesser.
(A: V, 140, xli, ll. 39937 f.)

887 Mais, se tu as bien fait, fay miex.
(D: II, 198, xiii, l. 700, III, 63, xvii, l. 1975)

888 Car qui aultruy blasme
Sa honte a tousdis. (C: II, cxlvii)

889 On fait les bledz à l'adventure:
Les uns en ont par abundance;
Les autres perdent leur croissance,
Tant leur survient d'adversité. (F: I, 2, 17 f.)

890 Bobance mondaine perit
Richesse & tresor diminue *etc.* (C: II, ccxxii)

891 Quant bonne chose est descouverte
On y a plus tost son regard. (A: III, 6, xxiv, ll. 17687 f.)
892 De bon conseil vient bonne consequence.
(A: V, 353, xlii, l. 44306)
893 Car jamais ung bon cueur ne ment. (F: III, 52, 112)
894 Au bon esprit chose bonne est plaisante,
Et aux fascheux, rudes et lasches veaulx,
Chose joyeuse est en tout desplaisante.
(G: III, 240, xxviii, ll. 28 ff.)
895 Souvent on raconte et retrait
Qu'a bon fait bon avoir a faire,
Car qui des bons est souef flaire;
Le mauvais ne prise une quille. (D: III, 154, xix, ll. 448 ff.)
896 Pour peu de chose bon regnom on efface.
(A: V, 2, xxix, l. 36564)
897 De bon service bon merite:
Qui sert bien Dieu en a bon gaige.
(A: III, 401, xxx, ll. 26493 f.)
898 Et en disant accorderay
La bouche au cuer. (D: I, 317, vii, ll. 120 f.)
899 Mais qu'on ayt la bource garnye
On a des dames a choisir. (E: I, 7, 6)
900 Le plus brief nous est le meilleur. (B: p. 369, l. 28120)
901 Puis que le membre capital
Est blessé, veullent ou non veullent,
Tous les autres membres s'en deullent:
C'est amphorisme solennel. (A: I, 73, iii, ll. 1871 ff.)
902 Justice, vous devez sçavoir
Que la chair est fresle et debile
Et l'homme aussi de soy fragile. (A: I, 353, xvi, ll. 8757 ff.)
903 Bé! qui va aux champs et ne chie,
Il ne fait pas ung gros estront. (G: I, 79, iii, ll. 171 f.)
904 Il n'empire pas qui bien change. (A: I, 214, ix, l. 5588)
Et n'est si hault prince
Cite ne prouince
Qui ne scayt changer. (E: I, 6, 10)
Il vient des inconveniens,
En peu de temps l'homme se change.
(A: V, 7, xxxix, ll. 36685 f.)
905 Chassé est qui le mal apporte. (G: III, 261, xxviii, l. 500)
906 Ainsi que le chat fist du lard,
Quant il y fust trouvé pendu.
On luy coupa auprès du cul
La queue, vueil que le sachiez. (F: III, 51, 46 f.)

907 Chaucun doit mettre son estude
Pour soy. (A: II, 348, xxiii, ll. 17106 f.)
908 Cheval hargneux une estable par soy. (F: III, 59, 256)
909 Mais, qui n'auroit nourry que ung chien,
De sa mort il luy feroit mal.
(A: IV, 231, xxxv, ll. 32316 f., 356, xxxvii, ll. 35265 ff.)
910 Mauldict soyt le petit chien
Qui abouaye abouaye abouaye
Qui abouaye & ne voit rien.
(E: II, 17, 14, IV, 14, 9; F: II, 33, 154)
911 Tu choisiras le bon, laissant le pire. (G: III, 307, xxx, l. 12)
912 C'est bien loin d'en combattre deux
A la fois. (F: II, 47, 393)
913 Qui bien commence, doit parfaire,
Ou son ouvraige riens ne vault. (A: V, 9, xxxix, ll. 36723 f.)
Qui commence et ne veult parfaire,
C'est mal faict. (G: II, 319, xvi, ll. 215 f.)
Une chose est bien formée
Où l'on ne treuve que redire;
Chascun a très souvent ouy dire:
Commencement n'est pas fusée. (F: III, 51, 85)
914 En tout fault aller par compas /
Car qui bien les choses compasse
Selon raison / il ne trespasse
Ses metes ne son droict passage. (C: I, ciii[v])
915 Car chose a grant peine conquise
S'en veult plus cherement garder. (B: p. 80, ll. 6249 f.)
916 Conseil est vng noble tresor
Qui est aux poures proffitable. (C: I, c)
Jamais nul par conseil nempire /
Mais sans conseil tout bien deduict
Jamais nul bien ne se conduict
Quen bon conseil / cela iay sceu. (C: I, c)
Conseil nest pas chose petite
Conseil garde le corps & lame
Conseil tient en paix vng royaulme
Conseil preserue les citez
Des perilz & aduersitez. (C: I, c)
Sire, il fault bien sur mains d'affaire
Avoir conseil. (D: VI, 144, xxxiv, ll. 1929 f.)
Qui plus ne veult bon conseil croire
En la fin voit son bien finé. (G: III, 146, xxiv, ll. 415 f.)
Son conseil est impertinent,
Qui nasquit de contumelie. (A: II, 382, xxiii, ll. [G 1972 f.])

917 Car convoiteux est durement. (D: II, 188, xiii, l. 407)
Sire, c'est convoitise et yre:
Ces deux l'omme pas ne despeschent,
Mais si le troublent et empeschent
Que veoir ne peut verité. (D: III, 253, xxi, ll. 258 ff.)

918 Car aux coquars monstrer fault qu'ilz sont foulx.
(A: IV, 295, xxxvi, l. 33831)

919 Car courroux engendre tout mal. (A: I, 188, viii, l. 4905)
Pense que le courroux du prince
Courrouce ceulx de la province.
(A: IV, 231, xxxv, ll. 32323 f.)
Après courroux il vient grant joye.
(A: V, 20, xxxix, l. 37011)

920 Se l'un y [*at court*] acquiert du regnon,
Ung aultre blasme y acquerra.
(A: IV, 119, xxxiii, ll. 29822 f.)

921 On de doibt croire un estranger,
Y n'amende poinct de changer. (E: III, 19, 15)

922 On croit aulcunesfois bien fort,
Dont le contraire est tout à plain. (F: I, 9, 140)

923 Cuer courrociez
Ne scet a la foiz que doit dire. (D: I, 10, i, ll. 194 f.)
Car cueur de destresse remply
Vault mieulx de bonne compaignie. (B: p. 195, ll. 14994 f.)

924 Vn delict faict desoublz les nus
Est sceu. (E: II, 4, 4)

925 Qui desplaisir d'aultruy machyne
C'est bien de droict qu'i soyt bany. (E: II, 4, 3)

926 Ung homme qui sçait bien le jeu
Des dez ja povreté n'aira. (G: I, 85, iii, ll. 229 f.)

927 Tousiours dieu ayde a ses amys /
Tousiours conforte ses seruans. (C: II, liv[v])
C'est bien vray dict, en chascun lieu,
L'on dict qui est ayme de Dieu,
Est ayme du monde n'est mye. (E: IV, 3, 5)
En petit de temps Diex labeure. (D: I, 162, v, l. 317)
Et aussi les gens font les armes,
Mais Dieu seul la victoire donne.
(A: IV, 127, xxxiii, ll. 29995 f.)
Qui ne sert Dieu ne fera ja beau faict.
(A: V, 139, xli, ll. 39905, 39915, 39925, 39930)

928 (C'est ung dit) dont on verra l'effait. (F: I, 12, 197)
Vous le dittes,
Mes au prouver gist le soubtil. (B: p. 114, ll. 8870 f.)

Chascun dit que ne sçays respondre. (F: I, 19, 330)

929 Si en mesnaige y a discorde
On ne sçauroit fructifier. (F: I, 4, 48)

930 Ainsi, nous dormans d'aventure
Par la pesance de nature
Qui ne peust pas tousjours veillier,
Mes luy esconvient sommeillier
Aucuneffois quoy qu'on s'efforce. (B: p. 403, ll. 30746 ff.)

931 Bon fait doubter aucuneffois,
Pour avoir plus grand certitude;
Si vault mieulx bonne doubte et rude
Que savoir trop presomptueux. (B: p. 69, ll. 5386 ff.)

932 Parlez a li doulcement;
Car lait parler chace et retrait
L'enfant, mais doulx parler l'attrait.
(D: III, 279, xxi, ll. 1076 ff.)

933 Mes il n'est douleur qui ne passe. (B: p. 160, l. 12220)

934 Qui aura bon droict sy le garde. (E: II, 4, 5)

935 Ung chascun doit bien carculler
Le droit chemin ou il veult tandre. (G: I, 154, v, ll. 211 f.)

936 Tels dueilz et telz afflictions
Bien souvent, qui n'y remedie,
Sont cause de grant maladie. (B: p. 374, ll. 28492 ff.)
Je say bien qu'il fault que nature
S'aquite, mais se m'en creez,
Si grant dueil mie ne ferez
Qu'en vailliez pis. (D: II, 244, xiv, ll. 352 ff.)
Estre n'en devez si engrant,
Sire; puis qu'il ne peut autre estre,
Pensez de vous en joie mettre:
C'est vostre miex. (D: IV, 368, xxviii, ll. 1455 ff.)
Autrement faire vous esteut,
Puis que ceste chose on ne peut
Amender. C'est tout dit en somme;
Laissiez se dueil, monstrez vous homme,
Et l'oubliez. (D: V, 23, xxix, ll. 607 ff.)
Je sçay bien qu'il fault que nature
S'aquite, mais aiez cuer fort,
Car il n'est si biau reconfort
Con de son dueil laissier aler,
Puis c'on ne le peut amender,
Vous le savez. (D: V, 224, xxxi, ll. 2067 ff.)
Dame qui prent plus que sa part
De dueil, son cueur en a le pis. (B: p. 155, ll. 11906 f.)

Il ne faut pas tel dueil mener:
Qui trop de courroux en soy prend,
Nature et raison l'en repprend. (B: p. 80, ll. 6233 ff.)

937 Quant guerre est entre enfans et pére,
C'est trop dure chose et amére,
Et les enfans trop griefment péchent
Qui le droit de leur pére empeschent.
(D: VI, 130, xxxiv, ll. 1513 ff.)

Car touz jours seult honneur venir
A l'enfant qui se veult tenir
Obediant et doubtant pére,
Et qui ne l'est si le compére,
Car mal en vient. (D: III, 280, xxi, ll. 1093 ff.)

Car on voit advenir souvent
Qu'enfans tenus chers en jeunesse
Ne viennent pas à grant prouesse,
Et ceulx qui prennent vaine gloire
A la fin sçauront le contraire. (F: III, 51, 17)

938 On doit son ennemy surprendre:
Qui empruncte ne peult choisir. (A: II, 365, xxiii, ll. 17351 f.)

939 Qui plus ne veult estre enseigné,
Il voit ou doit voir qu'il est nisse.
(G: III, 146, xxiv, ll. 417 f.)

940 Car de toux maulx je [*Envye*] suis le chef.
(A: II, 343, xxiii, l. [G 918])

Envye est tousjours a la court. (A: IV, 116, xxxiii, l. 29742)

Enuie
Qui a tout mal les cueurs excite. (C: I, xiii[v])

Ie [*Envye*] fais les vns des haultz descendre,
Les aultres ie les fais monter. (E: I, 10, 7)

Jamais ne valut rien envye. (A: VI, 163, xliv, l. 47902)

941 Ung petit derreur au principe
Est grant en fin ie vous promect
Comme le philosophe mect
Au quint de sa metaphisique. (C: I, xviii[v])

942 Il fault eschapper en effect,
Qui est en ung mauvais passaige.
(A: IV, 151, xxxiv, ll. 30488 f.)

943 Mais esperance les deçoit. (G: I, 124, iv, l. 111)

944 Selon lestat doit on lhostel parer. (C: II, ccxx[v])

945 On ne fait pas a sa devise
En pays estrange. (A: III, 383, xxx, ll. 26111 f.)

946 Car voiagiers en lieu loingtain
A peine sont secourus d'ame. (A: II, 123, xix, ll. 11701 f.)

947 Quant c'est faict c'est faict.
(A: II, 166 f., xx, ll. 12768, 12776, 12784, 12788, III, 24 f., xxiv, ll. 18075, 18082, 18089, 18093; C: II, clxxxvii, ccxl; D: I, 388, viii, l. 1015; F: I, 12, 197, 22, 381, III, 53, 148)
Mais remède n'y a: c'est faict.
(A: IV, 206, xxxiv, l. 31743)
C'est faict, il n'y fault plus penser. (F: I, 19, 347)
Puisqu'il est fait, il faut qu'il soit. (B: p. 393, l. 29975)
948 Vous auez tort
Rien na faict qui autre naduienne. (C: II, xciiii[v])
949 On dit maintes foys
Qu'il a tant faict qu'il n'en peult plus [mais?]
On le doibt bien laisser en pays,
C'est une autorité commune. (F: II, 36, 203)
950 Fay à aultruy ce que veulx qu'on te face. (F: II, 34, 175)
951 Qui bien fera le trouvera;
Qui fera mal a l'opposite;
Le mauvais son mal portera,
Et le bon selon son merite. (A: I, 92, iv, ll. 2385 ff.)
952 Car on dit par auctorite
Qui faict mal / il hayt la clarte. (C: I, xxxiii[v])
953 J'ay grant peur que n'en faciez rien.
Vous faictes assez de parolles;
Mais quoy! c'est tout. (F: I, 10, 172 f.)
954 Chascun ne faict pas ce quil veult /
Tel cuy de bailler qui recoit /
Tel a trop qui a tort se deult /
Conuoitise plusieurs decoit.
Tel pense que a seurete soit
Que sa pensee chet en doubte /
En fin verite se percoit
Tel menace qui fort redoubte. (C: II, clxx)
955 On ne saroyt par trop farder
Le penser qu'on a sur le cœur. (G: III, 68, xxi, ll. 282 f.)
956 Ils ne suyvent pas le dicton,
Que si bien enseigne Caton,
Quand il dit que feindre simplesse,
En temps et lieu est grand sagesse.
(G: III, 319, xxx, ll. 325 ff.)
957 Liberte, richesse et beaulte.
Ce sont les trois biens d'une femme. (E: III, 1, 15)
Quant une femme a le corps beau,
Elle en est plus tost mariee. (G: I, 73, iii, ll. 99 f.)

Y ne fault poinct faire de doubte
Que l'homme qui a belle femme,
Combien que sage on le reclame,
Bien estimé en plusieurs lieux,
Qui soyt mys au nombre des dieux,
Eust il cent mille francs de rente,
Sy sa femme ne se contente,
Y sera badin en tout poinct. (G: III, 62 f., xxi, ll. 158 ff.)
Mais, femmes desirent sçavoir
Tousjours quelque novalité. (A: IV, 31, xxxi, ll. 27818 f.)
Pensée de femme est tost changée.
(A: IV, 317, xxxvii, l. 34356)
Et que penser de femme tost aller. (C: I, iv[v])
Car trop muable est cuer de femme. (D: II, 158, xii, l. 1033)
Quant une femme est à son aise,
Elle est de nature maulvaise
S'elle ne le peult endurer. (F: I, 26, 90 f.)
Tantost riz, tantost pleurs et lermes,
Tantost courroucer, tantost paix;
Autrement ne fut il jamais
Des femmes: il vient de nature. (G: II, 86, x, ll. 1209 ff.)
Femmes ont tousjours le regnom
De parler. (F: II, 44, 354)
Femmes n'ont jamais le bec clos. (F: I, 3, 30)
Vous verriez plus tost Lucifer
Devenir ange salutaire
Que une femme eust un peu de repos
Et soy taire ou tenir manière. (F: II, 30, 109)
Toujours femme demande ou tence,
Sans avoir paix à l'environ. (F: I, 14, 227)
Cantelle de femme est trop fine. (A: V, 317, xlii, l. 43636)
Il n'est rien que femme ne affine. (A: IV, 24, xxxi, l. 27652)
Femmes sont fines a merueilles. (E: II, 4, 20)
Il n'y a homme, tant soyt fin
Et tant est la teste fine,
Que fine femme enfin n'afine. (E: III, 4, 23)
A! il n'est c'une femme fine
Pour quelque fin tour auiser. (E: III, 12, 15)
Vous aues veu quelle finesse,
Que pour trouuer une fin esse,
Souldain il n'est que femme fine. (E: III, 12, 23)
Contemplez en effect
Qu'il n'est finesse que d'une femme. (F: I, 16, 288)
Il n'est ouvrage que de femme. (F: II, 44, 357)

Mieulx vauldroict asaillir un deable
Que d'asaillir aucunes femmes. (G: III, 76, xxi, ll. 461 f.)
Et croy qu'il n'est homme sur terre
Qui sceut avoir plus durre guerre
Que d'ugne femme discordante. (A: V, 31, xxxix, ll. 37294 ff.)
Et sy la femme d'avanture
Est mauvaise de sa nature,
Qu'el veuille fraper ou mauldire. (G: II, 316, xvi, ll. 158 ff.)
De meschief folle femme affame. (G: II, 40, x, l. 395)
Mainte se tient pour preude femme,
Par faulte de la requerir;
Qu'elle sauve son los et fame,
Car elle n'en scet où querir. (F: I, 14, 241)
Tousiours ycy discort,
Ce n'est que nature de femmes;
Plus sont haultaines que gens d'armes,
A leur auys mais du tout rien. (E: II, 7, 12)
Car quant les femmes sont metresses
Elles y doibuent les bres porter. (E: I, 5, 25)
Seigneur, merveille est de ces femmes:
Ilz sont toutes tressages dames,
Mais a la foiz sont si lunages
Que vous verrez que les plus sages
Sont les plus nices. (D: VI, 60, xxxiii, ll. 1763 ff.)
Voirement qui en femme met
Son cuer, bien le doit on blasmer,
Car on y treuve moult d'amer
Ainçois que l'en en viengne au bout.
(D: I, 326, vii, ll. 382 ff.)
Oncques femme aultrement n'en fit:
C'est leur nature, a tout compter,
Que de perdre bien et gaster. (B: p. 207, ll. 15979 ff.)
On dit que pour faire grant chére
Compaignie ne vault riens sans femme.
(A: VI, 11, xliii, ll. 44579 f.)
De femme croire, c'est follye de s'en plaindre.
(A: V, 353, xlii, l. 44307)
Femme est pour tout faire ou deffaire.
(A: VI, 38, xliii, l. 45227)
Mais, ainsi que je puis comprendre,
Femmes peuent donner entendre
Des faulcetez aucunes fois. (A: III, 79, xxv, ll. 19035 ff.)
Honme qui a garde de femme
N'a pas toujours euvre lessée. (A: VI, 42, xliii, ll. 45328 f.)

On dit que femme ne sçait rien,
Et si faict, si faict, si faict bien. (A: VI, 96, xliv, ll. 46483 f.)
Car femme seulle est bien a prendre.
(A: II, 134, xix, l. 11967)
Sy une femme en est serue,
La clef de son con est perdue. (E: I, 2, 12)
Aussi je veulx certifier
Que le cas est à femme laict
Fair (de) son maistre son varlet,
Tant soit[-il] sot ou mal aprins. (F: I, 4, 48)
On doit tenir femme pour sotte,
Qui prent mary sans le cognoistre,
Et qui de son servant s'assotte
Pour en faire son privé maistre. (F: II, 33, 140)
Communement on dit cela,
Tant soit à Paris comme à Rome:
A femme de bien ung fol homme,
Et à quelque meschante femme
Ung bon homme. (F: I, 10, 154)
Or sa, desployés moy une once
Du sçavoir que on dit feminique. (G: II, 93, x, ll. 1350 f.)
De femme qui, par sa paresse,
Fait un pet au lieu d'une vesse,
Et puis se trouve un pied de nez,
Gardez vous d'y estre trompé. (G: III, 317, xxx, ll. 253 ff.)
Ha! que trop coquin ou trop chiche
Se sent qui cherche femme riche! (G: III, 309, xxx, ll. 61 f.)
Roy Ostes, je vous jur par m'ame
Tel cuide avoir femme touz seulz
Qu'a li partissent plus de deux.
(D: IV, 341, xxviii, ll. 648 ff.)
Car l'homme faict la femme telle
Qu'i la veult ou doulce ou rebelle
Ou en luy n'a poinct de raison. (E: I, 5, 29)
Le dit de Cathon fault garder
Qui dit louange de la femme.
Souffre-la quant el est sans blasme,
Et la supporte patiemment. (F: I, 1, 6)
Ma foy, ma femme, un homme sage
Ne s'enquiert jamais de sa femme,
Que le moins qu'il peult. (F: II, 24, 32)
On doit beste homme reputer,
Beste plus qu'une beste mue,
Que femme sçait suppediter. (A: VI, 25, xliii, ll. 44894 ff.)

Encor est hom plus abusé
Qui cuide en soy ou pense avoir
A sa voulenté le vouloir
De femme; faire ne se peult.
Ou l'homme veult elle ne veult;
Ou ne veult, elle veult tout oultre.
(A: VI, 22 f., xliii, ll. 44837 ff.)

958 Fort à ferrer a tousjours fer qui loche. (F: III, 59, 256)

959 Fille sans amy est bien beste. (F: II, 48, 414)
Une fille est tost affollée. (A: II, 274, xxii, l. 15417)

960 Et mal conduit son avangarde
Celluy qui la fin ne regarde. (B: p. 211, ll. 16296 f.)
Noz maistres qui moult travaillèrent
Pour nous enseigner nous baillèrent
Par leur escript ung très beau cas.
En latin c'est: *Quicquid agas*
In primo respice finem.
Qui est à dire en françoys,
Que, quelque chose que tu fays,
Regardes comme tu la fays.
Tu la doitz faire sagement.
Note dont premièrement
Que en pourra estre la fin. (F: III, 51, 8 f.)

961 Il n'est finesse qu'on ne face. (E: II, 4, 8, 15, 30)

962 Car fol est qui cuyde estre saige. (G: III, 213, xxvii, l. 43)
Folz est cil qui autrui desvoie,
Qui entrez est en bonne voie. (D: I, 202, iv, ll. 1533 f.)
Et tant il est fol qui se fie
Aux raporteurs plains de mefaict. (E: II, 7, 11)
Il est fol qui se glorifie. (A: IV, 403, xxxviii, l. 36381)
Sire, les folz ont en despit
Les choses qui sont, pour un point,
Qu'il cuident qu'il ne soient point,
Et s'efforcent moult d'avoir celles
Qui ne sont pas. (D: III, 254, xxi, ll. 268 ff.)
Folz est et de senz trop ligier
Et presumptueux, qui jugier
Son seigneur ose. (D: VI, 144, xxxiv, ll. 1942 ff.)
Fol est qui se mesle d'amis
Et d'enfans; c'est abusion;
A gens de bien n'est point promis.
Fol est qui se mesle d'amis. (F: I, 8, 126 f.)
Et fole estes de refuser
Chose que vueille. (D: VII, 43, xxxvii, ll. 1116 f.)

Car la parole est abolye
D'vn fol, fust-il roy, duc ou compte. (E: II, 6, 32)
Car vng fol mot mal entendu
A vng quidam mal recite
Peust esmouuoir vne cite. (C: II, clxviii)
De folle vie maleureuse
Fin souvent vous verrés tenir. (G: II, 100, x, ll. 1481 f.)
Ceste folle veult tout avoir. (F: II, 50, 444)

963 Ce n'est pas tout que d'estre fort;
Mais c'est le tout, pour abreger,
Quant l'on est en quelque danger
Trouver fault manyere et stille
D'en eschaper & estre abille,
En euitant la mort & blame. (E: III, 13, 37 f.)

964 Celluy est fol qui fortune ne doubte. (A: I, 185, viii, l. 4851)
Contre fortune la diverse
Un charestier rompt son fouet. (G: III, 291, xxix, ll. 273 f.)
Mais Fortune vers moy s'adresse,
Qui me tourne son faulx visage. (E: III, 3, 27 f.)
Quant de Fortune me récolle,
Elle est, par Dieu, maulvaise beste;
Car tant souvent roulle et bricolle
Qu'il semble quel(le) soit une folle. (F: I, 9, 130)
Fortune, tu m'es bien contraire,
Contraire dès que je fuz né. (G: I, 131, iv, ll. 249 f.)
Se fortune vous enuironne
Pour vous faire des maulx porter
Ou vous faict tirer a sa tonne
Bruuage trop aigre a gouster
Ja ne vous fault desconforter /
Car el ne regarde personne /
Et a qui luy plaist elle donne. (C: I, cxxvii)
Helas fortune / helas fortune / helas
Seray ie ainsi demourant en tes laz
Dolent & las
Me feras tu doncques languir tousiours
Comme vng grant fol de ma vie tesbas.
Vng iour suis bas / hault lautre / tu rabas. (C: I, cxxxvii[v])
Plaindre me doy de ta durte.
Fortune felle & rigoureuse (C: I, clxxx[v])
Ha! fortune, faulce ennemye,
Fortune, beste deguisee
Et de tout mal faire advisee,
C'est les tours que tu sces jouer:
Mon dueil cuides faire muer. (B: p. 102, ll. 7840 ff.)

Ha! fortune, chose soubdaine,
Plus variable et incertaine
Que chose nee,
Trop diversement t'es tournee
Devers la povre infortunee
Qui plus n'attens
Que la mort me perse tout ens. (B: p. 155, ll. 11891 ff.)
Veue ma vie fortunee,
En rigueur de fortune nee,
Et en bruit de desesperance! (B: p. 162, ll. 12374 ff.)
Ha! fortune tres variable,
Variant variablement,
Tu m'as fait faire ung jugement. (B: p. 402, ll. 30661 ff.)
Fortune n'est point permanente,
Et si n'y a princes ne roys
Que souvent elle ne tourmente.
(A: VI, 184, xlv, ll. 48370 ff.)
Fortune qui le cas varie
La grant temps durement greue. (C: I, cxliii)
En fortune n'a rien de seur. (A: VI, 148, xliv, l. 47604)
Il ne fault que ung cop de fortune
Pour faire maistre le servant,
Et du maistre le pousuyvant:
Les biens du monde bien peu durent.
(A: V, 7, xxxix, ll. 36675 ff.)
Fortune a plusieurs es amye /
Mais a moy trop es ennemye
Et pleine de crudelite. (C: I, xii)
M'amie, mettez en deport
Les maux qu'ore avez par fortune;
Car aux uns est dure et enfrune,
Doulce aux autres, par verité.
En li n'a point d'estableté.
Souvent honneur amaine a honte.
(D: IV, 292, xxvii, ll. 1503 ff.)
Sa [*Fortune's*] roue nest iamais constante
Elle est de nature inconstante /
Mais tousiours tourne & tournera /
Tel regne en bruit / & rit & chante
Qui puis aura vie meschante
Tel na rien qui enrichira. (C: I, cxxvii[v])
Fortune m'a en sa roe hault monté;
A son hault choix, de son desir et vueil,
En sa roe m'a haultement levé.
(A: VI, 57, xliii, ll. 45690 ff.)

Fortune, il n'en est pas en toy,
Fortune, beste merveillable:
Toy et ta roue detestable
Mettons au sanglant pis tourner. (B: p. 80, ll. 6229 ff.)
Ha! Fortune, tant m'es perverse!
A bon droit or de toy me plains
Et com dolente me complains,
Qui m'as mis ou hault de ta roe
Et m'as puis jetté en la boe. (D: V, 61, xxix, ll. 1726 ff.)
Fortune du hault de sa roe
M'a bien jetté en my la boe
Et mise en dure adversité,
Selon la grant prosperité
Et l'onneur ou je soloie estre. (D: V, 187, xxxi, ll. 917 ff.)
Ha! Fortune, conme tu m'as
A ce cop du hault de ta roe
Jetté jus et mis en la boe!
Trop as pris vers moy grant rancune
Et trop m'es diverse et enfrune,
Quant tant me fais honte et annuy.
(D: VI, 189, xxxv, ll. 543 ff.)
Il nous mettera à la roue de fortune;
C'est pour nous faire avoir les oreillons. (F: III, 59, 258)
Et ay volé du premier sault
Jusques cy par roe de Fortune. (G: II, 188, xii, ll. 65 f.)

965 Hayne de fréres est treslourde. (A: II, 357, xxiii, l. 17171)

966 Quant vient ainsi une fureur
De loing fuir est bien propice. (G: II, 284, xv, ll. 103 f.)

967 Mal as recordé ta lecon
Dedans le livre de Cathon,
En ce lieu là, sans dire ho,
Qui dit: *Luxuriam fugito.*
Il dict qu'on doibt fuyre luxure
Pour ce qu'on faict à Dieu injure,
Et est peché moult desplaisant. (F: III, 51, 81)

968 Malureux donq l'homme
Qui se fye en somme
Au bras de la chair!
Heureux se doibt dire
Qui de Dieu desire
Son secours chercher! (E: I, 6, 11)

969 Filz, s'elle mesmes ne se garde,
Je ne la pourroie garder. (D: V, 26, xxix, ll. 698 ff.)

970 Ung homme ne se peult garder
De son heur, soit bon ou mauvais. (A: II, 362, xxiii, ll. 17287 f.)

971 Bon fait son chastel et son corps
Garder touzjours. (D: II, 236, xiv, ll. 130 f.)
972 Laissez ce dueil / laissez laissez
Rien ny vault le gemir ou plaindre. (C: I, clxxx[v])
973 Gentillesse fault soustenir
Qui la pourroit entretenir. (F: I, 12, 202)
974 Cil qui de glave frappera
Du glave aussi pardu sera. (B: p. 248, ll. 19165 f.)
La sentence est en l'escripture
Escripte contre lui trop dure;
Je ne say se vous la savez:
Dire la veuil, or entendez:
'Qui de glaive ferra autruy,
A glaive ira le corps de lui.' (D: I, 139, iii, ll. 1005 ff.)
Car tu trouveras par escript,
Aussi l'Evangille le dit,
Que ceulx qui de glayve ferront
Pour certain de glayve mourront. (F: I, 1, 4)
975 Cela est vsance de guerre. (C: I, cliii[v])
Conte Grimault, grant foleur brace
Qui guerre sanz raison esmeut. (D: IV, 17, xxiii, ll. 438 f.)
Par mon serment on dit bien voir
Vng vaillant homme ou quil se treuue
Quant en vne guerre sespreuue
Il treuue tousiours a combatre.
(C: II, cxl[v] [misnumbered clF])
Par la guerre cheut en ruyne
Qui sesbat a chauffer telz baings. (C: I, clxvi)
Ou est guerre justice est morte. (A: V, 263, xlii, l. 42572)
976 Riche abbit l'homme trompe. (A: VI, 137, xliv, l. 47385)
977 Car Cathon[net] ne le veult mye,
Qui commande, qui bien veu l'a,
Et dit: *Cum bonis ambula*,
Hante les bons, tu seras bon. (F: III, 51, 74)
978 Car de tant que chose est plus haulte
Et en puissance plus unye,
S'il chet qu'elle face deffaulte,
De tant doit estre mieulx pugnye. (B: p. 33, ll. 2478 ff.)
Car de tant que l'omme est plus hault,
Et a plus grant bien evocqué,
Quant il chet qu'il a delinqué,
Sa pugnicion est plus griefve. (B: p. 365, ll. 27782 ff.)
Qui plus hault monte qu'il ne doibt,
Quant ung fol homme a tout perdu,
Tantost chascun le monstre au doyt. (G: I, 262, ix, ll. 382 ff.)

979 Où est Helaine qui fust sy belle?
Et la grand Deesse Sybelle,
Ou Iudic plaine de paresse? (E: III, 1, 14)
980 S'on auoyt la force Hercules,
La beaulte d'Absalon le gent,
Auec la valeur Achiles,
Amour ne faict rien sans argent. (E: IV, 8, 30)
981 Une heure hausse, une autre abesse.
(D: V, 63, xxix, l. 1806)
982 Sy maintenant veulx estre heureulx,
Escoute, regarde, & tais toult. (E: III, 2, 9)
983 Et sçés bien que l'homme est beste
Ce il n'a un peu d'aisement. (F: I, 10, 176)
984 Les hommes font bien les batailles
Et Dieu de iustice & gloyre
Donne a qui y plaist la victoyre. (E: I, 6, 6)
985 Avoir de l'onneur terrien
Aucunes fois est dangereux. (A: IV, 301, xxxvi, ll. 33970 f.)
L'honneur mondain a l'homme est peu durable.
(A: IV, 383, xxxvii, l. 35926)
On dit souvent que les honneurs
A quoy on vient muent les meurs.
(D: VII, 155, xxxviii, ll. 991 f.)
Honneurs muent les condicions
Aucunes foys. (G: II, 219, xiii, ll. 71 f.)
986 Car ire empesche le courage
Et faict mainte iniure enomir. (C: I, cvi[v])
987 C'est grande follye
A homme d'avoir jalousye
De chose où n'a aulcun dommaige. (F: II, 37, 211)
988 Les jeunes ne sont point [plus] seurs
Que les vieulx, vous le sçavez bien. (F: II, 36, 193)
En jeunes gens n'y a pas grant sagesse.
(A: V, 4, xxxix, l. 36600)
Mais il fault excuser ieunesse
Qui trop quiert suyure sa plaisance
Sans soy armer de temperance
Qui refrene les passions. (C: I, cvii)
Car en jeunesse le monde est variable,
Dont je crains fort qu'en la fin ne se change[nt].
(F: III, 52, 89)
Jeunesse viellesse desprise. (A: IV, 335, xxxvii, l. 34768)
989 Du jour au lendermain survient
Tout autrement qu'on ne propose. (G: II, 328, xvii, ll. 3 f.)

Car par advanture il y a
En ung seul jour autant de peine
Com aura en une sepmaine. (F: I, 1, 2)

990 Tel est joyeulx qui bien tost pleure! (A: II, 373, xxiii, l. [G 1732])

991 Ce n'est pas parlé d'ung sage homme
De juger de chose improveue
Si en haste sans l'avoir veue. (B: p. 153, ll. 11729 f.)

992 Car juges qui n'entent
Ce qu'on dit loyal jugement
Il ne peut rendre. (D: III, 225, xx, ll. 1105 ff.)
Car comme Cathon nous afferme,
Ire qui excede hors terme
Empesche fort l'entendement
Qu'il ne face vray jugement. (B: p. 80, ll. 6236 ff.)

993 Il n'est si vaillant laboureur
Qui ne s'ennuy de labourer. (F: I, 6, 66)

994 Aussi ceste raison est vive,
Que a laver la teste d'ung asne
On n'y pert rien que la lescive. (G: III, 147, xxiv, ll. 427 ff.)

995 Car lhomme non plus que vne beste
Nauroit en soy de liberte. (C: I, cv)

996 Je suppose que temps sera
Que ie mesbatte vng peu a lire
Meilleur moyen ne scay eslire
Ne plus gente occupation. (C: I, xc[v])

997 Quant les loupz si ont bien ullé,
Ilz s'en vont querir a mengier. (G: I, 99, iii, ll. 405 f.)

998 Mal finer doibt qui en mal veult naistre.
(G: II, 101, x, ll. 1507, 1509)
L'homme qui le mal ymagine
Et en son coeur a la racyne
Doibt estre des aultres pugny. (E: II, 4, 3 f.)
Nature humaine est inclinée
A faire plus tost mal que bien. (A: I, 203, ix, ll. 5304 f.)
Car tous humains nez
Sont a plusieurs maulx inclinez. (A: I, 244, xi, ll. 6269 f.)
C'est voir que les maux a cheval
Viennent, mais a pié, sire doulx,
S'en vont. (D: VI, 241, xxxvi, ll. 333 ff.)

999 Car trop doubteuse est maladie
Dont on renchiet. (D: IV, 262, xxvii, ll. 600 f.)

1000 Gens mariez ont assez peine,
A bien considérer leur cas,
L'ung tracasse, l'autre pourmaine. (F: I, 3, 21)

On y peult dire marri age:
Par mettre *marri* devant *aige*,
Les ungz en meurent devant aage. (G: III, 128, xxiv, ll. 46 ff.)

1001 Car maulvaistié est de tel(le) sorte
Que, où elle est, beaulté est morte. (F: I, 10, 166)

1002 Je te dy bien dit le prophéte,
Qui dit des mauvais qu'a ce chéent
Que leurs maux sur leurs chiés leur chéent,
Et il dit voir. (D: III, 358, xxii, ll. 1384 ff.)

1003 Car mauvaise nouvelle empire
En la bouche d'ung frivoleur. (B: p. 395, ll. 30085 f.)

1004 Helas il a perdu la main
Pour soy trop fier aux medecins
Qui font malades ceulx qui sont sains. (C: I, lvii)
N'est ce grand dommaige qu'on n'ose
Monstrer son mal au medecin
Et faire cracher au bassin
Ceulx la que tant je n'oze dire?
(G: III, 246, xxviii, ll. 142 ff.)
Riens n'y vauldra la medecine
Après la mort. (B: p. 154, ll. 11738 f.)

1005 C'est que les aprentis
Tousjours les meilleurs maistres sont. (F: II, 36, 194)

1006 Le meilleur sens que je y voie
C'est de tenir moyenne voie. (B: p. 180 f., ll. 13923 f.)

1007 Tel a menacer se dispose
Qui moins en seurete repose. (C: II, cxiii)

1008 C'est bon menger que d'une heure,
Entendés vous bien? de sanglier. (G: I, 66, iii, ll. 15 f.)

1009 De mesprendre n'est pas merveille,
Puis que repentir on s'en veille,
Mais merveille est quant on mesprent
Et on ne s'amende et repent. (D: VI, 132, xxxiv, ll. 1575 ff.)

1010 Mais je recorde pour certain
Que a toutes gens c'est grant folie
De mettre son cueur trop a plain
En quelque chose près ou loing:
Aulcunes foys bien n'en prent mye.
(A: III, 46 f., xxv, ll. [G 3188 ff.])
J'ay ouy dire, certain en suys,
Que une chose tant desirée,
Et la ou tant son cueur est mys,
Bien acoup on en voit les fins,
Et si n'a pas grande durée. (A: III, 48 f., xxv, ll. [G 3230 ff.])

1011 De moins que neant on faict maintes reproches.
(F: III, 59, 256)

1012 Le monde fut bien nestié,
En bien peu de temps, de Templiers. (G: I, 82, iii, ll. 207 f.)

1013 Dea, monsieur vault bien madame. (E: IV, 8, 24)

1014 Superbes montaignes
Aux humbles campaignes
On void esgaller
Par grosses riuieres
Bruyantes & fyeres
Qui les font grouler. (E: I, 6, 11)

1015 Il fault que tout meure. (A: I, 168, viii, l. 4419)
Touz fault morir. (D: III, 260, xxi, l. 469)
O mort, mort, tu monstres bien comme
Tu es commune a tout humain. (A: I, 161, vii, ll. 4249 f.)
Car la mort est a tous comune. (A: II, 102, xviii, l. 11168)
La mort a toute nation,
Aage, estat et condition
Indifferemment fait effort. (A: II, 49, xvii, ll. [EF 986 ff.])
Dieu ne a regart n'a chapeau ne a couronne.
Quant il luy plaist donner mortel assault,
En ung instant sans auchun cry le donne,
Sans envoier messagier ne herault. (G: I, 205 f., vii, ll. 75 ff.)
Ha! faulce Mort,
Qui le povre et riche remords,
Tu prens tousjours ce qui vault mieux.
(G: II, 280, xv, ll. 23 ff.)
Se la mort vient,
A qui sommes obligez tous,
A gré prendre vous la convient. (A: II, 82, xviii, ll. 10666 ff.)
Car pour mourir tous sommes faiz.
Mort est deue a toute personne. (A: II, 85, xviii, ll. 10733 f.)
La mort prent tout et n'espergne ame.
(A: II, 263, xxi, l. 15163)
Et qu'il fault
En fin que la mort donne assault
A toute humaine creature. (A: III, 424 f., xxx, ll. 27073 ff.)
Fol est qui s'en mellencollie,
Puis que aussi bien mourir convient.
(A: II, 209, xx, ll. 13862 f.)
Mourir convient; mort est maistresse
Qui n'espargne foyble ne fort. (A: II, 323, xxiii, ll. 16604 f.)
Quant la mort vient, il la fault prendre.
(A: IV, 330, xxxvii, l. 34671)

A la mort ne puis reculler. (A: III, 186, xxvi, l. 21426)
Contre mort remede n'y vault. (B: p. 24, l. 1689)
Tu es seure
Que une foys la mort seure,
Aspre et dure
Tous endurer convient,
Et fault en gré prendre quant elle vient.
(A: I, 137, vi, ll. 3579 ff.)
Car vne fois mourir nous fault. (C: I, clxii[v])
Dame, puis qu'en ce monde nez
Sommes, une foiz nous convient
Touz et toutes morir. (D: V, 278, xxxi, ll. 591 ff.)
Combien que mort soit inhumaine
A toute creature humaine,
Si la dis je en comun langage
Humaine, car, chose certaine,
Quant ce vient a l'heure souldaine,
Il fault tous passer ce passage. (A: I, 145, vii, ll. 3790 ff.)
Tu mourras, il est tout certain,
Et ne sçays ennuyt ou demain.
Tu ne sçais l'heure de ta mort. (F: III, 63, ll. 354 f.)
La mort prent les vngs sur les lictz
Et les autres a leur aduenture. (C: II, clxvii)
Toutesfois, nous l'advertirons
Que sommes tous venus de cendre
Et en cendre retournerons. (A: IV, 330, xxxvii, ll. 34673 ff.)
Ainsi fault que chascun s'en aille
En terre dont il est venuz:
De ce pas n'eschappera nulz
Qu'il ne li faille trespasser
Ce monde et par la mort passer
Jusques au jour du jugement. (D: VII, 30, xxxvii, ll. 734 ff.)
La fin, sire, c'est la mort, voir,
A quoy on vient. (D: III, 260, xxi, ll. 462 f.)
Mes enfans, or vous recordez
Des povretés de corps humain,
Ennuyt vif et puis mort demain.
Helas! c'est bien grant vanité,
Quant il n'y a jour de certain,
En tout l'estat de humanité. (A: I, 138 f., vi, ll. 3619 ff.)
Or n'avons nous point de demain;
Tel est ennuit en grant santé,
Qui porte la mort en son sain
Et demain en terre bouté. (A: I, 161, vii, ll. 4253 ff.)

Ennuyt vivans et demain mors;
La vie d'homme est bien petite. (A: II, 84, xviii, ll. 10707 f.)
Puisque mort l'a voulu saisir
Cessez vostre dolent tristesse:
La mort est de telz fais maistresse,
Que riens n'en revient pour gemir. (B: p. 192, ll. 14816 ff.)
Mon seigneur, tel deuil concevoir
Ne faire a vous pas n'appartient.
Puis que morte est, il la convient
En terre mettre. (D: I, 306, vi, ll. 1546 ff.)
Qui bien meurt il ne perit pas. (A: II, 50, xvii, l. [EF 1000])
C'est tout ung quand nous serons mors
Pour avoir en servaige esté. (A: III, 182, xxvi, ll. 21304 f.)
Mes fréres, il fault mourir jeune
Ou a la fin devenir vieux. (A: IV, 335, xxxvii, ll. 34775 f.)
Car sage qui son fait entend
Eschappe la mort quand il peust. (B: p. 330, ll. 25262 f.)
Tel cuide vivre plus d'un an
Qui meurt dans trois jours. (G: II, 328, xvii, ll. 11 f.)

1016 Ce que ce monde voy muable,
Cheant d'eur en meseur,
Et c'on n'y vit point asseur,
Ainçois n'y a que vanité,
Le me fait faire, en verité. (D: VI, 284, xxxvi, ll. 1645 ff.)
Le vouloir de l'homme est muable,
Et ne sçait on que se peult estre.
(A: IV, 89, xxxiii, ll. 29110 f.)

1017 Tout ce passe,
Ce que nature a compassé. (F: II, 36, 191)

1018 Negligence bien souvent cause
Soudainement un grant meschef. (A: V, 239, xlii, ll. 42056 f.)

1019 Noblesse vient de noble cœur
Et non pas d'un vilain moqueur. (G: III, 37, xx, ll. 146 f.)

1020 On veoyt qui a grand paine peult
Se nourir qui aultre nourist. (G: II, 311, xvi, ll. 80 f.)

1021 Ases voyt on de telz nouices
Qui en seruant font beaulx ofices,
Mais quant y viennent a puissance;
Y veulent faire a leur plaisance
Et sy on leur dict vn seul mot,
Y iectent la pinte & le pot
A la teste. (E: III, 14, 13)

1022 Offense a dieu est forte a reparer
A sage tiens qui vers luy ne mesprent. (C: II, ccxx[v])

Offence d'esgalle action
Veult esgalle pugnicion. (B: p. 32, ll. 2349 f.)

1023 En ouvrage où (en) rien ne s'acqueste,
C'est grant follie d'y quester. (F: I, 14, 236)

1024 Sage est louurier quen raison sexercite
Selon le faict fault loeuure preparer. (C: II, ccxx[v])

1025 Que sert oyseau en mue? (E: IV, 1, 18)

1026 Gens oysifz ne songent nul bien. (A: III, 55, xxv, l. [G 3374])

1027 Si fault il avoir pacience
Quant on ne peult reméde mettre
Et quant divine sapience
En ce point l'a voulu permettre. (A: I, 125, vi, ll. 3257 ff.)
Puis quil est ainsi ordonne
Il fault tout prendre en pacience. (C: I, cxxxvii[v])
Chacun prendra en pacience,
C'est le plus fort puisqu'il est prest. (B: p. 426, ll. 32536 f.)

1028 Il fault prendre en gré l'aventure. (B: p. 104, l. 8022)

1029 Paier fault l'ouvrier selon l'euvre
Et aux quoquars leur bienvenue. (G: I, 268, ix, ll. 515 f.)

1030 Pain est principalle viande. (A: III, 179, xxvi, l. 21236)

1031 Tel prent grant plaisir a veoir paindre
Qui ne sairoyt bien faire un traict. (G: III, 58, xxi, ll. 63 f.)

1032 Paix est bonne et la fault attraire
L'un avecques l'autre, qui peut. (A: II, 276, xxii, ll. 15464 f.)
Car quant deux gens ont vng debat
Adoncques est la paix monstree
Quant lune partie est oultree
Et surmontee. (C: II, xvii)
La paix nous avons; mais, combien
Que nous l'ayons, c'est qu'on la garde.
(G: II, 357 f., xviii, ll. 5 f.)

1033 Paresse est mauvaise de soy. (B: p. 242, l. 18684)

1034 Aucunes fois a l'estourdy
On parle que on ne sçait que on dit.
(A: III, 291, xxviii, ll. 23939 f.)
On ne seroyt tenir les gens
De parler & les faire taire. (E: II, 17, 15)
Il fault qu'on en parle en tout lieu. (F: III, 52, 107)

1035 La parolle ne fait pas tout;
Il y fault ouvrer de main mise. (A: I, 253, xi, ll. 6507 f.)
Car bien souuent vne parolle
Faict les amys estre ennemys. (E: III, 1, 20)

1036 On dit qu'a chose homme ne tent
Dont il ne parviengne a effect. (D: IV, 3, xxiii, ll. 2 f.)

1037 Tu sçais que jamais on ne vit
Peché impugny. (A: IV, 178, xxxiv, ll. 31131 f.)
1038 Ie trouue erreur cache,
Que cestuy la veult vn pesche reprendre
Du quel il est tache & empesche. (E: II, 14, 30)
1039 Tout pescheur doibt porter la somme
De tous les pesches qu'il a fais. (E: II, 2, 22)
1040 Trop ardemment aymer pecune
Fait gens aller oblique voye. (G: II, 219, xiii, ll. 83 f.)
Que mauldicte soit la pecune
Qui cueur gentil decepuera. (C: I, clxiiii)
1041 Après coup perdu n'est nul courre. (B: p. 343, l. 26351)
Ce qui est pardu est pardu. (B: p. 344, l. 26410)
1042 Si com petite medicine
Souvent de grant douleur delivre. (D: III, 271, xxi, ll. 806 f.)
1043 Pour peu de chose il vient beaucoup de mal. (F: III, 59, 256)
1044 Le peuple menu
Qui croit bien de legier et trop.
(B: p. 175, ll. 13457 f.; C: I, xxxiii, lxxi)
Toutesfois on croyt de leger. (C: I, clxiiii)
Le peuple n'est pas fort estable,
Et si est de ligier commeu. (A: IV, 279, xxxvi, ll. 33431 f.)
1045 Le congé prendre
Ne doit pas sambler si mauvais
Veu que ce n'est pas pour jamais:
Ung peu de temps va tost passant. (B: p. 231, ll. 17879 ff.)
1046 Catin, pitié mault (*sic*) mieulx qu'envie
En vertu, se disent les sages. (F: I, 14, 228)
Pitye se doibt tourner aulx dames. (E: IV, 8, 25)
1047 Il n'est rien qui ne vienne a planche.
(A: II, 388, xxiii, l. [G 2149])
1048 Nulz ne reviennent pour plourer
Ne pour force larmes jecter. (A: III, 53, xxv, ll. [G 3334 f.])
Le plourer n'y vault riens jamais. (D: II, 52, ix, l. 1418)
Fors plourer pour celui qu'avoir
Ne poez, ne n'en arez point. (D: I, 255, vi, ll. 23 f.)
Riens n'y vault ne plorer ne plaindre. (B: p. 377, l. 28747)
Nous voyons bien
Que lamenter rien ne proffite. (A: III, 237, xxvii, ll. 22621 f.)
A lamenter ne gaigne rien. (A: IV, 160, xxxiv, l. 30705)
Sire, vous ne gaignez pas maille
A plorer ny a lamenter. (A: IV, 165, xxxiv, ll. 30831 f.)
Il est mort! Plorer rien ne gaigne.
(A: IV, 317, xxxvii, l. 34349)

Il nous est force d'endurer,
Car rien ne vault le murmurer.
(A: IV, 345, xxxvii, ll. 35024 f.)
Pleurer vous peut estre nuisant,
Seigneurs, et sachiez riens ne vault. (D: I, 115, iii, ll. 308 f.)
Par pleurs ne par quelque soucy
Certes ne le poons avoir. (B: p. 377, ll. 28744 f.)
La ou l'une pleure l'autre chante. (A: II, 186, xx, l. 13316)

1049 Ceux qui plus ont plus envis meurent. (G: I, 248, ix, l. 150)

1050 Homme ne se doit avancer
De porter mauvaises nouvelles.
(A: IV, 226, xxxv, ll. 32201 f.)

1051 Qui ne peult ne peult. (A: VI, 194, xlv, l. 48641; F: I, 6, 66)

1052 Or cognoiz je maintenant bien
Que povre homme est touz jours bas mis,
Et quc nul ne li est amis
S'il n'est riches et plain d'avoir. (D: VI, 194, xxxv, ll. 705 ff.)
Helas! povres gens sont honnys. (G: III, 195, xxvi, l. 383)
On veoyt mainct pauvre qui s'en deult.
(G: II, 311, xvi, ll. 76, 79, 82)

1053 Povreté après grant honneur
Vient aucunes fois. (A: V, 38, xxxix, ll. 37469 f.)
Car il nest chose qui tant blesse
Comme pourete a noblesse. (C: I, cxxvii)

1054 Telle cuide estre la première
Qu'est la dernière de la danse. (F: I, 14, 249)

1055 Mes a le prendre est la maistrise. (B: p. 241, l. 18631)

1056 Lisez: Promettre et rien tenir. (F: I, 8, 124)

1057 Par prudence, honneur et sagesse,
Le page deuyent grand seigneur. (E: III, 14, 23)
Ung homme prudent doit porter
Sa fortune & calamite. (C: I, cxxxii[v])

1058 Oultre puissance riens ne gist,
C'est une maxime en nature. (B: p. 34, ll. 2548 f.)

1059 Qui plus ne veult qu'on le punisse,
Il veoit ce qu'il ne demandoit. (G: III, 147, xxiv, ll. 419 f.)

1060 La queue deffault a ung singe
Quant ne couvre ses genitoires. (G: I, 85, iii, ll. 235 f.)

1061 Que fera le rain, quant la souche
Est morte? Certes il morra. (D: II, 52, ix, ll. 1408 f.)

1062 Considére que gens reaulx
Ont aucuneffois plus de maulx
Que n'ont simple gens mecaniques.
(A: IV, 239, xxxv, ll. 32491 ff.)

1063 On doit son reconffort querir
De celluy qui peust secourir
Et donner joye. (B: p. 333, ll. 25548 ff.)
1064 Il fault que chacun ait son régne. (A: VI, 152, xliv, l. 47676)
1065 Mon pére, c'est a vous follye,
Quant de rémede il n'y a mye,
De si fort vous desconforter. (A: III, 53, xxv, ll. [G 3325 ff.])
Bo, il ne fault point tant gemir;
A tous maulx on trouve remède. (F: I, 18, 322)
1066 Car le droit dit qu'il fault
Autant rendre conme on a pris. (D: II, 365, xvi, ll. 496 f.)
1067 On me repayt de promesse souuent;
Mais tout cela ne rent mais sens content. (E: I, 23, 14)
1068 Fi de richesse et de soucy!
Il n'est vie si bien nourrie
Qui vaille estat de pastourrie. (B: p. 59, ll. 4646 ff.)
1069 Rire avecques ceulx qui riront
Il n'est pas de meilleure vie,
Et puis laissez parler envie. (F: II, 29, 94)
La ou l'un rit l'autre murmure. (A: II, 186, xx, l. 13315)
On voyt mainct riche qui s'en rit.
(G: II, 311 f., xvi, ll. 77, 83)
1070 Ung rost, s'il n'est souvent tourné,
Il se brusle et pert sa saveur. (F: I, 14, 238)
1071 Un roy se doit trop plus garder
De pechier, a bien regarder,
Qu'une autre personne ne fait,
Soit en parler ou soit en fait. (D: V, 221, xxxi, ll. 1980 ff.)
Car il nest plus seure deffence
A vng roy / ne plus seur logis
Que lamour des loyaulx subgitz.
Le roy na point mestier de garde
Qui son peuple en amytie garde. (C: I, clvii[v])
1072 Et a ce Salemon s'acorde
Qui dit: 'Le sage craint folie
A faire, et le fol trop s'i fie.' (D: I, 106, iii, ll. 48 ff.)
Celuy est saige qui s'enfuyt
Pour mieulx le danger eviter. (F: III, 53, 163)
N'est pas sage qui ne ressongne. (B: p. 202, l. 15570)
Car celluy est sage qui veille
A ses besongnes de bonne heure. (C: I, cxxvii[v])
1073 L'homme sain est plus de guesté
Mile foys que n'est le malade.
(G: I, 186, vi, ll. 76 f., 79, 82 f.)

Fy de thresor! Je ne desire
En se monde qu'avoir Sancté. (G: I, 188, vi, ll. 115 f., 118 f.)

1074 De sault allant à sault venant
N'aura point mès faicte qu'il viengne. (F: III, 53, 155 f.)

1075 Mon amy, c'est belle vertu
De sçavoir de chascun mestier. (F: I, 1, 7)
Car tout sauoir gist en experience. (E: I, 4, 3)
Vous deuez entendre & scauoir
Qu'il nest tresor que de scauoir. (C: I, clxxix)
C'est belle chose d'aquerir
Sçavoir, quant on peult, en jeunesse,
Pour avoir repos en viellesse. (G: III, 204, xxvi, ll. 532 ff.)
Celuy qui n'apete sçavoir
Et a son profit ne procure
Et qui n'a de rien faire cure,
Chascun le repute pour beste. (G: III, 204, xxvi, ll. 526 ff.)

1076 L'homme ne peult estre refaict,
Sy n'a science en fin de compte. (E: III, 9, 8)
Par science l'homme hault monte. (E: III, 9, 8)
Car ainsi l'enseigne Cathon:
Instrue qui possint inopem deffendere vitam
Cum tibi sint nati nec opes tunc artibus illos.
Cathon dit: Se tu as enfans
Qui soyent povres et non puissans,
Telement que ne puissent vivre
De ce que ta rente leur livre,
Aprens-leur mestier ou clergie
Dont ils puissent gaigner leur vie,
On ne les peult mieux heriter
De meilleur œuvre pour s'ayder,
Car il n'est trésor ne finance
Qui vaille tant que faict science.
Car on peult perdre par fortune
L'heritage et la pecune;
Mais on ne pert point sapience
Qu'on a aprins en son enfance. (F: III, 51, 9 f.)
Car science n'est desprisée,
Comme on dit, que par ignorance.
(A: VI, 229, xlv, ll. 49385 f.)
Science alleguee a vng fol
Est perdue chascun le voit. (C: II, ccii[v])

1077 Maint sel faict fondre faulse raffe. (G: II, 73, x, l. 975)

1078 Tel semble estre bonne personne
Qui est vn tres mauuais pinard.

Tel est fin et qui mot ne sonne
Qui est vn tres rufe regnard. (E: I, 15, 22)

1079 Se de vostre serf faites maistre,
S'iert grant folour. (D: I, 168, iv, ll. 489 f.)
Car qui serf a pitié se moustre
N'est pas serf, non, mais il passe oultre,
Car il est de bien enseigneur
Et se preuve de touz segneur. (D: III, 199, xx, ll. 311 ff.)

1080 Maleureux est qui sert autruy. (A: I, 264, xii, l. 6719)
Car qui sert de couvert venin,
La mort le suit pour son loier. (B: p. 285, ll. 21816 f.)
On doit fouyr servaige. (A: II, 348, xxiii, l. 17107)

1081 Servans doibvent estre loyaulx
A leur maistre en toute saison. (A: I, 19, i, ll. 469 f.)
Servant doit craindre son seigneur,
Et ne doit quelque chose faire
Qui luy puisse ou doibve desplaire,
S'il veult en fin avoir merite. (A: V, 48 f., xxxix, ll. 37785 ff.)

1082 Il fault bien que les serviteurs
Resjouissent les souverains. (A: IV, 119, xxxiii, ll. 29804 f.)

1083 Je vous dy bien tout a ceste heure
Qu'il vault mieulx qu'un seul homme meure
Que beaucoup de peuple perisse.
(A: II, 351, xxiii, ll. [G 1136 ff.])
Mieulx vault qu'ung homme soit grevé
Et ung puissant peuple sauvé
Que pour ung seul homme sauver
Ung peuple se doye grever. (B: p. 204, ll. 15699 ff.)

1084 Sire, fault tout considerer:
Mieulx vault de souffrir ung tel fol
Que d'emprendre sur nostre col
Ung fardeau qui n'est point portable.
(B: p. 216, ll. 16673 ff.)

1085 Il n'est point de plus maulvais sours
Que ceulx qui ne veullent ouyr. (F: II, 35, 188)

1086 Un sot ne sera pas un sage. (G: III, 61, xxi, l. 122)
Car en soties n'a que follye. (G: II, 197, xii, l. 255)
Le plus sot y est le plus saige. (F: I, 15, 263)

1087 On ne scet pas ce qu'il survient
En toute bonne compaignie. (A: II, 74, xvii, ll. [F 1611 f.])

1088 Tousjours n'est pas temps de soy taire;
Mais la langue est si dangereuse
Qu'on ne peult a chacun complaire.
(A: V, 142, xli, ll. 39984 ff.)

Taire vault miex tant c'on conmande
Parler; car tant c'on s'en abstient,
En son pouoir parole on tient,
Ce n'est pas doubte. (D: IV, 271 f., xxvii, ll. 884 ff.)

1089 Car tant plus on tarde a la prinse
Tant plus doux en est le repos. (E: II, 11, 22)

1090 A tel deserte tel paiement. (A: IV, 46, xxxi, l. 28136)

1091 Ung temps ne peult tousjours durer.
(A: IV, 206, xxxiv, l. 31753)
Le Temps Chascun faict et deffaict. (G: III, 23, xix, l. 289)
Qui vouldroit veoir le Temps jadis,
On le trouveroit aux croniques. (G: I, 71, iii, ll. 83 f.)
Mais quoy, le temps pase n'est plus,
Tout s'en va, on n'en parle plus,
On ne tient compte des amys. (E: II, 7, 13)
Pére, il est un temps qu'il convient
Amer, en autre fault hair,
Temps de paiz et temps d'envair,
C'est a dire temps de bataille. (D: III, 280, xxi, ll. 1098 ff.)

1092 De tempter dieu nest pas licite
A son esgal se doit on comparer. (C: II, ccxx[v])

1093 C'est tien pour tien. (F: II, 34, 175)

1094 Il ne se fault point tormenter
D'une chose qu'on ne peult faire.
(A: II, 276, xxii, ll. 15462 f.)

1095 Celuy qui aucun tort feroit
Ne seroit pas homme notable. (A: IV, 86, xxxiii, ll. 29056 f.)
On le congnoit bien, on le voit:
Mieulx vault que soit a tort que a droit.
(A: V, 206, xli, ll. 41370 f.)

1096 Combien que c'est chose possible,
Toute voie n'est pas loysible. (D: VII, 211, xxxix, ll. 467 ff.)

1097 Traïson retourne a son maistre.
(A: IV, 290 f., xxxvi, ll. 33711, 33719, 33727)
Qui fait traison traison dessert;
La mesure qu'il a offert
Luy doibt retourner bien acoup.
(A: II, 384, xxiii, ll. [G 2037 ff.])
Telle est la fin de trahison,
Car quand ung trahitre dechet,
Chacun se rit, s'il luy meschet,
Et ma trahison decherra,
Car en la fin m'en mescherra. (B: p. 283, ll. 21680 ff.)

1098 Tel se treuve en gros acidens
Qui en pence bien eschaper. (G: III, 58, xxi, ll. 59 f.)
1099 Se l'homme ne vit par Tricherie,
Il ne viendra jà à honneur. (F: III, 63, 391)
1100 Cé-tu point bien que on dit qu'enfin
Le compaignon n'est point bien fin,
Qui ne trompe son compagnon. (F: II, 27, 79)
1101 Car souvent tel y va courant
Que puis s'en retourne en plorant. (G: III, 311, xxx, ll. 109 f.)
1102 Sans doubter,
Il ne nous en fault point vanter
En quelque lieu ne hault ne bas,
Et prenez en gré noz esbas. (F: II, 27, 79)
1103 Qui ayeroit de la veneson,
On pourroit faire des pastés. (G: I, 72, iii, ll. 87 f.)
1104 Il n'est homme, s'il ne devie,
Qui ayt rien plus cher que la vie. (A: II, 66, xvii, ll. [F 1402 f.])
Remembre toy
Que ma vie n'est que ung peu de vent
Qui est variable souvent. (A: V, 40, xxxix, ll. 37538 ff.)
1105 On veoyt a l'oeuil d'aultruy tout aultre
Vn petit festu odieulx;
Mais on ne voyt poinct vne poultre
Qu'on a deuant les yeulx. (E: II, 14, 26)
1106 On dict, par la foy de mon corps,
Qu'en quelque lieu qu'on abonde
On ne voyt rien qui ne va hors. (E: III, 18, 5)
On voit les gens aucunesfoys,
Et ne sait-on comme il est. (F: II, 34, 169)
1107 Verité ne fault point qu'on taise. (A: V, 243, xlii, l. 42136)
1108 Qui ne pourra vivre mourra. (A: II, 388, xxiii, l. 17527)
1109 On chasse vice par vertu. (C: II, lxxxi[v])
1110 Au propos de Cathon le saige
Ce qui s'ensuyt en brief langaige:
Multorum cum facta senes et dicta recenses
Fac tibi succurrant juvenisque feceris ipse.
Quant tu seras en ta vieillesse
Et racompteras ta prouesse
Et les beaulx faicts de plusieurs gens,
Fais dès maintenant que les tiens
Te puissent alors secourir,
Et de ce te puisses servir
Que aprins auras en ton temps. (F: III, 51, 19)

1111 Les vieulx ont regné, il souffit;
Chascun doit rener a son tour.
Chascun pense de son proffit,
Car après la nuyt vient le jour. (G: I, 120, iv, ll. 29 ff.)

1112 Iamais amour n'entra en teste
De vilain ie le congnoys bien. (E: I, 7, 13)

1113 Vray est que du vin la liqueur
Rend vigoureulx l'entendement
Le prenant modereement;
Mais qui le prend oultre raison,
Y prend pour son esprit poyson. (E: II, 9, 11)
Cathon note et met avant
Qu'on se doibt tremper bien souvent
En bon vin, quant il s'avisa
Dire: Vino te tempera. (F: II, 23, 17)

1114 Dames vous saues qu'il fault viure
Ainsy qu'on peult. (E: II, 17, 9)
I'ayme trop myeulx
Viure sain poure, ioyeulx & gent,
Que d'auoir soulcy & argent. (E: IV, 13, 7)
Qui plus vit de monde, plus vit. (E: IV, 10, 23)
L'homme yure n'a nulle raison. (E: II, 9, 12)

NOTES

CHAPTER I

1. *A Manual of the Writings in Middle English* (New Haven, 1916), pp. 539 ff.

2. These are: the liturgical Shrewsbury Fragments; the Newcastle *Noah's Ark*, both in O. Waterhouse, *The Non-Cycle Mystery Plays* (EETS., ES., CIV, 1909); and the Bodley *Burial and Resurrection*, ed. F. J. Furnivall for the New Shakspere Society, Series VII (1882).

3. See B. J. Whiting, *Chaucer's Use of Proverbs* (Cambridge, Massachusetts, 1934), p. 9.

4. In these comparisons allowance is not made for the proverbial material, mainly sententious, in Chaucer's prose.

5. See J. E. Wells, *Manual*, p. 548.

6. p. 49, v, 3 f.; p. 78, ix, 6, 12; p. 98, xi, 41.

7. p. 4, i, 88 f., p. 5, 1, 129, 136 f.; p. 52, vi, 19 f., p. 54, vi, 70; p. 68, viii, 141, p. 72, viii, 238, p. 76, viii, 390 f.; p. 149, xiv, 287, p. 155, xiv, 465; p. 197, xix, 70, p. 203, xix, 258; p. 295, xxv, 81 f.; p. 327, xxvii, 52, 60 f.; p. 356, xxix, 106, p. 360, xxix, 206, p. 365, xxix, 360, 361.

8. p. 42, iv, 82.

9. There are two comparisons in this play: p. 95, x, 308; p. 97, x, 368.

10. p. 162, xv, 70 f.

11. p. 192, xviii, 195 — the play's only proverbial phrase.

12. Cf. pp. 30 ff.

13. Cf. pp. 24 ff.

14. p. 274, xxiii, 527.

15. p. 258, xxiii, 2; p. 265, xxiii, 232; p. 268, xxiii, 324, 327; p. 269, xxiii, 361; p. 270, xxiii, 399, 406; p. 271, xxiii, 429.

16. p. 310, xxvi, 144; p. 325, xxvi, 623.

17. There are seven proverbial phrases here: p. 341, xxviii, 111; p. 344, xxviii, 168; p. 346, xxviii, 210; pp. 347 f., xxviii, 225, 258; p. 350, xxviii, 299; p. 352, xxviii, 345, 347.

18. There are four proverbial phrases here: p. 389, xxxi, 71; p. 391, xxxi, 145, 146, 147.

19. p. 24, iii, 58; p. 25, iii, 62 f.; p. 26, iii, 120; p. 29, iii, 200 f., 224 f.; p. 32, iii, 298; p. 33, iii, 336; p. 34, iii, 364; p. 35, iii, 406; p. 38, iii, 506, 515; p. 39, iii, 525.

20. p. 169, xvi, 98 f., 101, 128; p. 171, xvi, 189; p. 172, xvi, 197; p. 173, xvi, 231; p. 175, xvi, 318; p. 178, xvi, 398; p. 181, xvi, 512 f.

21. p. 281, xxiv, 82 f.; p. 283, xxiv, 155; p. 290, xxiv, 339.

22. p. 12, ii, 88, 89; p. 13, ii, 123, 141; p. 15, ii, 226; p. 17, ii, 283, 297; p. 18, ii, 311; p. 19, ii, 369; p. 21, ii, 439; p. 22, ii, 449. The remaining proverbial phrase is Abel's: p. 17, ii, 285.

23. In addition to those mentioned hereafter there is one phrase in the play which may perhaps be called ecclesiastically proverbial: p. 115, xii, 487; cf. p. 140, xiii, 737 f.

24. Jack uses two proverbial phrases: p. 106, xii, 180, 186.

25. He uses three proverbial phrases: p. 101, xii, 21, 32 f., 38.

26. He uses four proverbial phrases: p. 102, xii, 64 f.; p. 103, xii, 93 f.; p. 113, xii, 424.

27. He also uses four proverbial phrases, the third doubly dubious: p. 117, xiii, 13, 37; p. 123, xiii, 215 f.; p. 138, xiii, 699 f.

28. p. 119, xiii, 101, 105; p. 123, xiii, 217; p. 127, xiii, 356 ff.

29. It is possible that his surprised comment when he sees the sheep in the cradle (Sagh I neuer in a credyll A hornyd lad or now [p. 135, xiii, 600 f.]) is one of the earliest references in English literature to the horns of cuckoldom, which were to become proverbial enough.

30. p. 123, xiii, 226, 232, 233 f.; p. 124, xiii, 245; p. 125, xiii, 278; p. 127, xiii, 344; p. 128, xiii, 389.

31. She uses two proverbial phrases: p. 129, xiii, 405, 407 f.

32. There are seven proverbial phrases in the play: p. 230, xxi, 80; p. 231, xxi, 94; p. 232, xxi, 129; p. 233, xxi, 166; p. 234, xxi, 210; p. 239, xxi, 354 f.; p. 240, xxi, 375.

33. There are three proverbial phrases: p. 243, xxii, 14 f.; p. 244, xxii, 55; p. 246, xxii, 99.

34. There are sixteen proverbial phrases in the play: p. 371, xxx, 128; p. 372, xxx, 163; p. 373, xxx, 204 f.; p. 374, xxx, 224 f., 236; p. 375, xxx, 263, 267 f., 269; p. 377, xxx, 314, 315, 316, 324; p. 378, xxx, 370; p. 384, xxx, 554 f.

35 The manuscript of this cycle (Cotton Vespasian D VIII) exhibits a curious coincidence with that of the Chester Plays (MS. Add. 10305). In this MS., among some scribbled proper names on fol. 91 (v), is the following in a later hand: 'wee that will not when we paie (*sic*) when we would we shall find [? *or* saie] nay.' Miss Block, p. xxxvi, says that a four-line version of this saying, with the first line missing, is on fol. 124 of the Chester MS.

36. p. l.

37. pp. xliii ff.

38. Cf. pp. 30 ff.

39. See A. de Montaiglon, *Recueil Général . . . des Fabliaux* (Paris, 1872), I, 162 ff.; J. Bédier, *Fabliaux*, 4th ed. (Paris, 1925), pp. 460 f.

40. See p. xxiv.
41. See p. xxiii.
42. He likes this saying well enough to use it again in his final speech (p. 68, l. 1140).
43. See pp. xliii–xliv.
44. pp. 13* ff.
45. See pp. 28*–30*.
46. Two, xi and xvi, contain none. There is no thirteenth pageant.
47. On the Vice, see especially p. 66.
48. Oswin Wandelt, *Sprichwörter und Sentenzen des altfranzösischen Dramas* (1100–1400) (Marburg, 1887). The paucity of available documents apparently forced Wandelt to eke out his proverbs with religious commonplaces to such an extent that approximately half of his entries do not belong in a collection of proverbs and sententious remarks.
49. Ed. Baron James de Rothschild (Société des Anciens Textes français), 6 vols. (Paris, 1878–1891). In the Appendix all quotations from this work are lettered A. It should be remembered that, while the division into separate plays is logical in most cases, it is the work of the editor.
50. See J. E. Wells, *Manual of the Writings in Middle English* (New Haven, 1916), p. 549.
51. I, pp. 259 ff., ll. 6609 ff.
52. II, pp. 30 ff., ll. [499 ff.]; 186 ff., ll. 13300 ff.; 199 f., ll. 13613 ff.; 206 ff., ll. 13791 ff.; 212 ff., ll. 13912 ff.; V, 5 ff., ll. 36635 ff.
53. III, pp. 88 ff., ll. 19264 ff.
54. VI, pp. 75 ff., ll. 46055 ff.; 98 ff., ll. 46514 ff.; 164 ff., ll. 47928 ff.; 172 ff., ll. 48100 ff.
55. III, pp. 226 ff., ll. 22381 ff. These scenes seem to have exerted an hitherto unnoted influence on the English Slaughter of the Innocents.
56. IV, pp. 348, ll. 35105 ff.; 371, ll. 35646 ff.
57. V, pp. 160 ff., ll. 40390 ff.
58. V, pp. 244 ff., ll. 42158 ff.; 254 f., ll. 42358 ff.; 265 ff., ll. 42619 ff.; 280, ll. 42911 ff.; 287 ff., ll. 43068 ff.; 298, ll. 43259 ff.; 316 f., ll. 43623 ff.; 343 f., ll. 44108 ff.; 350, ll. 44229 ff.
59. VI, pp. 138 ff., ll. 47415 ff.; 153, ll. 47699 ff.
60. VI, pp. 188 ff., ll. 48485 ff.
61. In all the humorous passages there occur four proverbs (II, p. 209, l. 13861; IV, 352, l. 35188; V, 290, l. 43123; VI, 194, l. 48633); five sententious remarks (V, p. 6, l. 36659; 266, l. 42640; 317, l. 43636; 338, ll. 43989 ff.; 350, ll. 44234 f.); and fifteen proverbial phrases, mainly simple comparisons (I, 271, l. 6848; II, 32, [ll. 560 f.]; 33, [ll. 592 f.]; 187, ll. 13322 f.; 200, l. 13645; III, 91, l. 19308;

226, ll. 22389 f.; 227, l. 22400 f.; IV, 349, l. 35119; V, 8, l. 36699; 245, ll. 42174 f.; 280, ll. 42903 f.; VI, 138 f., ll. 47415 f.)

62. I, 347, ll. 8598 f.; 378, ll. 9354 f.

63. II, 107, l. 11291; 108, ll. 11302 f.; 130, ll. 11867 ff.

64. II, 146, ll. 12280 f.; 152, l. 12410; 174, ll. 12985 f.

65. II, 344, [ll. 927 f.], [l. 929], [ll. 930 f.], [l. 933], [ll. 935 f.]; 350, [ll. 1098 f.].

66. IV, 119, ll. 29804 f., 29818 ff.; 127, ll. 29995 f.; 128, ll. 30017 f.; 151, ll. 30488 f.; 165, ll. 30823 f.; 178, ll. 31125 f.; 179, l. 31156; 180, l. 31181; 207, l. 31769; 231, ll. 32316 f.

67. IV, 401, l. 36336.

68. IV, 402, l. 36344.

69. IV, 402, l. 36345.

70. IV, 406, l. 36474.

71. IV, 408, l. 36513.

72. I, 293, l. 7352; III, 185, l. 21388; V, 127, l. 39647; 319, l. 43687.

73. I, 378, ll. 9354 f.

74. III, 244, ll. 22801 f.

75. IV, 206, l. 31753.

76. V, 62, l. 38085.

77. Ed. Gaston Paris and Gaston Raynaud (Paris, 1878). R. Lebègue (*Romania*, LXX [1934], 218 ff.), criticizes adversely the text of this edition.

78. I have used a copy of the edition printed by the Brothers Angeliers in 1540, owned by the Harvard College Library. The work is in two volumes: *Le Premier volume du triumphant Mystere des Actes des Apostres translate fidelement a la verite Historiale/ escripte par sainct Luc a Theophile etc.*, and *Le Second Volume du Magnificque Mystere des Actes des Apostres / Continuant la narration de leur Faictz et gestes etc.*

79. For the various problems concerning the *Actes* consult Raymond Lebègue, *Le Mystère des Actes des Apotres* (Paris, 1929). That Simon Greban was the author was the opinion of the first editor and printer, Guillaume Alabat (see I, sig. a ii[v]).

80. *Miracles de Nostre Dame par Personnages*, ed. G. Paris and U. Robert (Société des Anciens Textes Français), 8 vols. (Paris, 1876–1893).

CHAPTER II

1. A workable definition is given by W. Roy Mackenzie, *The English Moralities from the Point of View of Allegory*, Harvard Studies in English, II (Boston, 1914), p. 9: "A Morality is a play,

allegorical in structure, which has for its main object the teaching of some lesson for the guidance of life, and in which the principal characters are personified abstractions or highly universalized types."

2. Morris P. Tilley, "Notes on *The Marriage of Wit and Wisdom,*" *The Shakespeare Association Bulletin,* X [1935], 57. It is likely that convention plays a larger part here than any desire on the author's part to exhibit Idleness as an unusually clever person. Earlier writers on the Vice had passed proverbs by with little more than mention. L. W. Cushman (*The Devil and the Vice in the English Dramatic Literature Before Shakespeare* [Halle, 1900], pp. 76–77) introduces his detailed list of Vice-motifs thus: "In this classification those motifs which the Vice has in common with other figures, such as oaths, obscenities, proverbs, phrases from foreign languages, and which are, therefore, not characteristic, are omitted." Later he quotes the woman-dodman-goose proverb which Sedition employs in *King Johan* (see above p. 100) and calls it 'a senseless comparison' (p. 112). From the following quotation it would appear that Eduard Eckhardt (*Die lustige Person im älteren englischen Drama* [Palaestrà, XVII, Berlin, 1902], pp. 207 f.) recognized one especial kind of phrase often, but not always, proverbial in the Vice's speech: "Ein spezielles Kennzeichen des Vice ist die Zote, die er häufig und mit Behagen als Mittel der Komik anwendet. In Zussammenhang mit der Zote stehen die zahlreichen frivolen und cynischen Redensarten, über die der Vice verfügt, ein Motiv, das uns wieder zu dessen Intrigantennatur zurückführt, und an seine oben (S. 206) erwähnten Spöttereien und Sarkasmen anknüpft. Mit den derben oder unflätigen Reden des Vice berühren sich nahe die Schimpfworte, die er, wie auch andere Gestalten, so gern und reichlich auf die ihn umgebenden Personen herabregnen lässt." Karl Pfeffer (*Das Elisabethanische Sprichwort in seiner Verwendung bei Ben Jonson* [Giessen, 1933], p. 20) mentions the Vice—'in den älteren Stücken'—along with other comic characters who make use of proverbs.

3. Strangely enough the least humorous of all the plays, *Everyman,* contains a goodly number of proverbs which, it may be, represent the author's compromise with comedy.

4. P. 102, ll. 425 f. Waterhouse reads *coot* for the MS *cot,* but Bradley, in his sheet of 'Corrections' inserted in the volume, rejects the emendation and says that 'cot' equals 'cat.' A. Brandl (*Quellen des weltlichen Dramas in England vor Shakespeare* [Strassburg, 1898], p. 31) suggests *wilgate* and translates *Durch geher.*

5. The speakers, however, are indicated in each case.

6. For a discussion of Medwall's other play, *Fulgens and Lucres,* see pp. 210 ff.

7. See J. Nichol's preface to *Sir David Lyndesay's Works*, Part V, p. xlv, EETS., ES., XLVII (1871).

8. The proverbs in Lyndsay's works have been extracted by J. Kissel, *Das Sprichwort bei . . . Sir David Lyndesay* (Nürnberg, 1892). A list of line references to his extractions from *The Three Estates* is on p. 41. The following, mainly Biblical quotations, scraps of Latin and pious generalizations, I have been unable to consider proverbial: ll. 249, 1056, 1060 f., 1462 f., 1586 ff., 1605 ff., 1609 ff., 1842 f., 1875, 1886 f., 1898 f., 1916 f., 1944 f., 2836, 2853 f., 2897 f., 2899 f., 3667 f., 3672 ff., 3745, 3780, 3784 ff., 3887 f., 4236 f., 4254 ff., 4470, 4492, 4535 f. He gives practically no proverbial phrases; cf. pp. 35–37.

9. This play could have been printed in such a way as to contain something less than eight hundred longer lines.

10. For a discussion of the play, with some account of its proverbs, see Celesta Wine, "Nathaniel Wood's 'Conflict of Conscience,'" *Publications of the Modern Language Association*, L [1935], p. 676.

11. Leroux de Lincy and Francisque Michel, *Recueil de Farces, Moralités et Sermons Joyeux*, 4 vols. (Paris, 1837), and Viollet Le Duc, *Ancien Théatre François*, Vols. I–III (Paris, 1854). I have considered moralities such plays as are so listed by L. Petit de Julleville, *Répertoire du Théatre Comique en France au Moyen-Age* (Paris, 1886). The moralities in question comprise Petit de Julleville's following numbers: 7, 8, 16, 17, 23, 24, 25, 28, 30, 32, 33, 34, 35, 36, 43, 47, 48, 50, 60, 62, 63.

12. See the statement of E. Eckhardt (*Die lustige Person im älteren englischen Drama* [Palaestra, XVII, Berlin, 1902], p. 121): "Als selbständige Dramengestalt ist ja der Vice der englischen Litteratur allein eigentümlich."

13. I regret my inability to consult the much mentioned *Bien Avisé, Mal Avisé* (Petit de Julleville, no. 13) which is about eight thousand lines long.

CHAPTER III

1. Ed. G. H. McKnight, *Middle English Humorous Tales in Verse* (Boston, 1913), pp. 21–24.

2. For a discussion of these French documents see L. Petit de Julleville, *Répertoire du Théatre Comique en France au Moyen-Age* (Paris, 1886), pp. 259 ff.

3. On the canon of Heywood's plays, all probably composed before 1525, see H. N. Hillebrand, 'On the Authorship of the Interludes Attributed to John Heywood.' *Modern Philology*, XIII, [1915], pp. 267 ff.; R. W. Bolwell, *The Life and Works of John Heywood* (New York, 1921), pp. 80 ff.; A. W. Reed, *Early Tudor Drama* (1926), pp. 118 ff.

4. See E. Eckhardt, *Die lustige Person*, p. 193.

5. *Pernet qui va au vin*, Viollet Le Duc, *Ancien Théatre François* (Paris [1854]), I, 195 ff.

5a. The proverbs which appear in the various plays by, or ascribed to Heywood have, however, been used by the most recent writer on Heywood as an argument, though only one out of many, in favor of unity of authorship; see R. de la Bère, *John Heywood, Entertainer* (1937), pp. 55, 60, 65, 68, 73, 82, 84, 86, 87, 93. Professor de la Bère's statements and suggestions that Heywood made constant use of proverbs in his plays and that this use is in some way peculiar to him are, as we have seen, of doubtful validity, and it is pleasant to observe that his other proofs of Heywood's authorship of the plays in question are less open to objection.

6. A. W. Reed, *Early Tudor Drama* (1926), pp. 105 ff.

7. A. R. Moon, "Was Nicholas Udall the Author of 'Thersites'?" *The Library*, VII [1926], 184 ff.

8. See Appendix.

9. Leroux De Lincy and F. Michel, *Recueil de Farces, Moralités et Sermons Joyeux* (Paris, 1837), III, No. 6.

10. Viollet Le Duc, *Ancien Théatre François* (Paris, [1854]), III, 249 ff.

11. But see Petit de Julleville's treatment, *Répertoire du Théatre Comique en France au Moyen-Age* (Paris, 1886), p. 162.

12. E. Picot, *Recueil Général des Sotties*, I [1902], iv.

13. Picot, I, 47 ff.

14. I, 47; cf. 49, and notes *passim*.

15. See Picot, III, 45 ff.

CHAPTER IV

1. See Flügel, p. 95.

2. *Troilus and Criseyde*, v, 505.

3. The same, ii, 397 ff.

4. More specific comments are reserved for a subsequent volume dealing primarily with Shakespeare's use of proverbs.

5. Sixth hundred of epigrams, no. 88 (Spenser Society, 1867), p. 214.

6. G. L. Apperson, *English Proverbs and Proverbial Phrases* (1929), p. 35.

CHAPTER V

1. See G. L. Kittredge, "Notes on Elizabethan Plays," *Journal of [English and] Germanic Philology*, II [1898], 8 f.; W. W. Greg, ed., *Sir Clyomon and Sir Clamydes*, Malone Society Reprints, 1913, pp. v f.; Tucker Brooke, ed., *Common Conditions*, Elizabethan Club Reprints, No. 1 (New Haven, 1915), pp. 83 ff.

INDEX I

NAMES AND WORKS

This index includes the plays treated, the authors and works mentioned in the text and notes, and other important proper names which have appeared in the discussion. Modern editors are not listed unless they have been cited or quoted for particular information.

INDEX II

VERBAL INDEX TO ENGLISH SAYINGS IN CHAPTERS I TO V

The following verbal index to the English proverbs and sententious remarks quoted in chapters I to V has been made with the hope that it may facilitate the location of particular sayings. No index of this sort, apparently, can be completely satisfactory, but the inclusion here of numerous short phrases, few of more than two words, ought to be of considerable assistance to the reader. When the second element in the phrase is an important word, as is the case in a vast majority of instances, it is entered separately. The reader must be warned, however, that this index is not to the stereotyped or "dictionary" forms of the sayings, but to the actual quotations in the text. Allowance, therefore, must be made for verbal variations and more than one word or phrase must be checked before there can be any certainty that all occurrences of a saying have been located.

Modern English spellings are used throughout and obsolete words are given the preferred forms of the *New English Dictionary*. Nouns found only in the plural are entered under the plural forms, except when a noun is listed with an adjective or verb of identical spelling. Words showing aphesis are entered with the full form. When a word or phrase is of importance in more than one saying on a single page the number of occurrences is given in brackets after the page number.

For the reader's convenience the index is preceded by lists of page references to the Latin sayings which are scattered through the plays and to the Wellerisms, since the former are not indexed at all, and the latter are not always easy to find by means of key words. With the exception of a single Italian proverb (p. 247) no foreign sayings, other than Latin, are found in the English plays.